Music for the Piano

A Handbook of Concert and Teaching Material from 1580 to 1952

by

JAMES FRISKIN

and IRWIN FREUNDLICH

Dover Publications, Inc.
New York

Published in Canada by General Publishing Company, Ltd., 30 Lesmill Road, Don Mills, Toronto,
Ontario.
Published in the United Kingdom by Constable
and Company, Ltd., 10 Orange Street, London WC 2.

This Dover edition, first published in 1973, is an
unabridged, slightly corrected republication of the
work originally published as Volume V of the series
entitled *The Field of Music,* edited by the late
Ernest Hutcheson, and published by Holt, Rinehart
and Winston, Inc., in 1954. A new Preface by Irwin
Freundlich and a new Biographical Appendix have
been added to the present edition.

International Standard Book Number: 0-486-22918-1
Library of Congress Catalog Card Number: 72-93608

Manufactured in the United States of America
Dover Publications, Inc.
180 Varick Street
New York, N. Y. 10014

To the memory of two notable contributors to the art of the pianist

ERNEST HUTCHESON and CARL M. ROEDER

ACKNOWLEDGMENTS

The writers wish to record with gratitude the courtesy and assistance of the following publishers:

G. Schirmer, Carl Fischer, J. Fischer & Bro., Associated Music Publishers, C. F. Peters, E. F. Kalmus, G. Ricordi, Galaxy Music Corporation, Boosey & Hawkes, Oxford University Press, Augener & Co., Alfred Lengnick, Elkan-Vogel Co., Salabert, Inc., Broude Bros., Leeds Music Corporation, Mercury Music Corporation, Southern Music Publishing Co., E. B. Marks.

The American Music Center and the American Composers' Alliance Library have both been most helpful.

Dr. Marion Bauer was kind enough to read through the section on American contemporary music; and Miss Isabel Marting, librarian of the Juilliard School of Music, has contributed valuable critical suggestions.

Preface
to the Dover Edition

Almost twenty years have passed since the first printing of *Music for the Piano* (Rinehart & Co. 1954). James Friskin (my former teacher and subsequent colleague on the Juilliard faculty) and I had labored on this volume with tenacity since 1947 in the face of very demanding professional schedules that severely limited our time and energy. The book was originally Volume V of the series *The Field of Music* under the general editorship of the distinguished Australian pianist Ernest Hutcheson, then President Emeritus of the Juilliard School of Music. Other volumes in the series included works on the concert band by Richard Franko Goldman, music for violin and viola by Hans Letz and two works on vocal repertoire and technique by Sergius Kagen.

During the years that have elapsed *Music for the Piano* went through three printings and became something of a classic manual for student, teacher and performer alike, a handbook that achieved widespread use especially throughout the United States and Canada. It is not too much to say that it was the first book of its kind in English to present a well-rounded treatment of the entire spectrum of the pianistic repertoire in a format making for quick and easy reference.

The decision to reprint *Music for the Piano* without attempting a revision was based upon several factors not the least of which is that the book is of permanent value in its original form containing, as it does, the thumb-nail characterizations by both Mr. Friskin and myself a propos not only the major works of the repertoire but many minor ones as well, reaching as far back as 1580 and including works up to 1952 which have become classic items in the modern repertoire. When one observes that our comments were not restricted to the solo literature alone but included works for four hands at one and two pianos and concertos for piano and orchestra (all within the covers of one book), the value of the work is clear.

A current list of American agent or parent companies of all leading music publishers may be obtained from the Music Publisher's Association of the U. S. A., 609 Fifth Avenue, New York City 10017. A new appendix (preceding the index) contains an alphabetical list of composers mentioned in the book who have died since the original edition was published.

Users of the reprint may find the following two works useful as supplements: *Short History of Keyboard Music* by F. E. Kirby (The Free Press, New York, 1966) and *Guide to the Pianist's Repertoire* by Maurice Hinson—edited by Irwin Freundlich (Indiana University Press, Bloomington, Indiana, 1973). The first is a most useful historical account (the best of its kind in English) and the second fills in many of the lacunae mentioned above but only within the realm of the solo piano repertoire. For readers of German the *Handbuch der Klavier-literatur* by Klaus Wolters (Atlantis Verlag, Zurich, 1967) is unexampled in scope, depth and insight.

It is with regret that I sign this preface alone, without the signature of my former teacher and colleague, the Scottish pianist of the formidable repertoire, James Friskin, who invited me, in 1947, to collaborate with him on the original venture. His passing in 1967 concluded a rich and eventful life in the service of music. However, the Dover reprint ensures the perpetuation of his work on *Music for the Piano* and makes available once again the many insights contained therein—the results of his great experience as concert artist and teacher of renown. It is in his memory that I affix my signature and note with gratitude the years of joint effort on the completion of our book. What it meant to my own development (I played at the keyboard every piece on which I commented!) was indescribable. May the fruits of our work over those years give pleasure and guidance to yet another generation of pianists through this reprint edition.

IRWIN FREUNDLICH

New York City
May, 1973

Preface
to the First Edition

When I was invited by the late Ernest Hutcheson, who was exercising general musical supervision over this series, to undertake the volume dealing with pianoforte music I hesitated, knowing something (though not all) of the magnitude of the task and the labor it would involve. I finally suggested that I have the assistance of Mr. Irwin Freundlich, who had, I knew, in his work in the classes of the Juilliard School, accumulated a considerable amount of material that would be of help in the book's preparation. I had specially in mind the period of early keyboard music (pre-Bach), and also much of the output of composers of our own time. Now that we have come to the end of our task, the value of Mr. Freundlich's contribution is evident; he has brought to it not only his already acquired knowledge, but also the results of an impressive further research.

The original plan was that I should myself undertake what has been called 'the main stream of music,' so far as it concerned the piano—roughly, from Bach to Ravel; and that my collaborator should deal with earlier and later periods. There has been a general adherence to this scheme; but in planning the book as a whole other subdivisions have appeared to be desirable, with the result that my extensive section on J. S. Bach appears, as of course it should, as part of the entire pre-piano section, the remainder of which has been dealt with by Mr. Freundlich. For a similar reason, Brahms rather than Ravel appears as the principal figure at the end of the period dealt with in Part II. My sections on Debussy and Ravel are placed with those that deal with recent developments.

Accordingly the final disposition of the material is as follows:

Keyboard music before the advent of the piano—Freundlich.
Pianoforte music from Haydn to Brahms—Friskin.
Pianoforte music of the twentieth century—Freundlich.
Music for four hands (one and two pianos)—Freundlich.
Music for piano and orchestra (one or more pianos)—Friskin.

The principal exceptions to the above are: J. S. Bach, Handel, Debussy, Ravel (Friskin)—Reger (Freundlich). There are also some minor composers of whose work one or other of us had some special knowledge that made an interchange convenient.

The listings in the appendixes have been made by Mr. Freundlich.

Sometimes for reasons of chronology, sometimes for reasons of style and idiom, deviations from an exact dividing line (an impossible one in any case) between our groupings have been made. The index will, it is hoped, avoid any difficulty of reference.

James Friskin

The purpose of this book is to provide, not of course a listing of the entire repertoire of the pianist, but an ample selection that will represent each composer fairly and with proper consideration of his place in the history of composition for the keyboard. The annotations are concerned largely with the technical requirements of the material, and also with its interpretative

treatment; they are intended to give the student, teacher, amateur and professional pianist some help in making a selection from the enormous mass
of music accumulated during the past three hundred and fifty years.

It should be said that the general aim is to include only material that has
real artistic value; consequently the large department of what are known as
"teaching pieces" has been ignored. On the other hand, while there is no
division into "grades," there is frequent indication of relative ease or difficulty. In the case of the outstanding figures of pianoforte literature there
is generally a short section with a separate list of easier compositions.

One minor problem has been presented by the decision whether or not
to include the names and compositions of composers who were prominent
in their day but whose reputation has faded and whose work has lost its general appeal. Sometimes there are single pieces by such composers, which
have still an old-fashioned charm—the names of Hummel and Czerny come
to mind—and some material illustrating this will be found in our list.

The output of a few major figures, whose compositions are of exceptionally even quality, will be found here almost entire. Schumann, Chopin,
Brahms, Debussy and Ravel are in this category. A very few lesser composers, too, have been given a similarly full treatment where ease of reference has seemed to justify a perhaps disproportionate award of space. On
the other hand, the two great names of Bach and Beethoven are associated
with a considerable number of insignificant pieces—e.g., many of Beethoven's
sets of variations—which can be dispensed with in a book of this kind.

As the book has been primarily designed for use in America, that fact
has had its influence in the listing of publishers and editions. Even at this
date the effect of the Second World War, in restricting the use of paper and
even in destroying publishing businesses in Europe, is still felt; a few of
the compositions named, it will be found, are at present out of print and only
accessible in libraries. In general we have taken care that the information
regarding editions is applicable to today's conditions.

It need hardly be said that the repertoire of the pianist includes a large
body of music not written for the piano at all. The years 1760-1770 may be
taken as an approximate starting point for the repertoire of the piano proper.
In the earlier years the harpsichord (in its various species), clavichord and
organ were at times used indiscriminately to perform keyboard pieces in
general, and even some of the great Viennese masters wrote for both harpsichord and piano. As for music of a still earlier period, the writers trust
that the extensive treatment given may stimulate further exploration of a
field that is too often dismissed as merely archaic.

Arrangements of music written for other instruments have as a rule
not been included. However, exceptions have been made in the case of some
notable transcribers—Liszt, Busoni, etc.

In dealing with the constantly increasing list of contemporary publications, which offer such great variety of idiom and where the question of
standards is apt to be perplexing, we have tried to be both as discriminating
and as impersonal as possible. But we cannot hope that we shall entirely
escape the accusation of unpardonable omissions—or, possibly, of inde-
fensible inclusions.

James Friskin
Irwin Freundlich

Contents

Part I
The Earlier Keyboard Music
(Before the Advent of the Pianoforte)

THE EARLIER KEYBOARD MUSIC
(before the advent of the pianoforte)

The earlier repertoire is much more extensive than is commonly supposed. Some of it has already been absorbed into the normal performing and study habits of students of the piano while the bulk of it remains unknown territory. We have become so accustomed to J. S. Bach on the piano that we often fail to realize his music predates the actual advent of the piano as an instrument in common use. The many fine keyboard composers who flourished before and during Bach's lifetime are almost completely neglected although, in many instances, transplanting their music to the piano offers problems no greater than those posed by keyboard music of the Leipzig master.

The lines are not so clearly drawn (in the earlier music) between organ, harpsichord (in all its forms) and clavichord pieces, but some knowledge of the sonorous possibilities of all keyboard instruments is useful to the pianist in arriving at satisfactory pianistic equivalents. It must be borne in mind that since the earlier keyboard music, in its original state, bore very few or no indications of tempo, phrase articulation (legato and staccato, slurrings, etc.) and dynamics, the editorial markings in most reprint editions are not the original markings of the composer. They are merely suggestions that attempt to serve as a crutch for students and performers who lack a solid grounding in matters of style and structure. Such editorial suggestions are most often open to question and eventual modification. Almost always the tendency is to do too much to the text, "filling out" the harmonies, overphrasing and using the dynamic indications of the Beethovenian and later romantic approaches, quite at variance with the musical outlook of the sixteenth, seventeenth and early eighteenth centuries.

This was an era that stressed homogeneity of sound, and the sharp opposition of terrace dynamics rather than a gradual transition by means of crescendo or diminuendo. The sforzando was nonexistent, as was the ability to mix sonorities with the damper pedal. But the ability to play legato and non-legato was present and there was a strong emphasis on a singing style in keyboard playing. It cannot be too strongly emphasized that there is no real substitute for a solid grounding in the materials of music and the historical development of the literature.

The editions suggested in this section are, to the author's knowledge, the best and most authoritative. Deviations are noted where they occur. It is hoped that this section of Music for the Piano will stimulate a widened interest in a fascinating segment of the repertoire. It goes without saying that any serious approach to playing these pieces requires a long and careful study of all the problems involved.

The English Virginalists (c.1580-1650)

From the viewpoint of the modern piano repertoire it is probably realistic to begin with a consideration of English keyboard music toward the end of the sixteenth century. The keyboard music before this period is mainly of interest to the historian and musicologist. However, the dances, variations on folk songs and dance tunes, the fantasies (or fancies, as they were then called), and the miscellaneous pieces in the repertoire after about 1580 exhibit a keyboard style independent of vocal and organ traits and are of sufficient interest to merit the attention of the present-day performer. To paraphrase Charles van den Borren, the great authority in this field, it is a music of half shades, rarely pathetic, on occasion weighty, speaking of joy, serenity, grief, love, hope, at times playful, with a feeling for nature, elegant, refined and sensitive, possessing an element of untamed wildness and spontaneous freshness. It is a music essentially English in flavor, based as it is on a solid core of English folk song.

Something over six hundred pieces come to us from this period, not all of which are of interest to us as pianists. None of this music was originally written for the concert stage, which was at that time nonexistent. The instrument on which it was played (the virginal) was a simple one-manual harpsichord incapable of dynamic contrast, but absolutely clear and precise in articulation, brilliant and small in sonority. A mere cursory leafing through of representative works reveals a wealth of pianistic devices unsurpassed until Domenico Scarlatti: complicated rhythmic figures, broken chords and intervals, scale passages, skips up to three octaves, tremolo and repeated note figures, etc.

The compositions of the English virginalists range in difficulty from extremely simple short pieces to long, complex works demanding much facility and control. They fall into various categories almost all of which make use of the variation principle.

Dance Types

The most rewarding pieces among the many dance genres are the pavanes and galliards, often thematically related and coupled to form a kind of rudimentary suite. Other dance pieces bear the titles Maske, Alman, Coranto, Ground, Gigge, Toy or simply Daunce.

Variations on Folk Songs and Dance Tunes

From the simple The Carman's Whistle of Byrd to the complex Walsingham variations of Bull stretches a rich literature built on folk and popular tunes of the day. The tunes are exploited in any number of ways, from simple chordal settings to various contrapuntal or keyboard idioms.

The Fancy or Fantasia

Among the precursors of the eighteenth-century fugue is the above-mentioned category. Usually, though not always, the fancy is a polyphonic composition built on one or more subjects posing the usual problems that arise in handling several moving parts on a single keyboard. Very often these fancies are intended for the organ and are more appropriately performed on that instrument. In some cases, as in the Running Fantasia of Gibbons, a more pianistic, prelude-like piece is the result.

4

The Prelude

Many pieces anticipate the étude-like preoccupations of later composers. Sometimes called Prelude, Preludium, Voluntary or even Fancy, they are characterized by running figures loosely bound together by simple chordal progressions. They provide useful miniatures that could very well substitute for some hackneyed Czerny étude in velocity. Similar pieces of very moderate difficulty abound in the volumes mentioned below.

Miscellaneous

A few descriptive pieces such as The Bells of Byrd and the Fantasia ("Faire Wether") of Munday are of some interest as examples of early program music. In this category are the miniatures of Farnaby and Bull bearing descriptive titles. They combine a fresh musical quality with craftsmanship and compelling charm. Other categories such as the plain-song variations are of no immediate interest to the present-day pianist.

Almost all English virginal music never departs from a signature of one or two sharps or flats, since it is basically modal in conception. It may be mentioned that the Hexachord Fantasia of Bull attempts to use all twelve tones in a kind of modulation through the circle of keys. Although the lack of key contrast creates a problem for modern ears accustomed to Tschaikowsky, Rachmaninoff and Wagner, the fresh melodic qualities, arresting rhythmic features, the endless procedures of variation, the lines of the more contrapuntal works, the vigorous straightforward march of simple harmonies or the more complex pianistic elaboration of their possibilities provide ample interest for the present-day musician.

An exact account of stylistic technicalities may be found in:

The Sources of Keyboard Music in England, Charles van den Borren, London: Novello & Co., 1913.
About Elizabethan Virginal Music and its Composers, Margaret H. Glyn, London: W. Reeves, 1934.

Collections

Fitzwilliam Virginal Book (FVB) (Fuller-Maitland and Barclay Squire), 2 Vols., Breitkopf and Härtel, 1899. Reprint editions by J. W. Edwards and Broude Bros.
    Two huge library volumes containing 297 pieces by almost all composers of the period, transcribed from the original manuscript into modern notation. The main source of English virginal music.
Selected Pieces from the Fitzwilliam Virginal Book (Fuller-Maitland and Barclay Squire), 2 Vols., Breitkopf and Härtel.
    A good selection of twenty-one pieces by Byrd, Morley, Bull, Giles Farnaby, Munday, Peerson, Philips, R. Johnson and Anonymous.
Selections from the Fitzwilliam Virginal Book (Margaret H. Glyn), 2 Vols., British and Continental Music Co. (through Associated Music Publishers).
    A new selection not duplicating the above, intelligently edited in modern notation (ornaments omitted) by the foremost English authority in the field.
Parthenia (Kurt Stone), Broude Bros., 1951
    Reprint edition in modern notation of the "Maydenhead of the first Musicke ever printed for the Virginals" (1611). Twenty-one pieces by Bull, Byrd and Gibbons. A facsimile edition of the original is also available through Reeves.

Twenty-Five Pieces for Keyed Instruments from Benjamin Cosyn's Virginal
  Book (Fuller-Maitland and Barclay Squire), J. & W. Chester.
    Pieces by Bull, Byrd, Cosyn, Gibbons and Anonymous.
Thirty Virginal Pieces by Various Composers (Margaret H. Glyn), Stainer
  & Bell (Galaxy Music Corp.).
    Pieces by Cosyn, Dowland, Holborne, Ed. Hooper, John and Robert
    Johnson, Lawes, Peerson and Tomkins.
Many pieces are reprinted in general anthologies such as Early Key-
board Music (EKM), Vol. I (Oesterle), G. Schirmer; Old Masters of the 16th,
17th and 18th Centuries (Niemann), Kalmus; and Antologia di musica antica e
moderna per il pianoforte (TPA), (Tagliapietra), Ricordi.
The reprint editions of single composers by Margaret H. Glyn contain many
pieces in shortened versions, but when such is the case they are so
indicated.
Schott's Anthology of Early Keyboard Music (Frank Dawes, ed.), 5 Vols.,
  Associated Music.
    Vol. 1 - Ten Pieces by Hugh Aston and others.
    Vol. 2 - Twelve Pieces from Mulliner's Book (c.1555).
    Vol. 3 - Seven Virginal Pieces (from British Museum Add.3).
    Vol. 4 - Eight Pieces from the Tomkins Manuscript.
    Vol. 5 - Fifteen Pieces from Elizabeth Rogers' Virginal Book (1656).
A new and apparently carefully prepared Urtext edition without tempo,
phrase markings or fingerings.

JOHN BULL (1562-1628)

Bull is traditionally known as the virtuoso among the English Virginalists,
since his larger works encompass many keyboard problems commonly
thought to have been initiated by later composers such as Scarlatti and
Clementi: passage playing of all kinds, repeated tones, double notes,
crossed hands, a variety of broken chord figures, tricky rhythms and
intricate counterpoint. At the same time, the shorter pieces are well
within the reach of the player of moderate ability and repay acquaintance,
if only for casual musicmaking in the home or studio.
    In addition to the general collections of English virginal music, the
following edition specifically devoted to the works of Bull may be
recommended:

Selected Works of John Bull (Margaret H. Glyn), Stainer & Bell (through
  Galaxy Music Corp.). Sixty of the 170 known works of Bull compiled in
  the following arrangement:
    Vol. I — Dances and Fancy Pieces
    Vol. II — Folksong Variations
    Vol. III — Pavans and Galliards
    Vol. IV — Plainsong and other Fantasie

Duke of Brunswick's Alman   Short dainty setting of quiet tune, varied with
                             simplicity and charm.
                             Selected Works, Vol. I.

Bull's Goodnighte   Eight short variations on a sturdy folklike
                             tune. Idiomatic keyboard figures. Straight-
                             forward and utterly disarming.
                             Selected Works, Vol. I

Pavana in G Major	Bright, sturdy. Three phrases, each with a flowing variation. Interesting scale inflections. In <u>Twenty-Five Pieces from Benjamin Cosyn's Virginal Book</u>, J. & W. Chester.
Dr. Bull's Juell	Courante in 6/4, three phrases with flowing, melodic variations. <u>FVB</u>, Vol. II, p.128.
Walsingham	Large-scale, complex set of thirty variations on an old pilgrim's tune, "As I went to Walsingham." A fantastic piece utilizing a rich variety of idioms providing a summary of English virginal keyboard speech. Difficult. Could be played with cuts. <u>FVB</u>, Vol. I, p.1. Edited, shortened reprint in modern notation in <u>Selected Works</u>, Vol. II.
The King's Hunt	Brilliant, effervescent, rhythmic. Three sections. Rapid passages for both hands. <u>FVB</u>, Vol. II, p.116. Various reprints.
Dr. Bull's My Selfe	Short gigue, dotted rhythms, two phrases each varied. <u>FVB</u>, Vol. II, p.257
My Greife	Short gigue. One instance of three against two in a single hand! <u>FVB</u>, Vol. II, p.258

WILLIAM BYRD (1543-1623)

Byrd is the great pioneer figure in English virginal music. The task of creating an idiomatic keyboard speech out of the essentially vocal music of Elizabethan England rested largely on the shoulders of the "The Father of Musicke." His style is deceptively simple when he so chooses. It conceals a knowing hand whose skill is revealed only by close study of every phrase. The performer must match the sensitivity of the composer if the result is to be at all satisfactory. While a tinge of melancholy often suffuses an entire piece (<u>Fortune, The Woods so Wild</u>), a buoyant, joyful exuberance is just as often projected through the straightforward setting of some contemporary dance tune (<u>Sellenger's Round</u>, <u>The Carman's Whistle</u>). The pieces listed below (a mere fraction of his output for the keyboard) include moderately difficult problems in rhythms and the satisfactory handling of imitative textures.

In addition to the general anthologies of English virginal music, the following editions specifically devoted to pieces by Byrd may be recommended:

<u>Fourteen Pieces for Keyed Instruments</u> (Fuller-Maitland and Barclay Squire), Stainer & Bell (through Galaxy Music Corp.).
<u>Forty-Five Pieces for Keyboard Instruments</u> (Stephen D. Tuttle), Lyrebird Press. A library edition.
<u>My Ladye Nevells Booke</u> (Hilda Andrews), J. Curwen and Sons. Forty-two pieces by·Byrd dating from 1591 and earlier, in a superb library edition.

The Bells	Descriptive variations over a ground bass. Sustained, climactic. <u>FVB</u>, Vol. I, p.274.
John come kisse me now	Buoyant, rhythmic set of fifteen variations on a four-bar tune. Requires dexterity and rhythmic precision. <u>FVB</u>, Vol. I, p.47.
Sellenger's Round	Eight variations on a dance tune. Some double thirds (left hand). <u>FVB</u>, Vol. I, p.248.
Rowland (Lord Willoughby's Welcome Home)	Two variations on a twenty-four bar section. Rousing, spirited. Not difficult. In <u>Fourteen Pieces</u>, Galaxy Music Corp.
Three French Corantos	Short dance pieces in 6/4. Easy. Ingratiating qualities. In <u>Fourteen Pieces</u>, Galaxy Music Corp.
Pavane and Galliard, the Earl of Salisbury	Short, rudimentary suite, easy. Neat, polished style. In <u>Parthenia</u>. Many reprints.
The Carman's Whistle	Eight variations on a popular tune. Light, cheerful. Some imitative counterpoint. <u>FVB</u>, Vol. I, p.214. Many reprints.
Fortune	Three variations on a twenty-four bar theme. Melancholy, flowing. Some running-passage playing. <u>FVB</u>, Vol. I, p. 254.
O Mistris Myne	Five variations on the Shakespearean song. Varied textures. Requires agility and sensitivity. <u>FVB</u>, Vol. I, p.258.
The Woods so Wild	Thirteen variations on a tune also set by Gibbons. Drowsy, atmospheric. Requires smoothness and sensitivity. <u>FVB</u>, Vol. I, p.266.
Pavans and Galliards	Of the <u>Pavians</u> (sic) and <u>Galliards</u> in <u>My Ladye Nevells Booke</u>, the first, third and fifth may be singled out for their sensitive, melancholy qualities.
Goe from my windoe	Variations on the tune set by Morley and Munday. Seven sections, mostly freely contrapuntal. Some passage playing, opposing meters. In <u>Forty-Five Pieces</u>, Lyrebird Press.

BENJAMIN COSYN (early 17th century)

<u>Twenty-Five Pieces for Keyed Instruments from Benjamin Cosyn's Virginal Book</u> (Fuller-Maitland and Barclay Squire), J. & W. Chester. The volume also contains pieces by other composers.

The Goldfinch	Sturdy folk tune, two phrases with vigorous rhythmic variants. Short, easy.
What You Will	Robust variations on vigorous, gigue-like tune. Broken-chord and broken-octave passages, both hands.

GILES FARNABY (c.1565-1598 ?)

Farnaby is essentially a miniaturist, a composer of ingenuity and good humor. In addition to the many collections of English virginal music in which Farnaby's works appear, the following edition devoted solely to his compositions may be recommended:

<u>Selected Works</u> (Margaret H. Glyn), Stainer & Bell (through Galaxy Music Corp.). Twenty-five of the fifty known pieces by Farnaby. Vol. I — Selected Pieces, Vol. II — Folk Song Variations.

Giles Farnaby's Dreame	Short, lyric.
His Rest	Short, easy, quiet.
His Humour	Four short sections, good natured, simple. Some unusual chromatics.
Mal Sims	Two phrases varied with brilliant passages. Catchy.
Tell mee Daphne	Expressive, flowing. Three short sections.
Pavan	Noble, ample melodic qualities, moderate motion. Three large sections.
Rosa Solis	Three light, brisk variations on a sturdy popular tune. Requires facility in passage playing.
Wooddy-Cock	Elaborate set of six variations. Requires facility and finger independence. Difficult. <u>FVB</u>, Vol. II, p.138.
Quodling's Delight	Four sections with flowing, lyric variations on a melancholy folk tune. <u>FVB</u>, Vol. II, p.19.
Tower Hill	Also attributed to Thomas Tomkins. Short, brisk variations on two square folk-song phrases. Easy. <u>FVB</u>, Vol. II, p.371.

ORLANDO GIBBONS (1583-1625)

The keyboard pieces of Gibbons reveal a composer of emotional depth. Some of the pieces possess a weight and density of texture that seem incompatible with the tiny instrument for which they were written. His pavans and galliards are among the most touchingly noble statements in early keyboard music. They are large, ample pieces in the traditional pavan arrangement; three phrases each treated to florid variation. At least one set of folk-song variations (<u>The Woods soe Wilde</u>) approaches an impressionist idiom, and the short pieces are full of a direct, unaffected manner of musical speech, easily accessible and thoroughly rewarding. The fancies (fantasies) are, in reality, free fugal pieces inclined to an organ-like style. They are about as well suited to the modern piano as the organ-style fugues of Bach in the "48".

In addition to the general anthologies of English virginal music, the following edition devoted exclusively to the works of Gibbons may be recommended:

<u>Complete Keyboard Works</u> (Margaret H. Glyn), Stainer & Bell (through Galaxy Music Corp. Fifty-two pieces in five books:
    Vol. I — Masks and Dances
    Vol. II — Variations
    Vol. III— Pavans and Galliards
    Vols. IV and V — Fancies

Lincolne's Inne Maske	Bright, forthright tune. Two phrases, each varied. Easy. Complete Works, Vol. I
The Queene's Command	Folk-dance tune, short, brilliant variations. Fast passages, both hands. In Parthenia. Reprints in Complete Works, Vol. II; EKM, Schirmer.
The Woods soe Wilde	Unusual set of nine variations on a modal tune. Great variety of treatment; flowing counterpoint, running figuration, drone basses, short gigue, imitative figures. Drowsy, impressionist sonorities. Complete Works, Vol. II.
The Lord of Salisbury, His Pavin, The Galliard	Companion pieces; the Pavin noble, stately, the Galliard with florid variations. Requires discerning musicianship. In Parthenia; Complete Works, Vol. III; EKM, Vol. I.
Pavan in G Minor	Richly expressive, weighty. Florid, melodic variations. Complete Works, Vol. III.
Galliard in C Major	Bold, brilliant. Requires dexterity and sensitivity. In Parthenia; Complete Works, Vol. III; EKM, Vol. I.
Fantazia of Foure Parts	Complex fugal work in four voices exploiting six subjects. Organ-like in style. In Parthenia; Complete Works, Vol. V; EKM, Vol. I.

Fancy in A re — Short fugal piece, intense. Flowing counter-point.
Complete Works, Vol. IV.

Preludium in G Major — Short running étude-like piece.
In Parthenia; Complete Works, Vol. IV; EKM, Vol. I.

JOHN MUNDAY (1563 ? -1630)

Goe from my Window — Serious, sustained set of variations (eight sections) on a tune popular with virginal composers. Variety of textures. Not easy.
FVB, Vol. I, p.153. Also in Selections from FVB, Vol. II.

Fantasia — Early example of program music depicting "Faire Wether," "Lightning," "Thunder," "A Cleare Day."
FVB, Vol. I, p.23.

MARTIN PEERSON (? -1650)

The Fall of the Leafe — Short, melancholy, sustained. Two phrases, each varied. Easy.
FVB Selections, Vol. II.

The Primerose — Dance tune. Two phrases, briskly varied.
FVB Selections, Vol. II.

PETER PHILIPS (1550 ?-1628)

Galliardo — Short dance, unusual, elastic meters.
FVB Selections, Vol. II.

THOMAS TOMKINS (? -1656)

Barafostus' Dream — Elaborate set of variations, eight sections. Difficult. Vigorous, rhythmic, great variety of keyboard figures.
FVB, Vol. II, p.94.

Worster Braules — Short, vigorous, dancelike. Unusual and characteristic in quality. Short.
FVB, Vol. II, p.269.

A Toye — Bouncing dance tune. Two phrases, each varied. Also attributed to Giles Farnaby.
In Thirty Virginal Pieces, Galaxy Music Corp.

Later English Composers

(Seventeenth and Eighteenth Centuries)

If the English Virginalists bequeathed a music truly national in style it must be said that the keyboard legacy of Purcell and his contemporaries does not exhibit similar traits. By the middle of the seventeenth century the English keyboard composers are writing suites or lessons, as they were sometimes called, or simple unrelated dance movements in French style. Occasionally there are toccatas or, later on, sonatas in the Italian style.

THOMAS ARNE (1710-1778)

The sonatas of Arne are characterized by a euphonious, ingratiating type of melody heavily indebted to both vocal song and instrumental dance. The texture is uniformly thin (two or three voices) and makes only very moderate technical demands on the player. They are published by Augener (available through Broude Bros.).

8 Sonatas or Lessons for the Harpsichord. These sonatas are mostly three
    movements, using binary suite structures.

Sonata No. II in E Minor	Wistful, lyric <u>Andante</u> (flowing triplets in 4/4), short <u>Adagio</u> in three voices, dancelike finale in 3/8.
Sonata No. III in G Major	<u>Prelude quasi Improvisazione</u>, robust, concerto-like <u>Allegro</u>, concluding <u>Minuet</u> with two variations.
Sonata No. V. in B-flat Major	Short minuet-like movement joined by short connecting flourish to a piquant, sensitive <u>Gavotta</u>.
Sonata No. VII in A Major	Bright, sunny. Imitative <u>Allegro</u> in busily moving sixteenths, flowing <u>Andante</u>, closing <u>Minuet</u> in 3/8.

JOHN BLOW (1648 or -9-1708)

Blow's keyboard works include four complete "setts" or suites and many single dance movements and short pieces (airs, preludes etc.) of which the most interesting are the chaconnes and grounds. The style has a bluff, direct quality not without a certain harmonic gaucherie.

Contemporaries of Purcell (Fuller-Maitland), J. & W. Chester.
    Vols. I and II are devoted exclusively to keyboard pieces of Blow.
Old English Composers (E. Pauer), Augener (through Broude Bros.).
    Vol. IV is devoted exclusively to Blow.
Some pieces are reprinted in Early Keyboard Music, Vol. I, G. Schirmer.

Ground in G Major	Seven variations on a five-bar ground. Variety of problems in imitative counterpoint and passage playing. <u>EKM</u>, Vol. I
Chacone in G Minor	Fifteen sections on a four-bar set of ground harmonies. Change of texture with each sec-

tion. Robust section in major, rapid passages, quiet ending.
EKM, Vol. I

Prelude in C Major — Short, étude style.
EKM, Vol. I

Courant in C Major — Short, easy, rhythmic 3/4.
EKM, Vol. I

Ground in G Minor — Lyric, melodic variations on a four-bar set of ground harmonies in 6/4.

Chacone in F Major — Elaborate set of variations on fourteen-bar theme. Great variety of textures, including humorous fugue in 9/8 and sonorous homophonic ending.
Old English Composers, Vol. IV.

Suite No. I in D Minor

Almand — Flowing, heavily ornamented melody.
Corant — Stately. Dotted rhythms, some imitation.
Minuett — Quiet, noble.
In Fuller-Maitland, Vol. I.

Suite No. IV in D Minor — One of his best suites, completely French in style.
Almand — Solo melody, two accompanying voices.
Saraband — Dotted rhythms, melody in a restricted compass.
Ayre — Rhythmic, gavotte-like.
Corant — Lyric rondeau with short Corant II as trio.
Minuett — Stately, restrained, short.
In Fuller-Maitland, Vol. I.

JEREMIAH CLARKE (1669 ?-1707)

The five suites in the edition listed below may be compared, for difficulty, with the easier movements in the French Suites of Bach. The problems are moderate, the style reminiscent of the French clavecinists.

Contemporaries of Purcell (Fuller-Maitland), J. & W. Chester.
Vol. V is devoted to Clark.

Suite No. IV in C Minor

Almand — Broken, syncopated melodic line against two accompanying voices.
Corant — Brisk 3/4, neat, rhythmic qualities.
Minuet — Short. Smooth, amiable, two voices.

WILLIAM CROFT (1677 ?-1727)

Croft leans very heavily on the French style. His miniature suite movements move with suppleness, ease and fluency, embellished with the usual "agréments" of the Clavecinists. The difficulties are moderate, less mechanical than musical, since the phrase demands neatness of stress and smoothness in execution. The rondeau, with its recurring theme separated by interpolated "couplets" provides the basic formal element for a large number of his pieces. The Ground in C Minor usually attributed to Purcell is probably by Croft (according to Fuller-Maitland).

Contemporaries of Purcell (Fuller-Maitland), J. & W. Chester.
    Vols. III and IV are devoted to Croft. Each volume contains six suites.

Suite No. III in C Minor

Ground	See under Purcell.
Almand	In the style of an air. Phrases separated by humorous two-bar refrain, basso solo.
Corant	Short rondeau, minuet style.

Suite No. V in B Minor

Almand	Dotted rhythms in 4/4 make way for a flowing ending.
Corant	Dotted rhythms, some imitation.
Saraband	Solo melody, simple textures.

Suite No. VIII in E-flat Major

	One of his best works.
Allemande	Flowing lines, some imitation.
Corante	Lively, neat rhythmic quality.
Menuett	Stately, short.
Gavott	From Suite No. X in E Minor. Good-natured rondeau, chordal textures, solo melody.

Suite No. XII in C Minor

Almand	Solo melody, some imitation, dotted rhythms.
Aire	A fine rondeau, humorous, sensitive. Could be used separately.
Saraband	Sustained melody, chordal. Flowing bass in eighth notes.
Minuett	Short rhythmic rondeau.

HENRY PURCELL (1658 ?-1695)

The keyboard speech of Purcell differs in every way from that of the earlier Virginalists. His is a music based primarily on continental models (both French and Italian), with the seventeenth-century suite genres serving as center of gravity. In few instances does he attain the essentially British folk character that marks the music of his English predecessors, nor the variety and profusion of keyboard idioms that were so immediately lost to the main stream of English music. Purcell's keyboard music is mostly miniature, confined to a two- or three-voiced texture. Much of it is simple and charming (short pieces and dances) while some of it is infused with the tender, expressive qualities we have come to associate with the composer of Dido's Lament.

Suites, Lessons and Pieces for the Harpsichord (William Barclay Squire), 4 Vols., J. & W. Chester.

The Suites are reprinted in <u>Early Keyboard Music</u>, Vol. I, G. Schirmer. See also Purcell album (A. M. Henderson, Ed.), Bayley and Ferguson (through G. Schirmer).

<u>Eight Suites</u>
These are three or four movements in length, often restricted and thin in content. Generally not difficult.

No. II in G Minor	One of the most distinctive of his suites. Moderate difficulty.
Prelude	Flowing sixteenths, invention style.
Almand	Dotted rhythms in moderato 4/4.
Corant	Light three voices. Solo melody, syncopated rhythms.
Saraband	Noble, quiet. Dotted rhythms.
No. IV in A Minor	Serious qualities.
Prelude	Short, freely improvisational.
Almand	Sixteenth-note motion in 4/4.
Corant	Dotted rhythms in 3/4.
Saraband	Three voices, solo melody, dotted rhythms.
No. VII in D Minor	
Almand	Florid, three voices. Dotted rhythms throughout.
Corant	Syncopated, broken melodic line in 3/4.
Hornpipe	Vigorous solo melody, rhythmic, catchy.
Lesson	Sensitive tune, saraband rhythm. Two phrases varied. Easy. Touching qualities, three thin voices. Vol. II.
Ground in C Minor	Also attributed to William Croft. Reiterated four-bar bass in walking eighths. Plaintive solo melody. Vol. III.
Toccata in A Major	Rambling, improvisatory. Constantly changing textures culminating in a gigue in 18/16, recitativo section, three-voiced fugato and final flourish. Vol. III.
Hornpipe in E Minor	Short, rhythmic, syncopated tune. Vol. III.
Air in G Major	Non legato, brisk tune. Catchy, easy. Vol. III.
A New Ground	Haunting, melancholy tune over a three-bar ground bass. One of his best pieces. Vol. IV.
Lilliburlero	Famous political song of the seventeenth century. Rollicking, easy, short. Vol. IV.

Sefauchi's Farewell

Quiet lament on the departure of a famous singer of the period. Three voices, simple. Vol. IV.

The French Clavecinists

French keyboard music from about 1650 to about 1770 is a music based on the dance. French ballet under the "ancien régime" colored every facet of French music and the Pièces de Clavecin from Chambonnières to Daquin testify to the sensitivity and resourcefulness of French composers who exploited and developed the subtle rhythmic and textural possibilities of the then-current dance forms. They gave us pieces in small forms, refined at times to the point of over-ripeness, delicate, often irregular in phrase structure, occasionally stereotyped in mechanical repetition of sections, intricately ornamented and completely individual in style. The ornamentation, so essentially wedded to the style, is carefully notated in the original editions (and authentic reprints) and can be dispensed with or altered only at the risk of destroying the music. The composers left many explanatory tables indicating the precise rendition of the graphic signs employed. There is simply no substitute for first-hand knowledge of these tables.

It must be remembered that although the French masters assembled various dances into collections governed primarily by similarity of key, the groupings are, by and large, haphazard and are not aimed at compositional unity. The implication for the performer is a certain freedom in selecting single movements for presentation as his inclination and good taste may dictate.

Whenever the term "rondeau" is mentioned (a structure basic to French clavecin music) the arrangement ABACAD....A is meant to be conveyed to the reader. The A section (rondeau) is almost invariably repeated in unaltered fashion and the B, C, D etc. sections (couplets) constitute the contrasting interpolated interludes. The term "chaconne" or "passacaille" does not indicate variations on a set of ground harmonies but merely indicates a special type of rondeau wherein the rondeau theme is usually in 3/4 time with certain stately rhythmic characteristics.

The solutions to the strange unbarred preludes are uncertain, since the notation only approximately indicates the actual note values executed. Tagliapietra has a few suggested solutions in his Antologia which may help the modern performer arrive at his own conclusions.

Collections

Les Clavecinistes Français (L. Diemer), 4 Vols., Durand.
   An anthology of works by F. Couperin, Daquin, Rameau, Dagincourt, Dandrieu, Lully and others.
Les Maîtres Français du Clavecin des XVII et XVIII Siècles (P. Brunold), Senart.
   Single works by French composers including lesser masters such as Le Roux and Le Begue.
Early French Piano Music (I. Philipp), Oliver Ditson and Co.

JEAN HENRI D'ANGLEBERT (1628-1691)

D'Anglebert uses a florid, heavily ornamented style throughout the unbarred preludes, rondeaux, chaconnes, variations and miscellaneous dance pieces that constitute the body of his works.

Pièces de Clavecin (Roesgen-Champion), Société Française de Musicologie.

A library edition containing the complete keyboard works. Many reprints in the usual anthologies.

Variations sur les "Folies d'Espagne"	Twenty-one variations on the famous "La Folia." Same ground harmonies throughout. New textures and rhythmic motion with each variation. Could be played with cuts. In TPA, Vol. VII.
Chaconne in D Major	Graceful eight-bar rondeau theme. Five lengthy couplets heavily ornamented. In EKM, Vol. 1.

JACQUES CHAMPION DE CHAMBONNIÈRES (c.1602-1672)

The founder of the French Clavecin school had his thirty suites published in 1670. They consist of dance movements (allemande, pavane, courante, sarabande, gigue, gailliard, and minuet) favoring a texture of three voices, heavily ornamented with the usual French "agréments." The descriptive subtitles that become the rule with François Couperin are often attached to the separate dances. Predominant among the problems to be met with by the pianist are clarity of parts, neatness of embellishments and a flexible though steady rhythmic pulse. More often than not (especially in the courantes) the phrase is irregular in length, asymmetrical and vacillating in meter.

Complete Keyboard Works (P. Brunold and A. Tessier), 1 Vol., Senart.

Tagliapietra (Antologie, Vol. VII), reprints six suites. See also Farrenc, Trésor des Pianistes, and many modern anthologies (EKM, Vol. I, etc.)

Suite in E Major

Allemande	Sedate, flowing, three voices.
2 Courantes	Lively, dotted rhythms, moving quarters in 3/2, 6/4.
Sarabande	Stately, light texture. In The Art of the Suite (Pessl), E. B. Marks.

Suite in G Minor

Pavane	Three sections, stately 4/4, four voices.
Gigue	Mostly three light voices, quarter-note motion in 3/4. Requires neat accentuation.
Courante	Dotted rhythms, crossed metric accents in 3/2, 6/4.
Gigue (en canon)	Light texture, three voices, canon in upper two parts. In TPA, Vol. VII.

Four Pieces — Many reprints.

Allemand (La Rare)	Dignified 4/4, four voices.
Courante	Shifting meters 3/2, 6/4.
Sarabande	Simple chordal motion.
La Loureuse	Flowing allemande.

LOUIS NICOLAS CLÉRAMBAULT (1696-1749)

Pièces de Clavecin (1704), (P. Brunold), Lyrebird Press. This volume
  contains two suites of which the second, listed below, displays sensitive
  musical qualities.

Suite in C Minor

Prelude	Free, unbarred improvisation, melancholy, introspective.
Allemande	Tender, expressive. Mostly three voices.
Courante	Lively, rhythmic, 3/2, 6/4.
Sarabande grave	Serious, florid melody, three voices.
Gigue	Solo melody, jig style in 12/8. Essentially chordal accompaniment.

FRANÇOIS COUPERIN (1668-1733)

The twenty-seven Ordres (collections of pieces or suites) that comprise the
four books of Pièces de Clavecin of François Couperin contain over two
hundred and twenty pieces, a rich source of pleasurable, subtle and sometimes startling music. They stamp the composer as a many-sided, ingenious artist who may be considered the summation and finest flower of
French clavecin music. Even to browse through these pieces is convincing
proof that Couperin is little known to present-day pianists and, when at all
played, is represented by single pieces which display only a very limited
aspect of his art ("Soeur Monique," "Le Carillon de Cythère," "Le Tic-Toc-
Choc," etc.). It is necessary to approach Couperin without any preconcep-
tions, for the books tell us many things that are often contradicted by the
music itself. If we expect a light style, we come across some weighty
allemande or grand passacaille to disprove it. If we expect traditional
harmonic procedures, we are astonished at the dissonant chromaticism en-
gendered by the complex ornamentation of some sarabande or rondeau.
Satire is present in abundance ("Les Fastes. . .," "Les Folies Françaises")
and a deft quality of characterization ranging from descriptions of natural
phenomena to states of emotion and individual portraiture (including himself) marks his entire output.

It may be said that the ornamentation, precisely notated and carefully
explained, is an integral part of the style and is indispensable to a proper
performance (with some allowable adjustments due to the differences between piano and harpsichord). No pianist who aspires to an understanding
of Couperin can dispense with a careful study of his treatise, L'Art de
toucher le Clavecin, in which he discourses at length on his style in general
and his pieces in particular.

Although most of the Ordres are not suitable for performance as a unit
because of the great number and unequal stylistic disposition of the com-
ponent pieces, the twenty-sixth and twenty-seventh Ordres, consisting of
five and four pieces respectively, are eminently suitable for programming
in toto. The eighth Ordre may be especially singled out for the significant
qualities of many of its ten movements.

Complete Works, 12 vols. (P. Brunold) Lyrebird Press. A sumptuous
  library edition.
  Vol. I contains L'Art de toucher le Clavecin.
  Vols. II-V contain the Pièces de Clavecin.

Pièces de Clavecin, (Brahms and Chrysander) 4 Bks., Augener (through Broude Bros.).

Bk. I (1713), Ordres 1-5
Bk. II (1717), Ordres 6-12
Bk. III (1722), Ordres 13-19
Bk. IV (1730), Ordres 20-27

An excellent edition, the best available on the market.

Pièces de Clavecin, (L. Diemer), 4 Bks., Durand (through Elkan-Vogel).
A student edition with dynamics added by the editor and the ornamentation written out in small notes in place of the original graphic symbols. There are many reprints of single pieces all of which should be checked with the above editions.

L'Art de toucher le Clavecin, Breitkopf and Härtel, 1933.
Original French, modern German and English translations in parallel columns. Not available on the present market. An accessible English translation is badly needed. There are also eight Préludes (illustrating the treatise) that have been reprinted separately by Fuller-Maitland (editor) with incorrect ornamentation.

Very useful for an understanding of the music is Wilfred Meller's excellent book on Couperin published by Dobson, London, 1950.

The following selection does not mean that there are no other pieces by Couperin worth playing. On the contrary, it has been a difficult task to make the following representative listing from his entire output.

Second Ordre in D Minor

Allemande (La Laborieuse)	Serious. Flowing sixteenths "a trifle dotted."
Première Courante	Classic French style, shifting meters, 3/2, 6/4.
Sarabande (La Prude)	Three voices, dignified quarter-note motion, solo melody.
Passepied	Lively, jumpy 3/8, middle section in major.
Rigaudon	Alla breve, quarter-note motion, two voices, lively.
La Florentine	Gigue in 12/16, two voices, light and tender.
Les Papillons	Gigue in 6/16, constant sixteenths in right hand, two voices.

Troisième Ordre in C Minor

Allemande (La Ténébreuse)	Weighty, dense texture, pitched in deep register, chordal, sonorous.
Les Regrets	Pathetic genre, melody with two accompanying parts.
La Favorite (Chaconne)	Serious, lyric rondeau with five couplets.

Quatrième Ordre in F Major

Le Reveille-matin	Light, simple texture in 12/8. Broken intervals, moderato motion.

Cinquième Ordre in A Minor

La Bandoline	Rondeau, lyric 6/8, moderato. Legato melody

with light bass. Three couplets.

Sixième Ordre in B-flat Major

Les Moissonneurs	Crisp, rhythmic Gavotte en Rondeau, three couplets.
Les Langueurs-Tendres	Three voices, tender solo melody.
La Bersan	Lively, light two voices, invention style, flowing sixteenths.
Les Barricades-Mistérieuses	Lively rondeau, broken chords throughout, no change of texture.
Le Moucheron	Gigue in 12/8. Forerunner of Bartók's From the Diary of a Fly!

Huitième Ordre in B Minor

La Raphaéle	Deep, profound qualities. Allemande. Compelling chromaticisms, variety of textures.
Passacaille	One of Couperin's finest pieces. Stately eight-bar rondeau theme, unusual harmonies. Eight couplets of varying length and texture. Lengthy, difficult. Requires musicianship.
L'Unique	Noble sarabande, curious phrases "vivement" inserted into a Grave movement. Dissonant acciaccaturas.

Neuvième Ordre in A Major

Le Bavolet-flottant	Tender rondeau, flowing sixteenths in 6/8.

Onzième Ordre in C Major

Les Fastes de la grande et ancienne Ménestrandise	Ballet scene in five acts. 1- The Notables and Judges enter in a stately Marche. 2- The Old Men and Paupers are depicted in a melancholy tune over a drone bass in minor. 3- The Jugglers and Tumblers disport themselves to a leaping air also over a drone bass in major. 4- The Cripples hobble along to dotted, disjointed rhythms. 5- Grand finale—the entire troupe is routed by the Drunkards, Monkeys and Bears. Running passages and fast left-hand broken octaves. Separate reprint by Lyrebird Press.

Treizième Ordre in B Minor

Les Folies Françaises ou les Dominos	Twelve characteristic pieces depicting the Foibles of the French, a kind of carnival scene suggested to Couperin by the masked figures (les Dominos) in the Mardi Gras procession. The pieces are variations over a ground set of

harmonies (eight bars long). A unique work.
Requires neatness of style, tonal imagination,
and sensitivity.

Quatorzième Ordre in D Major

Le Carillon de Cythère — Euphonious, three voices in higher registers suggesting carillon timbres.

Le Petit-Rien — Light two-voiced rondeau, minuet style. Two couplets.

Seizième Ordre in G Minor

La Distraite — Tender, legato rondeau, distinctive chromaticisms. Uneasy, agitated melody.

Dix-Septième Ordre in E Minor

La Superbe, ou la Forqueray — Noble allemande, one of Couperin's best. Flowing sixteenths over walking eighths.

Les Petits Moulins à Vent — Rapid, scurrying imitative figures, two voices, light, clear style.

Les Timbres — Euphonious, melodic rondeau, three and four voices, uniform texture.

Dix-Huitième Ordre in F Major

Soeur Monique — Melodic rondeau, simple accompaniment, three couplets.

Le Tic-Toc-Choc — Uniform broken-chord texture, close position, a "pièce croisée" (for two manuals). Parts may be raised or lowered an octave to facilitate execution (on Couperin's authority).

Vingt-Unième Ordre in E Minor

La Couperin — Moderato motion, quasi-allemande, flowing sixteenths. Quiet charm

Vingt-Deuxième Ordre

L'Anguille — Two voices, animated invention style. Writhing figures to suggest the "Eel."

Vingt-Quatrième Ordre in A Major

L'Amphibie — Complex, lengthy Mouvement de Passacaille. Changing tempo and textures.

Vingt-Sixième Ordre in F-sharp Minor

La Convalescente — Allemande, suave, flowing sixteenths, three voices.

La Pantomime — Vigorous, marked, dotted rhythms. Lively, jumpy qualities.

Vingt-Septième Ordre in
B Minor

L'Exquise	Flowing allemande, three voices.
Les Chinois	Gigue-like 6/4, rapid rhythmic 2/4, ending with slow dignified 3/4.
Saillie	Lively dance, constantly moving sixteenths in 2/4. Three voices, some imitation.

LOUIS COUPERIN (1626-1661)

This lesser known uncle of the more famous Francois Couperin is a composer of sensitivity and originality. His works comprise a series of unbarred, improvisatory preludes, many dance movements (not organized into unified suites), many passacailles and chaconnes, a fantaisie and a tombeau. All these are collected in a magnificent library edition published by Lyrebird Press:

Complete Keyboard Works in one volume (P. Brunold).
Many separate pieces have been reprinted in the usual anthologies.

Passacaille in G Minor	Stately four-bar ground bass with twenty double variations pre-eminently lyric in character. Some chromaticism. In TPA, Vol. VIII.
Tombeau de Monsieur de Blancrocher	Lament in F. Improvisatory, intense, serious. Single reprint by Lyrebird Press.
Chaconne in D Minor	Dignified, serious, lyric eight-bar rondeau theme. Four interpolated couplets, varying in texture. In EKM, Vol. I.
Sarabande en canon	Canon between upper two voices. In EKM, Vol. I.

JEAN FRANÇOIS DANDRIEU (1684-1740)

The pieces listed below by Dandrieu are intimate, mostly lyric, of engaging quality and moderate difficulty. They may be found in Les Clavecinistes francais, Vol. II (Diemer), Durand and in Early French Piano Music, Vol. I (Philipp), Oliver Ditson and Co.

La Gémissante	Melancholy, lyric rondeau in three voices. Cf. Gretchen am Spinnrad of Schubert!
L'Empressée	Lively. Running eighths against quarters, two voices.
La Favorite	Euphonious rondeau, two smooth voices. Two "doubles" each with increasing animation.
La Lyre d'Orphée	Introspective, tender melody, three legato voices.
Les Tendres Reproches	Moderato motion in 3/4. Lyric. Syncopated, broken line in soprano, steady quarters in bass.

Le Caquet	Humorous. Busily moving sixteenths in repeated tones simulating cackling.
Les Tourbillons	Buoyant, rapid, lively, good humoured. Passage playing, some imitative figures.

From Le Concert des Oiseaux:

L'Hymen	Short, light melodic section with two "doubles" becoming increasingly animated.
Les Amours	Short. Two and three lyric voices.
Le Ramage	Bold figuration. Requires some dexterity.

LOUIS CLAUDE DAQUIN (1694-1772)

Daquin's style is light, graceful and not excessively ornamented. The difficulties are only moderate.

Pièces de Clavecin (1735), (P. Brunold), Senart (through Salabert). Four suites containing from two to ten pieces assembled without any close relationship.

Deux Rigaudons	Rhythmic, buoyant, two-voiced rondeau, two couplets with three-voiced texture. Short Rigaudon in major serves as trio.
Les Vents en Couroux	Descriptive piece, "the sea disturbed by winds and storms." Lively scale passages divided between the hands. Fairly long.
Les Trois Cadences	An early experiment in double-note trills. Animated, lengthy.
Courante	Animated, sonorous. Arpeggios and broken chords.
L'Hirondelle	Animated, lengthy rondeau. Close passage playing, imitative figures, two voices throughout.
Le Coucou	Lively rondeau on the call of the cuckoo. Close position finger passages. Many reprints. The entire suite from which this piece comes is reprinted in Art of the Suite (Pessl), E. B. Marks.
L'Amusante	Tender, lyric rondeau in E minor.
La Melodièuse	Graceful, euphonious rondeau in C minor. Pathetic genre.

CHARLES DIEUPART (? -1740)

The following suite was known to J. S. Bach and copied out by him in his own hand. It is in The Art of the Suite (Pessl), E. B. Marks.

Suite in F Minor

Ouverture	Traditional French overture. Stately opening, fugued middle section.

Allemande	Flowing sixteenths in 4/4, profusely ornamented.
Courante	French style, shifting meters in 3/2.
Sarabande	Square phrases, traditional sarabande rhythm.
Gavotte	Gay, crisp
Menuet	Rhythmic. Imitative figures
Gigue	Light three-part counterpoint, eighth-note motion in 6/8.

DUPHLY (1716-1788)

The three pieces by Duphly mentioned below have a flavor reminiscent of Domenico Scarlatti both from the viewpoint of formal structure and pianistic style. They all require finger dexterity, brilliance and neatness in phrasing.

La Van Loo	Lively, running figuration. Crisp, effective movement in two sections.
La Victoire	Descriptive piece, trumpet fanfares, brilliant passages contrasting with lyric melodies.
La Villeroy	Lively, brilliant opening, contrasting subordinate idea. Two fairly long sections. Effective broken-octave passages both hands.

ELIZABETH JACQUET DE LA GUERRE (c.1664-1729)

Pièces de Clavecin (1707), (P. Brunold), 1 vol., Lyre Bird Press. This very slim collection contains a dozen dance pieces individual in character.

Sarabande in G Major	Dignified, intense. Unusual progressions. Dotted rhythms.

JEAN BAPTISTE LOEILLET (1680?-1730 ?)

Suite in G Minor

Allemande	Dignified. Dotted rhythms throughout.
Courante	Italian style. Robust 3/8.
Sarabande	Florid melody, dotted rhythms, block chords.
Minuetto	Animated 3/4, lengthy.
Gigue	Vigorous 12/8. (This piece exists in a difficult pianistic metamorphosis by Leopold Godowsky.) In Alte Meister, Vol. III (Pauer), Breitkopf and Härtel.

See also Monumenta Musicae Belgicae (J. Watelet), Antwerp, 1932-1938, Vol. I, for other suites by this composer.

JEAN BAPTISTE LULLY (1633 ?-1687)

Air Tendre	Plaintive solo melody, floridly embellished.
Courante	Italian style, 3/8, constant eighth-note motion.
Gigue	Animated 12/8, flowing.

Many reprints of the above three pieces.

JEAN PHILIPPE RAMEAU (1683-1764)

The keyboard style of Rameau is quite different from that of his younger contemporary, François Couperin. Of the fifty-three pieces remaining to posterity from his pen, a large number display a treatment of the keyboard that stresses a more ample sonority including arpeggio figures, passages for alternating hands, runs over an extended range and, in general, greater "pianistic" breadth. The original Durand edition contains Rameau's short treatise De La Méchanique des doigts Sur Le Clavessin, in which he sets forth a few interesting ideas on the use and position of the fingers, wrists, and elbows. The stress is never on force or power, always on suppleness, naturalness and roundness. In his remarks on some pieces in the 1736 collection he says that the tempo of most of them is on the fast side. However, he cautions, "always remember that it is much better to err on the side of slowness rather than speed: when one really has a piece, one unconsciously grasps the style and soon one feels the true tempo."

Pièces de Clavecin, (Saint-Saens), 1 Vol., Durand (through Elkan-Vogel). Contains the four collections of pieces dating respectively from 1706 (10 pieces), 1724 (21 pieces), 1736 (16 pieces), 1741 (5 arrangements from the Pièces en Concert. Also a single piece (La Dauphine) from 1747. The reprint edition does not contain the short treatise mentioned above.
Selected pieces, Heugel (through Mercury Music).
Many reprints in various anthologies.

Suite in E Minor

Allemande	Noble, grand in style, moving sixteenths in 4/4.
Courante	Classic French style, shifting meters in 3/2, 6/4.
Gigues en Rondeau	Two gigues, one in minor, the second in major. Two- and three-part playing in 6/8.
Le Rappel des Oiseaux	Simulated bird calls, light, transparent, two voices.
Rigaudons	Two movements, the second with a "double." Rhythmic.
Musette en Rondeau	Pastoral, quiet, lyric.
Tambourin	Rhythmic, direct, homophonic, pedal bass throughout.
La Villageoise	Lyric, three-voice rondeau, animated variation last half.

Pieces in lyric, pathetic, cantabile style:

Les Tendres Plaintes	Two and three voices, two couplets each sixteen bars long.
Les Soupirs	Mostly three voices, broken, "sobbing" melodic line.
L'Entretien des Muses	Three voices, legato, lyric, smooth.
L'Enharmonique	Graceful three-voice texture. Unusual chromatic progressions.

Pieces of broad pianistic scope:

Les Niais de Sologne	Rondeau with two doubles becoming increasingly complex.
Les Tourbillons	Rondeau, quiet beginning. Bravura arpeggio figuration split between the hands.
Les Cyclopes	Large scale rondeau. Wide variety of pianistic devices: repeated chord tones, arpeggios, crossed hands, broken chord figures, trills, etc.
Les Sauvages	Strong, assertive style. Two and three voices.
L'Egyptienne	Brilliant. Broken-chord figuration, imitative figures.
La Dauphine	Ample, noble, combining a variety of technical devices with lyric passages.

Pieces in smooth, flowing style, homogeneous in texture:

La Joyeuse	Rondeau, simple scales and broken intervals.
La Follette	Two and three voices à la gigue.
Fanfarinette	Same as above.
Les Tricotets	Rondeau, flowing eighths in 6/8.
L'Indifferente	Melancholy, flowing.

Miscellaneous:

La Poule	Humorous tour de force, built on a motive derived from the clucking of the hen. The "doux" (piano) and "fort" (forte) are Rameau's own indications.
Les Trois Mains	Hands constantly overlapping and crossing to simulate "three hands." Alternation of lyric playing and passage work.
Gavotte with 6 Doubles (Variations)	The variations offer problems in scales for both hands, alternating hands, broken intervals and repeated notes for both hands.

Early Italian Keyboard Music

The organ is the center of gravity for early Italian keyboard music. The sixteenth century produced an imposing accumulation of keyboard compositions largely contrapuntal in texture. The ricercari, fantasie, capricci, and canzoni (all precursors of the later fugue) that comprise this literature are not easily adaptable to the modern piano. However, in the rambling improvisatory style of the Italian organists there developed, in conjunction with the exploitation of fugal textures, a tradition of toccata writing that made its way from sixteenth-century masters such as Merulo, Cavazzoni and the Gabrielis through Frescobaldi and his German pupil Froberger to J. S. Bach. The toccata is Italy's specific contribution to early keyboard music and many of the toccatas of this period are suitable for performance on the modern piano. Many sets of variations (often called partite) mark the literature along with a host of dance styles such as the corrente, balletto (often a metric variant of the corrente), passacaglia and ciaconna (chaconne).

It was Italy that gave birth to the piano (Cristofori, 1709) and with the early and middle eighteenth century the Italian keyboard sonata occupies a prominent place in the literature. The light homophonic style of a Platti or a Pergolesi prepares the way for the pre-classic sonatas of a Paradies or a Rutini. The thin, flexible keyboard writing is in strong contrast to the earlier baroque style of Frescobaldi or Michelangelo Rossi—a style often florid, powerful and strange to modern ears. The chromaticism of these earlier masters is wild, daring and extravagant (Rossi, Toccata 7).

Domenico Scarlatti is a figure bridging over the baroque to the "modern" pianism of Muzio Clementi (late eighteenth and early nineteenth century). However, many of the characteristic elements of his musical speech are Spanish in origin, taking their harmonic, rhythmic and textural patterns from Spanish dance and guitar music.

There is much in the literature of early Italian keyboard music to commend itself to the attention of amateur, professional, student and teacher alike: depth and strength of utterance in the earlier masters; charm, wit, brilliance, suavity and an engaging patheticism in the pre-classic composers. In general this is an eminently idiomatic keyboard music. Modern pianism leans heavily upon these early Italian composers.

Collections

L'Arte Musicale in Italia (L. Torchi), 7 Vols., Ricordi.
> A library edition. Volume III contains compositions for keyboard instruments by composers of the sixteenth, seventeenth and eighteenth centuries. Included are Cavazzoni, Frescobaldi, A. Gabrieli, G. Gabrieli, B. Pasquini, E. Pasquini, Porpora, M. Rossi, Zipoli and others.

Cembalisti Italiani del Settecento (Benvenuti), Ricordi.
> 18 sonatas by Bertoni, Galuppi, Manfredini, Paganelli, Paladini, Paradies, Peroti, Pescetti, Rutini, Sales Pompeo, Sammartini, Serini.

I Classici della musica italiana (d'Annunzio), 36 Vols., Milan, 1919-21.
> The following volumes in this general series contain keyboard works. This is not an Urtext edition. All pieces are heavily edited.
> Vol. 6—G. Cavazzoni,   Vol. 11—F. Durante,
> Vol. 8—M. Clementi,   Vol. 12—G. Frescobaldi,

Vol. 18—G. B. Martini,   Vol. 29—P. G. Sandoni e Serini,
Vol. 22—P. D. Paradies,   Vol. 31—D. Scarlatti,
Vol. 26—M. Rossi,   Vol. 33—F. Turini,
Vol. 27—G. Rutini,   Vol. 36—D. Zipoli.
Italian Sonatas of the 18th Century (de Paoli), J. & W. Chester.
  Six sonatas by Galuppi, Paradies, Martini and Rutini.
Ancient Italian Masters (Vitali), 2 Vols., Ricordi.
  Pieces by Frescobaldi, Grieco, Pollaroli, Pasquini, Zipoli, Marcello,
  Pescetti, Scarlatti, Rutini, Durante, Grazioli, Galuppi, Turini, Porpora,
  Martini, Paradies.
Early Italian Piano Music (Esposito), Oliver Ditson and Co.
  Pieces by many of the above composers.

DOMENICO ALBERTI (c.1710-c.1740)

Sonata in G Major   Flowing Allegro with predominance of Alberti
Op. 1 No. 8   basses. Presto assai in 3/8, mostly in two
                           voices. Light texture. Some problems in
                           ornamentation.
                           In Thirteen Keyboard Sonatas of the 18th and
                           19th Centuries (W. S. Newman), University of
                           North Carolina Press.

AZZOLINO BERNARDINO DELLA CIAJA (1671-1755)

Six Sonatas, Op. 4 (1727) Each sonata consists of a toccata, a canzone
                           (fugal piece), and two short pieces loosely con-
                           nected called "tempi" (precursors of Scarlatti's
                           one-movement sonatas). The end movements
                           are in the same keys, the middle ones have
                           varied tonics. Improvisational style of the
                           toccatas is bold and daring. Separate move-
                           ments could be played alone.

Sonata in G Major (from
the above)
  Toccata   Bela Bartók has transcribed this sonata com-
  Canzone   plete (Carl Fischer). Unusual Toccata—the
  Primo tempo   Canzone is a study built on a repeated tone—
  Secondo tempo   the last two sections a moto perpetuo and a
                           quiet pastoral finale.

See also three sonatas published by C. Bratti & Co. (Florence), full of
startling stylistic details.

DOMENICO CIMAROSA (1749-1801)

32 Sonatas   In three collections, Eschig, Paris.

                           One-movement sonatas, easy to moderate
                           difficulty, homophonic in style, light and trans-
                           parent in texture. Scales, Alberti basses,
                           broken-chord figures, conventional figuration
                           and harmonies.

FRANCESCO DURANTE (1648-1755)

Sonate per Cembalo divise in Studii e Divertimenti (c.1732)	Six <u>Studii</u> paired with as many movements called <u>Divertimenti</u>; the former in duple, the latter in triple meter, both in the same key.

Some movements are free fugues or canons. General predominance of skips and crossed hands. Light, pointed style, much passage playing.

4 Toccatas	One-movement keyboard pieces, perpetually moving. Nos. 1, 2 and 3 are prototypes of the later motorlike toccatas of Clementi, Czerny, Schumann and Prokofieff. No. 4 is a quiet allegretto.

To be found in <u>I Classici</u>, Vol. 11. Various pieces reprinted in Kalmus, <u>Old Masters</u>; <u>TPA</u>, Vol. III; and Farrenc, Vol. IX.

GIROLAMO FRESCOBALDI (1583-1643 or 4)

The history books speak of the greatness of Frescobaldi. His name commanded respect not only in his own day, for we know that in a later period J. S. Bach studied the music of the Italian assiduously and even copied out the entire <u>Fiori Musicali</u> by hand. But of what use is a man's fame if we do not play his music? Frescobaldi today is a composer still to be discovered by pianists of our time. His style is somewhat strange to modern ears since the music comes from a period when modern harmonic practices had not yet crystallized into the familiar tonal concepts of a later day. The forms are mostly sectional with a tendency toward looseness and discursiveness, especially in the toccatas. But there was a time when the style of J. S. Bach was considered heavy, pedantic, abstract and outmoded. The partitas, canzoni, toccatas and miscellaneous pieces of Frescobaldi offer a source of unexplored riches for the enterprising musician who desires to depart from the conventional repertoire.

Frescobaldi wrote no fugues in the sense that J. S. Bach did. The <u>Fugue in G Minor</u> in <u>EKM</u>, Vol. I, is spurious. (See the article by Benvenuti in <u>Rivista Musicale Italiana</u> 1920.) However, he did write many pieces in fugal style according to the current practices of the early seventeenth century. These include the canzone (or canzone francese), capriccio, ricercare and fantasia.

The canzoni are of moderate difficulty, posing the usual problems of polyphonic playing. The subjects have a popular swing since many of them derive from popular tunes of the day. The pieces themselves are in two to seven sections, each section changing meter and style but often retaining the subject in rhythmic and melodic alteration. The texture is prevailingly contrapuntal except for passages preceding the cadences. These are often declamatory, demanding freedom of treatment, both rhythmically and dynamically.

The capricci are similar to the canzoni but add some special compositional difficulty, such as a piece on the call of the cuckoo or one in which all the dissonances resolve upwards.

The ricercari offer similar problems in fugal playing but are likely to move more slowly than the canzoni (the subjects are in long notes) and are generally more suitable to the organ.

The partitas are, in actuality, sets of variations. They demand facility, rhythmic precision and imaginative musicianship. Some of the longer ones might be performed with judicious omissions since Frescobaldi himself sanctioned cuts in some of his own works.

The dances include various correnti, balletti, passacagli and ciaconne. They are all short, eminently suited for players of moderate ability and use- ful as encore numbers. Three of the seven correnti in the Ricordi collection are linked to balletti, forming a rudimentary suite. The corrente in triple meter serves as variation of and contrast to the balletto in duple meter. The irregular phrase structure adds to the freshness and charm of the pieces.

The toccata of Frescobaldi is a vehicle for free musical outpouring. It is sectional, in turn improvisatory, fugal, homophonic, declamatory or "pianistic." The music demands a free style of execution and is unplayable without some study of the famous Preface to the Toccatas of 1614. Trans- lations of the Preface may be found in Novello's publications: Ornamenta- tion, Vol. I (Edward Dannreuther), and The Interpretation of the Music of the 17th and 18th Centuries (Arnold Dolmetsch). In addition to his discussion of rubato, tempo, execution of the passages, trills, etc., Frescobaldi suggests that the player may cut various sections as suits his pleasure. Tempi vary according to the changing emotional content of the piece.

Complete Keyboard Works (Pierre Pidoux) 5 Vols., Bärenreiter (through Concordia Music Publishing Co.) Unedited text.
>Vol. 1 Fantasie 1608, Canzoni alla Francese, 1645.
>Vol. 2 Capricci, Ricercari and Canzoni alla Francese, 1626.
>Vol. 3 Toccate, Partite, Balletti, Ciaconne e Passacaglie, 1626.
>Vol. 4 Toccate, Partite etc. 1637.
>Vol. 5 In preparation.

De Santis of Rome has published the following three fine volumes edited by Fernando Germani: Vol. I—12 Toccatas (from the first book of toccatas, 1614-1616); Vol. II—11 Toccatas (from the second book of toccatas, 1627); Vol. III—Fiori Musicali (toccatas, kyrie, canzoni, capricci, ricercari in open score using the C clefs).

The Fiori Musicali is also published by Peters and is now available.

Ricordi has published the following volumes edited by Felice Boghen in modern notation including altered bar lines, added tempo markings, dynamics and phrasing, none of which is distinguished from the original text: 25 Canzoni, Correnti and Balletti, 5 Partite, 16 Ricer- cari, Sette Toccate, Nove Toccate.

Boghen has also done 15 Capricci for Senart of Paris.

There are many reprints of single works in the various anthologies.

See also Torchi: L'Arte Musicale in Italia, Vol. III; Tagliapietra: Antologia, Vols. IV and V; and Farrenc: Trésor des Pianistes, Vol. II.

Canzone in A Minor (Dopo la Pistola)	From the Fiori Musicali. Two short sections, four-part counterpoint. Lyric and rhythmic contrasts. No. 10 in Canzoni, Ricordi. Also in Old Masters, Kalmus.

Canzone in G Major	Five sections contrasting in mood and motion. Same subject transformed metrically. Requires dexterity and musicianship. No. 7 in <u>Canzoni</u>, Ricordi.
Canzone in F Major	Five contrasting sections. Buoyant. Problems in handling imitative counterpoint. No. 8 in <u>Canzoni</u>, Ricordi. Also in <u>EKM</u>, Vol. I.
Partite sopra La Folia	Six variations (not on the traditional <u>La Folia</u> theme.) Moderate problems in simple part-playing and easy keyboard figuration. Each variation has a short ripresa or refrain.
Cento Partite sopra Passacagli	Lengthy, complex work. Many unusual ideas including metric changes, rhythmic movement, modulations and insertion of dance styles into the variations. Could be played with cuts. In Vol. III of the Bärenreiter edition.
Partite sopra l'Aria della Romanesca Partite sopra Ruggiero Partite sopra La Monicha	These three partitas are generally more complex and intricate than the above, especially from a pianistic angle. They demand independence of finger, facility and musicianship. Could be played with cuts as authorized by the composer.
La Frescobalda	Short set of variations some of which are marked as dances (<u>Gagliard</u>, <u>Corrente</u>). In <u>Evolution of Piano Music</u> (C. Sachs), E. B. Marks.
Correnti and Balletti	Short dance movements, irregular phrase structure. Many reprints. Several could be linked into a group.
Toccata in D Minor	Sectional: declamatory opening, imitative melodic figures, improvisatory flourishes, short fugato, robust close. Not long or difficult. No. II in <u>Nove Toccate</u>, Ricordi. No. VIII in Vol. II of the De Santis edition.
Toccata in F Major	Sectional, varying textures: free imitative counterpoint, florid melodic figuration, improvisatory passages, block chordal background etc. No. 8 in Vol. III of the Bärenreiter edition.
Toccata in G Minor	Assertive, flowing, changing textures. No. III in Vol. III of the Bärenreiter edition.

BALDASSARE GALUPPI (1706-1785)

The elegant, polished sonatas of Galuppi contain many delightful details. They are not long and are of moderate difficulty. Bongiovanni of Bologna publishes a collection of 12 Sonatas and there are many reprints of single sonatas in the usual anthologies. See also TPA, Vol. XII.

Sonata in D Major	Suave, melodic Adagio, brilliant, light Allegro, sonorous, majestic slow section, effective gigue-like finale. In Pièces de Clavecin of the 17th and 18th Centuries (B. Selva), Senart (through Salabert). Many reprints.
Sonata in A Major	Florid, melodic Andantino, assertive Allegro (imitative figures, passage playing), light concluding Presto. In Cembalisti Italiani del Settecento (Benvenuti), Ricordi.
Sonata in A-flat Major	One movement, solo melodies, light accompaniment. Suave. In Italian Sonatas of the 18th Century (de Paoli), J. & W. Chester.
Sonata in D Major	Fresh, brisk Allegro, animated melodies with Alberti basses. Dignified Menuetto. In Italian Sonatas of the 18th Century (de Paoli), J. & W. Chester.

GIOVANNI BATTISTA GRAZIOLI (1755-1820)

Sonata in G Major	Flowing Moderato, Adagio in pathetic genre, dainty Tempo di Minuetto as finale. The Adagio has been reprinted separately. In Alte Meister, Vol. IV (Pauer), Breitkopf and Härtel.

BENEDETTO MARCELLO (1686-1739)

Toccata in C Minor	Curious study in repeated double notes, persisting throughout the piece. Requires some stamina. Effective. In Early Italian Piano Music (Esposito), Oliver Ditson. Also in Italian Masters (I. Philipp), International Music Co.
Sonata in B-flat Major	Quiet, meditative opening movement in dotted rhythms. Assertive, three-voiced Allegro, orchestral in style. Decisive Allegro in G Minor, broken-chord figuration. Short processional closing movement, chordal textures, dotted rhythms. Many reprints. Bartók has transcribed this work for modern piano (Carl Fischer).
Concerto in D Minor	Transcribed for keyboard solo by J. S. Bach from a work originally intended for oboe. Eminently worthy of performance. Concerto

grosso style. See especially the noble, florid
<u>Adagio</u>.
In volume of Bach Concerto transcriptions
published by Peters.

PADRE GIAMBATTISTA MARTINI (1706-1784)

The most famous counterpoint teacher of his time, master of Johann Christian Bach and Mozart, wrote sonatas from two to five movements in length
including occasional suite movements. The styles range from florid,
declamatory slow movements, aria, siciliano, Italian corrente, allemande
and minuet to complicated fugal movements and straightforward keyboard
pieces including short sets of variations.

12 Sonatas, Op. 2 (1741)	In <u>I Classici</u>, Vol. 18. Also two sonatas in <u>TPA</u>, Vol. XII. Various reprints.
Prelude and Fugue in E Minor	Flowing prelude, étude style, similar to two- part invention. Smooth three-voice fugue in 6/8, moving sixteenths. In <u>Early Italian Piano Music</u> (Esposito), Oliver Ditson.
Sonata in E Major	Brisk <u>Allegro</u> in two voices, minuet-like movement, dignified. Concluding <u>Aria</u> over pizzicato bass with two light figural variations. In <u>Italian Sonatas of the 18th Century</u> (de Paoli), J. & W. Chester.

PIETRO DOMENICO PARADIES (1710-1792)

A composer of invention, wit and brilliance. His handling of the keyboard
within the bounds of late eighteenth-century Italian writing is masterly and
completely characteristic in treatment. The sonatas are in two movements,
the first of which are more ample in scope than the second, exploiting a
variety of textures and full pianistic figurations. The second movements
are more homogeneous in texture and generally shorter. They contain a
varied and often tricky pianism, including all the brisk figures and ornamentation of the Italian cembalists. To do them full justice requires
clear articulation, a neat finger dexterity, precise rhythm and, by way of
contrast, a sensitive lyricism. The <u>12 Sonate de Gravicembali</u> (London,
1754) are in <u>I Classici</u>, Vol. 22. Especially to be noted are:

Sonata No. I in G Major	Flowing <u>Allegro</u>, melodic. Brisk <u>Vivace</u> in 3/8.
Sonata No. 3 in E Major	Brilliant, vivacious <u>Presto</u> in 3/8. Aria <u>Larghetto</u> in 4/4.
Sonata No. 6 in A Major	Opening <u>Vivace</u> in 3/4, concluding <u>Allegro</u> in 2/4, a perpetual motion (the famous <u>Toc- cata</u>, often played separately). Many reprints.
Sonata No. 10 in D Major	Similar to No. 6 in design and texture; the final movement also a perpetual motion (in minor).
	See also Farrenc, Vol. XIV (10 sonatas); and <u>TPA</u>, Vol. XII.

Sonata in B-flat Major	Quietly flowing, lyric opening movement. Animated <u>Giga</u> in 12/8, triplet eighth-note figuration in right hand. In <u>Italian Sonatas of the 18th Century</u> (de Paoli), J. & W. Chester.

BERNARDO PASQUINI (1637-1710)

One of the most important Italian keyboard composers between Frescobaldi and Domenico Scarlatti. The sonatas of Pasquini are often in a single movement, short, not difficult, written in a kind of workaday contrapuntal idiom stressing sequences. Works in <u>Torchi</u>, Vol. III; <u>TPA</u>, Vol. VIII; <u>Farrenc</u>, Vol. III; <u>Selection of Pieces composed for the Harpsichord</u> (Shedlock), Novello, 1895; and <u>EKM</u>, Vol. I.

Sonata in F Major	Four sections, generally contrapuntal, short. <u>EKM</u>, Vol. I.
Toccata sul Canto del Cucu	Toccata in A built on the descending third characterizing the call of the cuckoo. Improvisatory sections leading to an allegro with florid passages playing around the motive. Various reprints. Also to be found in <u>I Clavicembalisti Italiani</u> (Rossi), Carisch, Milan, 1946.
Partite di Folia Partite di Bergamasca	Variations on well-known tunes of the seventeenth century.

There are also other toccatas, ricercari and canzoni francesi.

ERCOLE PASQUINI (c.1580- ?)

Canzona Francese	Three-sectional, fugal. Melancholy, lyric subject, three voices. Requires fine legato, sensitive balance. In <u>Early Italian Piano Music</u> (Esposito), Oliver Ditson. Many reprints.

GIOVANNI BATTISTA PERGOLESI (1710-1736)

Volume I of the complete edition of Pergolesi's works (Amici della Musica da Camera, Rome) contains six sonatas and three suites, all in a light, transparent, homophonic style. The sonatas are short, one-movement affairs of very moderate difficulty. The third suite, in D, contains the following <u>Gavotta</u> made famous in a later day by Stravinsky in his <u>Pulcinella</u> suite.

Gavotta con Variazioni in D Major	Light, elegant gavotte and four variations, using more and more animated figuration. Should be reprinted. Easy.

GIOVANNI BATTISTA PESCETTI (c.1704-1766)

Sonata in C Minor	Opening <u>Allegro</u> in assertive two- and three-part counterpoint in moving quarter notes.

Melancholy slow movement. Light, concluding Presto in two voices, triplet eighths in 2/4. In Cembalisti Italiani del Settecento (Benvenuti), Ricordi.

Allegretto in C Major

Crisp sonata movement in Scarlatti style, two light, clear voices. Imitation, perpetual passage playing in right hand. Fine encore. In Cembalisti Italiani, Vol. I (M. Vitali), Ricordi.

Sonata in G Minor

In TPA, Vol. XII.

GIOVANNI PICCHI (early 17th century)

Balli d'arpichordo (1620)

Dances for harpsichord in different styles. See especially the Ballo alla Polacha (Polish Dance), the Ballo Ongaro (Hungarian Dance) and the Ballo Detto "Il Steffanni."

Each dance in duple meter has its "nachtanz" in triple meter forming a rudimentary suite. The dance tunes are varied. Mostly chordal accompaniments with refreshingly archaic parallel harmonies.

TPA, Vol. V, Ricordi (12 Dances).

GIOVANNI PLATTI (c.1700-1762)

Sonata in D. Major, Op. 1, No. 1

Adagio in two voices. Light-textured Allegro, homophonic. Unusual Largo, sensitive and touching, both melodically and harmonically. Bouncing Presto finale. In Thirteen Keyboard Sonatas of the 18th and 19th Centuries (W. S. Newman), University of North Carolina Press.

MICHELANGELO ROSSI (17th century)

This pupil of Frescobaldi possesses a style that is daring and extravagant. In his toccatas one may find declamatory recitative, fugatos, chromatic passages of a completely unexpected nature and flowing keyboard figures that alternate in the musical fabric with that freedom of expression characteristic of seventeenth-century Italian baroque music. This is a musical speech that reveals strength and intensity. His works may be found in:

I Classici della musica italiana, Vol. 26 (Alceo Toni), Milan.
L'Arte Musicale in Italia, Vol. III (Torchi).
Antologia, Vol. VI (Tagliapietra).

The Andantino and Allegro in Early Keyboard Music, Vol. I (Schirmer), attributed to Michalengelo Rossi belong to a period about a hundred years later (probably Lorenzo di Rossi, 1720-1794).

Ten Correnti	Short, simple dances, three-voiced texture, some shifted meters. Bartók has linked Nos. 5, 1 and 2 into a transcribed arrangement stressing increased sonority by the use of octave doublings. (Carl Fischer)
Toccata No. 1 in C Major	Sectional: motives in imitation, lyric and flowing counterpoint, buoyant fugato, vigorous ending. Transcription by Bartók (Carl Fischer).
Toccata No. 7 in D Major	Unusual in its harmonic instability. See especially the daring chromatic progressions of the final page.
Toccata No. 9 in A Minor	Sectional, varying textures. Vigorous ending. Transcription by Bartók (Carl Fischer).

GIOVANNI RUTINI (1725-1797)

| Twelve Sonatas, Op 1 and Op. 2 | Mostly two movements, some with introductory or interpolated largo or recitative (cf. No. 2). Homophonic, light-textured pianism. Nos. 5 and 6 are full of a winning lyricism, grace and sensitivity. Moderately difficult but tricky, demanding agility and lightness. In I Classici, Vol. 27. See also TPA, Vol. XIII. Many reprints. |

ALESSANDRO SCARLATTI (1659-1725)

Unlike his son Domenico, the elder Scarlatti did not devote the bulk of his creative energies to composition for keyboard instruments. However, he left some works of interest that merit inclusion in this volume. They are unrestrained, freely flowing works full of the element of continual expansion characteristic of so much baroque keyboard music.

7 Toccatas for Clavier	Etude style, mostly two voices. Passage playing of all sorts, double notes (No. 7), polyphonic playing (fugues in Nos. 4, 5 and 6) and a few simple dance styles (corrente in No. 4, gigue in No. 7). (Rio Nardi), Bärenreiter
Toccata Nona	Dramatic, brilliantly effective. Requires strong passage playing, boldness, scope. In Early Italian Piano Music (Esposito), Oliver Ditson.
Fugue in F Minor	Same motion as the fugue in Op. 110, Beethoven. Legato, flowing three voices. In Early Italian Piano Music (Esposito). Oliver Ditson.
Toccata in D Minor	In five sections, the last of which is a set of Variazioni sulla "Follia di Spagna." One of his best keyboard works. In TPA, Vol. IX.

DOMENICO SCARLATTI (1685-1757)

If the earlier Italian composers leave one in doubt as to the instrumental intent of their music (in the sixteenth century, pieces are written "appropriati per cantare e sonare d'ogni sorti di stromenti"—suitable to be sung and played on all kinds of instruments—and even Frescobaldi does not always clearly distinguish between organ and harpsichord music), the same cannot be said of Domenico Scarlatti, keyboard composer par excellence. He may be reckoned, along with his seventeenth-century predecessor Froberger and his nineteenth-century successor Chopin, in the class of musicians whose style and entire manner of thinking in sound was almost completely conditioned by the peculiar and characteristic demands of keyboard writing. Scarlatti's keyboard works (numbering approximately 550) are for the harpsichord. The style is idiomatic keyboard speech to the highest degree and, as such, perfectly suited to performance on the modern piano. The ingenuity of the figuration, the unorthodox character of the harmonies, the preoccupation with timbre, unusual dissonances, characteristic sonorities (often unexpectedly thin and lacking in inner voices) and the liberal use of cross relations make for a modern-sounding music fascinating to study and play.

Scarlatti's long sojourn in Spain accounts for many of the above traits.* From the Spanish guitarists came the plangent sonorities resulting from chords characteristic of that instrument's tuning. From Spanish dance came the bouncing rhythms (especially the jota) that permeate many of the movements in 3/8, 6/8 and 12/8 time. Special bass progressions may be traced to elements in popular Spanish music. And, of course, the over-all quality of the music is completely dominated by the thinking of a musician who loves the touch of his keyboard. The most ingenious repertoire of technical problems is here to be solved: scale and arpeggio figuration of all kinds, broken chords and intervals, trills, leaps up to four octaves, crossed hands, octaves, double-note passages in thirds and sixths, fast repeated notes, smooth contrapuntal playing, etc. The music is completely healthy and buoyant, on occasion pathetic and, in the best of the pieces, constantly surprising in unexpected details of sonority. For the player this demands precision above all; precision in rhythm, timbre and phrasing, with sparing use of the damper pedal.

It is a pity that so few of Scarlatti's sonatas are honored by pianists. May the following stimulate interest in those many fine pieces that deserve the attention of student and professional alike.

Opere complete per Clavicembalo ordinate in Suites di 5 Sonate ciascuna
(Complete Works for Harpsichord arranged in Suites of 5 Sonatas apiece) (Alexander Longo), Ricordi, 10 vols. and 1 supplement, comprising 545 sonatas.

The numbering of the pieces in this edition constitutes the standard manner of referring to Scarlatti's sonatas. Longo has arranged them in "suites" (a perfectly arbitrary device of his own) grouping the

---

*For further discussion of this interesting point cf. The Music of Spain (Gilbert Chase), Norton & Co., 1941, pp. 108-113.

pieces according to key. The numbering and ordering has no relationship to time of composition, since the chronology has not yet been
determined. All marks of dynamics, phrasing, accentuation, etc., are
not original and should be adhered to very sparingly, using the baroque
conception of terrace dynamics and echo effects rather than the long
crescendo and diminuendo of the nineteenth and twentieth centuries.
Variants in the original sources are noted. It is probable that other
sonatas by Scarlatti exist.

Among the many useful smaller collections are:

60 Selected Sonatas (unedited), Breitkopf and Härtel (through Kalmus).
20 Selected Sonatas (a partial reprint of the above), Kalmus or Associated
  Music Publishers.
27 Selected Sonatas, Boston Music Co. (an especially interesting set).
25 Sonatas (A. Longo), Ricordi (a selection from the complete edition).
24 Sonatas (J. Friskin), 2 Vols., J. Fischer & Bro.
10 Sonatas (A. Loesser), Mercury Music (unusual, rarely played).
35 Sonatas, 2 Vols., Carl Fischer (an excellent, unhackneyed collection).

The editions of Czerny, Sauer (Peters), Tausig and Von Bülow are not
true to the original texts and contain changes in harmonies, keys and voice
parts and, on occasion, added doublings which are stylistically inept.

The following listing, though by no means indicative of all the sonatas
of Scarlatti that merit study and performance, will at least constitute a
guide to the many riches that lie at hand.

Pieces in lyric, cantabile style, moderately flowing:

Longo No.	Time Sig.	Key	
33	3/4	B Minor	Three- and four-part weaving, melodic counter-point. Melancholy. Requires sensitive legato. (Carl Fischer)
103	3/4	D Major	Two and three voices, cantabile. (Friskin)
124	3/4	G Major	Flowing, amiable, unusual harmonic progres-sions.
142	3/8	E Flat Major	Flowing cantilena, Spanish flavor, ingenious dissonances.
147	4/4	B Minor	Expansive, sonorous qualities.
187	4/4	F Minor	Pathetic genre, unusual.
191	¢	A Major	Short. Light, ingratiating, smooth figuration.
256	3/8	C-sharp Minor	Weaving counterpoint, three voices. Enharmon-ic modulations, legato.
312	3/8	G Minor	Two and three voices, short, flowing melodic style.
383	2/4	F Minor	Aria type, graceful, "moderato" motion.
449	3/4	B Minor	Popular guitar style "with its harmonization of a melody by descending to the octave below and its chordal passage work lying between the

Longo No.	Time Sig.	Key	
			widely spaced march of the outer parts" (Chase). Haunting quality, requires sensitivity.
497	3/4	B-flat Major	Aria style, extremely simple, light counterpoint, dignified, overlapping phrases. A gem.

Pieces in dance style:

3	3/8	C Major	Unusual. Witty changes of meter and texture. Dotted, jagged rhythms. One of the best.
14	6/8	D Major	Boisterous. Spanish elements. Scale rushes. (Friskin)
23	3/4	E Major	Dignified. Echo effects, horn calls, Spanish rhythms.
28	3/8	F Major	Contrasting phrases, good-humoured, quiet, subtle.
104	6/8	C Major	Most popular and best known. "Jota" style. (Many of the sonatas in 3/8, 6/8 or 12/8 bear the influence of the Spanish jota.)
105	6/8	C Major	Primarily rhythmic in content. Repeated chords.
110	6/8	D Minor	Two voices. Requires lightness, rhythmic propulsion. Ingratiating in quality.
117	3/8	F Major	Fascinating rhythmic play. Pointed, neat style. Requires dexterity.
120	6/8	F Major	A bouncing dance. Broken chords, trills inside three-note block chords. Simple, straightforward harmonies. A gem.
125	6/8	G Major	Similar to 105. Left-hand skips. Requires vivacity.
134	3/8	A Minor	Vigorous, ingenious rhythmic study. Simultaneous trills in both hands, broken octaves and sixths, left-hand octaves. Requires quickly shifting thumb.
165	12/8	D Major	Brilliant gigue. Requires rhythmic verve.
188	6/8	F Major	A bouncing dance. Genial, healthy qualities.
205	3/8	C Major	Syncopated rhythms, percussive, zestful. Difficult octave leaps in left hand.
279	3/8	F Major	
282	3/8	C Minor	Excellent dance pieces, Spanish flavor.
290	6/8	G Major	
349	3/8	G Major	Minuet motion, capricious, humorous, light, short, not difficult.
369	3/8	A Major	Quick changes of texture and motion. Crossed hands. Easy, rapid figuration. Reminiscent of C. P. E. Bach.

Longo No.	Time Sig.	Key	
372	3/4	E Major	Charming minuet built on a single motive. Should certainly be reprinted. Requires grace and sensitivity.
384	3/8	F Major	Brisk, brimming over with vitality. Completely joyous. Requires agility. (Friskin)
387	12/8	G Major	Sparkling gigue. Light, neat, staccato style. (Friskin)
446	12/8	B Major	Plaintive, flowing style, moderato.
457	3/4	C Major	Unusual minuet. Florid melody, haunting dissonances. Should certainly be played extensively. (Boston Music Co.)
465	3/8	D Major	Richly varied textures. Horn call, trills, octaves, fast repeated notes, suspensions, cross relations, parallel fifths, leaps over the hands, shifted meters. One of the best. (Friskin)
467	3/3	E Minor	Interesting sonorities and metric changes. Flowing movement. Should be reprinted.
479	3/8	E Major	Close position finger work, short, brilliant.

Pieces tending to deal with special technical problems:

107	4/4	D Major	Double thirds and sixths, horn fanfare, crossed hands, interesting timbres, difficult.
109	3/8	D Major	Horn call, scales, quick changes of register, arpeggios, broken octaves.
119	3/4	F Major	Complete repertoire of technical problems: fast repeated notes, double sixths, broken sixths and octaves. Awkward and interesting.
127	3/4	G Major	Brilliant arpeggios, scales, passages, crossed hands, excellent étude.
129	3/4	G Major	Brilliant figures for both hands.
133	4/4	A Major	Flowing, repeated-note étude. Interesting broken-chord figures.
136	2/4	A Minor	Thirteen variations on a twelve-bar theme. Alberti basses, broken chords, scales, rapid triplet figuration, repeated tones. Good for basic pianistic problems.
148	2/4	B Minor	Vital rhythmic qualities, repeated notes. Ingenious.

Longo No.	Time Sig.	Key	
166	4/4	F Major	Square, running figuration. Somewhat reminiscent of Handel (Fantasia in C). Orchestral style.
174	2/4	C Major	Ingenious triplet figures, wide left-hand leaps, a witty piece.
184	3/4	G Major	Breathless, scurrying scales and broken chords over the entire length of the keyboard after a harmless opening. Unexpected changes.
210	12/8	D Major	Leaping bass figures. Double notes in both hands. Unusual and difficult.
215	12/8	D Major	A crossed-hands piece to end all crossed-hands pieces! Constant leaping. Double sixths also.
232	3/8	G Major	Breezy arpeggio étude. Wonderfully buoyant and extroverted. Fast triplet sixteenths.
262	3/4	D Major	Descending arpeggios over the length of the keyboard. Delightful contrasting material. (Boston Music Co.)
266	¢	D Minor	Useful study for scales, broken chords, close position passage work.
325	3/4	E Major	Rich rhythmic study, unexpected details, suspensions, syncopations.
345	¢	A Major	Frequently performed, perpetual motion, skips over the hands, running eighths.
380	3/8	E Minor	An extended piece, interesting syncopations concealing the initial meter. Running figures confined to a single hand. Clean, thin timbre.
415	3/8	D Major	Unusual, percussive. Unorthodox, varied textures. Fast repeated notes, broken chords, arpeggios, leaps over the hands. Quite long.
417	3/8	D Major	Sparkling, close position passage work, scurrying figures, rapid scales and arpeggios. A delight to play.
422	3/8	D Minor	A kind of toccata. Repeated notes over long stretches. Broken chords, skips.
429	2/4	A Minor	Vigorous, harsh, impulsive. Sonorous tone clusters.
461	C	D Major	Passage playing, both hands. Melodic interludes. Leaps over the hands. (Friskin)
487	3/8	G Major	Study for left hand. Passage playing, some difficult, quick adjustments, broken thirds, sixths and octaves. (Friskin)

Longo No.	Time Sig.	Key	
495	C	A Major	Brilliant. Repeated notes, alternating hands, passages in both hands, scale rushes, double thirds, leaps over the hands. Melodic episodes. (Friskin)

FERDINANDO TURRINI (or TURINI) (1740-1812)

5 Sonatas	In I Classici, Vol. 33. Two or three movements, full of a pianism that leads directly to Clementi. No. 5 is a brilliant three-movement work in D-flat major with a slow middle movement in B-flat major (pathetic genre). Demands a brilliant, assured pianism.
Presto in G Minor	In I Clavicembalisti Italiani, Carisch (Milan, 1946). Brilliant, perpetual motion with figuration over the full range of the keyboard. Etude style. See also TPA, Vol. XIII. Many reprints.

DOMENICO ZIPOLI (c.1765- ?)

Works in I Classici, Vol. 36; Torchi, Vol. 3; TPA, Vol. X, Various reprints.

30 Versi	Short preludes and fugal pieces in two, three or four voices. Nos. 5, 10, 15, 20 and 25 are canzoni (fugal pieces). Style varies from sustained chord passages, smooth three-part counterpoint, free prelude to étude-like pieces. No. 30 is a pastorale (with organ pedal part) that has been transcribed by Bartók. (Carl Fischer)
Suite in B Minor	Prelude, Corrente, Aria, Gavotte. Moderate difficulty, charming. Many reprints. The collection also contains several other suites and two partitas (variations).

Spanish Successors of Scarlatti

Spanish Successors of Scarlatti

Spanish keyboard music of the seventeenth and eighteenth century is sporadic and limited. Music for vihuela and guitar seems to have occupied first place in the attention of Spanish musicians. However, Joaquin Nin has collected and edited a rich and varied selection of Spanish successors of Domenico Scarlatti (published by Max Eschig, Paris). All the pieces are in one movement and the great majority are relatively easy, disarming and distinctive.

Vol. I—Seize Sonates Anciennes d'Auteurs Espagnols (1925).
Vol. II—Dix-sept Sonates et Pièces Anciennes d'Auteurs Espagnols (1928).

MATEO ALBENIZ (1760 ?-1831)

Sonata in D Major (I)	Popular dance style. Theatrical. Not difficult. Excellent program opener. Fanfare effects.

PADRE RAFAEL ANGLES (1730-1816)

Adagietto in B-flat Major (II)	Short, expressive, simple. Square phrases, pathetic, easy.
Sonata in F Major (II)	Simple, homophonic, running passage work, quasi-perpetual motion.
Aria in D Minor (II)	Florid melody, sonorous, organ-like accompaniment.
Fugatto (sic) in B-flat Major (II)	Playful, quasi-fugal, vigorous.

CANTALLOS (born c.1760)

Sonata in C Minor (I)	Tricky, light, veiled qualities, repeated notes, some octaves. Animated dance.

PADRE NARCISO CASANOVAS (1747-1794)

Sonata in F Major (II)	Alberti basses, transparent, Haydnesque, quasi-menuetto, lyrical, easy.

MATEO FERRER (1788-1864)

Sonata in D Major (I)	Pianistic, à la Clementi, varying textures, fully developed classic Sonata-Allegro, sonorous.

FREIXANET (born about 1730)

Sonata in A Major (II)	Short, simple, two and three voices.

PADRE JOSÉ GALLES (1781-1836)

There are six sonatas by Galles in Vol. II (B-flat major, C minor, A-flat major, B minor, C major and F major). They are all Italian in style, with simple melodies and classic pianistic figures. That in B minor may be singled out for especially engaging qualities.

PADRE FELIPE RODRIGUEZ (1759-1814)

Rondo in B-flat Major (II)   Quasi-menuetto, simple and charming.

PADRE VICENTE RODRIGUEZ (1685 ?-1761)

Sonata in F Major (II)   Two- and three-voice texture, dancelike.

BLAS SERRANO (born c.1770)

Sonata in B-flat Major (I)   Flowing, singing, homophonic style.

PADRE ANTONIO SOLER (1724-1783)

Padre Soler probably studied with Scarlatti. The texture of his keyboard speech is akin to the Italian master and is full of delightfully characteristic traits. The sonatas in this collection are eminently suitable for performance. The following may be singled out:

Sonata in D Major (I)	Brilliant, popular style, fast repeated notes, broken chords.
Sonata in F-sharp Minor (I)	Lyrical, gently moving, demands neatness and sensitivity.
Sonata in G Minor (I)	Light dance type, delicate.
Sonata in D-flat Major (I)	Brilliant keyboard piece, repeated notes, alternating hands.
Sonata in G Minor (I)	Boisterous dance, especially interesting left-hand figures running throughout the entire piece.
Sonata in F-sharp Major (I)	On the lyric side, dancelike, melodic contrasting section, crossed hands, smoothly flowing, engaging qualities.
Sonata in C Minor (II)	Moderately moving, three sections to each part. Demands smoothness and nuance.

Early Portuguese Keyboard Music

EARLY PORTUGUESE KEYBOARD MUSIC

Just as Joaquin Nin has done a service for the early Spaniards so has Santiago Kastner done the same for the early Portuguese composers. In his Cravistas Portuguesas (Old Portuguese Keyboard Music, Schott) he has assembled some rich specimens from the seventeenth and eighteenth centuries. The style does not, on the whole, seem to display indigenous Portuguese qualities so much as a general assimilation of more universal features. The hand of Scarlatti lies heavily on Carlos Seixas, the outstanding figure, whose warm personality shines through the clear, light texture of his music. Manoel Coelho shares a more sixteenth-century viewpoint in his organ-like ricercare, while Frei Jacinto and Sousa Carvalho speak more in terms of the seventeenth and eighteenth centuries respectively. The contemporary pianist may be inclined to bypass this music because of its light texture and brevity, but a proper tempo, neat phrasing and clear, straightforward dynamic contrasts lead to unexpectedly interesting and convincing results.

SOUSA CARVALHO (? -1798)

Toccata in G Minor — In two parts: a dramatic Allegro)(two and three voices) in two sections with contrasting textures and themes, lyric Andante in 3/8 (rondo), expressive and compelling. Entire piece requires contrasts in touch and imaginative "registration."

MANOEL RODRIGUEZ COELHO (1583- ?)

Premeiro Tento do Premeiro Ton — Long organ-like ricercare in Dorian mode on several subjects. Four-part counterpoint.

FREI JACINTO (Seventeenth Century?)

Toccata in D Minor — Two sections à la Scarlatti. Interesting chromatic clashes. Three voices, spirited.

CARLOS SEIXAS (1704-1742)

This most important Portuguese keyboard composer of the eighteenth century was very possibly a pupil of Domenico Scarlatti. The toccatas of Seixas are, in fact, short one-movement sonatas in Scarlattian mold (two sections, each section repeated). They are occasionally followed by a minuet or gigue often in a contrasting key. Although the style gravitates around a thin two- or three-voiced writing, the content of the toccatas ranges from slow movements in pathetic genre to dramatic, vigorous allegros demanding facility and sureness of execution. In some ways (phrase structure and general texture) they are more reminiscent of the Telemann Kleine Fantasien or the Handel keyboard pieces. The following may be singled out for special mention:

Toccata in F Minor — Bold, vigorous motives in imitation. Some passage playing. Excellent opener. Short.

Toccata in G Minor	Walking quarters, assertive melodies, strong rhythms, passage playing.
Toccata in D Minor	Bravura passage playing. Requires strength and agility in repeated notes. A brilliant and effective piece, one of the best.
Minuet in A Minor	Winsome, melancholy, sensitive.
Toccata in G Minor	Lyric moderato in two voices. Wandering, melancholy effect.
Toccata in E Minor	Broken intervals and repeated notes. Linked with a short, unusual Adagio and a tiny Minuet. Could be played as a short suite with the toccata da capo.
Toccata in D Major	Bright moderato in 4/4.
Toccata in B Minor	Spirited 3/8. Imitative motives, passage playing.
Toccata in D Minor	Sensitive Largo in 2/4, moving eighth notes, two imitative voices. Charming, easy.

Early German Keyboard Music

(Through J. S. Bach, his sons, and Handel)

German keyboard music by composers preceding and surrounding J. S. Bach falls into several distinct types: pieces in French style (suite movements such as the allemande, courante, sarabande, gigue, minuet, gavotte, etc., the orchestral-like French overture, and the tombeau of the French lutenists); pieces in Italian style (the contrapuntal canzone, capriccio, ricercare, fantasia, the rhapsodic toccata, the light "galant" style of the pre-classic sonata) and the more specifically German fugue (often coupled with a free toccata-like fantasia or a prelude in any one of a number of styles). The variation form persists as a frequent keyboard piece and the chaconne and passacaglia are closely allied to it in concept (in distinction to the French treatment of pieces by the same name).

It may be mentioned that the suites of many of the earlier German masters, such as Froberger, are organized into definite groupings of three, four or more pieces to be played as a unit and, though the style is French in character, the concept of a unified grouping is a German addition that one does not find, for example, in François Couperin, in whose works the organization of the suite movements seems more haphazard. The miniature, intimate character of these seventeenth-century suites may be accounted for at least partially by the fact that many of them were originally meant for the sensitive and tonally subtle clavichord.

All the musical currents of the seventeenth century fed the mighty stream that is J. S. Bach and it is perhaps not too much to say that the overwhelming emphasis placed upon the music of that greatest of all masters has unnecessarily obscured and cast into an unmerited oblivion many of the fine craftsmen who preceded him and many of those who functioned in his day. Froberger, J. K. F. Fischer, Gottlieb Muffat and Telemann are interesting composers in their own right. Present-day pianists can do worse than explore their pieces suggested below. They require a rhythmic precision, clarity of phrase, neatness of style and a general musicianship that, in many cases, will provide more than a superficial test.

CARL PHILIPP EMANUEL BACH (1714-1788)

The keyboard music of this most gifted son of J. S. Bach stretches over a creative period of about forty-five years. The output was indeed voluminous. Over four hundred pieces for solo keyboard instruments and about fifty concertos exist, many of which are still in manuscript. By and large this represents a totally unexplored field for contemporary pianists. The style varies from a thin two voices to a more florid, heavily ornamented melodic manner and, on occasion, free recitative with truly idiomatic keyboard flourishes. Although C. P. E. Bach is often rhythmically abrupt, harmonically bold and generally striking, a sensitive "espressivo" infuses his entire work. For the present-day pianist the problem is to recapture the characteristic phrase elements and weld them into a unified whole. The passages and rhythms require agility and deftness, the melodic line, heavily laden with ornamentation, demands careful, precise study and an ever-present singing legato. Bach's Essay on the True Manner of Playing Keyboard Instruments is available in a very serviceable English translation

48

by William J. Mitchell (W. W. Norton, 1949), and it is to this source that
the pianist must go for an authentic solution to many of the problems
involved.

It cannot be emphasized too strongly that editions other than the Urtext
must be used with care. Philipp Emanuel's original markings for phrasing,
touch, dynamics and tempo are completely adequate. Von Bülow's edition
of Selected Sonatas, published by Peters (also International Music), is
representative of most reprints. The text (including notes, touch and
dynamics) is altered, voices are added and original markings suppressed
and replaced. The result is useless for the serious student.

The following editions are all excellent:

Clavier Sonaten und freie Fantasien, nebst einigen Rondos fürs Fortepiano
für Kenner und Liebhaber (Krebs), in six collections, Urtext, Breitkopf
and Härtel.
  A first-class edition of his most important keyboard works, at present
  out of print but available in many of the larger libraries.
Klavierwerke (H. Schenker), 2 Vols., Urtext, Universal Edition
(through Associated Music).
  An excellent selection from the above, containing complete sonatas and
  single movements. Schenker's Beitrag zur Ornamentik, a valuable
  treatise on ornamentation and style, was written to accompany this
  edition. It is as yet untranslated.
Kurze und Leichte Clavierstücke (O. Vrieslander), Universal Edition.
  Twenty-two short pieces of moderate difficulty displaying the art of
  spinning out a piece by the subtle variation of repeated phrases.
The Prussian Sonatas (R. Steglich), 2 Vols., Nagel's Musik-Archiv, Nos. 6
and 15 (through Associated Music).
  Six sonatas, three in each volume. An excellent Urtext edition.
The Württemberg Sonatas (R. Steglich), 2 Vols., Nagel's Musik-Archiv,
Nos. 21 and 22.
  Six sonatas, three in each volume. Same as above.
18 Probestücken (E. Doeflein), 2 Vols., Schott (through Associated Music).
  Example pieces for his Essay on the True Art of Playing Keyboard
  Instruments, organized into six sonatas, three pieces in each sonata.
Sonatas and Pieces (K. Herrmann), Peters.
  Short pieces, a Rondo in E-flat Major, four sonatas and the Folia
  variations.
Farrenc in Le Trésor des Pianistes reprints 65 sonatas and four rondos
in Vols. XII and XIII. This largest single source is, of course not
available on the present market but is to be found in many of the large
libraries.
Other separate pieces have been reprinted in collections featuring the sons
of Bach by Universal Edition and Mercury Music (W. Newman) among
others.

Sonata in A Major (1742)	No. 6 of the Prussian Sonatas. Light, scurrying Allegro, introspective, intense slow movement with bold harmonic strokes and a bright closing rondo.
Sonata in G Minor (1746)	Long, bold free fantasy with running passages, recitatives, cadenzas etc., an Adagio with florid melodic content and an Allegro assai, chromatic and unusual. The entire work is

striking and not easy.
In <u>Sons of Bach</u> (W. Newman), Mercury
Music.

From the collections for "Kenner und Liebhaber" (Connoisseurs and
Amateurs), 1779-1787:

Sonata in A Minor	Rapid, abrupt motives in a capricious opening movement. Quiet, tender, "sighing" slow section leading to a playful finale. In Schenker, Vol. I.
Sonata in F Minor	Bold, vigorous, dramatic <u>Allegro assai</u>, florid, melodic <u>Andante</u>, short, lyric <u>Andantino grazioso</u>. A difficult work. In Schenker, Vol. II.
Sonata in G Major	Melodic opening movement leading by abrupt transition to an intense, short slow movement in F-sharp minor again moving abruptly to gay, rapidly changing finale. In Schenker, Vol. I.
Sonata in A Major	Long, brilliant work, the end movements requiring dexterity and assertiveness, the slow movement florid and highly ornamented. In Schenker, Vol. I.
Rondo in B Minor	Two simple voices. A tour de force in the pathetic genre. In Schenker, Vol. II.
Rondo in G Major	Rich, lengthy, florid variation-rondo, graceful, subtle, with unexpectedly amazing excursions into remote keys. Requires a fluent, skillful musicianship. In Schenker, Vol. II.
Fantasy in C Major	A most unusual piece. Light, joking <u>Presto</u> alternating with two contrasting lyric sections culminating in an unexpectedly expansive closing cadence. In the sixth collection.

From the "18 Probestücken" (1753)

Allegro Siciliano e scherzando	Short, graceful Mozartean <u>Siciliano</u> in F-sharp minor. In Vol. II.
Allegro di molto in F Minor	Rapid étude-like piece, crossed hands, running sixteenths in close position, contrasting lyric episodes. In Vol. II.
Fantasia in C Minor	Magnificent free fantasy of great scope and boldness. Mostly unbarred. Requires mature musicianship. In Vol. II.

Miscellaneous pieces:

Abschied von meinem Silbermannischen Claviere (1781)	"Farewell to my Silbermann Clavichord." Rondo in pathetic genre, rubato. Single, florid melody, simple accompaniment, striking harmonies. In The Bach Family, Universal Edition.
Various "Characterstücke"	Short pieces mostly in the French style with descriptive titles: La Stahl, La Bach, Les Langueurs Tendres, etc. Many of these pieces are modeled after the rondeaux of Couperin.
	The famous Solfeggietto belongs to a host of similar teaching pieces.
12 Variations auf die Folie d'Espagne	Most unusual imaginative treatment of the famous La Folia theme. (The bare set of chords used by Philipp Emanuel could be replaced by a more interesting version of the theme). Unorthodox motives, rhythmic changes, keyboard figuration in turn expressive and brilliant. In Sonatas and Pieces (Herrmann), Peters.
Rondo in E-flat Major	Lengthy, lyric essay requiring fine legato and subtle "espressivo." In Sonatas and Pieces (Herrmann), Peters.

JOHANN CHRISTIAN BACH (1735-1782)

The youngest son of Johann Sebastian ("ein Mann von Weltkenntnis"—a worldly-wise man) was, in a material sense, the most successful of all the Bachs. For many years he was a dominant figure in the musical life of London. His keyboard works, written with an eye to the trade, are suave, polished and completely Italianate in their lightly-flowing homophony. The young Mozart learned much from him and even today there is still much to enjoy in the smooth "singing allegros" and transparent pianistic figuration that marks his style. The difficulties are moderate with the accent on legato and cantabile playing. It may also be mentioned that Johann Christian was the first musician in England to perform solo on the then modern pianoforte (1768) and his activity as pianist was an influential factor in securing for that instrument the pre-eminent place it has since occupied.

10 Sonatas (L. Landshoff), 2 Vols., Peters.

Sonata in C Minor, Op. XVII, No. 2	An outstanding piece. Sprightly Allegro; tender, suave, singing Andante, brisk, closing, operatic Prestissimo of great vigor and vitality. In Vol. I, No. 5, Peters.
Sonata in C Minor, Op. V, No. 6	Serious, weighty Grave leading to vigorous rhythmic fugue in three voices. Light, gavotte-like finale. In Vol. II, No. 9, Peters.

| Sonata in G Major, Op. V, No. 3 | Flowing <u>Allegro</u> and light <u>Allegretto</u> with four variations. Generally suave and singing in style. Not difficult. In Vol. II, No. 10, Peters. |
| Sonata in B-flat Major, Op. XVII, No. 6 | Graceful, flowing <u>Allegro</u>, quiet <u>Andante</u> and brilliant gigue-like <u>Prestissimo</u> in 12/8. Requires finish and clear passage playing. In <u>Sons of Bach</u> (W. Newman), Mercury Music. |

JOHANN SEBASTIAN BACH (1685-1750)

A comprehensive acquaintance with the most important constituents of
J. S. Bach's enormous output is an indispensable part of the musician's
equipment. Large blocks of material—e.g. the Inventions, Suites, Partitas,
and the forty-eight Preludes and Fugues of the <u>Well-tempered Clavier</u>—
should be familiar as a whole. Therefore no apology is made here for a
detailed commentary on the main groups of his keyboard compositions.

Editions

The most satisfactory edition on the whole is still that of Hans Bischoff,
originally published by Steingräber. Most of it has been reprinted in
America by Kalmus. For the average pupil, however, some further anno-
tation by the teacher will be found necessary. Mugellini's edition of the
<u>Well-tempered Clavier</u> has many virtues—a good text, good fingering,
useful analytical notes and interpretation of the ornaments and generally
sensible phrasing, with a perhaps too-ready adoption of staccato, in some
of the livelier movements, for eighth notes where these alternate with
passages in sixteenths. (The Mugellini edition is issued in America by
Carl Fischer.) The edition of the Suites and Partitas bearing Mugellini's
name is for some reason less carefully phrased. The Schirmer reprint
of Czerny's edition of the <u>Well-tempered Clavier</u> has only one virtue—
careful fingering. The text is often poor, and the phrasing is frequently
misguided. The Schirmer edition of the Suites and Partitas (Czerny, etc.)
has a generally good text with some erratic, sometimes grotesque, dynamic
indications and occasionally demonstrably wrong phrasing.

Busoni's edition of the <u>Well-tempered Clavier</u> (Schirmer) has a good
text, phrasing which is almost invariably sensible (though a notable exception is to be found in the subject of the <u>Fugue in D-sharp minor</u>, I. 8), and
a general treatment which is the product of a fine musical mind, though
many features are extremely personal. The edition of Edwin Hughes
(Schirmer) is careful and conservative, and has the advantage of a comparison of various previous editions. An edition that should also be mentioned is that of Percy Goetschius (Ditson) who, although his text is based
on that of Czerny, has corrected many errors and has made a clean sweep
of Czerny's phrasing. There is perhaps, for the pianist, a too-exclusive
reliance on legato, this edition going to the opposite extreme from
Mugellini's.

An edition of the <u>Well-tempered Clavier</u> that is in a class by itself is that
of the great scholar D. F. Tovey, issued by the Oxford University Press.
The text is presented with no editorial additions; but accompanying it there
are not only a most illuminating general introduction, but also separate
notes, referring to both text and performance of each prelude and fugue,
which are unique in the light they throw on problems of the interpretation
of Bach.

The firm of Peters reprints the excellent text of the Well-tempered Clavier provided by Franz Kroll, who edited the same material for the Bach-Gesellschaft. There are no editorial phrasings or dynamics.

Scholarly editions of the Well-tempered Clavier are published by the English firms Novello and Ashdown.

The complete edition of the Bach-Gesellschaft, formerly published by Breitkopf and Härtel and for years unobtainable, has recently been reprinted by J. W. Edwards, Ann Arbor, Michigan. This library edition is on the whole to be regarded as authoritative for reference.

Elementary Material

The following collections of simple pieces are useful as an introduction to Bach for pupils in the earlier stages:

First Lessons in Bach (Walter Carroll), 2 books, G. Schirmer.
The Children's Bach (E. Harold Davies), Oxford University Press.
Bach—Easy Piano Compositions (Cuthbert Harris), Warren & Phillips,
    London
Bach volume in Master Series for the Young (Edwin Hughes), G. Schirmer.
Introduction to Bach (John Thompson), Willis Music Co.
Bach Album (John Thompson), Schroeder & Gunther. Includes some
    arrangements.
Bach for Beginners (Charles Vincent), 2 books, Boosey & Hawkes.
Bach—26 Easy Pieces in Progressive Order (Oscar Beringer), 2 books,Augener.
Bach verklärt (Persis Cox), E. C. Schirmer. A collection of shorter
    pieces with no editing.

The Little Clavier Book of Anna Magdalena Bach is issued by various publishers:
    Kalmus.
    Peters—Twenty Easy Pieces (Sauer).
    Augener—Twenty Easy Pieces.
    International Music Company—Twenty Easy Pieces (Sauer) and
        Twelve Selected Pieces (Philipp).

Twenty Pieces from the Little Clavier Book of W. Friedemann Bach are
    published by J. Fischer and Bro. (edited by G. Maier).

Short Preludes and Fugues

Collections of these, containing generally more advanced material than the preceding, are issued by:

    Kalmus (Bischoff) 28 pieces.
    Peters (Ruthardt),revision of Czerny, 24 pieces.
    Schirmer (Mason) 24 pieces.
    Schirmer (Buonamici) 18 pieces including 6 by W.,F. Bach.
    Augener (Franklin Taylor).

Fifteen Two-part and Fifteen Three-part Inventions

These form an excellent introduction to the problems of contrapuntal playing. It may be observed that the three-part Inventions are in general more difficult than most of the material in the Suites and Partitas. Among available editions are the following:

Schirmer (Mason, Busoni or Czerny).
Kalmus (Bischoff).
Peters (Czerny or Urtext).
C. Fischer (Czerny).
Suggested selection:
  Two-part Inventions - Nos. 1, 6, 8, 9, 13, 14.
  Three-part Inventions - Nos. 2, 3, 5, 8, 9, 11.

Six French Suites
Editions: (Bischoff) Kalmus, (Mugellini) Ricordi, (Czerny) Schirmer,
  (Czerny) Peters.

No. 1, in D Minor	The Allemande and Courante (The latter of the "French" type) present some of the most complicated fingering problems in this series of suites. The Sarabande and Minuets are straightforwardly expressive, with some contrapuntal interest. The Gigue is of the exceptional slow-moving type in quadruple dotted-note rhythms that is found again in the gigue of the sixth partita.
No. 2, in C Minor	The simplest of the suites, none of its movements having any technical difficulty. The texture is generally two-voice—easier than most of the two-part Inventions.
No. 3, in B Minor	Has a highly organized Allemande of no great technical difficulty. The "French" Courante is slightly more taxing in its fingering problems. The Sarabande gives in its counterpoint an opportunity for careful balance of tone. The Anglaise, Minuet and Trio, and Gigue are all tuneful and fairly simple.
No. 4, in E-flat Major	Has the simplest Allemande of the series. The Courante is not much more difficult than the "Italian" one of No. 2; the Sarabande is simpler than that of No. 3. The authentic slurs in the Gavotte and Minuet (clearly indicated by Bischoff) should be noted. The most difficult movement to present effectively is the Gigue, with some trills that need careful management.
No. 5, in G Major	The finest of the French Suites. The beautiful Allemande is a test for musical phrasing; the Courante and Bourrée tax the player's rhythmic control; the Sarabande is easy and melodious; the Gavotte and Loure call for delicate accentuation; and in the brilliant and popular Gigue a more severe test of technique and rhythm is met with than anywhere else in this series.
No. 6, in E Major	Also a suite of fine quality. The contrapuntal passages of the Allemande offer alternatives

of tonal balance that can add interest to the repeats. The <u>Courante</u>, <u>Gavotte</u> and <u>Bourrée</u> are similar to those of No. 5. The <u>Sarabande</u>, with opportunity for rich tone in its chords, the <u>Polonaise</u> and the <u>Minuet</u> are all easy. The <u>Gigue</u> is less brilliant than that of No. 5, but two left-hand passages, with accompanying right-hand trills, need steady control. The position of the <u>Minuet</u> in the Bischoff edition seems less effective than that in other editions which place it between the <u>Bourrée</u> and the <u>Gigue</u>.

Six English Suites
Editions - as for French Suites.

No. 1, in A Major

The <u>Prelude</u> has an improvisatory character, compared with the firmly organized preludes of the remaining five English Suites. The <u>Allemande</u> has complicated part-writing and less clearly defined material than is found in the others of the series. Another difficulty in the way of presenting this suite as a whole lies in the fact that there are two <u>Courantes</u> (like all those in the English Suites, of the French type), with a further redundancy in two variations for the second. The <u>Sarabande</u> is notably beautiful and warmly expressive, and the two <u>Bourrées</u> are appealing - the second specially so. The <u>Gigue</u> is rather slow-moving and less sparkling than its five companions.

No. 2, in A Minor
No. 3, in G Minor
No. 4, in F Major
No. 5, in E Minor
No. 6, in D Minor

The preludes of all these five suites are lively allegros in an extended ABA form; No. 6 has in addition an introductory section in slower tempo. The allemandes of Nos. 2, 3 and 5 are similar in character and tempo; the rolling triplets in No. 4 and the thirty-second notes in No. 6 prescribe a slightly slower speed. The five courantes are all comparatively simple in texture, with some occasional care needed in managing the ornamentation. In Nos. 2, 3 and 6 it is recommended that the "double" of each half of the sarabande be used for the repeat. Between the sarabande and the gigue each suite has a pair of alternating lighter movements - bourrées in No. 2, gavottes in Nos. 3 and 6, minuets in No. 4, and passepieds in No. 5—all individually pleasing and not difficult. The gigues are brilliant (No. 4 outstandingly effective); in No. 2 the short trills serve as a restraint on the tempo; Nos. 5 and 6 are somewhat more exacting technically than the others.

Seven Partitas
Editions—as for the Suites (Ricordi gives selection only).

In contrast to the general uniformity of the English Suites, the Partitas
show an unusual variety both in their character and in the arrangement of
their movements. Even the inclusion of the standard allemande, courante,
sarabande and gigue, which are always found in the Suites, is not invariable; the second Partita has no gigue, and the seventh no allemande. There
are introductory movements of widely differing characters, ranging from
the short Praeludium of No. 1 to the extended and weighty French Overtures of No. 4 and 7 and the equally imposing Toccata of No. 6. Besides,
there are numerous short interpolated movements which vary the conventional scheme.

No. 1, in B-flat Major	The most delicate of the series. In the Alle-mande the two measures before the double bar warn against too fast a tempo. In the Sara-bande, on the other hand, care is needed lest the underlying rhythm be lost through a tempo that is too slow. The Gigue is quite unlike any other similarly named movement of Bach (with hand-crossings that suggest Scarlatti and Italian influence); some very discreet pedaling is advisable.
No. 2, in C Minor	More weighty than No. 1. The andante of the opening Sinfonia needs careful phrasing. The Sarabande, with its totally different texture from No. 1, has nevertheless a similar under-lying harmonic and rhythmic structure. The tempo of the Rondeau should be guided by the triplets in measures 86 and 87. The brilliant and highly organized Capriccio presents problems of technical control greater than are to be met with elsewhere in the Partitas, except perhaps in the Gigue of No. 4.
No. 3, in A Minor	This, which appeared originally with No. 6 in one of the collections bearing the name of Anna Magdalena, is a partita with curiously dissimilar and somewhat inconsistent individ-ual movements. Starting with a Fantasia having the texture and character of a two-part invention (much expanded), followed by a florid Allemande not unlike that of the sixth Partita, it continues with a light Italian Courante, a so-called Sarabande with no trace of sarabande character, a Burlesca and Scherzo (both slight), and a Gigue of quite serious and weighty type. Technical difficulty is throughout moderate.
No. 4, in D Major	A fine work, starting with a French Overture consisting of an imposing Grave and extended contrapuntal Allegro. The Allemande has a depth of feeling unequaled in Bach's movements

of this type; it demands a fine sustained cantabile. The rhythmic "French" Courante is,
exceptionally, in 6/4 time throughout. Next
come three technically simple movements -
Aria, Sarabande and Minuet - and the Partita
ends with a most brilliant, effective, and
technically exacting Gigue.

No. 5, in G Major

The Praeambulum is a bright and lively movement, without excessive difficulty, that gives
scope for a good finger technique. The Allemande is weightier, calling for a smooth
legato in its rolling triplets. The Italian
Courante has technical requirements and a
musical character like the Praeambulum.
The Sarabande, in its unusual rhythm, is almost as far from the typical sarabande as
that of No. 3; the interpretation of its ornaments is not always easy. The delicate Tempo
di Minuetto, with its fascinating cross-rhythms
and absence of technical difficulty, and the
equally simple Passepied are followed by an
exceptionally complicated Gigue which poses,
especially by reason of the trills in the second
half, difficult digital and interpretative
problems.

No. 6, in E Minor

The most severe of the Partitas. The first
movement, entitled Toccata, consists of an
improvisatory introduction leading to an extended fugue which contains a few problems of
fingering and tonal discrimination. The Allemande recalls in its dotted rhythms the Allemande of No. 3. The Italian Courante has a
simple two-voice texture, but a larger form
than usual, with definite first and second
subjects. A quite slight Air is followed by the
most complicated and abstruse of all the
sarabandes, requiring a firm rhythmic grasp
if it is to be presented intelligibly. A Tempo
di Gavotta provides some light relief, and the
Partita ends with a fine, but austere Gigue—
in a quadruple rhythm like that of the first
French Suite; the prevailing texture is a complicated three-voice counterpoint.

**No. 7, in B Minor
(Overture in the
French Style)**

This, published separately by Peters, Ditson's
Musicians' Library, and others as Overture in
the French Style, is included in the Kalmus
volume reprinting the Bischoff edition of the
Partitas. It was published by Bach together
with the Italian Concerto, and it contains
"piano" and "forte" directions indicating that
it was intended for a harpsichord with two
keyboards.

The first movement is a French <u>Overture</u> like that of the fourth Partita, with an additional section at the end, returning to the opening slow tempo. There is no allemande. A French <u>Courante</u>, with some diverting cross-rhythms, is followed by two pairs of alternating dance movements (<u>Gavottes</u> and <u>Passepieds</u>) which are tuneful and technically simple. The <u>Sarabande</u> is one of Bach's finest, deeply expressive and full of interesting detail. A third pair of lively dance movements (Bourrées) and a rhythmically vital <u>Gigue</u> follow. The last movement, unique in the Suites and Partitas, is an <u>Echo</u> which makes entertaining use of the two manuals of the harpsichord. These can be appropriately represented by using the "una corda" pedal for the echoes.

The Well-tempered Clavier
For editions see introduction to this section.

In the following tabulation some indication of the salient requirements for performance on the piano is attempted:

Book I

1. Prelude	Delicacy and evenness.
Fugue	Legato - tonal discrimination between voices played by the same hand.
2. Prelude	Moderate tempo in first half, allowing increase of speed in second part - compare structure of tenth prelude.
Fugue	Rhythmic vitality.
3. Prelude	Even finger technique.
Fugue	Rhythmic control and vitality—independence of finger in double-note passages.
4. Prelude	Legato cantabile - phrasing.
Fugue	Presentation of the design and management of tone with regard to climax.
5. Prelude	Even finger technique.
Fugue	Grasp of design and planning of climax.
6. Prelude	Even finger technique—suggestion of harmonic subtleties.
Fugue	Tonal discrimination between different voices.
7. Prelude	Grasp of design - planning of climax.
Fugue	Rhythmic vitality - even finger control.
8. Prelude	Cantabile, together with rhythmic flow.
Fugue	Grasp of design, economizing tone with view to climax.
9. Prelude	Legato cantabile - phrasing.
Fugue	Finger control and evenness.

The Well-tempered Clavier, Book I

10. Prelude	Expressive cantabile - even finger control in second half.
Fugue	Even finger technique.
11. Prelude	Smooth legato and careful phrasing of the dominant figure.
Fugue	Legato cantabile, with phrasing of imitative entries.
12. Prelude	Expressive legato.
Fugue	Planning of tone in relation to the design, with contrast in episodes.
13. Prelude	Legato cantabile.
Fugue	Careful voice leading.
14. Prelude	Even finger technique.
Fugue	Legato cantabile - careful phrasing of counter-subject and passages derived from it.
15. Prelude	Strong finger technique.
Fugue	Even control, emphasizing structural features (e.g., inversion of subject) by variety of tone.
16. Prelude	Phrasing and legato.
Fugue	Tonal discrimination between different voices.
17. Prelude	Rhythmic vitality.
Fugue	Phrasing and legato.
18. Prelude	Phrasing and legato.
Fugue	Cantabile - tonal discrimination between different voices.
19. Prelude	Legato cantabile - careful voice leading.
Fugue	Delicacy - accurate tonal balance.
20. Prelude	Rhythmic vitality.
Fugue	Grasp of design, with economy of tone to build climax.
21. Prelude	Even finger technique.
Fugue	Rhythmic vitality—independence of finger in double-note passages.
22. Prelude	Rhythmic flow—expressive phrasing.
Fugue	Legato cantabile—tonal discrimination in voice-leading.
23. Prelude	Phrasing - accurate finger control.
Fugue	Balancing of voices - legato.
24. Prelude	Legato cantabile.
Fugue	Grasp of the large design and planning of climax - contrast of tone in episodes not founded on main subject.

Book II

| 1. Prelude | Grasp of design - legato. |
| Fugue | Even finger technique. |

The Well-tempered Clavier, Book II

2. Prelude	Phrasing—independence of finger.
Fugue	Tonal discrimination and balance of tone in voice leading.
3. Prelude	Delicacy and evenness—rhythmic vitality in latter part.
Fugue	Delicate staccato in sixteenth-note diminution of fugue subject - careful building of climax toward quarter-note augmentation.
4. Prelude	Expressive legato - rhythmic flow.
Fugue	Even finger technique and control.
5. Prelude	Strong finger technique - clear grasp and presentation of design.
Fugue	Legato cantabile - tonal discrimination between two voices in same hand.
6. Prelude	Even finger technique.
Fugue	Control of finger - legato and phrasing of individual voices.
7. Prelude	Expressive phrasing and legato.
Fugue	Voice leading - planning of climax.
8. Prelude	Legato - rhythmic flow.
Fugue	Legato cantabile—tonal discrimination in voice leading—planning of climax.
9. Prelude	Phrasing - expressive legato.
Fugue	Grasp of design - legato cantabile - clear voice leading.
10. Prelude	Smooth legato - musical phrasing.
Fugue	Rhythmic vitality and drive.
11. Prelude	Legato - singing quality in sustained notes - rhythmic continuity and grasp of design.
Fugue	Light touch, non legato—even finger technique and rhythmic control.
12. Prelude	Expressive legato phrasing.
Fugue	Rhythmic vitality - even finger technique.
13. Prelude	Phrasing - legato - rhythmic flow.
Fugue	Rhythmic vitality and delicacy.
14. Prelude	Smooth legato - musical phrasing.
Fugue	Clear grasp of design - careful planning of tone in relation to climax.
15. Prelude	Finger technique - rhythmic drive.
Fugue	Delicate finger staccato - clear delivery of two-voice countersubject with singing tone in tied notes.
16. Prelude	Presentation of design, with steady rhythmic flow.
Fugue	Rhythmic vitality - planning of climax.

17. Prelude	Holding of long rhythmic lines, leading to successive re-entries of main subject - economy of tone before final climax.
Fugue	Smooth legato—grasp of design—tonal discrimination in voice leading.
18. Prelude	Expressive legato phrasing.
Fugue	Control of smooth legato, with sufficient delicate accentuation to make the main subject clear—economy of tone.
19. Prelude	Legato - tonal discrimination between two voices in same hand.
Fugue	Rhythmic vitality and control.
20. Prelude	Legato and phrasing.
Fugue	Rhythmic drive, with powerful delivery of final climax.
21. Prelude	Smooth legato, with careful phrasing.
Fugue	Balance of tone in playing of two voices in same hand—clear presentation of new countersubject entering after cadence on dominant.
22. Prelude	Expressive legato - tonal discrimination in voice leading.
Fugue	Careful management and economy of tone for building of climax, with feeling for the design's architecture.
23. Prelude	Even finger technique.
Fugue	Grasp of structure - steady rhythmic flow toward the cadences.
24. Prelude	Legato, with rhythmic drive.
Fugue	Rhythmic vitality and control.

Seven Toccatas
Editions: (Bischoff) Kalmus, (Hughes) Schirmer.

Of these, five (D major, D minor, E minor, G major, G minor) are early works, with less interest in the sections requiring technical mastery and contrapuntal skill than in those that are emotionally expressive. The Toccatas in F-sharp minor and C minor are mature compositions, that in C minor being specially effective.

Toccata in D Major	In six sections: 1. An introductory bravura passage recalling the opening of the great organ prelude in the same key. 2. An allegro with a lively motive which persists, with some contrasting material, throughout - much variety of touch and tone is requisite to maintain interest. 3. A short passage of emotionally expressive recitative. 4. A tranquil andante, founded on a two-voice theme in invertible counterpoint, calling for expressive legato. 5. A second recitative, of dramatic character. 6. A fugue of an easy-going sort, best treated

with a humorous approach—it makes no attempt at any real contrapuntal development. Bischoff's metronome mark ($\flat$ = 108) allows playing of the passages in thirty-second notes toward the end without slackening of tempo.

Toccata in D Minor

A work of unequal interest. Its five sections are: 1. An introduction suggesting, as does that of the Toccata in D Major, organ style. 2. A sustained slower section with a good deal of expressiveness in its persistent suspensions. 3. A rather dull and repetitious fugue. 4. The most striking part of the piece, an adagio of moving character, developing a short theme in rising and falling thirds with remarkable expressive power. 5. A fugue with character similar to that in section 3.

Toccata in E Minor

In four sections: 1. A few simple measures of uniform texture, serving as introduction. 2. A section in moderate tempo resembling, in its structure and development from a two-voice invertible theme, the fourth section of the Toccata in D Major. 3. A dramatic section with sharply contrasting material that lends itself to imaginative treatment. 4. A short fugue, not very enterprising, but with somewhat greater interest than those in the Toccata in D Minor. It should be said that Bischoff's notes indicate that the copies by various hands of the different manuscript sources leave some doubt as to the final authority of any text.

Toccata in G Major

The three sections are: 1. A rhythmically vital allegro that stands well by itself. 2. An adagio, the opening expressive phrase of which is later reduced to simple elements which are developed contrapuntally. 3. A fugue which starts promisingly but becomes repetitious and has a curiously inconclusive finish.

Toccata in G Minor

There are three distinct sections: 1. A brilliant opening flourish leads directly to thirteen measures of an expressive ruminating adagio. 2. A lively allegro in B-flat major somewhat like section 2 of the Toccata in D Major and again requiring much tonal variety to maintain interest, concludes with eleven measures of an adagio similar to that of the first section. 3. A lengthy fugue with primitive counterpoint recalling the final fugue of the D-major Toccata and presenting, with its repetitions and absence of climax, a severe test of the player's resources of touch and tone.

Toccata in F-sharp Minor

Five extended sections follow one another without any real break other than a pause on a perfect cadence at the end of the third. 1. Some brilliant opening passages lead to a series of broad and dignified sequences followed by (2) a nobly expressive slow movement developing a simple four-note motive in three- and four-voice counterpoint. Section 3 is a very effective and brilliant fugue (<u>Presto e staccato</u>) —the most difficult movement in the clavier toccatas. Then follows (4) a unique section consisting almost entirely of single-bar sequences, sometimes rising, sometimes falling, suggesting Bach's experience in improvisation, and ending, through a passage of rhythmical diminution, in a powerful climax. This subsides in (5) a second fugue, in a quietly expressive allegretto, which brings the toccata to an end, through a cadenza-like series of sequences, with a tranquil final statement of the subject in full harmony.

Toccata in C Minor

This fine piece has three connected sections, the first two each ending in a half close on the dominant and leading directly to the next. 1. A vigorous opening bravura passage with material of arresting character. 2. An adagio of great emotional power, founded on a scale motive that lends itself to expressive contrapuntal treatment both in direct and in inverted form. 3. A long fugue, with a striking subject, developed with constant vitality and variety, but nevertheless demanding and offering opportunity for much musicianship and technical resource in the presentation of its interesting structure. The opening section of this fugue comes to a pause on the dominant, and is followed by a renewed development with a fresh countersubject. The ingenious "shifting of step" through which this new counterpoint, on its last three appearances, holds the attention should not be overlooked and should be emphasized in performance.

Italian Concerto

This, with the <u>Partita in B Minor</u>, was published by Bach as the second part of the <u>Clavierübung</u>. It is designed for a harpsichord with two manuals, and the original indications "piano" and "forte" (the words written in full) refer to their alternation. The piece is of moderate difficulty, the first and third movements being similar in design to the preludes of the second, third, fourth, and fifth English Suites, and demanding the same rhythmic

control. The slow movement consists of a
continuous flow of highly expressive cantabile,
with a persistent figure of accompaniment in
the left hand. It cannot be doubted that the
"singing style" which Bach mentions in his
introduction to the Inventions is here called
for, or that we are justified in exploiting to
the full the tonal and expressive resources of
the modern pianoforte.
Published by Kalmus (Bischoff); Schirmer
(Bülow); Ditson (Prout); Peters (Urtext).

Chromatic Fantasia and Fugue

This piece is in a class by itself for its harmonic daring and emotional inspiration. The
Fantasia has affinities with the great organ
Fantasia in G Minor and the organ Toccata in
D Minor. Bischoff's editing is most satisfactory. Though there are no excessive technical
difficulties, a high degree of interpretative
maturity is called for, especially in the delivery of the recitative section of the Fantasia.
Bülow's edition, with its very personal treatment of the text and amplification through
octave doubling, etc., is from its point of view
an extremely able piece of work. However,
its arbitrariness is hard to justify. Prout, in
a volume published by Ditson in the Musicians' Library series, gives a careful and
conservative edition whose value should be
recognized.
(Editions—as for the Italian Concerto).

Fantasia and Fugue in A Minor

A fine and comparatively unfamiliar piece.
The Fantasia is written in a style that suggests the organ; the Fugue, with two subjects -
first developed separately and finally combined
in a masterly climax - is by no means easy,
but is one of Bach's most effective clavier
compositions.
Published by Ditson (Prout).

Fugue in A Minor (with arpeggio introduction)

One of Bach's longest clavier fugues; its subject in continuous sixteenth notes and its
uninterrupted moto perpetuo call for considerable finger control. It has a fine and effective
climax, and affords opportunity for a great
variety of color. The suggested interpretation
of the introductory measures in the Schirmer
edition is unsatisfactory—a simple arpeggio
treatment, like that of similar passages in the
Chromatic Fantasia, is decidedly preferable.
Published by Ditson (Prout); Schirmer (Bülow).

Fantasia in C Minor

A short and attractive piece showing Italian
influence. The Bülow edition published by

Schirmer should be compared with that of Bischoff or the Bach-Gesellschaft for correction of the ornamentation, etc. In the Ditson Musicians' Library is a more scholarly edition by Prout.
Published by Ditson (Prout); Schirmer (Bülow).

Capriccio, "On the departure of a beloved brother"

This early composition (moderately easy, except the final fugue) has a special interest as being Bach's only experiment in the field of instrumental program music. It was written at the age of nineteen, but it already shows remarkable emotional power (e.g., in the central "Lament") and vitality.
The Kalmus and Marks reprints contain, as Bischoff states, in the first two sections of the piece an excessive amount of ornamentation, much of it of doubtful authenticity.
Published by Kalmus (Bischoff); Marks (reprint of the old Peters edition); J. Fischer (Friskin).

Aria with Thirty Variations (Goldberg Variations)

Only the exceptional pupil is likely to be equal to the demands of this piece (originally for harpsichord with two keyboards), which displays so many aspects of Bach's genius.
Those demands are more interpretative than technical; indeed, except for the special difficulty, in a few variations, caused by the crossing of the hands, this composition is technically much easier than many of the preludes and fugues of the Well-tempered Clavier.
Kalmus's reprint of the Bischoff edition is the most serviceable for the pianist. Ralph Kirkpatrick's edition has much interesting information and embodies fine and careful scholarship, though the text is more designed for the harpsichordist.
Published by Kalmus (Bischoff); Peters (Urtext edition); Schirmer (Kirkpatrick).

WILHELM FRIEDEMANN BACH (1710-1784)

The clavier works of Wilhelm Friedemann are little known and seldom played. They combine within themselves the older contrapuntal style and the lighter, thinner, more homophonic treatment of the contemporary music of his time. His output for the keyboard is divided among sonatas, fantasias, fugues, polonaises, concertos and miscellaneous short pieces. There are interesting works in all categories. They display an original turn of mind, sensitivity and a fund of sentiment. This latter is especially pronounced in the dramatic sections of the fantasias, such pieces as the fugues in F minor and C minor, and those polonaises that stress an expressive chromaticism.

Six Sonatas (F. Blume), 2 Vols., Nagel's Musik-Archiv, Nos. 63 and 78.
A fine selection from various periods of his life.

<u>8 Fugues</u> (c. 1778) and <u>12 Polonaises</u> (c.1765) Urtext, Peters.
In one volume. The Polonaises have also been printed by Universal Edition (J. Epstein).

Farrenc also reprints a suite and four fantasies in Vol. X of <u>Le Trésor des Pianistes</u>.

Sonata in G Major (c.1744)	Curious opening movement alternating between an expressive <u>Andantino</u> phrase and an <u>Allegro di Molto</u>. <u>Lamento</u> in pathetic genre, three voices, chromatic. (Reprinted separately in <u>The Bach Family</u>, Universal). Scurrying <u>Presto</u> in 6/8, running eighths, two voices, imitative figures. No. I in Vol. I, Nagel.
Sonata in D Major (c.1744)	One of his most characteristic works. Predominantly three-voiced texture. Rhythmically tricky <u>Un poco Allegro</u> in invertible counterpoint, light, elegant. Dignified, chromatic <u>Adagio</u>. <u>Vivace</u> in rapid triplet eighths requiring dexterity. No. IV in Vol. II, Nagel.
Sonata in D Major (c.1778)	Light two voices throughout. Mozartean opening movement; serious, lengthy duet in 2/4 (Grave); closing, good-humoured running <u>Vivace</u>, triplet sixteenths in 3/8. No. V in Vol. II, Nagel.
Capriccio in D Minor	An agitated, dramatic fantasy. Three main textures: <u>Allegro di molto</u> in broken chords, <u>Grave</u> recitativo with dotted rhythms, flowing three-voice fugue. In <u>Clavier Musik aus alter Zeit</u>, Bk. I, (L. Kohler), Litolff.
12 Polonaisen (1764)	No one piece similar to any other. Those in pathetic genre most effective: No. 2 (C Minor), No. 4 (D Minor - very short), No. 6 (E-flat Minor), No. 8 (E Minor), No. 10 (F Minor).
Fugue in C Minor	Energetic, massive. Dotted rhythms, vigorous, propulsive sixteenths, three voices, not easy. In <u>Alte Meister</u> (E. Pauer), Vol. I.
Fugue in D Minor	Melancholy, introspective, three voices, chromatic, short. Flowing 16th-note triplets in 3/8. No. 4 in Peters. Also in <u>Harvard Anthology of Music</u>, Vol. II.
Fugue in F Minor	Sustained, chromatic, intensely expressive, lengthy, three voices, walking eighths and quarters in 2/4. No. 8 in Peters.
Sonata in E-flat Major (1748)	Three movements. In <u>Sons of Bach</u> (W. Newman), Mercury Music.

DIETRICH BUXTEHUDE (1637-1707)

Distinguished predecessor of J. S. Bach, chiefly known as keyboard composer by his works for organ. The keyboard works mentioned below have
been recently discovered and are available in a fine Urtext edition (edited
by Emilius Bangert), printed by Wilhelm Hansen, Oslo, 1944, and available
through Broude Bros.

Clavier Works (in one volume)	19 Suites, 6 sets of Variations, 3 anonymous pieces. The Suites are short, similar to those of Fro-berger and Pachelbel, probably originally for clavichord. Mostly, but not always, they consist of allemande, sarabande, courante, gigue, with an occasional "double", or two dances of like nature (two sarabandes). Easy to moder-ate difficulty. Excellent "house music." The Variations are mostly figural in character. Those on the tune "La Capriccioso" (bearing a vague resemblance to one of the tunes in the "Quodlibet" of the Goldberg Variations) are most extended, containing thirty-two "partite" with some ingenious keyboard treatment within a very restricted harmonic range (probably dictated by the unequally tempered tuning of Buxtehude's keyboard).

JOHAN ERNST EBERLIN (1702-1762).

Präludium and Fugue in E Minor	Quiet, expressive Präludium, trio-sonata tex-ture. Chromatic Fugue, basically in three voices, walking eighth notes, intense, pathetic. In Alte Klavier Musik, Bk. III, Peters.
6 Preludes and Fugues	In Trésor des Pianistes, Vol. 12 (Farrenc).

JOHANN KASPAR FERDINAND FISCHER (1650-1746)

The most important master of the suite between the time of Froberger and
the Bach-Handel period. Fischer is an especially interesting composer
working mostly in miniature; short dances, preludes, fugues etc. Many
of his works deserve to be reprinted not only because of their moderate
difficulty but also the high level of their craftsmanship and musicality.
In his own words it is "eine etwas stillere musik" (a somewhat more quiet
music), much of it originally devoted to the intimate and subtle Clavichord.

Sämtliche Werke für Klavier und Orgel,(Ernst von Werra), Breitkopf and
  Härtel, 1901.
Selections in Old Masters. . . .(Niemann), Kalmus.
    The Art of the Suite, (Yella Pessl), E. B. Marks.
Selected Keyboard Works, Schott (through Associated Music).

Musicalisches Blumenbüschlein (1696)	Eight suites, each preceded by a praeludium. The dances include allemande, courante, sara-bande, gavotte, menuet, ballet, rondeau, cana-ries, passepied, passacaille (French style), bourrée, branle, amener, gigue, plainte and chaconne.

	Special attention must be called to Suite No. 5 in E Minor; a short, expressive Praeludium coupled to an Aria (adagio) with eight Variations. Demands neatness, clarity and fine balance of parts. Also Suite No. 8 in G Major; a Praeludium in the style of a free fantasy followed by a Chaconne, noble and eminently worthy of performance. Also in Old Masters, Kalmus.
Musicalischer Parnassus (1738)	Nine suites called Parthien, each named after one of the nine muses. Introductory movements include praeludium, ouverture, toccatina, tastada, harpeggio (broken chord prelude), and toccata. In addition to the dances mentioned above there also appear a Ballet anglois, Air anglois, and a Rigaudon. Both series of suites are generally less sophisticated and shorter than Bach's, but none-the-less have great charm and variety of invention.
Ariadne Musica (1715)	Twenty short preludes and fugues ordered in chromatically ascending keys. Omitted are F-sharp Major, E-flat minor, G-sharp Minor, B-flat Minor and D-flat Major. A kind of miniature "Well-tempered Clavier," including five quiet ricercari on subjects derived from old chorale tunes.
Blumen-Strauss (1735)	Eight sets of pieces, each including a prelude, six fugues and a finale, all very short. Fischer includes a table of ornaments in the Musicalisches Blumenbüschlein.

JOHANN JAKOB FROBERGER (1616-1667)

Froberger ("un homme très rare sur les épinettes" - a rare one at the spinet) seems to have devoted his energies exclusively to keyboard writing. In his music we find the Italian toccata-style of his teacher Frescobaldi, the pre-fugal genres of early seventeenth-century masters, the laments or tombeaux in memory of a great personage (cultivated by the French lutenists and clavecinists) and, above all, the first solid organization of the suite into the basic dances: allemande, courante, sarabande and gigue. The emotional content of his music ranges from the quiet beauty of his short dance movements to the restless, rhapsodic, improvisational sections of his ingenious toccatas and laments. Both Handel and Bach esteemed his music highly.

Complete Keyboard Works, Denkmäler der Tonkunst in Oesterreich (Monuments of Music in Austria), Breitkopf and Härtel Vols. IV, VI (2), X (2). A library edition comprising 25 toccatas, 8 fantasias, 6 canzoni, 18 capricci, 4 ricercari, 30 suites.
Selections in TPA, Vol. 6; Old Masters, Kalmus; Froberger album, Peters; and Selected Keyboard Works, Schott.

Suite in E Minor	A lovely, quiet variation-suite. Each dance has a "double" except the <u>Gigue</u> (which exists in two versions, one in duple and one in triple meter). Easy and short. (Peters)
Toccata in D Minor	Best known of the toccatas: improvisatory recitative, flowing fugue, gigue-like closing section. Short, impressive. Excellent opening number. In <u>EKM</u>, Vol. I. Better version in <u>EPM</u> (Sachs)
Lamento (sopra la dolo-rosa perdita della Maesta di Ferdinando IV, Re di Romani....)	Remarkable piece packed with expressive qualities. To be played "fort lentement à la discrétion sans observer aucune mésure" (very slowly, in good taste without keeping a strict beat). The opening movement of a <u>Suite in C</u>. (Peters)
Fantasia in Phrygian Mode	Prototype for Bach's Fugue in E Major in Bk. II of the "48" (Peters)
Partite auf die Mayerin	Variations on a popular tune of the seventeenth century. Medium difficulty. Variety of simple figuration, some sections in dance styles. Many reprints.

CARL HEINRICH GRAUN (1701-1759)

Gigue in B-flat Minor	Brilliant, virtuoso style, rapid triplet eighths in 2/4. Humorous. Broken chord figuration, crossed hands. Excellent program opener or encore. In <u>Old Masters</u>, Kalmus.

GEORGE FREDERICK HANDEL (1685-1759)

Easy Compositions

<u>Twenty Little Dances</u>, Schott. Quite elementary material.
<u>Pieces for Harpsichord</u> (Squire and Fuller-Maitland), Schott. These are a
   little more advanced.
<u>Twelve Easy Pieces</u> (Hans von Bülow), Schirmer.
<u>Twenty-two Pieces</u> (Buonamici), Schirmer. Slightly more advanced technic-
   ally than the von Bülow volume.
<u>Fourteen Easy Original Pieces</u> (Oscar Beringer), Augener. Arranged in
   progressive order.
<u>A Set of Pieces</u> (Harold Bauer), Schirmer. Edited freely.

Suites

The harpsichord suites of Handel do not deserve the comparative neglect with which they are treated. While they do not reach the heights of the greatest of Bach's works of the same type, and have less technical perfec- tion, they have special qualities of charm and melodiousness. Fugal move- ments, and short sets of variations, very simple in structure, are frequent features. The pieces described as variations, chaconnes and passacaglias do not really differ in their essential treatment, and the names might be used interchangeably.

Editions

The first eight suites were published by Handel himself, and are reproduced by leading publishers today. Other suites, chaconnes, etc., appear in varying successions in different editions. Both Peters and Augener print two volumes—with eight suites in each. Kalmus reprints the edition of W. Dorr in two volumes, the first having the eight of Handel's publication, and the second a number of suites, chaconnes, etc., which follow the order of the Handel Society's edition. (Kalmus's text has few editorial marks.)

Suite No. 3 in D Minor	This has a short Prelude consisting of brilliant passage-work; a three-voice Fugue without much climax; a tuneful Allemande and Courante; then an extremely florid Air with five quite simple variations; finally, a vigorous Presto with material that is also used in one of Handel's organ works.
Suite No. 5 in E Major	Starting with a solid and placid Prelude, contrapuntal in character, this suite continues with an Allemande and Courante which are pleasant without being particularly striking, and ends with the familiar Air and variations commonly entitled "The Harmonious Blacksmith." (These are oftenest played separately.)
Suite No. 7 in G Minor	A short French Overture is the opening movement; the usual allemande and courante are replaced by an Andante and Allegro, both two-voice; a Sarabande, presenting its characteristic rhythm in simple chords, and a short Gigue follow; the Passacaglia which ends the suite, founded on a four-bar phrase, is a short example of a type of which there are two much longer specimens—each on an eight-bar theme—running to as many as twenty-one and sixty-two variations.

JOHANN PHILIPP KIRNBERGER (1721-1783)

Fugue in D Minor	Rapid gigue in 12/8. Three voices. Robust, vigorous. In Alte Meister, Vol. I (Pauer), Breitkopf and Härtel.
Fugue in D Major	Animated 6/8, two voices in running 16ths. Requires facility.. In Alte Meister, Vol. I (Pauer), Breitkopf and Härtel.

Fugue in F-sharp Minor	Three voices. Introspective, legato, chromatic. In Alte Meisterstücke (Epstein), Universal Edition.
Tanzstücke	Collection of dance pieces. Schott((Hermann), through Associated Music.
	For other pieces by this pupil of J. S. Bach see Trésor, Vol. 10 (Farrenc); and Old Masters of the 16th, 17th and 18th Centuries (Niemann), Kalmus.

JOHANN LUDWIG KREBS (1713-1780)

Partita No. 2 in B-flat Major

Preludio	Florid arioso, reiterated chord and interval accompaniment.
Fuga	Lengthy, sustained, chromatic, four voices.
Allemande	Flowing, three voices, smooth, melodic.
Corrente	Snapped, dotted rhythms in 6/4. Animated.
Sarabande	Florid melody, chordal accompaniment.
Burlesca	Robust, animated alla breve, rhythmic.
Menuet I, II and III	A large rondeau (I, II, I, III, I). Vigorous, with two trios in minor on the quiet side.
Gigue	Two voices, 3/8, moving sixteenths. In Alte Meister, Vol. II (Pauer), Breitkopf and Härtel.

Partita No. 6 in E-flat Major

Preludio	Free improvisational passages leading to four-voice fugato and concluding flourish.
Fuga	Lengthy, animated, dancelike, three voices, 3/4.
Allemande	Flowing, three voices.
Corrente	French style.
Sarabande	In E-flat minor! Complex, florid melody lavishly ornamented.
Bourrée	Rhythmic, animated, robust.
Polonaise	Two light voices, dignified.
Gigue	Lengthy, rapid, two voices, fugal style in 12/8. In Alte Meister, Vol. II (Pauer), Breitkopf and Härtel.

JOHANN KUHNAU (1660-1722)

The keyboard music of this dignified predecessor of J. S. Bach at Leipzig's Thomas Kirche has, by and large, been relegated to oblivion. The complete works may be found in the Denkmäler deutscher Tonkunst, Vol. IV, first series. They comprise:

1 - Neuer Clavier Übung, Part I (1689), consisting of seven partitas.
2 - Neuer Clavier Übung, Part II (1692), consisting of seven partitas and a sonata in B-flat major.
3 - Frische Clavier Früchte or 7 Sonaten von guten Invention und Manier (1696).

4 - Musicalische Vorstellung einiger Biblischer Historien in 6 Sonaten (1700).

The last of these are by far his most interesting works for keyboard and are famous examples of eighteenth-century program music. Each of these "musical representations of some Bible stories" is preceded by Kuhnau's own colorful summary of the biblical episode pertaining to each sonata. They are unique, loving accounts and warrant translation into English. The sonatas themselves contain many interesting passages and movements, although it is somewhat difficult to program an entire work for performance. A complete reprint is available in a handsome "Urtext" edition by Kurt Stone for Broude Bros.

The Biblical Sonatas are:

Sonata I	The Battle between David and Goliath. See especially the Trembling of the Israelites, using the chorale Aus tiefer Not, the battle itself, with the phrases depicting David's slingshot and Goliath's fall. In Old Masters, Kalmus.
Sonata II	Saul cured by David's music making. Bold chromaticisms and daring figuration to depict Saul's melancholy.
Sonata III	Jacob's Marriage.
Sonata IV	Hiskias, sick unto death and then recovered.
Sonata V	Gideon, Saviour of Israel.
Sonata VI	Jacob's death and burial.

GOTTLIEB MUFFAT (1690-1770)

One of the most important masters of German keyboard music after Bach and Handel. In his 12 Concerti and in the Caecilia Ode Handel made good use of movements by Muffat. An interesting composer worth looking into. His works may be found in Farrenc, Vol. 7, DTÖ, Vol. III, Pt. 3. Separate suites and pieces are reprinted in EKM, Vol. II; Art of the Suite (Pessl) E. B. Marks; and Old Masters, Kalmus. See also G. Muffat: Partiten und Stücke, Schott.

Componimenti Musicali per il Cembalo (1735-1739)	Six suites and a ciaconna. The basic suite movements (allemande, courante, sarabande and gigue) are preceded by long introductory movements (as in the Bach English Suites) called "overture" (French), "prelude" or "fantaisie." Various "galanterien" such as the minuet, rigaudon, bourrée, hornpipe etc. are inserted before (and even after) the gigue.
	In true French style these suites are abundantly ornamented. Muffat has a Table of Ornaments attached to the Componimenti explaining the solutions to the graphic signs. The material itself is elaborate, ornate,

sometimes startling in harmonic detail, ranging from a lovely, flowing cantabile in the allemandes through the melancholy elegance of the sarabandes to the gay brilliance of his finales.

Movements such as the Sarabande in Suite III and the Allemande, Minuet and Sarabande in Suite IV can be programmed or studied separately to good advantage.

Suite IV (B-flat major) is complete in EKM Vol. II.
Suite II (G minor) is complete in The Art of the Suite.

The Ciaconna has thirty-eight variations (five in minor) on the same bass that Bach uses in the first eight bars of the Goldberg Variations.

12 Toccatas and 72 Verstl	Each toccata is followed by six short fugues. Originally for liturgical use but also "for beginners to learn from" ("als behelf für Anfänglinge"). Several toccatas in TPA, Vol. VIII.

JOHANN PACHELBEL (1653-1706)

Pachelbel bridges the musical gap between Froberger and J. S. Bach. He wrote voluminously for all the keyboard instruments of his day (harpsichord, clavichord, organ) in all the accepted genres. The fantasy, ricercare, fugue, chaconne, toccata, suite and variation all found expression in his creative work. Many of his pieces are possible on the modern piano although in some cases (involving pedal parts for organ) they necessitate adaptation to the single keyboard.

The keyboard works may be found in the Denkmäler der ·Tonkunst in Bayern, II, Vol. I; IV, Vol. I; and in the Denkmäler der Tonkunst in Österreich, VIII, Vol. II. See also TPA, Vol. IX, and the reprint edition published by Bärenreiter (through Concordia Music).

Hexachordum Apollinis (1699)	In DTB, II, I. Six arias with figural variations. Broken chord techniques, passage playing, contrapuntal problems. See especially Aria V in A Minor. In Masters of the Cembalo, Peters.
Musicalische Sterbensgedanken (1683)	In DTB, II, I. "Musical Meditations on Death." Choral variations. See especially those on "Alle Menschen müssen sterben," a choral setting with eight "Partitas."
Ciacona in Dorian mode	In DTB, II, I. Four-bar chaconne bass with thirty-one variations. Vigorous, energetic. In Masters of the Cembalo, Peters.
17 Suites	In DTB, II, I. Four basic suite movements (allemande, courante, sarabande, gigue)

with occasional interpolated movements.
Light-textured, intimate "house music."
Short, not difficult.
See especially <u>Suite in E Major</u> in <u>Masters of the Cembalo</u>, Peters.

94 Fugues on the
Magnificat

Short fugues on material derived from the
hymn to the Virgin Mary.
In <u>DTÖ</u>, VIII, II.

Fugue in E Minor
(Phrygian)

Three voices, scherzando. Repeated tones,
light, joking quality.
In <u>Old Masters</u>, Kalmus; and <u>Early Keyboard Music</u>, Schirmer.

Fugue in F Major (4/4)

Three voices, rhythmic scherzo.
In <u>Old Masters</u>, Kalmus.

Fugue in F Major (12/8)

Four voices, pastoral quality, moderato.
In <u>Old Masters</u>, Kalmus.

Ricercar in F-sharp
Minor

Double fugue on two vigorous subjects. Clean,
strong lines, three voices. Not long.
In <u>Masters of the Cembalo</u>, Peters.
See also the Pachelbel album published by
Schott (through Associated Music).

SAMUEL SCHEIDT (1587-1654)

Song Variations for
Clavier

Three sets of variations published by Schott
(Associated Music Publishers) on melodies
popular in Scheidt's day. From his <u>Tabulatura Nova</u> (1624). Both homophonic and contrapuntal in treatment.

Variations on the English
song "Fortune"

Five variations, moderate difficulty, three in
lyric, flowing counterpoint, two in running
passage playing. Sensitive, melancholy.
Universal Edition. (Epstein)

JAN PIETERSZON SWEELINCK (1562-1621)

Although most of the music of the great Dutch master (the famed "maker"
of German organists) has not been performed on the modern piano, it may
be well to indicate the extent of this composer's keyboard music and to
suggest one or two pieces to serve as introduction to his style. They are
all for mature students or professionals. The keyboard music is Vol. I of
the complete works:

<u>Werken Voor Orgel En Clavecimbel</u> (Max Seiffert), G. Alsbach and Co.,
Amsterdam, 1943.
Some variations are published by Schott (Erich Doflein) and are available
through Associated Music Publishers.

18 Fantasies and
1 Ricercar

Large-scale extended fugal works employing
not only imitative treatment of one or several
subjects but also running passage work and
broken-chord figuration of all kinds. The

opening <u>Fantasia Chromatica</u> may be singled
out as especially impressive. Six of the
fantasias are in "Echo" style, a device of
baroque writing that persisted through J. S.
Bach (see the final movement of the <u>Ouvertüre
nach Französischer Art</u>).

13 Toccatas	Pieces combining free passage playing with fugal sections.
25 Choral Preludes	Specifically for organ. Variations on well-known chorales.
7 Sets of Variations on Secular Songs	Very possible on the modern piano. Especially noteworthy are the six variations on the Dutch song "Mein junges Leben hat ein End," a masterly work eminently suitable for performance. Problems in imitative counterpoint, fine balance of parts. Keyboard figures in the style of the English virginalists with whom Sweelinck was acquainted. Single copies published by Senart (available at Salabert, New York).
5 Sets of Variations on Dance Tunes	Same as above.

GEORG PHILIPP TELEMANN (1681-1767)

A composer of a prodigious output in all fields of music. "First among
the Germans was he to use lightness and naturalness in the melodies of his
Arias. He leaned much on the French style but also has much that is
particular to himself" (Chr. D. Ebeling, 1770). Polish, grace and fluidity
are the chief marks of his light-textured keyboard style. The <u>Fantasies</u>
and the <u>Easy Fugues</u> contain many fine cameos, a delight to play, and useful as teaching material, concert repertoire or "house-music." Although
moderate in difficulty they demand finish, lightness and an easy, fluent
mechanism with fine control of tonal nuance. Depth and dramatic impact
are absent from this master of the "style galant"; freshness, wit and an
easy grace are everywhere present.

Fantasies pour le Clavessin; 3 Douzaines	Three dozen keyboard pieces mostly in two or three voices except for the slow sections, which often use block chords as accompaniments to sensitive aria-like melodies. Every even-numbered <u>Fantasie</u> may be used as a B section to the preceding odd numbered one; e.g., after <u>Fantasie No. 2</u> Telemann marks "Si replica la prima fantasia." The first and third dozen are ABA in plan with B always in contrasting tempo or key. The second dozen are in four sections usually in the order: moderate (or slow), lively, moderate (or slow), lively. The final lively section is very short, providing a kind of catch ending. It is probably in style to fill in tastefully the

middle voices in the bare two-voiced airs that often serve as contrasting B sections. Especially to be noted from the above are:

From the first dozen:

No. 2 (D minor)	Bold, forthright two-voiced Presto, short Adagio as B section.
No. 5 (F major)	Bouncing Vivace with Largo in D Minor.
No. 6 (F minor)	Winsome minuet, pathetic genre.
No. 8 (G minor)	Running Vivace, rhythmically interesting, short Aria as contrast.

From the second dozen:

No. 1 (C minor)	Two voices throughout: Tendrement, vivement, tendrement, très vite.
No. 3 (B minor)	Ditto: Pompeusement, allegrement, pompeusement, gaiment.

From the third dozen:

No. 2 (D minor)	Easy two-voiced Vivace with more extended, tender Largo section, arioso style.
No. 12 (B-flat major)	An outstanding piece. Short rondeau in moderate tempo with tender arioso (G minor).
	The Fantasies are published by Bärenreiter and are available in a reprint by Broude Bros.
Easy Fugues and Short Pieces	A selection of six from the "20 little Fugues for Organ or Clavier." The fugues are in two voices, only lightly contrapuntal, and are each followed by several short vivacious movements homophonic in style, often dancelike in character. (International Music Co.) Also see Farrenc, Vol. IX.

GEORG CHRISTOPH WAGENSEIL (1715-1777)

Four Divertimenti	South German equivalent of the Prussian and Württemberg Sonatas of C. P. E. Bach. Three- and four-movement works, homophonic in style. Light texture, conventional pianistic figuration with unexpectedly charming turns of phrase. Florid slow movements, Haydnesque minuets, light, spirited finales. Nagel's Musik-Archiv, No. 36 (through Associated Music).

Part II
Pianoforte Music from Haydn to the Early Twentieth Century

ISAAC ALBENIZ (1860-1909)

Album of Eight Pieces

This small volume contains pieces that are comparatively simple technically and not specially important musically, though exhibiting characteristic charm. (Boston Music Co.) The following may be mentioned:

Cadiz	
Cuba	These are tuneful and technically easy.
Tango	
Seguidilla	Makes a brilliant effect, while lying easily for the hand.

Iberia

The twelve pieces in this series are much more elaborate than the above, more difficult, and the most representative of Albeniz's compositions. The fundamental harmonies are simple, but they are frequently accompanied by liberal ornamentation and figuration which present complicated technical problems (Edition Mutuelle). (Nos. 1 to 6 also reprinted by E. B. Marks of New York.) A salient feature is a primitive insistence on a single rhythm, or on similar rhythms, throughout an entire piece. The titles are mostly taken from the names of Spanish towns, or of particular districts or local features therein. With the exception of Nos. 1, 2 and 6, these compositions are rather lengthy, and sometimes repetitious.

No. 1—Evocation	Not difficult. Has tonal and lyrical charm, and needs good legato.
No. 2—El Puerto	Lively and attractive, with driving rhythm - requires a good deal of keyboard facility.
No. 3—Fête-Dieu à Seville	One of the finest, musically, of the series. It is exacting, with some quasi-orchestral passages that are not easy to make fully effective; but for a pianist with mature technique it is rewarding.
No. 4—Rondeña	Much of this piece, which is somewhat difficult to interpret, is in alternating bars of 6/8 and 3/4 time; a central lyric episode provides contrast. One problem is the disentangling of the essential melodic line from a surrounding texture that is sometimes complicated.
No. 5—Almeria	Starting, as does Rondeña, with an extended opening section on a persistent tonic bass, this has a middle section of folk-song character, and of great beauty. Of moderate difficulty and easier to present than No. 4.
No. 6—Triana (Gypsy quarter of Seville)	A sparkling and brilliant piece, with rapid shifts of keyboard position that add to its difficulty. (Some of these can be eliminated by redistribution of the hands.) A good rhythmic sense is essential.
No. 7—El Albaicin (Gypsy quarter of Granada)	Has a xylophone-like introduction, the hands alternating in staccato single notes and chords,

leading to a cantabile theme developed with complicated accompanying figuration. The climax requires large tonal resources.

No. 8—El Polo
(Andalusian song and
dance)

A few introductory measures lead to a mournful theme in "sobbing" broken rhythm. This persists throughout the piece (one of the less difficult of the series), and the monotony of rhythmic movement makes great demands, for the maintenance of interest, on the pianist's tonal variety.

No. 9—Lavapies
(People's quarter of
Madrid)

Another complicated piece in a persistent rhythm, many passages depending for their effectiveness on accurate balance of tone, with emphasis of inner notes in the texture. Requires endurance and strong technique, particularly in the rapid successions of staccato chord handfuls.

No. 10—Malaga

Lively and fairly difficult; an alternative cantabile theme is given to the left hand, against a complicated right-hand accompaniment.

No. 11—Jerez

The longest of the set, with elaborate detail in the accompaniment to its characteristic tunes. Here the deliberate rhythmic monotony referred to above is noticeable.

No. 12—Eritana
(An inn outside Seville)

Has a similar rhythmic quality to that of "Triana," with a thicker texture and less variety. Needs great rhythmic vitality.

Navarra

One of Albeniz's last compositions, completed (the final twenty-six measures) by de Severac. It has all the national flavor found in the Iberia series, with less excessive complication in the keyboard writing than in many of these. The central section has a powerful climax making use of the full tonal resources of the instrument. Edition Mutuelle, reprinted by E. B. Marks.

EUGEN D'ALBERT (1864-1932)

D'Albert's compositions for piano solo consist of a number of early works, all displaying a solid nineteenth-century technique.

Suite in D Minor, Op. 1

The five movements (Allemande, Courante, Sarabande, Gavotte, and Musette and Gigue imitate in a pleasing way the character of a Bach suite, with somewhat easygoing contrapuntal texture.
(Bote & Bock. Schirmer has reprinted the Gavotte and Musette.)

Clavierstücke, Op. 16

No. 1 - Waltz in A-flat
Major

Asks for good legato octaves. The material is pleasing, without strong character; there is a good deal of variety of texture.

No. 2 - Scherzo in F-sharp Minor	Effective and brilliant. Requires deft finger technique, accurate staccato chords and good singing tone.
No. 3 - Intermezzo in B Major	A graceful study for various touches - legato (single and double notes) and staccato (finger and hand).
No. 4 - Ballade in B Minor	A well-constructed piece requiring good cantabile, and full power in its climaxes. (Peters)

Transcriptions

D'Albert also deserves mention as a transcriber of two important works of Bach for the organ.

| Prelude and Fugue in D Major | The arrangement of this has been carried out with reverence and faithfulness to the original; in these respects it compares favorably with Busoni's version. D'Albert's is also considerably less taxing technically. (Bote & Bock) |
| Passacaglia in C Minor | Also an able and conscientious transcription. It presents in its climactic passages considerable difficulties in regard to pedaling, and it needs a large hand. (Bote & Bock) |

CHARLES HENRI VALENTIN ALKAN (1813-1888)

A large number of études by this composer are now difficult to obtain; they present ingenious and formidable technical problems, "effects peculiar to the instrument carried to the very verge of impossibility." Their actual musical substance is comparatively slight.

| The Wind | A good example of Alkan's gifts. Rapid chromatic scales in either hand accompany a cantabile melody in the other. Later, a melody in octaves, for thumb and fifth finger, has to be played together with tremolando figures for the inner fingers of the same hand. (Schirmer) |

ANTON ARENSKY (1861-1906)

Most of Arensky's piano pieces are of a light salon character - well made and effective.

| Basso ostinato, Op. 5, No. 5 | A clever and attractive passacaglia - not difficult, and with more serious and solid musical quality than is found in much of Arensky's work. (Augener) |
| Près de la mer, Op. 52, No. 4 | Mainly left hand cantilena, with right hand accompanying figuration. (Carl Fischer) |

| Près de la mer,
Op. 52, No. 5 | Easy staccato double notes, and legato chords.
(Carl Fischer) |
| Etude in F-sharp Major,
Op. 36, No. 13 | Has a melody carried by the left hand, with accompanying scales in the right. Requires a fair degree of technical advancement.
(Schirmer) |

MILI BALAKIREFF (1837-1910)

| The Lark | A popular arrangement of the song by Glinka. It requires some keyboard facility.
(Schirmer) |
| Islamey | A most original virtuoso piece - brilliant and technically very exacting.
(Carl Fischer) |

LUDWIG VAN BEETHOVEN (1770-1827)

The teacher's need for a wide acquaintance with the main groups of com- positions, which has been stressed in the case of J. S. Bach, is equally apparent here. In particular, the thirty-two sonatas which have a unique place in the literature of the piano, demand a general familiarity.

Editions of the sonatas

The "Urtext" edition of Breitkopf and Härtel, reprinted in the United States by Kalmus, is useful for reference and as an indication, by compari- ison, of the additions and alterations of the various editors.

Heinrich Schenker's edition (Universal Edition) has a dependability similar to that of the Urtext. It has some individual fingering, and is backed by profound scholarship.

The edition of Artur Schnabel (Simon and Schuster) is characterized by extreme reverence for the composer, and an invariable desire to make clear his musical intention which results in the crowding of the page with innumerable tempo indications, etc., though care has always been taken to distinguish the editor's marks from the composer's. The text has been carefully compared with original sources, and only in rare cases leaves any doubt as to its authority.

The firm of Peters now prints the sonatas in an edition by Max Pauer with very little injection of the editor's personal views.

The widely circulated edition of Bülow and Lebert, originally published by Cotta in Stuttgart, and mainly reprinted by Schirmer, has been subjected to a good deal of justified criticism on account of its sometimes arbitrary treatment of the text and of its frequent obscuring of the larger outlines of the structure through exaggerated inflections. Opus 13 and Opus 31, No. 3 are obvious examples of this.

Casella's edition, published by Ricordi, is notable for its excellent fingering and pedaling; the phrasing is logical, though it sometimes takes unjustified liberties with the original.

D'Albert's edition has been reprinted by Carl Fischer, and has good features without being outstanding.

Two good European editions that should be noted are those of Heugel (Moszkowski), and Breitkopf and Härtel (Lamond).

Finally, the English edition of Tovey and Craxton (the Associated Board edition) is notable for the illuminating commentary by D. F. Tovey, which is valuable in the same way as his notes, previously referred to, on the <u>Well-tempered Clavier</u>.

Editions of the Variations

    Schirmer (Bülow and Lebert)
    Kalmus (Ruthardt)
    Augener

The other large group of Beethoven's pianoforte compositions, the sets of variations, are less uniformly important than the sonatas. Like the latter, they present a wide range of technical and interpretative difficulty. In the edition published by Schirmer, the most important sets are contained in the first of the two volumes; most of those in the second are early and technically easier. Certain individual sets are also obtainable singly.

Editions of Miscellaneous Works

    Peters (Ruthardt)
    Kalmus (Ruthardt)
    Universal Edition (through Associated Music Publishers)
    Augener

Volumes containing the bagatelles, rondos, <u>Andante in F</u>, <u>Fantasia</u>, Op. 77, and some less important compositions, are issued by the above publishers. Single pieces and sets are also published by Schirmer, Augener and others.

Easier Compositions

The following may be suggested as of comparatively easy access:

    The short piece entitled "Für Elise"
    Two easy sonatas in G and F major
    Variations on a Swiss theme
    Easy variations in G major
    Variations in G major, on "Nel cor più non mi sento" (this piece is
        particularly useful as embodying fundamental techniques in a simple
        form).
    Eleven Bagatelles, Op. 119
    Two sonatas, Op. 49, Nos. 1 and 2

Also the following volumes:

    <u>Easy Pieces</u> (Bülow and Lebert), Schirmer
    <u>Twelve Easy Pieces</u> (Beringer), Augener
    <u>Sonatinas</u> (including boyhood compositions), Kalmus, Peters, and Augener
    <u>Contra-Dances</u> and <u>German Dances</u>, Schirmer
    <u>Dances</u> (complete), 2 vols., Augener
    <u>Ecossaises</u>, Augener (Also Schirmer, and Associated Music Publishers—
        (arranged by Busoni)

Thirty-two Sonatas

Sonata in F Minor, Op. 2, No. 1	A work of moderate technical demands: precision in the treatment of the triplet sixteenths in the first movement, a practical fingering for the right-hand legato fourths in the <u>Trio</u> of the third movement, and a flexible left hand for the triplet basses of the finale.

Sonata in A Major, Op. 2, No. 2	The most interesting of the three sonatas in this opus. The chief difficulties are in the treacherous canonic passages in the development of the first movement and the powerful staccato triplets for both hands in the second episode of the Rondo. The left hand of the Rondo's second subject is hard for a small span. The beautiful slow movement presents some interesting tonal problems.
Sonata in C Major, Op. 2, No. 3	A sonata on a large scale. A good broken-chord and broken-octave technique has to be developed to meet the requirements of the first movement; accurate rhythmic control is essential for the groups of three eighth-notes in the Scherzo; in the finale a taxing finger passage has to be mastered eight bars from the beginning, and the accompaniment of the second theme needs a fluent left-hand tremolo — the movement also gives exercise to the pianist's staccato chords and octaves.
Sonata in E-flat Major, Op. 7	This sonata contains some difficulties that are exceptional for that period. In the first movement, e.g., there are the legato octaves in the latter half of the exposition, and the rapid broken octaves, a little later, which need not only speed but power. A fine rhythmic sense is essential in the slow movement, and a flowing legato in both the third and fourth. In the finale the central episode has some special discomfort caused by the transference to the right hand of passages that are appropriate to the left.
Sonata in C Minor, Op. 10, No. 1	The first movement presents no great difficulty, and contains valuable musical and technical material. The beautiful slow movement has only two passages with any serious technical problem, where a varied ornamental version of the start of the second subject has to be carefully fitted into the tempo. The finale is more taxing, needing good fingers, accurage staccato and firm rhythmic control.
Sonata in F Major, Op. 10, No. 2	Another sonata with comparatively simple first and second movements, but with a finale that requires a certain virtuosity — a good staccato, fluent fingers and strong broken octaves.
Sonata in D Major, Op. 10, No. 3	A very fine and quite difficult work. The lively first and last movements need good broken octaves, sixths and rotation technique generally, with strong finger work. The slow movement has an emotional depth that makes it a landmark in Beethoven's development. The

main technical difficulty in the third movement
is the maintenance of evenness in the triplets
of the <u>Trio</u> at the necessary tempo to match
the <u>Minuet.</u>

**Sonata in C Minor,
Op. 13
(Pathétique)**

The popularity of this sonata often causes it
to be attempted by players who are not equipped
for the difficulties of the first movement,
which requires a well-developed left-hand
tremolo for the opening passage of the allegro
and its tiring expansion at the recapitulation.
The remaining movements are on a smaller
scale and are less exacting, but a finished
interpretation is nevertheless a substantial
achievement.

**Sonata in E Major,
Op. 14, No. 1**

A moderately easy sonata, with some slightly
treacherous broken thirds in the fifth and
sixth bars. With occasional modification to
accommodate small hands the whole is within
the capacity of a good student in the early
stages.

**Sonata in G Major,
Op. 14, No. 2**

Another sonata with only moderate technical
demands, and with charming musical quality,
which does not always appear in a schoolroom
performance—the repeated D of measures 9
and 11 is a test of the player's sensitiveness.
The main difficulties are to be found in the
left hand staccatos of the first movement's
development, the balance of tone in the first
variation in the <u>Andante,</u> and the clear accentuation of the opening measures of the last
movement.

**Sonata in B-flat Major,
Op. 22**

Beethoven himself expressed particular satis-
faction with the polished workmanship of this
sonata, and it invites as much technical finish
in its performance. A free forearm is a
requisite for the rotation passages of the first
movement—a warm singing tone for the <u>Adagio</u>
—rhythmic swing and precision for the <u>Menuet-
to,</u> with clear finger technique in the alternative section in G minor—smooth legato in the
main subject of the <u>Rondo,</u> which otherwise
resembles, in its technical requirements, the
first movement.

**Sonata in A-flat Major,
Op. 26**

An interpretative problem is the finding, in the
<u>Andante con variazioni,</u> of a tempo which, con-
trary to frequent practice, will serve for the
theme and the five variations. In the <u>Scherzo</u>
two measures have somewhat difficult legato
thirds. Careful pedaling and clear distinction
between tenuto and staccato are needed for the
funeral march. The <u>Rondo</u> is, incidentally, an
excellent study in rotation technique.

Sonata in E-flat Major, Op. 27, No. 1	Rhythmic and tonal control of a high order is needed for a finished performance of this unpretentious-seeming work. Among the difficulties are: accurate treatment of the syncopations in the latter part of the section in 3/4 time — maintenance of continuity in the extremely slow tempo of the <u>Adagio</u> — a steady tempo in the rapid changes of position in the transition from first to second subject in the final <u>Allegro</u>.
Sonata in C-sharp Minor, Op. 27, No. 2 (Moonlight)	The popular title favored by those who are unacquainted with any but the first movement is inevitable in a book of reference. A special requirement, not easy to attain, is the maintenance of a cantabile together with a general pianissimo. In the second movement a fine rhythmic swing has to accompany the moderate tempo. A well-developed technique is needed for the third, with its broken chords, tremolos and staccato chord passages.
Sonata in D Major, Op. 28 (Pastorale)	This sonata also has a popular title not initiated by Beethoven, but perhaps less inappropriate than that of Opus 27, No. 2. An apparently unpretentious work, it requires for its proper effectiveness a mature musicianship. A smooth legato in the outer parts of the second subject section, with a correct balance of tone between them and the inner accompaniment, is quite difficult, especially for a small hand. The combination of legato-chord playing and staccato bass at the opening of the <u>Andante</u> is another problem. The tempo of the <u>Scherzo</u> may well be guided by the left hand of the <u>Trio</u>. The start of the <u>Rondo</u> has the only definitely "pastoral" sound in the sonata.
Sonata in G Major, Op. 31, No. 1	A good finger technique in the first movement and the utmost finish for the old-fashioned graces of the <u>Adagio</u> are here needed. The <u>Rondo</u> has some left-hand passages that are difficult for a small span.
Sonata in D Minor, Op. 31, No. 2	One of the outstanding works of the middle period. An adequate hand technique, for the two-note slurs of the first movement, has to be developed. The very slow <u>Adagio</u> is a severe test of rhythmic continuity. In the last movement the mechanical effect of a too-rapid tempo should be sternly guarded against.
Sonata in E-flat Major, Op. 31, No. 3	This brilliant sonata needs in the first movement a good trill and a hand technique that allows accurate definition of the slurs in the second subject. The following <u>Allegretto</u> is a fine hand staccato study. The <u>Minuet</u> and <u>Trio</u>

are best taken at the same tempo. There are some difficulties of coordination between right and left hand, at the necessary speed, in the finale, which also requires a good finger staccato for the opening figure in the left hand, etc.

Sonata in G Minor, Op. 49, No. 1

A generally easy little sonata, with only occasional problems for the technique of a young player, such as the smoothness of the thirds in the left hand at the opening of the first movement, and the staccato of the main theme of the <u>Rondo</u>.

Sonata in G Major, Op. 49, No. 2

Decidedly easier than Opus 49, No. 1.

Sonata in C Major, Op. 53 (Waldstein)

Requires a powerful and brilliant technique. The first movement, for its proper effect, needs a particularly acute sense of its larger rhythmic shape, with the avoidance of too much modification of the tempo at the entrance of E major. The introduction to the <u>Rondo</u> demands, especially in its first nine measures, exact observance of time values; and the <u>Rondo</u> itself, equally taxing with the first movement, has a special problem in the glissando octaves of the coda. These, risky on most modern pianos, are acceptably represented by some arrangement like Bülow's.

Sonata in F Major, Op. 54

A sonata in two movements, with none of the usual formal characteristics. The first movement has two alternating subjects, the first a naively humorous one which in its variations requires careful phrasing, and the second a vigorous passage in staccato octaves and sixths which calls for some endurance. The smooth delivery of the toccata which constitutes the second movement gives an opportunity for all possible beauty of touch.

Sonata in F Minor, Op. 57 (Appassionata)

This has emotional and dramatic qualities that invite the player to give free rein to his temperament. The sonata asks for great reserve power. A salient difficulty in the first movement is in the "rotation" passage in the second part of the second subject, where both speed and large tone are necessary. It may be worth while to draw attention to the need for observance of Beethoven's direction, for the fortissimo chord at the end of the <u>Andante</u> (introducing the finale), that the left hand, but not the right, should be arpeggiated. Bülow's fingering for the principal figure of the finale (12434321 etc.), which has been widely adopted, does not seem really satisfactory. 12353132 or 12354321 may be recommended instead.

Sonata in F-sharp Major, Op. 78

In this two-movement sonata, the main danger in the allegro of the first movement is the adoption of a tempo too fast for the right breadth of treatment; in the second movement the need for clear definition of the two-note slurs should be a restraint upon excessive speed.

Sonata in G Major, Op. 79

A small sonata with most of the difficulty in the first movement, where the hand crossings require careful practice. The simple and beautiful Andante can be mastered by quite inexperienced players, and the humorous Vivace has no real hazards.

Sonata in E-flat Major, Op. 81a (Les adieux, l'absence et le retour)

Technically and interpretatively one of the most difficult of the sonatas. In the first movement there are two notoriously treacherous passages of legato double notes and rapid staccato chords. The central Andante needs care in the relation of its tempo to that of the opening Adagio; there is a risk that the similarity of some of the figures may lead to identity of tempo. In the finale the necessarily fast tempo is nevertheless restrained by the slurs in measures 9 and 10.

Sonata in E Minor, Op. 90

A two-movement sonata exhibiting already Beethoven's latest style; not of excessive difficulty - an unlabored delivery of the left-hand sixteenth-note accompaniment of the second subject of the first movement presenting the main technical problem. (This taxes a small hand.) Exact treatment of the energetic opening two-measure phrase (with the eighth-note rests) is an obvious point. It is less obvious that in the passage in the second subject referred to above the real difficulty in the first four measures is that of obtaining a genuine cantabile in the syncopated octaves of the right hand. The leisurely second movement has an almost Schubertian quality, and requires the most expressive legato in its details.

The latest sonatas

The last five sonatas of Beethoven, together with the variations, Opus 120, on a theme by Diabelli, present the most profound and subtle interpretative problems encountered in the work of any composer for the pianoforte. Part of the difficulty comes from the often deceptive simplicity of the musical ideas themselves, which are yet invested with a depth of emotion and almost prophetic exaltation that ask for exceptional qualities of dedication and musical insight, if any adequate performance is to be attained.

There are no compositions which so greatly repay the pianist's lifelong study.

Sonata in A Major, Op. 101

This is not the least difficult of the last five. In fact, two of its movements, the second and the fourth, show Beethoven's characteristic disregard of the mere convenience of the player, considerable practice being required before the awkwardness of some of the writing is overcome. It may be observed that an important technical need here is a free lateral movement at the wrist joint.

At the outset we are faced with the problem of finding a tempo which carries out Beethoven's direction —"etwas lebhaft, und mit der innigsten Empfindung"—i.e., reconciliation of a flowing movement with an extremely expressive delivery which deprives no detail of its meaning. The following march is frequently played too fast. Even Bülow's metronome mark — $\mathcal{P} = 80$ —seems to err in that direction, and a slightly slower speed makes for both dignity and rhythmic accuracy. The tempo of the short slow movement can be gauged from the necessity of a leisurely delivery of even the most rapid of the turns in its latter half. The final allegro, like the march, can suffer technically and become musically trivial if any tempo faster than Bülow's $\mathcal{P} = 120$ is adopted.

Sonata in B-flat Major, Op. 106 (Hammerklavier)

The combined musical and technical demands of this sonata make the most exacting of all tasks that a pianist can undertake. The difficulty for the listener is no less, the only remedy being sufficient familiarity through repeated hearings, to which the exceptional scale of the work and consequent infrequent performance are obstacles.

Beethoven's metronomic indications are, for our instruments at least, impracticable, most notably in the first movement and in the Adagio. The probability that the comparatively weak tone and slight sustaining power of even the best piano at Beethoven's disposal are responsible for his $\mathcal{P} = 138$ (for the opening allegro) is confirmed by the opposite extreme $\mathcal{P} = 80$ in Weingartner's orchestral transcription. Even Bülow's 112 is fast, and a flexible tempo which rarely exceeds $\mathcal{P} = 92$ is recommended. For the Scherzo $\mathcal{P}' = 72$ might replace $\mathcal{P}' = 80$, and the Adagio might average $\mathcal{C} = 80$. The final fugue can hardly with safety and clarity go beyond Bülow's $\mathcal{P} = 132$, and had better be somewhat slower.

The need for a breadth and authority that
will match the vastness of the conception is
evident. Some passages in the first movement
and in the fugue are very difficult for a small
hand. In the Scherzo a real technical problem
is posed by the need for both accuracy in the
prevailing rhythmic figure and sufficient
delicacy in its accentuation. The slow movement – one of the most profound and moving
of all Beethoven's creations – requires the
utmost depth and beauty of tone, and an emotional sensitiveness that is alive to all the
implications of a passage like, for example,
the amazingly expressive ornamentation at
the return of the main theme. The fugue calls
for exceptional finger control and great care
to husband tonal resources, so as to avoid
their premature exhaustion and to achieve a
genuine climax.

**Sonata in E Major,
Op. 109**

The first movement of this is a difficult one
to make easily intelligible; it is in extremely
concentrated sonata form, with the two contrasted key centres (E and B) of the exposition presented in two contrasted tempi. The
adagio which comprises the second of these
sections is actually a theme and single variation, and the realization of this should help to
make it rhythmically coherent. The central
Prestissimo has the same uniformity of texture as the first movement of Opus 101, though
it is very different in character; both are in
extremely condensed sonata form. The beauty
and expressiveness of the theme of the elaborate concluding set of variations should not
cause the player to take too slow a tempo.

**Sonata in A-flat Major,
Op. 110**

This sonata is perhaps the least difficult,
technically, of the last five. In the first
movement, the number and variety of the
(mostly short) pieces of material make it no
mean task to achieve rhythmic continuity and
integration. Care should be taken to avoid too
wide a range of tempo. The tempo of the
second movement can be gauged from the dual
necessity of giving vent to Beethoven's explo-
sive humor and of restraining from any sense
of hurry the right hand's figuration in the
central section. In the introductory adagio
which follows, Beethoven has indicated the
fluctuations of tempo quite clearly. The original pedaling for the crescendo on the A-flat
minor chord at the start of the arioso, with
the chord sustained through the first measure

of the melody, is quite practicable even on a
modern instrument. In that movement and in
the later variation in G minor the expressive
features of the bass need as much attention as
the cantabile of the right hand. The fugue,
with its smooth counterpoint, in marked contrast to the harshness of much of the fugal
writing in Opus 101 and Opus 106, has as an
important technical requirement the choice of
a fingering which will give a legato that is
not dependent upon pedal. The latter should
be used sparingly. The final speeding up
(after the meno allegro in E-flat) should be
arrived at gradually, with no sudden jerk into
a faster tempo when the fugue subject enters
in the bass.

**Sonata in C Minor,
Op. 111**

As a whole, this great work is less exacting
technically than either Opus 101 or Opus 106.
For the stormy allegro of the first movement,
the same accurate judgment of tempo that has
been urged in the case of other movements of
the late sonatas is needed. Some modification
of the original impetus, at the entry of the
lyric phrase that introduces the key of A-flat,
is unavoidable. A general tempo that does not
exceed $\mathbf{\cdot} = 132$ will allow this without an exaggerated slackening that would disrupt the
design. The variations of the second movement
would lose their point if the successive doublings of the number of notes in a beat were not
supported by maintenance of the same tempo.
It may be noted that many performances of the
fourth variation are spoiled by a too-rapid
delivery of the subtle alternative versions in a
high octave in triplet thirty-second notes,
which reduces them to a meaningless ear-
tickling jingle with no regard for the continual
play of expressive detail.

Variations

In the section on easier compositions three sets of variations have been
included. Those now listed are the most important musically, and make
greater technical demands.

**24 Variations in D Major,
on Righini's arietta,
"Venni amore"**

This large set of variations is actually an early
work, but it shows an astonishing imaginative
range and power. Its difficulties are considerable, and a well-developed mechanism is
needed to cope with them.

**12 Variations in A Major,
on a Russian theme**

A set of average difficulty—technically and
musically on a par with a sonata like Opus 2,
No. 1.

6 Variations in F Major, Op. 34, on an original theme	An interesting experiment, but one which Beethoven did not repeat; the key-note of the first five of the variations dropping by alternate major and minor thirds from the previous tonic. Technically, the variations are of moderate difficulty.
15 Variations in E-flat Major, Op. 35, on a theme from "Prometheus"	The theme is the one from the <u>Prometheus</u> ballet used later for the finale of the <u>Eroica</u> symphony. This is a much more exacting work than Opus 34, and it makes technical demands similar to those of the sonatas of the middle period such as Opus 53 and Opus 57.
32 Variations in C Minor	These have a special place in the student's pianistic development, as they provide a compendium of most of the elements of a well-rounded technique. Their historical position between the <u>Chaconne in D Minor</u> of Bach and the finale of the fourth symphony of Brahms is also interesting. It is hardly too much to say that every student who has the necessary equipment should learn them. The expression marks of the composer are very meager, but Bülow's elaborate editing (in the Schirmer edition) should be accepted with reserve.
6 Variations in D Major, Op. 76	This set has for its theme the familiar Turkish March from the <u>Ruins of Athens</u>. It has intimations of Beethoven's later style and characteristic humorous touches. The difficulties are only moderate.
33 Variations in C Major, Op. 120, on a waltz by Diabelli	This monumental work invites comparison with Bach's <u>Goldberg Variations</u>, and it has an even greater emotional range which calls for interpretative gifts of a high order. A clue to the correct approach may often be found in suggestions of string-quartet style in the texture, Beethoven's mind having turned more and more in that direction when he composed these variations. The technical difficulties are considerable without being excessive.

<u>Miscellaneous</u>

From the volumes of miscellaneous pieces previously listed certain compositions deserve separate mention for their musical importance.

7 Bagatelles, Op. 33	All comparatively easy, with the exception of the brilliant No. 5.
Rondo in C Major, Op. 51, No. 1	Not more difficult than the sonatas of Opus 14.
Rondo in G Major, Op. 51, No. 2	A larger and more difficult work than the <u>Rondo in C</u>, calling for extreme sensitiveness and refinement of touch.

Andante in F Major	This, originally intended for the slow move-ment of the sonata, Opus 53, has some of the musical characteristics of the <u>Rondo in G</u>, and contains an exacting octave passage at the be-ginning of the coda.
Fantasia, Op. 77	This piece gives some idea of Beethoven's method of extemporization, with temperamen-tal outbursts alternating with passages of gentle expressiveness.
11 Bagatelles, Op. 119	For the most part quite simple.
6 Bagatelles, Op. 126	Characteristic later Beethoven, with a pro-fundity of feeling that their slight appearance would not lead one to expect.
Rondo a Capriccio, Op. 129 (Rage over a lost penny)	A posthumously published piece, technically rather difficult, and boisterously humorous in character. There is some uncertainty as to the exact period of its composition.

WILLIAM STERNDALE BENNETT (1816-1875)

The Lake	Gentle andante cantabile melody, with figure in legato sixths providing a suggestion of the title. (Schirmer; Augener)
The Millstream	Rapid legato triplets, with some double-note passages, requiring digital adroitness. (Schirmer; Augener)
The Fountain	Non legato triplets—a good étude.
Toccata in C Minor	Musicianly, fairly taxing, with mainly right-hand passage work.

ALEXANDER BORODIN (1834-1887)

Au Couvent	This imaginative and individual piece is the first in a suite, the remaining numbers of which are much more conventional. It is technically quite simple. (Schirmer)

JOHANNES BRAHMS (1833-1897)

Most of the pianoforte music of Brahms calls for a certain degree of maturity, both technical and musical. Warmth and depth of tone are prime requirements; virtuoso brilliance (particularly a brilliant finger technique) is less in evidence - one might say that Brahms rarely asks one to play a scale. A certain type of arpeggio passage, laid out in handfuls, with the fifth finger passing over the thumb or the thumb passing under the fifth finger, is characteristic. The total of compositions for piano alone is not large, when compared with that of Beethoven or Chopin, and Brahms's self-criticism allowed very little that was unrepresentative of his highest standards. Consequently, here again is a case where a comprehensive ac-quaintance with the entire output is to be aimed at.

Editions

Most of Brahms's compositions were originally published by the firm of Simrock, whose edition, prepared with great care, was a model. It is now out of print, but when copies are procurable, it can be regarded still as an "Urtext." Certain works have been printed by Simrock's successor —the Universal Edition—with detailed editing. An excellent unedited issue of the last four sets of piano pieces is printed by Breitkopf and Härtel (American agents—Associated Music Publishers). The Peters edition of the complete piano works (also reprinted by Kalmus) edited by Sauer is trustworthy, with occasionally questionable pedaling. The firm of Schirmer has printed various editions, the most recent one bearing the authoritative name of Mandyczewski. (The four late sets of pieces have been edited for Schirmer by Carl Deis with care and freedom from interference with the directions of the composer.) A good edition is also published by the English firm of Augener (American agents—Broude Bros.)

Three Sonatas

These are all early works, written before Brahms's pianoforte style was fully formed.

Sonata in C Major, Op. 1	This has a fine opening movement, and a finale which is structurally more satisfactory than that of either of the other two sonatas. The poetical Andante and variations antedate all other material in the sonatas. The Scherzo has a grand sweep, and, like the rest of the work, needs a big technical grasp.
Sonata in F-sharp Minor, Op. 2	The earliest of the sonatas (with the exception of the Andante of Opus 1). A powerful octave technique is requisite for the opening movement, with its fiery impulse; great warmth of tone for the Andante; and a large hand for one passage in the Scherzo. The finale is rather weak and unconvincing.
Sonata in F Minor, Op. 5	The finest and longest (with five movements) of the three, which retains its place in the repertory through its romantic character and warmth of feeling. Some of the writing, particularly in the first and last movements, is clumsy and difficult. The edition of Harold Bauer, published by Schirmer, incorporates modifications which simplify many of the more unpractical passages; these should be compared with Brahms's original text.
Scherzo in E-flat Minor, Op. 4	This, the earliest of all Brahms's published pianoforte compositions, is more consistent in style than the sonatas. It is comparatively difficult, has a fiery youthful impulse and requires a good deal of physical power.

Four Ballades

Ballade in D Minor, Op. 10, No. 1	The most striking of the four, inspired by the Scottish ballad Edward. The tragic atmosphere

suggested by the texture of the opening phrases, with the melodic line doubled in the midst of the bass chords, is worthy of note. The piece contains no special technical difficulty.

Ballade in D Major, Op. 10, No. 2	The combination of a smooth legato melody with extended chord positions in the opening section presents a little difficulty, and the staccato of the central section needs careful practice.
Ballade in B Minor, Op. 10, No. 3	An imaginative piece, with some difficult rapid finger passages for both hands asking, especially in pianissimo, for accurate tone control.
Ballade in B Major Op. 10, No. 4	A fine cantabile melody is the main feature, with a mysterious middle section suggesting the influence of Schumann.
Sixteen Waltzes, Op. 39	These were originally written for four hands. In the solo form Nos. 14, 15, and 16 have been transposed a half tone downward. These waltzes owe something to the numerous similar pieces of Schubert, but have more subtlety of phrasing. Most of them are not difficult, and it is easy to make a selection. When the whole series is played the inconclusive No. 16 can be followed by a repetition of the familiar No. 15.

Six Sets of Variations

Variations on a theme by Schumann, Op. 9	These, using one of Schumann's <u>Bunte Blätter</u>, Opus 99, as a theme, contain much that is poetical and beautiful, with some early crudities. They require a well-developed technique.
Variations on an original theme, Op. 21, No. 1	A fine set, which is however hard to present to an audience, largely because the beauty and nobility of the theme throw into the shade the succeeding variations, which come as something of an anticlimax. They are more difficult than Opus 9.
Variations on a Hungarian theme, Op. 21, No. 2	The earliest, and on the whole the least valuable of the variations. They nevertheless contain much useful technical material, and their moderate length is also, from the teacher's point of view, in their favor.
Variations and Fugue, on a theme by Handel, Op. 24	In these we have one of the great masterpieces of variation form, with the pianoforte style fully matured and the whole design developed to a noble climax in an enormously effective fugue. The difficulty of the work for present-day pianists is considerable but not excessive.

Variations on a theme by Paganini, Op. 35, Books 1 and 2	These two sets present the most formidable technical demands of any of Brahms's compositions, and may be regarded as a compendium of his idiomatic pianoforte characteristics. They are brilliantly effective; the second is slightly easier than the first, which has obstacles for a small hand (e.g., in Variation 2).

30 Short Pieces
Op. 76, 79, 116, 117, 118, 119.

These are all examples of Brahms's mature pianoforte style; they display uniformly finished workmanship.

Capriccio in F-sharp Minor, Op. 76, No. 1	A cantabile melody of the same type as that in the fourth <u>Ballade</u>, and with a similar accompaniment, alternates with passages of sweeping handfuls of arpeggio. Expressive warmth and depth of tone are needed.
Capriccio in B Minor, Op. 76, No. 2	This popular piece requires a delicate staccato and accurate keyboard sense.
Intermezzo in A-flat Major, Op. 76, No. 3	The legato syncopated chords in the upper part of the keyboard, against the staccato left-hand accompaniment, make an interesting color effect.
Intermezzo in B-flat Major, Op. 76, No. 4	A simple piece with smooth cantabile.
Capriccio in C-sharp Minor, Op. 76, No. 5	More difficult than most of the shorter compositions, with complicated rhythmic details. Requires power and breadth of style.
Intermezzo in A Major, Op. 76, No. 6	Rather easy, perhaps less distinguished than its neighbors; it needs a smooth legato.
Intermezzo in A Minor, Op. 76, No. 7	Also rather simple; there are some elementary problems of balance in the texture.
Capriccio in C Major, Op. 76, No. 8	One of the most masterly of Brahms's shorter piano pieces, complicated in rhythm, and extremely original. Needs an intelligent musician.
Rhapsody in B Minor, Op. 79, No. 1	The longest of these thirty pieces. In some places it is difficult for a small hand. There is scope for much fire and passion.
Rhapsody in G Minor, Op. 79, No. 2	A fine composition, with an originality which its familiarity may cause to be overlooked. It, too, requires warmth of feeling and full tone.
Capriccio in D Minor, Op. 116, No. 1	This fiery piece needs firm rhythmic control to make its persistent syncopations intelligible. The legato diminished seventh arpeggios in octaves for the left hand can only be tackled easily by one with a large span.

Intermezzo in A Minor, Op. 116, No. 2	A duet-like opening has a lower part with, it should be observed, equal importance with the upper. The flickering broken octaves of the middle section are not easy to present with accuracy and delicacy.
Capriccio in G Minor, Op. 116, No. 3	Needs power and full tone.
Intermezzo in E Major, Op. 116, No. 4	Warm singing tone, with careful balance of melody and accompanying voices, is needed for this beautiful piece.
Intermezzo in E Minor, Op. 116, No. 5	Original and somewhat elusive. The melody, in detached two-note slurs, is accompanied by ingeniously placed harmonies. Not difficult.
Intermezzo in E Major, Op. 116, No. 6	The cantabile phrases of the main section appear alternately in an inner part and at the top of the accompanying chords. Grateful and technically simple.
Capriccio in D Minor, Op. 116, No. 7	Requires power and breadth of style. Effective and not excessively difficult.
Intermezzo in E-flat Major, Op. 117, No. 1	The charming folk melody of this requires well-individualized fingers for a clear distinction from the surrounding octaves in the same hand.
Intermezzo in B-flat Minor, Op. 117, No. 2	The finest and most elaborate of the three Intermezzi in this set. Careful phrasing of the two-note slurs in the opening section is wanted, with warm full tone in the subsequent thematic transformation in D-flat.
Intermezzo in C-sharp Minor, Op. 117, No. 3	Has a wistful charm in its main section, and interesting color in the distribution of its texture.
Intermezzo in A Minor, Op. 118, No. 1	Has fine sweep and power, and subtleties of part-writing which should be analysed attentively. Not difficult.
Intermezzo in A Major, Op. 118, No. 2	One of the most melodious of the short pieces. Singing legato throughout. Musically free phrasing, with carefully adjusted rubato in places, is requisite.
Ballade in G Minor, Op. 118, No. 3	Calls for a fiery delivery in its main section, and extreme legato in the duet-like middle part. Some technical power and accurate pedaling are required for the clear and strong definition of the principal theme.
Intermezzo in F Minor, Op. 118, No. 4	Has interesting color effects, without special melodic distinction, in its canonic structure. Not easy to present intelligibly.

Romance in F Major, Op. 118, No. 5	The melodic interest at the outset, it should not be overlooked, is in the lower notes of the right hand and the upper notes of the left. Warmth of feeling and full tone are main essentials, with delicacy for the variations of the central section.
Intermezzo in E-flat Minor, Op. 118, No. 6	An outstanding masterpiece, notable for the mysterious color and atmosphere of the opening and the powerful central climax. Discreet pedaling is important—also choice of tempo (andante, not adagio).
Intermezzo in B Minor, Op. 119, No. 1	Full singing tone, carefully balanced against the accompaniment, is needed.
Intermezzo in E Minor, Op. 119, No. 2	The opening, with three rhythmical variations, in the minor, of the central section's straightforward tune in the major, has an elusive quality rather like that of Opus 116, No. 5. Delicacy of treatment is needed.
Intermezzo in C Major, Op. 119, No. 3	A popular piece that is often mistakenly phrased. The pedaling in some editions is excessive and interferes with the necessary lightness, grace and humor. The subtle cross-rhythm (3/4 against 6/8), sometimes crossing the bar-line, is notable.
Rhapsody in E-flat Major, Op. 119, No. 4	Requires powerful chord playing and feeling for climax. The A-flat section, which should be played with as little pedal as possible, to enable the legato melody to stand out clearly against the staccato accompaniment, and the coda offer the main technical difficulties.

FERRUCIO BUSONI (1866-1924)

Busoni's actual musical invention seems in general to lag behind his mental power and imagination, so his original compositions, which in many respects show a daring that anticipated some later developments, have not been widely performed.

Nuit de Noël	This unpretentious and little-known piece is attractive and imaginative. (Durand)
Sonatinas	Several compositions bearing this title have varying degrees of communicativeness. The Sonatina ad usum infantis is perhaps the most approachable and the Sonatina seconda the most enigmatic. (Breitkopf and Härtel)
Indianisches Tagebuch, Op. 47 (Indian Diary)	These short pieces on American Indian themes may be recommended (especially Nos. 1 and 3) as showing Busoni in a sympathetic aspect as a composer. (Breitkopf and Härtel)

Fantasia contrapuntistica	An enormous work in which, after an impressive introduction, there are presented three fugues, three variations of these fugues, and a final combination of their subjects not only with themselves but with the main subject of Bach's <u>Art of Fugue</u>. A performance would tax both the mental and technical powers of the pianist and the concentration and receptiveness of the listener. (Breitkopf and Härtel)

<u>Transcriptions</u> of works by J. S. Bach

These are in most cases extremely effective from the pianist's point of view, but they often need correction through comparison with the original.

Prelude and Fugue in D Major	An effective arrangement, thicker in texture and less faithful to the original, of the familiar work already transcribed by d'Albert. (Breitkopf and Härtel)
Toccata and Fugue in D Minor	The arrangement of this by Tausig is more often heard, but Busoni's version has merits of its own and is in some respects more scholarly. (Breitkopf and Härtel; Schirmer)
Toccata, Adagio and Fugue in C Major	One of the best of Busoni's transcriptions. It should be compared with the organ version, and the end of the fugue, in particular, can be restored with advantage. (Breitkopf and Härtel; Schirmer)

<u>Chorale Preludes</u>

Wachet auf (Sleepers, wake)	A popular transcription, which (especially in the treatment of the appoggiaturas in the counterpoint) is misleading. (A more accurate version is published by Schirmer in a volume of transcriptions by Henderson.) A nice feeling for balance of tone is a requisite.
Nun komm' der Heiden Heiland (Now comes the gentiles' Saviour)	An exceptionally beautiful chorale prelude, demanding fine singing tone and expressiveness in its florid ornamentation.
Ich ruf' zu dir, Herr (I call on Thee, Lord)	A simple treatment of the unornamented chorale tune, with flowing arpeggio accompaniment in the inner voice.
Nun freut euch, lieben Christen (Rejoice, beloved Christians)	The chorale appears in an inner part; the rapid counterpoint above it presents difficult fingering problems.
Chaconne for violin	This has many features of interest and has achieved popularity; a somewhat more faithful version, based on Busoni's, has been made by Siloti (published by Carl Fischer). (Breitkopf and Härtel; Schirmer)

EMMANUEL CHABRIER (1841-1894)

Habanera	Rather elementary harmonically, and technically simple. (Boston Music Co.)

Pièces pittoresques

Paysage	A lengthy piece presenting some unusual rhythmical problems testing the pianist's control of tonal balance.
Mélancolie	Requires smooth legato.
Tourbillon	Rapid finger passages and repeated chords.
Sous bois	The main technical problem lies in the soft legato chord passages.
Mauresque	Legato and staccato thirds, in detached two-note slurs, present a Moorish dance rhythm.
Idylle	Flowing cantilena, with accompanying repeated thumb in same hand.
Danse villageoise	Has a lively rhythm - not difficult.
Improvisation	Has no great digital difficulty, but has interesting rhythmical combinations.
Menuet pompeux	Requires good rhythm - a useful exercise for staccato chords.
Scherzo-valse	A brilliant finger staccato study. (Enoch)
Bourrée fantasque	Difficult and brilliantly effective. (Enoch; E. B. Marks)

CÉCILE CHAMINADE (1857-1944)

Automne	Has a sentimental melody that makes it popular. It lies easily for the hand. (Schirmer)
Scarf Dance	Graceful and rhythmical—technically easy. (Schirmer)
Toccata	A useful study of moderate difficulty, well written for the instrument. (Schirmer)
La fileuse (The Spinner)	This is decidedly effective, and demands more advanced technique—particularly, good finger work. (Schirmer)

FRÉDÉRIC CHOPIN (1810-1849)

Chopin's pre-eminent position as a composer for the piano, together with the fact that, with the exception of a few posthumously published pieces, his work is remarkably even in quality, makes a thorough acquaintance with his entire output desirable. The greater part of it demands a well-developed technique, calling upon every resource of the modern pianist—depth of tone, finger dexterity, endurance in hand staccato, powerful chord playing, etc. On the musical side are harmonic originality, melodic invention, warm sentiment and poetry—all of a high order that gives their possessor a place that is unique in the history of his art and of his instrument.

Editions

There is no completely satisfactory edition of Chopin. That of Carl Mikuli (reprinted in America by Schirmer) is perhaps as trustworthy as any, with the carefully annotated edition of Franz Kullak (Schlesinger), which is at present difficult to obtain. The complete edition of Breitkopf and Härtel (reprinted by Kalmus) should also be consulted. Scholtz's edition, published by Peters, is generally reliable. The edition of Klindworth (reprinted in England by Augener with revisions by Scharwenka) shows extreme care, but is over elaborate, and suffers sometimes from the editor's arbitrary interpretation of the original. A similarly careful edition, the work of Brugnoli, is issued by Ricordi, and has valuable comparisons of various texts; it, too, suffers from overediting. The edition published by the Oxford University Press, professing to reproduce the text of the original Paris edition and of Chopin's manuscripts, without alteration or addition, is useful for comparison. It has, however, defects arising from insufficient scholarship in its preparation and from carelessness in proofreading. It is also marred by such glaring misstatements as the claim of exact reproduction of the manuscript text of the F minor étude without opus number. Other editions that have merit are those of Debussy (Durand), Friedman (Breitkopf and Härtel) and Merrick (Novello).

The edition of Alfred Cortot (Salabert) has a special place because of the elaborate and interesting suggestions for the solution of technical problems through the practice of related exercises.

Finally, the edition of the Frédéric Chopin Institute (Polish Music Publications), which is, at the time of writing, gradually becoming available, may prove to be an authoritative source through its extensive notes. The Preludes, Ballades and Impromptus have already appeared, and these volumes make a favorable impression.

Easier Compositions

Preludes: Op. 28, Nos. 4, 6, 7, 9, 14, 15, 20.
Waltzes: Op. 34, No. 2; Op. 64, No. 1; and the six published posthumously; two as Op. 69, three as Op. 70, and the one in E minor without opus number.
Nocturnes: Op. 15, No. 3; Op. 32, No. 1; Op. 37, No. 1; and Op. 55, No. 1.
Mazurkas: Op. 6, Nos 2 and 4; Op. 7, Nos. 1, 2, 3, 4 and 5; Op. 17, Nos. 2, 3 and 4; Op. 24, Nos. 1, 2 and 3; Op. 30, No. 2; Op. 33, No. 3; Op. 41, No. 2; Op. 50, Nos. 1 and 2; Op. 63, No. 2; and the eight published posthumously as Op. 67 and Op. 68.

Twenty-four Preludes, Op. 28

Perhaps no other collection of piano pieces contains within such a small compass so much that is at the same time musically and technically valuable

No. 1, in C Major	Calls for a free forearm rotation—singing tone in right-hand thumb.
No. 2, in A Minor	Right-hand cantabile, with left-hand double-note accompanying figure which can be facilitated for a small hand by taking the top notes with the right-hand thumb.
No. 3, in G Major	The technical problem is in the left-hand running accompaniment, which it is difficult to play evenly and softly at full speed.

No. 4, in E Minor	Right-hand cantabile, with much harmonic subtlety in the left hand's accompanying chords, which invite discreet emphasis of salient points.
No. 5, in D Major	Requires flexible lateral adjustment at wrist joint.
No. 6, in B Minor	Left-hand cantabile—"bebung" accompaniment in right.
No. 7, in A Major	A natural simplicity is the obvious requisite.
No. 8, in F-sharp Major	Right-hand thumb cantabile, with accompanying figuration in the remaining fingers, presents a somewhat difficult problem in muscular co-ordination.
No. 9, in E Major	A duet between bass and upper right hand, with bold modulation in central climax asking for full tone.
No. 10, in C-sharp Minor	A short piece with light finger passages, giving scope for imaginative treatment of the similarly constructed four-bar phrases.
No. 11, in B Major	Another short prelude, in a moto perpetuo; one or two groups of legato double notes are difficult for a small hand. A melody is ingeniously implied, partly in cross-rhythm.
No. 12, in G-sharp Minor	One of the most difficult of the series, requiring a powerful hand technique, and accurate control to avoid a too-prominent right-hand thumb.
No. 13, in F-sharp Major	Has an expressive cantabile; and in the middle part a real problem is the proper tonal balance between the different strands of the texture.
No. 14, in E-flat Minor	A good rotation study—not too difficult.
No. 15, in D-flat Major	Another cantabile prelude, with a dramatic crescendo in the middle.
No. 16, in B-flat Minor	A short prelude with difficult passage work requiring powerful and well-schooled fingers.
No. 17, in A-flat Major	Requires good control of upper right-hand fingers for melody with simultaneous chords in the same hand.
No. 18, in F Minor	Demands strong fingers and rhythmic drive, with great power.
No. 19, in E-flat Major	A difficult piece, asking for free forearm rotation and flexible lateral adjustments; also, skillful phrasing of the melody.
No. 20, in C Minor	A simple chord study.
No. 21, in B-flat Major	A smooth delivery of the legato double notes of the accompaniment is the main difficulty.

No. 22, in G Minor — The left-hand octaves have two staccato passages that call for a little endurance; on the whole the difficulty is not excessive.

No. 23, in F Major — A short prelude with melodic implications like those of No. 11. In spite of the direction - sempre legato - it has been reported that Chopin played it with a non-legato articulation (which is effective).

No. 24, in D Minor — This requires dramatic power for the passionate phrases of the right hand, and rotational freedom for the taxing figures of accompaniment.

Prelude in C-sharp Minor, Op. 45 — A fine piece, almost anticipating Brahms in its emotional quality—not difficult except in the double notes of the cadenza near the end.

Twelve Etudes, Op. 10

The Etudes, Opus 10 and Opus 25, almost without exception, ask for virtuosity of a high order; and their length, greater than that of the preludes, necessitates considerable endurance.

No. 1, in C Major — A valuable étude for development and strengthening of the hand through broken-chord passages with alternate contraction and wide extension.

No. 2, in A Minor — One of the most difficult of the series; the chromatic scale passages for third, fourth and fifth fingers of the right hand, with accompanying chords in the same hand for first and second fingers, make an étude of great technical value.

No. 3, in E Major — The opening section has a cantabile melody, with accompaniment in the same hand, requiring careful tonal balance and delicately adjusted rubato. In the middle section is a cadenza with wide extension, in double notes, that needs a fairly good span.

No. 4, in C-sharp Minor — An excellent finger study for both hands.

No. 5, in G-flat Major — The familiar study on black keys, asking for a free rotation.

No. 6, in E-flat Minor — A comparatively easy piece, with an expressive cantabile in the right hand, and accompanying figuration - partly in the right and partly in the left.

No. 7, in C Major — An étude in double notes, requiring powerful fingers, and with a difficult tonal problem in the distinct articulation of the melodic line in the fifth finger.

No. 8, in F Major	Brilliant finger passages, sweeping up and down over four octaves, and demanding smooth manipulation of the thumb, accompany a left-hand melody that is a test of good pedaling.
No. 9, in F Minor	A left-hand accompaniment, with continuously rotating forearm, supports a panting theme that drives to a passionate climax. One of the less difficult études, in spite of some wide extensions.
No. 10, in A-flat Major	A tiring étude for the right hand, which has a continuous octave position with rotation from single notes for thumb to sixths for second and fifth fingers. There are ingenious variations of touch and rhythm.
No. 11, in E-flat Major	An étude in extended arpeggiated chords for both hands, carrying a melody which needs care in its phrasing.
No. 12, in C Minor	The so-called "Revolutionary Étude," which reverses the technical problems of No. 8 - the sweeping accompaniment now being in the left hand, taxing its endurance, with fiery and dramatic statements in the right.

Twelve Etudes, Op. 25

No. 1, in A-flat Major	Has a phrasing problem similar to that of the Prelude in E-flat major, though it is technically easier.
No. 2, in F Minor	A delicate finger study; in the right hand a slight accent on the second and fourth quarter of the bar should be felt if the long triplets of the left are not to cause confusion.
No. 3, in F Major	A light and independent action from the wrist for each beat constitutes an appropriate technique. From measure seventeen onward there are harmonic inflections that can be indicated through the left thumb.
No. 4, in A Minor	This depends for much of its charm on careful distinction between the different versions of the main idea, through staccato, legato and varying degrees of tenuto in the upper voice.
No. 5, in E Minor	Again an étude offering a number of ingenious touch variations applied to the same thematic material; the middle section has a left-hand cantabile melody with an accompaniment in sweeping figuration that lies well for the right hand.
No. 6, in G-sharp Minor	The well-known étude in thirds. The technical requirements are: (a) independence of finger action, (b) absence of rotational stiffness in the forearm, (c) an accurately poised upper arm.

No. 7, in C-sharp Minor	A duet between a left-hand cantilena and a subordinate melody for right hand, which also accompanies with soft chords for the lower fingers. A test for rhythmic flow and tonal balance.
No. 8, in D-flat Major	Etude in sixths, with similar technical requirements to those of No. 6. The extra stretch is taxing for a small hand.
No. 9, in G-flat Major	This "butterfly" étude, except for the powerful central crescendo, justifies its popular title by the delicacy of the persistent figure with its combination of legato slur and octave staccatos. A certain amount of endurance is required.
No. 10, in B Minor	An étude in rapid legato octaves, to be classed with No. 6 and No. 8. A small hand will be severely taxed by the proper degree of finger action combined with the span of the octave.
No. 11, in A Minor	The brilliant chromatic figuration is responsible for the "Wind Study" title. The skillful pianoforte writing makes the piece sound even more difficult than it is. To conquer it, a just balance of finger and rotation technique is needed.
No. 12, in C Minor	An étude requiring a powerful weight touch for the lowest notes, carrying the theme, and free rotational adjustments for the sweeping rise and fall of the accompanying arpeggios.

Trois Nouvelles Études

These, without opus number, were written for the instruction book of Moscheles and Fétis.

No. 1, in F Minor	Combines a right-hand melody in quarter-note triplets with a left-hand accompaniment in eighths.
No. 2, in A-flat Major	The melody is carried at the top of right-hand legato chords while the left accompanies in eighths (two against three).
No. 3, in D-flat Major	An exercise in the combination in the same hand of legato and staccato.

Nocturnes

The main essential in these compositions is an expressive cantilena, with a wide range of tone, together with the carefully adjusted and balanced rubato which the emotional content calls for.

Nocturne in B-flat Minor, Op. 9, No. 1	Singing legato required, both in single notes and in octaves.
Nocturne in E-flat Major, Op. 9, No. 2	The most hackneyed of the nocturnes—a comparatively easy piece—single-note cantilena.

Nocturne in B Major, Op. 9, No. 3	A particularly original nocturne, with a wide range of emotion; in the stormy middle section much depends upon the restless figure of accompaniment.
Nocturne in F Major, Op. 15, No. 1	Another piece of outstanding originality, with a placid main section, sometimes daring in harmony, and a sharply contrasted central part, requiring a powerful left hand in the opening measures.
Nocturne in F-sharp Major, Op. 15, No. 2	This popular composition has an attractive main theme, elaborately ornamented in its continuation and later recapitulation; there is in the middle section some characteristically novel figuration.
Nocturne in G Minor, Op. 15, No. 3	One of the easier nocturnes, with useful exercise in legato chord playing in the latter half.
Nocturne in C-sharp Minor, Op. 27, No. 1	A fine and tragic piece. The opening section has an accompanying figure calling for unusually wide extension in the left hand; in the middle is a powerful climax with big tone.
Nocturne in D-flat Major, Op. 27, No. 2	A smooth cantilena alternates with varied presentments of the material, introducing broken rhythms and slurs which require a delicate hand touch.
Nocturne in B Major, Op. 32, No. 1	A simple piece, with an original and dramatic close.
Nocturne in A-flat Major, Op. 32, No. 2	Not much more difficult than the preceding; the middle section offers good practice in the maintenance of a melodic line in the outer fingers while playing supporting chords in the same hand.
Nocturne in G Minor, Op. 37, No. 1	One of the simpler nocturnes. It has a more ornamental melodic line than Opus 15, No. 3, and has similar legato chord passages in the contrasting section.
Nocturne in G Major, Op. 37, No. 2	The popularity of this composition is due to the Venetian tune which alternates with the opening phrases in legato thirds and sixths. The latter require care to get evenness of tone control.
Nocturne in C Minor, Op. 48, No. 1	This fine work makes the most imposing instrumental effect of any of the nocturnes, with its huge crescendo, enhanced by some almost Lisztian octaves. The agitato recapitulation also presents some problems of tonal balance and control.
Nocturne in F-sharp Minor, Op. 48, No. 2	A placid and not particularly difficult piece, with an individual character and an original treatment

of the recapitulation, which is cut abruptly short in order to lead to a leisurely, very beautiful, coda.

Nocturne in F Minor, Op. 55, No. 1	Easy, except for the cadenza-like coda, which requires careful fingering. The same formal feature (shortening of the recapitulation) as in the preceding nocturne is to be noted.
Nocturne in E-flat Major, Op. 55, No. 2	A very fine and comparatively unfamiliar piece, characteristic of Chopin's later style. The main technical problem is to be found in the duet-like passages for right hand, with the lower voice subordinated but individual.
Nocturne in B Major, Op. 62, No. 1	Another composition of Chopin's creative maturity. The free rhythmic structure of the opening is notable and should be carefully analyzed to obtain an intelligent performance. At the same time a delicate control of tone, discriminating between upper and lower voices, is needed. Here again, as in Opus 48, No. 2 and Opus 55, No. 1, there is a much shortened reprise with a poetical coda.
Nocturne in E Major, Op. 62, No. 2	A popular piece, with a broad cantilena, followed by an agitated central part which contains the only serious technical problem—that of independent control of the outer fingers carrying the main melody, while subordinating the accompanying chords in the same hand.
Nocturne in E Minor, Op. 72	This, published posthumously, is an unpretentious and structurally simple nocturne having a sustained cantilena, which is only broken by a wildly passionate, floridly ornamented, version of the main theme, forming a central climactic point. There is little technical difficulty.
Nocturne in C-sharp Minor (no Op. No.)	A poverty-stricken nocturne in C-sharp minor, disinterred comparatively recently, has obtained a measure of popularity. It is quite unrepresentative of the composer, and its performance does his reputation no service.

Ballades

The four Ballades contain some of Chopin's most poetical and inspired ideas, with a wide range of emotion, from gentle sentiment to fiery brilliance. They are all of considerable technical difficulty.

Ballade in G Minor, Op. 23	The first thirty measures or so, easy technically, are actually the most difficult interpretatively. Later, some rapid legato octave scales need a strong mechanism; and the coda taxes a small hand, with the demand for a powerful rotation technique in passages resembling those of the Étude, Opus 10, No. 10.

Ballade in F Major, Op. 38	Again, as in Opus 23, the opening page of this piece, and the similar material later, are tests of the pianist's musical sensitiveness. The sections marked "presto" need endurance in various types of technique—strong finger work, rotation passages like those in the coda of Opus 23, and free hand action from the wrist.
Ballade in A-flat Major, Op. 47	On the whole the least difficult of the four. The second subject (entering first in F major) requires careful phrasing and pedaling. The climax which starts its preparation with the change of key signature to four sharps has the only serious mechanical difficulties—it asks for good left-hand finger technique and a powerful rotary action in the right.
Ballade in F Minor, Op. 52	This ballade, among the finest of Chopin's later pieces, calls for specially imaginative treatment. The phrasing of the flexibly constructed main subject is no easy problem. A notable technical feature is the frequency of double-note passages, with some exceptionally tricky ones in the strenuous coda.

Scherzos

The four Scherzos, in comparison with the Ballades, emphasize more the element of instrumental brilliance, though three of them (Nos. 1, 2 and 4) have contrasting sections of a lyrical character. All are technically exacting.

Scherzo in B Minor, Op. 20	Perhaps the most easily accessible of the four. It contains a comparatively small amount of material, which—it may be worth while to note—is in the principal section of a kind particularly valuable for the encouragement of a free arm condition in approaching and leaving the keyboard. The central "Molto piu lento" has its problems of phrasing, rubato, and tone production through weight touch; and the fiery coda has some taxing rotation passages.
Scherzo in B-flat Minor, Op. 31	This familiar scherzo makes a wide variety of technical demands—rhythmical chord playing, singing legato in the lyrical alternating melody of the main section, and brilliant finger technique. Some of the widely extended broken chords can be facilitated for small hands by an adroit division between right and left.
Scherzo in C-sharp Minor, Op. 39	Powerful octaves are needed for the principal theme, though the passages are not exceptionally tiring or difficult. At the "Meno mosso" the

four-bar chord phrases, with the connecting eighth-note passages, test the player's feeling for rhythmical balance. The coda requires strong fingers.

Scherzo in E Major, Op. 54	A typical example of the later Chopin. In contrast to the other three scherzos, this asks for great delicacy in both chord playing and finger technique. The piece is somewhat diffuse, but amply repays study; it has a fine lyrical middle section.

Impromptus

Of these four pieces the finest, and slightly the most difficult, is the second, in F-sharp. The first, in A-flat, and the posthumously published Fantaisie-Impromptu are somewhat alike in character and are of moderate difficulty.

Impromptu in A-flat Major, Op. 29	This has finger passages that lie easily for the hand, with only a little problem in two measures of double-note technique.
Impromptu in F-sharp Major, Op. 36	A more extended structure than the ABA of the other three. Sensitive phrasing of the main theme, and reliable finger technique for the passage work of the peroration are requisites.
Impromptu in G-flat Major, Op. 51	The least familiar of the series; it contains some legato thirds and sixths which are troublesome for a small hand.
Fantaisie-Impromptu in C-sharp Minor, Op. 66	Somewhat like the Impromptu in A-flat in character and in technical requirements. Grateful finger passages alternate with a central episode of appealing lyricism.

Polonaises

Chopin's national feeling finds expression in these stately compositions. There is a wide range of pianoforte and technical difficulty.

Polonaise in C-sharp Minor, Op. 26, No. 1	Prevailingly lyrical in character, and of not more than moderate difficulty.
Polonaise in E-flat Minor, Op. 26, No. 2	Also not very difficult; rhythmical chord passages are frequent. The general character is wild and tragic.
Polonaise in A Major, Op. 40, No. 1	The so-called "Military Polonaise." Rhythmical chord playing is again prominent; the piece can easily be made trivial by too fast a tempo.
Polonaise in C Minor, Op. 40, No. 2	A noble piece, with a stern, somewhat gloomy main subject, and only slight relief in the A-flat section. It has no excessive difficulty.
Polonaise in F-sharp Minor, Op. 44	Perhaps the finest of the polonaises, technically exacting and calling for a continuous rhythmic

drive. A barbaric passage with an insistent repeated rhythm leads to a central mazurka, after which the polonaise returns and culminates in a coda with a majestic climax.

Polonaise in A-flat Major, Op. 53	The best known of the polonaises; the octave crescendo in the left hand, accompanying the E-major theme, is so tempting to the virtuoso that its speeding up, with similar treatment of the whole piece, often vulgarizes the performance.
Polonaise-Fantaisie in A-flat Major, Op. 61	A discursive but emotionally profound example of the later style. After a short introduction, using a harmonic progression of two chords for a kind of motto, and foreshadowing the main theme, the latter enters complete. But the music soon becomes episodic and gives the player a definite problem in its integration for the hearer. A meditative central "Piu lento" supplies part of the material for a magnificent coda, which ends the piece splendidly. This work again has considerable technical difficulty, though of a kind less spectacular than in Opus 44 and Opus 53.
Polonaises in D Minor, B-flat Major and F Minor, Op. 71, Nos. 1, 2 & 3	These, published posthumously, are neither very exacting technically nor significant musically.
Andante spianato and Polonaise in E-flat Major, Op. 22	This was written with an orchestral accompaniment which can easily be dispensed with in performance. It is brilliantly effective; and while it requires a good command of the keyboard, it is less difficult than it sounds.

Waltzes

• The waltzes are of two kinds—those which are brilliant and dashing, with glittering pianoforte effect, and others, slower in tempo, of a pensive and expressive character. The main criticism that may be made is that the conventional waltz bass often seems to lead to harmonies that are unenterprising and obvious, with much tonic-and-dominant alternation. In general there is not more than moderate technical difficulty.

Waltz in E-flat Major, Op. 18 Waltz in A-flat Major, Op. 34, No. 1	These are good examples of the brilliant type, with passages that lie well for the hand and make an easy effect.
Waltz in A Minor, Op. 34, No. 2	A slow waltz of great charm; technically easy.
Waltz in F Major, Op. 34, No. 3	Less distinguished than most of these pieces; harmonically easygoing and unadventurous.

Waltz in A-flat Major, Op. 42	A fine example of the brilliant group, with a fascinating cross-rhythm in its main musical idea. A little more taxing than its companions.
Waltz in D-flat Major, Op. 64, No. 1	The so-called "Minute Waltz." Fluent finger passages lying easily for the hand make up most of the material, with a short sostenuto contrasting phrase. Easy and effective.
Waltz in C-sharp Minor, Op. 64, No. 2	Another popular waltz, with much individuality in its musical ideas—three in number, and well contrasted. Not difficult.
Waltz in A-flat Major, Op. 64, No. 3	This and Opus 42 are perhaps the most distinctive of the waltzes. Here one finds the subtlety characterizing Chopin's latest work; the syncopations of the main theme, the unconventional rhythmic organization of the C-major theme in the left hand, and the bold modulations toward the end all provide unusual interest.
Waltzes in A-flat Major and B Minor, Op. 69, Nos. 1 & 2	These are of the gently expressive type —easy and graceful.
Waltzes in G-flat, A-flat & D-flat Major, Op. 70, Nos. 1, 2 & 3	Except the opening and close of No. 1, these are again quiet and expressive, in moderate tempo, and with no technical difficulty.
Waltz in E Minor (without opus number)	A popular and effective waltz, not difficult, though of the brilliant type.

Mazurkas

Nothing in Chopin's whole output contains so much that is original and harmonically daring as do the finest of these characteristic products of Polish genius. Over fifty in number, they range from compositions of extreme simplicity, suitable for a student of moderate equipment, to others displaying amazing subtlety and sometimes of some technical difficulty. But there is hardly any that has not its special appeal. The following have outstanding features.

Mazurka in A Minor, Op. 17, No. 4	A plaintive piece, starting and ending with a four-bar "motto" which finishes "in the air" on an inversion of a triad. The harmony varies from extreme chromaticism to simple tonic-and-dominant over a drone bass.
Mazurka in C Major, Op. 24, No. 2	Notable for a Lydian mode tune, using a B-natural with a tonic F.
Mazurka in B-flat Minor, Op. 24, No. 4	Has a very original two-voice main idea, and dies away at the end in a mournful coda using fresh material.
Mazurka in C-sharp Minor, Op. 30, No. 4	Has a departure from convention in the chromatic descent of the seventh chords just before the final "fade-out."

Mazurka in D Major, Op. 33, No. 2	A mazurka of strong character notwithstanding the deliberate simplicity of its harmony, which gives it a primitive and rustic flavor.
Mazurka in C-sharp Minor, Op. 41, No. 1	Modal influence may be traced again here in a persistent Phrygian D-natural in the key of C-sharp minor.
Mazurka in C-sharp Minor, Op. 50, No. 3	The opening and close are unusually contrapuntal in contrast to the simply harmonized melody of the middle section.
Mazurka in B Major, Op. 56, No. 1	Interesting for its succession of keys: B—E-flat (i.e., D-sharp, the mediant)—B—G (submediant)—B.
Mazurka in A Minor, Op. 59, No. 1	Here again is much contrapuntal interest. The ingenious return of the principal subject in G-sharp minor is also worthy of note.
Mazurka in A-flat Major, Op. 59, No. 2	This has one of the most charming melodies in the mazurkas, and an astonishing passage of chromatic harmony leading to a delightful coda.
Mazurka in F-sharp Minor, Op. 59, No. 3	A spirited main theme and a central one with exceptionally sophisticated rhythm characterize this piece. A tendency toward contrapuntal treatment is seen in the passage introducing the recapitulation, and again in the one leading to the coda.
Mazurka in F Minor, Op. 68, No. 4	This sad and beautiful little piece was Chopin's last composition. Extreme chromaticism and a striking modulation to A major are salient features.

Sonatas

Chopin's compositions in this form have of course to be regarded from a point of view somewhat different from that of the great classical masters. The formal balance of Haydn and Mozart is replaced by a romantic freedom already foreshadowed by Beethoven, a freedom that permits great flexibility in performance.

Sonata in C Minor, Op. 4	This can be disregarded. It was published after Chopin's death and is quite unrepresentative; the first and last movements, in particular, consist of a vast amount of (often very difficult) passage work that has little real musical interest.
Sonata in B-flat Minor, Op. 35	Chopin's greatest work in a large form, completely original and successful from beginning to end. The grandeur of the conception calls for a similar quality in the performance, with command of a wide range of tone. The broken rhythms of the opening of the first movement

need careful pedaling if the full agitated effect
is to be achieved. The combination, in the
masterly development, of this rhythmic idea
with the "motto" stated in the first two
measures of the sonata has to be delivered
with a powerful left arm. The Scherzo, too,
makes more than average technical demands,
with again very thoughtful and discreet pedaling—see, for example, the problem presented
by the eight bars before the "Piu lento."
Strong rhythm for the funeral march and absence of sentimentality for the Trio are main
necessities. The extraordinary and eerie
finale (owing something in its structure to
J. S. Bach) has some fingering problems. Its
effect can be enhanced by very momentary and
discreet pedaling at a few places.

Sonata in B Minor, Op. 58	This is structurally less happy than Opus 35, the development of the first movement being somewhat labored, and the central section of the slow movement also showing a less sure grasp. But there is so much beauty in the material of the work as a whole, with a very brilliant and effective finale, that it has an assured place in the repertory. The first movement has some tricky double-note pas-sages; the Scherzo requires a fluent finger technique, and its Trio leaves some doubts as to the exact text, particularly in regard to ties; in the slow movement it may be suggested that the 4/4 tempo of the opening and close should become "alla breve" in the discursive central part. No pianist without brilliant finger technique and firm rhythm can success-fully cope with the demands of the exciting finale.
Variations in B-flat Major, Op. 12, on "Je vends des scapulaires"	A quite attractive and not exceptionally difficult piece; technically effective.
Bolero, Op. 19	Of moderate difficulty, effective, and of the same musical calibre as the Variations in B-flat.
Tarantelle, Op. 43	Brilliant and effective, with less musical sub-stance than Opus 12 and Opus 19, and not more difficult.
Allegro de Concert, Op. 46	An imposing piece, with Bellini-like cantilena alternating with exacting passage work; it suggests an orchestral background and has been so arranged by Nicodé.
Fantaisie in F Minor, Op. 49	A masterly composition, brilliant and difficult, requiring strong fingers and control of a wide

range of tone. Structurally, one of Chopin's most successful large designs.

Berceuse, Op. 57   An extraordinary tour-de-force consisting for the most part of a simple alternation of tonic and dominant harmony with inexhaustibly ingenious figuration superimposed. It requires great delicacy and sure finger control.

Barcarolle, Op. 60   One of the great compositions of Chopin's maturity, original and very refined and subtle harmonically. Control of singing tone, and differentiation between two voices in the same hand, with powerful weight touch for climaxes, are main essentials.

Three Ecossaises, in D, G, and D-flat Major   These, published posthumously, are pleasant trifles of no musical importance - technically easy.

Rondos, Op. 1, 5 and 16   The rondos can be disregarded.

MUZIO CLEMENTI (1752-1832)

Clementi, the father of modern pianoforte playing, left, apart from his technical studies, a large amount of serious pianoforte and concerted music, some of which even evoked the admiration of Beethoven.

Sonatinas (Op. 36, 37 and 38)

The sonatinas are still familiar items in the training of the young, and they (particularly the six, Opus 36) have an appeal for any musical child. (Schirmer, etc.)

Sonatas

The sonatas have not retained the same popularity, but their musical quality and finished workmanship entitle them to respect. Two volumes, containing twelve sonatas, are published by Schirmer.

Sonata in D Major, Op. 40, No. 3   This is a somewhat large-scaled work; the first of its three movements, after a short introduction in the minor in slow tempo, has an allegro with a considerable technical range, of about the same difficulty as those of Mozart. The slow movement has real emotional quality, and the final Rondo has an interesting feature in a canon (founded on the principal subject and taking the place of the usual third theme) which may well have had its influence on the second movement of Beethoven's Opus 101. (Schirmer, No. 11)

Sonata in B-flat Major, Op. 47, No. 2   This is slighter than the preceding, but it has its place in musical history because of a "contest" with Mozart, in the presence of the emperor Joseph II, in which Clementi played it. (The opening theme was appropriated by Mozart for

the overture to <u>Die Zauberflöte</u>.) The two
fermata bars toward the close of the first
movement are evidently intended to provide
an opportunity for an extemporized cadenza.
(Schirmer, No. 12)

CARL CZERNY (1791-1857)

Variations, Op. 33, on a
theme by Rode (La
Ricordanza)

There are five variations - three of them of a
florid Hummel-like type. They have a certain
interest as a rather rare survival from the
numerous works of a composer whose reputation rests, perhaps unfairly, entirely upon his
pedagogic productions.
(International Music Co.).

Toccata, Op. 92

This may have suggested to Schumann the
composition of his toccata in the same key.
Czerny's is largely concerned (as is Schumann's) with the exploitation of double-note
technique—mainly in the right hand.
(Schirmer).

LEO DELIBES (1836-1891)

Passepied (from
"Le roi s'amuse")

A charming trifle, quite easy, which calls for
delicate and sensitive treatment and invites a
comparison with the passepied in Debussy's
Suite Bergamasque.
(Schirmer)

ERNST VON DOHNANYI (1877-   )

Dohnanyi has produced a large number of compositions marked by an exceptional command of traditional nineteenth-century technique and idiom,
often influenced by Brahms. He has, however, an individual quality of his
own, and the feeling for the piano to be expected from one who has had a
distinguished career as a soloist.

Four Rhapsodies, Op. 11 (Doblinger, Universal Edition).

No. 2, in F-sharp Minor

This is less taxing than it sounds; the octaves
of its bombastic climax are not really difficult.
It contains phrases of Hungarian character
recalling Liszt, and a charming contrasting
cantilena.
(Willis Music Co.)

No. 3, in C Major

More difficult and brilliant than No. 2. Its
rapid staccato double notes and octaves require
a mature technique.
(Willis Music Co.)

Winterreigen, Op. 13

This series is of moderate difficulty, and has a
wide range of mood.

Tolle Gesellschaft
(The Madcaps)

No. 8 of Winterreigen - has passages in rapid
sixths and thirds which are somewhat taxing— a

good double note technique is needed. It is a
lively piece, with an amusing accelerando
that bears out the title.
(Schirmer; E. B. Marks)

Suite - Humoresken, Op. 17

March	On a ground bass of four notes. It has a vital rhythmic drive, and is not very difficult.
Toccata	A brilliant and effective display piece, lying well for the hand.
Pavane (from the sixteenth century) with variations	A very musicianly set, starting in G major, with the last variation in B major, leading to:
Pastorale	A clever canonic piece requiring good legato and nice control of tone.
Introduction & Fugue	Elaborately worked out, with a good deal of humor in its contrapuntal devices. A good staccato study. (Universal Edition)

Six Concert Etudes, Op. 28

No. 5, in E Major	An elaborate piece, with hands constantly alternating in arpeggio figures, developed to an imposing climax.
No. 6, in F Minor	The popular Capriccio in F Minor, a firework display which produces a dazzling effect when its difficulties are conquered. (Rozsavolgyi & Co. Reprints by Boston Music Co. and E. B. Marks)
Ruralia Hungarica, Op. 32a	Seven pieces which employ folk-song material, including some that are comparatively easy. (Rozsavolgyi & Co.)

Concert Transcriptions

Waltz from Delibes's "Naila"	An elaborate and effective virtuoso piece, with a climax involving a contrapuntal combination of two themes. Difficult and physically taxing.

Two Waltzes of Johan
Strauss

Schatzwalzer ("Zigeuner-baron") Du und Du ("Fleder-maus")	These are less exacting than the Naila waltz, though still requiring an advanced technique for their adequate performance. The Strauss melodies are irresistibly charming.

JOHANN LADISLAW DUSSEK (1761-1812)

A prolific composer whose compositions are almost forgotten today. The
two following pieces give a fair idea of his style:

La Chasse	A few measures of introduction in slow tempo lead to a pleasing 6/8 allegro; the naive "horn"

passages suggest the title and are not without attractiveness—they have also technical value, as a simple exercise in hand staccato. (Schirmer).

Sonata in B-flat Major, Op. 9, No. 1　This consists of two movements only, with no slow movement. The first is a solid structure of conventional design and material, and varied technical demands of Mozartian type. The second—Allegretto grazioso—is a rondo of gentle character, harmonically rather unenter-prising. (Schirmer).

ANTONIN DVORAK (1841-1904)

Without offering any technical novelty, the numerous short pieces of Dvorak generally have much of the individual flavor of his larger works. Unfortunately, most of them are hard to obtain at present—e.g., the thirteen Poetic Tone Pictures and the eight Humoresques, both originally published by Simrock. Single pieces from these have been reprinted by Schirmer, as is indicated below.

Dumka a Furiant, Op. 12　These twin pieces, subtitled "Elegy" and "Bohemian National Dance," have freshness and no particular technical difficulty. Some passages in the "Elegy" require careful balancing of tone where the melodic line passes from right to left hand. The dance has a vigorous rhythm. (Augener).

Poetic Tone Pictures, Op. 85

No. 3 - In the old castle　A simply expressive piece, somewhat Grieg-like in character. (Schirmer).

No. 8 - Goblin Dance　Lively and rhythmical, of moderate difficulty, with some effective hand staccato passages and an expressive central contrasting section. (Schirmer).

Humoresques, Op. 101

No. 7, in G-flat Major　The only one of the series readily available, and the only one that has become popular. (Schirmer). But No. 1 in E-flat minor and No. 5 in A minor are both vigorous and attractive and might well be revived.

These three compositions from Opus 85 and Opus 101 are included in a volume of ten (including some arrangements) published by Schirmer.

Slavonic Dances, Op. 46 and 72　These are similar in their character to the Furiant of Opus 12. (Simrock, through Associated Music).

MICHEL DVORSKY (Pseudonym of Josef Hofmann) (1876-)

Penguine   The most immediately appealing of "Three
                            Impressions"; it requires considerable keyboard
                            facility.
                            (Schirmer).

GABRIEL FAURÉ (1845-1924)

It is easy to underestimate the compositions of Fauré for piano. There is
about them a sort of aristocratic reserve, and they do not always make their
full impression on a first acquaintance. It may also be admitted that a number of them show so much similarity of character that there is an effect of
repetitiousness. Nevertheless, we have here a master of his craft, with
invariable technical finish, distinction and real individuality. The complete
list of pianoforte pieces is a long one; many of the best are among the thirteen Nocturnes, thirteen Barcarolles and six Impromptus, from which a
selection has been made here. It should be said that Fauré generally demands some technical maturity.

Three Songs without   These are, like all Fauré's compositions, well
    Words, Op. 17   written for the instrument, and they are easier
                           than most of those here selected.
                           (Hamelle; International Music Co.; Schirmer).

Berceuse, Op. 56, No. 1   Melodious and not difficult.
                           (Hamelle; Schirmer)

Barcarolles

Barcarolle No. 1, Op. 26   A short piece, consisting mainly of a flowing
                           cantabile with effective accompanying figuration.
                           (Hamelle; International Music Co., Schirmer).

Barcarolle No. 4, Op. 44   Very effective pianistically; individual and dis-
                           tinctive.
                           (Hamelle; International Music Co.; Schirmer).

Barcarolle No. 5, Op. 66   The most elaborate of the series; it has interest-
                           ing rhythmic and harmonic features—it is
                           somewhat elusive on first acquaintance.
                           (Hamelle; International Music Co.).

Barcarolle No. 6, Op. 70   Similar to No. 1.
                           (Hamelle; International Music Co.; Schirmer).

Barcarolle No. 7, Op. 90   A short piece in Fauré's later, more austere
                           style.
                           (Heugel).

Barcarolle No. 10,   Another short and simple piece, of somewhat
    Op. 104   wistful character.
                           (Durand).

Impromptus

Impromptu No. 2, Op. 31   The most popular of Fauré's piano pieces;
                           fluent and effective finger passages, and a
                           pleasantly tuneful central section.
                           (Hamelle; International Music Co.; Boston Music
                           Co.).

Impromptu No. 4, Op. 91	Starting with a syncopated theme of more rhythmic than melodic interest, and having a middle section with some subtle harmony, this is a good example of Fauré's later style. (Heugel).
Impromptu No. 5, Op. 102	Has an étude-like character; interesting for its experiments with the whole-tone scale. (Heugel).

Nocturnes

Note should be taken of the interesting and valuable comments of Roger Ducasse, printed in the Hamelle edition of the first eight nocturnes.

Nocturne No. 1, Op. 33, No. 1	An extremely original piece with some striking pianoforte effects. (Hamelle).
Nocturne No. 6, Op. 63	Perhaps the finest of the nocturnes; a very powerful piece, with a masterly development— a real test of the player's musicianship. (Hamelle).
Nocturne No. 7, Op. 74	Shows skillful and elaborate workmanship equal to that of No. 6, and makes similar demands on the musical intelligence. (Hamelle).
Nocturne No. 13, Op. 119	A grave and noble composition in Fauré's later manner. A somewhat severe principal theme is given out in a freely contrapuntal texture; a middle contrasting section of more purely pianistic character leads to a powerful climax, with a return to the opening and a quiet close. Repays close study. (Durand).

Preludes

The nine Preludes, Opus 103 (Heugel), are unequal in quality, but at least four call for special mention.

Prelude No. 2 in C-sharp Minor	A rapid moto perpetuo in triplets (each divided between the two hands) providing an interesting étude.
Prelude No. 3 in G Minor	An easy cantabile piece with a good deal of harmonic interest.
Prelude No. 6 in E-flat Minor	An interesting canon - a good legato study.
Prelude No. 8 in C Minor	Repeated note staccato, with legato counterpoint.
Theme and Variations, Op. 73	This set of eleven variations, apparently written in 1910 for a competition of the Paris Conservatoire, has much interesting pianoforte writing, but a less skillful organic structure than we

meet with in the finest of the nocturnes. A
certain absence of climax detracts from the
total effect.
(Hamelle; International Music Co.).

JOHN FIELD (1782-1837)

Field's chief title to fame is as the inventor of the nocturne, the romantic
type afterward developed by Chopin and further distinguished by Fauré.
The volume published by Schirmer (also Augener) reproduces Liszt's interesting essay, prefatory to a series of six nocturnes issued in 1859. The
technical demands are generally quite moderate.

Eighteen Nocturnes

No. 1 in E-flat Major

This sets the pattern for a number of these
compositions - a melody in the right hand,
quite simple, yet with an individual native
flavor; accompanied by a left-hand broken-
chord figure of unvarying shape.

No. 4 in A Major

The finest of Field's nocturnes; it has more
than the usual variety and emotional range.

No. 5 in B-flat Major

Quite short—for the most part resembling No. 1,
but with a contrasting passage in chords.

No. 7 in A Major

A charming piece, extremely simple harmonically, and owing a great deal of its attractiveness
to the delightful florid variations of the thematic
material.
(Schirmer; Augener).

Rondo in E-flat Major

This, edited by Bülow, may serve as a favorable
example of Field's work in more extended form.
(Schirmer).

CÉSAR FRANCK (1822-1890)

Eighteen Short Pieces

This volume contains easy pieces of slight importance, most of them written originally for
harmonium, but some more suited to the piano;
they have enough interest to make them suitable
as simple teaching material and as introduction
to Franck's style.
(Peters).

Prelude, Chorale and
    Fugue

In the three sections of this important work
prime requirements are depth of tone and a
good legato; the contrapuntal complexities of
the Fugue presuppose a good mental grasp, with
careful tonal discrimination and phrasing in the
treatment of each voice.
(Litolff; Peters; Kalmus).

Prelude, Aria and Finale

The technical and musical qualities asked for by
the Prelude, Chorale and Fugue are again needed
here; the Finale also calls for good wrists, a

facile octave technique, and brilliance in
finger passages.
Well edited by Harold Bauer for the Boston
Music Co. Original edition, Hamelle.

Prelude, Fugue and
Variation

This piece, transcribed for piano by Harold
Bauer, is easier than the two larger compositions mentioned above. Its gentle expressiveness is most appealing. The Fugue needs
careful phrasing; and the concluding Variation,
adroit balancing of tone.
(Durand).

NIELS GADE (1817-1890)

The Children's Christmas
Eve

This set of six simple pieces can be recommended as providing pleasing elementary
teaching material.
(Schirmer).

Aquarellen, Op. 19

These are also suitable for beginners; they are
influenced by Schumann, and exhibit neat
workmanship.
(Schirmer).

ALEXANDER GLAZOUNOFF (1865-1936)

Glazounoff's technically expert craftsmanship has not sufficed to keep
much of his large output in the present-day repertoire. A good selection
is to be found in a volume published by the Leeds Music Corporation, and
single pieces are issued by other firms. The following are representative:

Gavotte in D Major,
Op. 29, No. 3

Tuneful—not for a small hand—otherwise not
difficult.
(Leeds Music Corp.).

Concert Study in C Major,
Op. 31, No. 1

A virtuoso piece, difficult and brilliant, with
double-note technique.
(International Music Co.).

Valse, Op. 42, No. 3

A suave, delicate salon piece—not difficult.
(Leeds Music Corp.).

Prelude and Fugue in
E Minor

Has an imposing prelude, and an elaborately
worked fugue, with complicated counterpoint.
(Schirmer; Leeds Music Corp.)

Variations in F-sharp
Minor, Op. 72

A fine work, requiring mature technique and
musicianship.
(International Music Co.; Leeds Music Corp.)

REINHOLD GLIÈRE (1875-1926)

Twenty-five Preludes,
Op. 30

Pieces of romantic nineteenth-century character,
technically accomplished and well written for the
instrument. Most of them require fairly advanced digital command.
(Jurgenson).

BENJAMIN GODARD (1849-1895)

Most of this composer's piano pieces are of a pleasing salon type..

Chopin	The graceful waltz with this title is not difficult. (Schirmer)
En route	A taxing staccato chord study. (Schirmer)
Le cavalier fantastique	A more than usually ambitious piece - it requires good hand technique. (Schirmer).
La chevaleresque	Encourages keyboard command, with passages for free arm and weight technique. (Schirmer)
Jonglerie	Good for a special type of technique - melody in alternating thumbs. (Schirmer)

LEOPOLD GODOWSKY (1870-1938)

Godowsky has a unique place among composers for his instrument because of his extraordinary technical skill and manipulative ingenuity. His numerous arrangement and paraphrases, too, cannot be ignored - their musical value is variable, and an occasional choice of harmony raises a difference of opinion as to its good taste, but as a whole they amply repay a thorough examination. The fingering, incidentally, is a perfect model. A small selection from Godowsky's output is presented here:

Triakontameron	Thirty pieces in triple time, not difficult and quite charming. (Schirmer)
Phonoramas (Java Suite)	Twelve pieces descriptive of Javanese scenes, requiring a mature technique. Starting with "Gamelan," the repeated notes of which imitate the instruments of a native band, these have a wide variety of pianoforte effect, often demanding tonal gradations and balances like those of Debussy. The suite as a whole is modern in feeling. (Carl Fischer)
Passacaglia	This has for a theme the opening measures of Schubert's Unfinished Symphony. It is a good example of Godowsky's accomplished musicianship, and its performance requires similar musical and technical attainments. (Carl Fischer)
Paraphrases of songs by Schubert	Of these, Haidenröslein and Das Wandern may be specially recommended; they are less difficult than some others of the series, and are most effective. (Carl Fischer)

Le Cygne (Saint-Saens)	Another paraphrase with amusing chromatic elaborations and contortions. (Carl Fischer).
Arrangements of Etudes by Chopin	These extend Chopin's technical range by transfers of the passages, in many cases, from right to left hand (e.g., in the étude in thirds). The difficulties are naturally great. (Carl Fischer).

LOUIS MOREAU GOTTSCHALK (1829-1869)

This early-American writer—immensely popular in his day—was a virtuoso whose musical intentions (to judge by the pieces he has left) were very clear indeed. His harmony is unenterprising, and there is an abundance of guitar-like passages and repeated chord technique, requiring a facility like that of the jazz pianists. His compositions are period pieces demanding an elegant and precise pianism before their true effect can be measured.

Of the following, the first three pieces are in a Gottschalk album published by Augener.

Danse Ossianique	Elegant and scintillating; not too long or difficult.
Le Banjo (Caprice Americain)	A rhythmic, spirited banjo imitation. Requires endurance and brilliance.
Pasquinade	A capricious piece that requires neatness and dexterity.
Bamboula	This evocation of a primitive dance is a fair example of Gottschalk's talent. (Schirmer).
Souvenir de Porto Rico (Marche des Gibarros)	There is a short introduction, then a theme and refrain (possibly a Puerto Rican folk song), and a set of continuous variations in popular nineteenth-century style. An interesting period piece both pianistically and musically. (Mercury Music).

ENRIQUE GRANADOS (1867-1916)

Spanish Dances (Four Books)

These are technically and harmonically simple. The three mentioned below are reprinted in America by Carl Fischer.

No. 4 Villanesca	Mainly a simple rhythmic tune on a drone bass.
No. 5 Playera	The most popular of the series. Not difficult, but requiring good rhythmic sense.
No. 6 Jota	A lively primitive dance—like No. 4, on a drone bass—harmonically elementary. (Union Musical Espanola)
Goyescas	Granados's most ambitious compositions for the piano. The six pieces of this suite have individual flavor and idiomatic pianoforte writing. With

the exception of No. 4, they are rather diffuse and lengthy, suggesting a gifted improviser rather than an expert craftsman.

Los Requiebros (Flattery)	Ingratiating melodic ideas are passed from one hand to another with complicated accompanying figures, often involving difficult double-note technique.
Coloquio en la Reja (Love Duet)	This needs expert balancing of tone. There is some involved piano writing and the melodic line is often much ornamented; great passion and sweep are necessary.
El Fandango de Candil	The texture of this dance is for the most part simpler than in the two preceding movements, though Granados's special type of double-note technical difficulty is much in evidence.
Quejas o la Maja y el Ruiseñor (Laments, or the Lady and the Nightingale)	This, the most popular of the set, is a romantic rhapsody, with many repetitions of one leading phrase. It calls for much freedom in its delivery, and gives the impression of an extemporization.
El Amor y la Muerte (Love and Death)	A dramatic piece which makes some use of the principal theme of No. 4. The most difficult, interpretatively, of the set.
Epilogo (Serenade of the Spectre)	Staccato dance rhythms suggest a guitar, accompanying a doleful chromatic motive. A flickering figure calls up imaginatively the picture of a ghostly figure which hovers about and finally disappears. (International Music Co.).
Intermezzo, from the opera Goyescas	This arrangement by the composer is unpretentious and melodious. (Schirmer).

ALEXANDER GRETCHANINOFF (1864-   )

This composer has produced a large number of pieces for children, all showing accomplished musicianship.

Four Pieces for Children, Op. 170	These are technically elementary; the fourth—Berceuse—is the most imaginative. (Hargail)
Twelve Little Sketches for Children, Op. 182	(International Music Co.).
Pastels—Five Miniatures, Op. 3	Early pieces, dating from 1894, more sophisticated than the above, and of moderate difficulty. (Original publisher—Belaieff).

EDVARD GRIEG (1843-1907)

Some of Grieg's most characteristic work is to be found in the series of volumes entitled Lyric Pieces. These short compositions have a strong national flavor and are influenced by the folk music of Norway. They are, almost without exception, technically simple and quite elementary in structure, with some similarity to Schumann's smaller pieces. The works on a larger scale are less completely successful. All the compositions below are published by Peters and by Schirmer.

Lyric Pieces, Book I, Op. 12

Arietta	A cantabile melody accompanied by arpeggios divided between the hands.
Waltz	Simple staccato passages, single notes and chords.
Watchman's Song	The main section states an unpretentious theme in two-bar rhythm, in legato parallel octaves and in chords; the middle contrasting passage is an elementary exercise in rhythmic accuracy.
Fairy Dance	Easy staccato chords and rotation passages.
Folk-tune	A mazurka-like cantabile.
Norwegian Melody	A vigorous rhythmic theme in a pedal bass.
Album-leaf	Naive right-hand melody, with alternating cantabile for left.
National Song	Rhythmic chord passages.

Lyric Pieces, Book III, Op. 43

Butterfly	Graceful figuration for the right hand, lying easily.
Solitary Traveler	Easy legato lyric passages.
Native Country	Another piece requiring smooth legato.
Little Bird	The short trills and tremolos offer good rhythmic training.
Erotikon	Expressive legato with a sentimental appeal.
To Spring	Has an emotional climax of an obvious kind, useful in early stages of musical development.

Two pieces from the remaining sets deserve mention:

Canon, Op. 38, No. 8	A useful contrapuntal study.
Nocturne, Op. 54, No. 4	Simple and effective; gives practice in playing rhythms of two against three in the same hand.
Sonata in E Minor, Op. 7	More exacting than the short pieces; but it is an early and not quite representative work.
Ballade, - Op. 24	This, in form of variations, begins well, but does not quite maintain its interest. It is technically more ambitious than most of Grieg's compositions for piano solo.
Holberg Suite, Op. 40	An effective transcription, by the composer, of a suite for orchestra in old style—of moderate difficulty; the <u>Prelude</u> is rather more exacting than the remaining movements.

GABRIEL GROVLEZ (1879-)

A Child's Garden | Six easy and imaginative pieces, by no means commonplace.
(J. & W. Chester).

L'Almanach des Images | A set of eight pieces, with accompanying poems—fairly easy.
(Augener).

Improvisations on London | These are more advanced technically, and are interesting.
(Augener).

CORNELIUS GURLITT (1820-1901)

Buds and Blossoms, Op. 107 | Simple elementary material, in the same category as the little pieces of Gade.
(Schirmer).

The New Gurlitt (2 vols.) | A recent republication—of similar usefulness to the above.
(Schott).

JOHANN WILHELM HÄSSLER (1747-1822)

German composer who functioned for many years in Moscow. After turning from the harpsichord to the then modern piano he wrote many "characteristic" pieces that may be considered forerunners of the small lyrical pieces of Schumann.

Twenty-Four Studies in Waltz Form | Through all the keys. Excellent pieces (middle grades) exploiting classic pianistic figurations in musically satisfying, unexpectedly charming miniatures. Should be widely used.
(Schott).

Der Tonkreis | Selected pieces in all the keys. Easier than the above, arranged in order of progressive difficulty.

Various sonata movements have been reprinted in collections of pre-classic masters.
(Schott, Carl Fischer, etc.).

Also see Farrenc, Vols. 9 and 16, and Nagel's Musik-Archiv for other sonatas, fantasias and "solos."

Gigue in D Minor | Hässler's most important keyboard piece (from the Sonatas, Op. 31) stemming from the gigue in Bach's B-flat Partita, containing interesting problems for advanced players.
In Early German Piano Music (Moszkowski), Oliver Ditson.

Fantasie in C Minor | Large-scale free fantasy. Declamatory sections, passage playing, contrapuntal textures, transparent.
In Alte Klavier Musik, Bk. III, Peters.

JOSEF HAYDN (1732-1809)

It is easy to underestimate the importance of Haydn both in the general course of musical history and as a composer for the piano. A close acquaintance reveals one of the outstandingly original masters of his art; and even though his greatness in other fields is more apparent, the qualities of his pianoforte sonatas and other shorter pieces are similar to those which distinguish the string quartets and symphonies. Among those qualities we may note particularly his freedom and absence of "squareness" in rhythmic structure, and of course his humor and inventive daring.

<u>Editions of the Sonatas</u>

Many of Haydn's compositions are still unprinted. However, the twenty sonatas in the Cotta edition (reprinted by Schirmer) give a representative selection. These are also reprinted by Kalmus in the same order, with fourteen more in a second volume. The most comprehensive edition available at the time of writing is that of Peters, with forty-three sonatas in four volumes. The interpolation, at the end of Volume I, as No. 11, of an insignificant sonata in G causes the next volume to differ in its numbering from the editions of Schirmer and Kalmus (the latter's No. 12, e.g., appearing in Peters as No. 13). All the most widely circulated editions give the sonatas in a succession that has no relation to the date of their composition—Peters rectifies this to some extent by giving at the end of Volume I a thematic index in chronological order. The Haydn Society is issuing an edition which is expected to include in due course all the pianoforte works.

<u>Editions of Variations and Miscellaneous Pieces</u>

A convenient volume containing the important pieces of this kind is published by Kalmus. Similar material has been issued by the Universal Edition, Augener and in the Ditson volume of selected pieces.

Material for the pianist of moderate advancement can be found in the following four sonatas—the numbering is that of Schirmer and Kalmus.

Sonata in C Major, No. 5	Simple staccato and rotation passages in the first movement; legato scales in the <u>Adagio</u>; dotted rhythms of minuet-like character in the finale.
Sonata in F Major, No. 20	The first movement has a good deal of variety in its material, including broken-chord passages divided between the two hands and rotation passages of a familiar and simple type; the central movement is an <u>Adagio</u> in simple binary Bach-like form; the lively finale gives good practice in the treatment of two-note slurs in hand touch.
Sonata in D Major, No. 7	Hand staccato and rotation passages predominate in the first movement of this popular sonata; the short <u>Largo</u> is a test of rhythmic steadiness; the finale resembles in its requirements the finale of No. 20.

Sonata in E Minor, No. 2	Again hand staccato technique, with some double-note legato passages, in the opening movement; the <u>Adagio</u>, somewhat florid in character, ends on the dominant, leading directly to an extremely simple finale, with almost constant Alberti-bass left-hand accompaniment.
La Roxelane (air varié) Arietta con variazoni, in A Major Arietta con variazioni, in E-flat Major Tema con variazioni, in C Major	In the same general category as the four sonatas mentioned above are these four sets of variations (all included in the Kalmus volume of miscellaneous compositions).

More exacting, and representative of Haydn's mature powers, are the four sonatas now listed:

Sonata in F Major, No. 13	This has an imaginatively humorous first movement; a florid <u>Adagio</u>—also in sonata form; and a final <u>Tempo di Menuetto</u> with ، some interesting variations of the principal subject at its recurrence.
Sonata in E-flat Major, No. 3	Here the first movement is on a large scale, and full of character; the <u>Adagio</u> is similarly spacious, with great depth of feeling; the finale is again in Haydn's favorite <u>Tempo di Menuetto</u>— this time rather simpler than in No. 13.
Sonata in C Major, No. 42 (Peters)	A little-known sonata, most original and humorous in its first and last movements. The <u>Adagio</u> appears separately in the Kalmus volume of miscellaneous pieces, with some slight differences of detail.
Sonata in E-flat Major, No. 1	This, the latest of Haydn's sonatas, appears in most editions, for some unexplained reason, as No. 1. The first movement is full of original features, with some startling modulations and unusual largeness of conception; the slow movement is in the surprising key of E major, with much refinement and expressive detail; in the finale there is a characteristic display of high spirits and instrumental brilliance.

The mature pianoforte compositions include also:

Variations in F Minor	One of the greatest and also most familiar of Haydn's pieces. A double theme—alternately in major and minor—has two variations; the recapitulation of the opening section is interrupted by a striking coda. A notable feature is the irregularity and freedom of the bar-grouping.

Fantasia in C Major	Actually a rondo, though it is founded mainly on developments of one theme. The whole composition has a boisterous, sometimes explosive, humor, with immense vitality and effectiveness.
Capriccio in G Major	A lengthy, pleasantly discursive piece in moderate tempo; there is much interest in its rhythmic structure and modulatory features.
	(The above three are in the Kalmus volume and are also published singly by Schirmer and others.)

It should be said that, even when a sonata of Haydn as a whole may not be of the highest quality, a single movement can often be found that can be performed separately. Examples of this that may be suggested are:

Sonata in E-flat Major, No. 12	Finale
Sonata in A-flat Major, No. 8	Adagio
Sonata in B Minor, No. 39 (Peters)	Finale

and the number can be multiplied indefinitely.

STEPHEN HELLER (1813-1888)

The gentle sentiment of many of Heller's pieces has largely lost its appeal. Others are still useful for the not-too-advanced student.

The Art of Phrasing, Op. 16	A series of rather simple studies containing a variety of material. (Schirmer).
Studies, Op. 45, 46 and 47	Also useful in early stages. (Schirmer).
Tarantelle in A-flat Major, Op. 85, No. 2	Superficial musically, but it lies well and produces an easy effect. (Schirmer).
Etude, Op. 138, No. 6 "Curious Story," Op. 138, No. 9	Both of these have some pedagogic value. (Schirmer).

ADOLF HENSELT (1814-1889)

Henselt may be fairly represented by one of his sets of études—they have special technical features (notably, their wide extensions) which give them a value of their own.

Twelve Etudes, Op. 2

No. 1	A study in broken chords, with extension of the hand beyond the octave.
No. 2	Broken chords with wide extensions, the broken octave being played with second and fifth fingers.

No. 3	Right-hand cantabile supported by broken chords divided between the hands.
No. 4	Legato-cantabile study, the melody at first in the left hand, then accompanied by counterpoint in the right.
No. 5	A valuable rotation study for both hands, requiring flexible lateral adjustments from the wrist.
No. 6	The popular "Si oiseau j'étais," featuring delicate passages, mainly in pairs of legato sixths and fifths, in alternating hands.
No. 7	An octave study, requiring comparatively little endurance because of its easy rhythmic figure.
No. 8	Presents a taxing problem in coordination—legato melody in one hand against staccato double notes in the other—two notes against three.
No. 9	A melody is played in either hand with the fifth finger while the thumb and second finger double it with repeated notes at an octave's distance—a useful study for lateral flexibility.
No. 10	Cantabile melody, in left and right hand alternately, is accompanied by brilliant finger passages recalling Chopin's Etude, Op. 10, No. 4.
No. 11	Legato octave cantilena for right hand with extended arpeggios for left.
No. 12	An octave melody for right hand, in a cross-rhythm, is combined with double notes for the inner fingers - a useful strengthening exercise.

JOHAN NEPOMUK HUMMEL (1778-1837)

Rondo in E-flat Major, Op. 11	A piece with an old-fashioned grace that can still please. (Schirmer).
Variations on a Gavotte by Gluck, Op. 57	These are innocently entertaining, and have much technical variety with only moderate difficulty. In the coda is a modulation that might have come from Beethoven. In Le trésor des pianistes, Schott, Breitkopf and Härtel.

VINCENT d'INDY (1851-1931)

French Folk Dances	These are quite easy. (Oxford University Press).

Twenty-four pieces (for children of all ages), Op. 74 (in the style of various composers)	The three books of these contain interesting material. (Rouart).
Contes de fées, Op. 86 (Fairy Tales)	(Rouart).
Cortège chevaleresque d'un prince charmant	An imposing march.
La fée Aurore	This has a melodiousness that is not obvious, and has some problems of balance.
Les petits marchands de sable	Melody in consecutive fifths—delicate and imaginative.
Apparition	Requires good rotation technique—not easy to interpret.
Ronde des villageoises	A straightforward and tuneful dance movement.
Sonata in E Major, Op. 63	An ambitious work, of great structural power, somewhat austere and very difficult, but repaying study. It owes something to Franck. After some introductory passages, the first movement consists of a fine set of variations. There follows a brilliant scherzo-like movement with a contrasting central section; the finale makes use of the theme of the first movement's variations in its complicated development. (Durand).
Fantasia on an old French air, Op. 99	This has an introduction, six whimsical variations, and finale. It is less complicated than much of d'Indy's work; the difficulties are moderate. There are humorous touches that are exceptional in his compositions, and that invite more frequent performance. (Heugel).

ADOLF JENSEN (1837-1879)

The Mill, Op. 17, No. 3 Will-o'-the-Wisp, Op. 17, No. 11 Elfin Dance, Op. 33, No. 5 Barcarolle in A-flat Major, Op. 33, No. 16	These represent fairly Jensen's numerous piano pieces, which have charm and pedagogical usefulness that place them in a class with those of Heller.

ANATOL LIADOFF (1855-1914)

Liadoff's very large output of pianoforte music ranges from a light salon type to extended and serious works. A wide selection can be found in the republications of the Leeds Music Corporation. The pieces mentioned belo represent two extremes.

La tabatière à musique (Musical Snuff-box)	This entertaining little piece, imitating in the upper octaves of the piano the tinkling of a musical box, is quite easy. (Schirmer).

Variations on a theme of Glinka, Op. 35	A weighty and musicianly set of twelve variations, requiring advanced technique. (Leeds).

SERGEI LIAPOUNOFF (1859-1924)

Études d'exécution transcendante, Op. 11 (Zimmermann)
(dedicated to the memory of Liszt)

Berceuse	Flowing cantabile right-hand melody (somewhat complicated figuration in the same hand at recapitulation) with left-hand arpeggio accompaniment.
Ronde des fantômes	A brilliant étude requiring speed, delicacy and power.
Carillon	Has bell effects, and owes something to Liszt's "Harmonies du soir." Demands big tone and powerful octaves.
Térek	Calls for strong rotation technique in both hands. The demands have something in common with those of Liszt's tenth Etude d'exécution transcendante.
Nuit d'été	A severe test of the power to maintain a legato melody with simultaneous figuration in the same hand.
Tempête	This, like No. 4, is strongly influenced by Liszt's tenth étude, with exacting rotation passages, all very effectively written.
Idylle	A placid pastoral, calling for a smooth double-note legato like that in the opening of Chopin's "Berceuse."
Chant épique	A virtuoso study, based on two persistent rhythmic motives which are developed with gradually increasing brilliance and much glittering octave technique.
Harpes éoliennes	This exploits tremolando passages like those in Liszt's "Chasse-neige."
Lesghinka	This owes frankly a great deal to Balakireff's "Islamey," but is more grateful and immensely effective. (Reprinted by E. B. Marks).
Ronde des sylphes	Here the debt is to Liszt's "Feux follets"—similar delicacy is required.
Elégie en memoire de F. Liszt	Two themes, one in the spirit of the opening of L.'s rhapsodies and the other of a barcarolle-like character, are developed with exaggerated Lisztian virtuoso devices and immense sonority.

FRANZ LISZT (1811-1886)

No pianist who desires to develop a complete equipment can ignore the compositions of Liszt. In two directions—musical and technical—they make special demands. On the musical side they exhibit declamatory—one might say, histrionic—qualities that call for a corresponding approach from the executant. The sentiment is sometimes superficial and the rhetoric, at its worst, becomes exaggerated and even vulgar; but when that has been admitted we have to realize that both sentiment and rhetoric give an opportunity for the development of freedom of expression and the discarding of hampering inhibitions that has undeniable value. At the same time Liszt asks for extremes of sonority and brilliance which tax all the player's muscular resources to the limit, and which have their own peculiar glitter. While he does not in originality of treatment surpass the achievements of Chopin, he does carry further the full exploitation of the piano's tonal range.

Editions

Schirmer prints the main groups of Liszt's compositions in editions by Joseffy, Gallico, etc., that are generally satisfying. The Peters edition (Sauer) and that of Breitkopf and Härtel (Busoni) are equally good. Dannreuther's excellent editions of the Concert Etudes, Paganini Etudes and Etudes d'exécution transcendante are published by Augener.

Easier pieces

Very little of Liszt's large output can be classed as easy. The following may be attempted by players of moderate advancement:

Consolations (Six pieces)
Ave Maria (from Harmonies Poétiques et Religieuses)
Valse oubliée in F-sharp Major
Au lac de Wallenstadt, and Eclogue (from Book I of Années de Pèlérinage)
Canzonetta del Salvator Rosa (from Book II of Annees de Pèlérinage)
Liebesträume, Nos. 2 and 3

Consolations

No. 1, in E Major (Andante con moto)	Twenty-five measures of easy legato and chord passages, intended as introduction to No. 2.
No. 2, in E Major (Un poco più mosso)	A more extended piece than the first, but with similar melodic features; the distribution of the melody, divided at times between right and left hand, presents a useful technical problem for beginners.
No. 3, in D-flat Major (Lento placido)	Like the simpler nocturnes of Chopin—a sustained right-hand cantilena, with broken-chord accompanying figures in the left.
No. 4, in D-flat Major (Quasi adagio)	States a slow, sustained theme with supporting chords, continuing later in dialogue between middle and low octaves of the piano.
No. 5, in E Major (Andantino)	Continuous cantilena with flowing accompaniment and no variation of texture.
No. 6, in E Major (Allegretto sempre cantabile)	A good, simple étude for weight touch and pedaling.

Liebesträume
(Dreams of love)

No. 1, in A-flat Major
(Andantino, espressivo
assai)

No. 2, in E Major
(Quasi lento, abbandon-
andosi)

No. 3, in A-flat Major
(Poco allegro, con
affetto)

These three pieces all have a similar sentiment, indicated by the romantic title. The
first has an incidental difficulty in a couple
of accompanied trills for right hand. The
second is the simplest. Both it and the
popular No. 3 have imposing central rhetorical climaxes, not difficult but requiring some
power.

Valse oubliée, in F-sharp
Major

A charming and delicate piece, with slight
technical demands.

Valse-Impromptu, in
A-flat Major

A light salon piece of the effective type later
made familiar by Moszkowski.

Harmonies poétiques et religieuses

From this series may be selected:

No. 2 - Ave Maria

Simple cantabile and chords; the words of the
Latin hymn were printed above the melody,
suggesting an actual vocal setting.

No. 7 - Funerailles

An impressive piece of the sombre character
indicated by the title. Good left-hand octaves
are needed for one of its fierce climaxes;
otherwise it is not of more than average difficulty. A fine vehicle for a player with
temperament.

Légendes

St. Francis preaching
to the birds

Has extended passages, combining a melody
with trills in the same hand, requiring delicate
finger technique.

St. Francis walking on
the waves

Here the left hand's broken octaves need a
certain endurance. The subsequent climax
employs tricks, perhaps a little cheap, that
make the piece a useful technical study.

Ballade in B Minor

A piece on a large scale that can be made effective with the necessary rhetorical and imaginative treatment. It exhibits a wide variety of
technical devices—broken and interlocking
octaves, chords sustained by the pedal while
the accompaniment travels widely over the
keyboard, etc.

Polonaise in E Major

This is less popular than formerly. The early
sections have no formidable difficulty, but the
charming variation of the main subject toward
the end, with its delicate figuration in the upper
register, requires skillful finger work.

Mephisto Waltz	One of the most technically exacting and most brilliantly effective of Liszt's compositions. It demands great power and immense rhythmic drive. A wide range of technical resources is called upon—strong fingers, untiring broken octaves, powerful chord playing, accurate skips—with, in the sentimental middle episode, fine singing quality and flexible rubato.

Années de Pèlerinage

Of the three series entitled <u>Années de Pèlerinage</u> (Pilgrim Years), the third is negligible, the first has more material calling for consideration, and the second is continuously interesting.

Book I (Suisse)

No. 2 - Au lac de Wallenstadt (At the lake of Wallenstadt)	Has a simple melody for right hand (afterward presented in an ingenious rhythmical variation) over an unconventional persistent accompanying figure.
No. 4 - Au bord d'une source (At the spring)	A charming and rather difficult piece, with original pianoforte effect, a feature of which is a clever distribution of the melodic line between right hand and crossing left hand.
No. 7 - Eglogue	Unpretentious and effective, without technical hazards for a hand of average span.

Book II (Italie)

No. 1 - Sposalizio (Marriage)	The title is derived from Raphael's painting of the betrothal of the Virgin Mary. In this, one of Liszt's finest pieces, a good left-hand octave technique is necessary for the central fortissimo climax.
No. 2 - Il Penseroso (The Thinker)	A solemn marchlike piece, quite simple technically, having, structurally and harmonically, features in common with some of Chopin's preludes.
No. 3 - Canzonetta del Salvator Rosa	A lively march, inspired by the gay verses printed along with the tune. Rhythmic vitality is the main requisite.
No. 4 - Sonetto 47 del Petrarca	Easy, except for a Chopin-like cadenza in double notes. A great part of the melodic material is presented in continuous syncopation.
No. 5 - Sonetto 104 del Petrarca	A declamatory composition, rather taxing technically, with highly-charged emotional quality, paralleling the agitated words of the poem.
No. 6 - Sonetto 123 del Petrarca	Of only moderate difficulty, lyrically charming and imaginative.
	(The Schirmer edition prints, with translations, the three poems illustrated in the Sonnets.)

No. 7 - Après une lecture de Dante (After reading Dante)	This is an ambitious piece of program music, entitled "Fantasia quasi Sonata." It develops three leading themes in free rhapsodical style, presenting them in wide dynamic variety and pianoforte texture. A striking technical feature is the almost entire absence of "finger passages." Powerful octaves and repeated chords abound, requiring well-developed arms and wrists; another main requisite is a good rotational technique.

Supplement à l'Italie—Venezia e Napoli

Gondoliera	Has a naive tune in thirds, ultimately accompanied by a trill in the same hand, and then transferred to the left hand, with right-hand figuration. Requires some dexterity.
Canzone	A short "Lento doloroso"—an exaggeratedly rhetorical cantilena with tremolando accompaniment—leading to the Tarantella.
Tarantella	A brilliant show piece, involving repeated-note finger technique; full cantabile for the central "canzona napolitana," with good double notes for the characteristic ornamentation; and free arm condition for the final virtuoso chord passages.

Hungarian Rhapsodies

Formerly, these provided the conventional concluding piece for the average recital, but they are less played now. However, the glitter of their technical brilliance can still dazzle, and no one need despise the possession of the uninhibited temperament that is essential for their most effective presentation.

Hungarian Rhapsody No. 2	This familiar and effective composition has become rather faded, and its constant reliance on alternating tonic and dominant harmony becomes tiresome. For a pianist with good wrists and forearm rotation it is not excessively hard.
Hungarian Rhapsody No. 6	The opening declamatory sections are more interesting musically than the brilliant conclusion. The octave passages of the latter, for both right and left hand, require endurance.
Hungarian Rhapsody No. 8	Has a fine opening section; the subsequent Allegretto is comparatively easy, and the final Presto is not really difficult for a normal hand.
Hungarian Rhapsody No. 11	Shorter than its companions, and musically interesting. Its finger passages ask for both delicacy and brilliance, and the closing Prestissimo gives opportunity for a powerful effect without too much difficulty.

Hungarian Rhapsody No. 12	This lengthy and popular piece needs good hand technique for some passages in two-note double-third slurs, and free rotational adjustments for its brilliant passage work in the closing section - and of course plenty of power for the final peroration.
Hungarian Rhapsody No. 13	Perhaps the most musically valuable of the Rhapsodies. It has a fine emotional quality in the opening <u>Andante sostenuto</u>, and interesting rhythmic structure in the concluding <u>Vivace</u>, where the rapid passages of repeated notes contribute a striking technical feature.

Two Etudes

Waldesrauschen (Forest murmurs)	This graceful piece (with its companion, two of Liszt's most successful shorter compositions) has for its main theme a suave cantilena accompanied by rotational figuration; in the later development the right and left hand proceed in double counterpoint, leading to an effective climax.
Gnomenreigen (Dance of the gnomes)	Delicate hand staccato is the salient feature of the opening section; the alternative theme is a searching test of finger technique and rotational freedom. The climax requires a good deal of power.

Three Concert Etudes

No. 1, in A-flat Major	Rather repetitious; its effective pianoforte writing and pleasing tonal quality do not compensate for the weakness of its sentiment. It has some value as a not-too-difficult exercise in the treatment of cantilena with varied accompaniment.
No. 2, in F Minor	Deservedly popular; an opening section, stating a Chopinesque theme in graceful arabesques, is repeated in varied guises, making great use of rising and falling chromatic scale passages. The central climax, with its chromatic thirds, is somewhat taxing; but in general, delicacy rather than power is required.
No. 3, in D-flat Major	Ascending and descending arpeggios accompany a melody disposed in alternating notes for right and left hand—the maintenance of evenness, while the left crosses over and back, presents the main technical problem.

Six Paganini Etudes

No. 1, in G Minor	An exacting exercise in the playing of a melody with accompaniment of a rapid tremolo in the same hand.

No. 2, in E-flat Major

An ear-tickling piece, the main technical hazards of which are contained in one or two passages of chromatic sixths for alternating hands, and others where Liszt has written chromatic scales in tenths for crossed hands (these have been simplified in Busoni's edition); a tonal climax exploits Liszt's favorite alternating "false octaves" with glittering effect.

No. 3, in G-sharp Minor
(La Campanella)

The most famous of the series, with dazzling technical display, mainly in the upper half of the keyboard. Here again Busoni has simplified, and sometimes enhanced the effect of, some passages - notably the difficult repeated notes in the second statement of the modulation to B major.

No. 4, in E Major

An entertaining reproduction of a violinist's arpeggio staccato study, with the passages conveniently disposed for alternating hands.

No. 5, in E Major
(La Chasse)

On the whole the easiest of the set, with attractive flute and horn effects in the main theme. It should be compared with Schumann's version in his Opus 3. The glissandos in the A-minor section can be divided between the hands.

No. 6, in A Minor

The most musically valuable of the six, a set of variations on a theme also used by Brahms and Rachmaninoff—Liszt holding his own well in that company. For a mature pianist the difficulties are not excessive.

Douze Études d'exécution transcendante

No. 1, in C Major
(Preludio)

A kind of opening flourish, as introduction to the set of studies. It has some Cramer-like sequences.

No. 2, in A Minor

Apart from one passage requiring expert finger technique in double notes, this calls principally for rapid and accurate chord playing. Its material is rather severe and unattractive.

No. 3, in F Major
(Paysage)
(Landscape)

A lyrical piece requiring sensitiveness in its cantabile and in the balancing and gradation of tone.

No. 4, in D Minor
(Mazeppa)

This is suggested by the famous cossack's ride; it needs great endurance and power. Except in the opening cadenza, the technical equip. ment called for is mainly that of wrist and arm.

No. 5, in B-flat Major
(Feux follets)
(Will o' the wisp)

In this delicate study, one of Liszt's best, the greatest difficulty is contained in the double-note passages of the first forty measures, which offer a formidable test. The remainder, while not easy, is considerably less exacting.

No. 6, in G Major
(Vision)

Another étude making large tonal demands in its powerful chords embedded in sweeping arpeggios; double-note tremolandos, crescendo, add to the climactic effect.

No. 7, in E-flat Major
(Eroica)

Again a wide range of tone, from piano to a powerful fortissimo in the octaves, for both hands, of the climax. The material is bombastic and somewhat undistinguished.

No. 8, in C Minor
(Wilde Jagd)
(Wild Chase)

One of the most taxing chord études in the literature of the piano, the maintenance of a tiring rhythm, with great power, requiring exceptional endurance.

No. 9, in A-flat Major
(Ricordanza)
(Remembrance)

This has a slightly cloying sentiment, but a richness of tonal effect that comes from an exact appreciation of the special qualities of the piano's different registers.

No. 10, in F Minor

This fine composition may take its place, for musical quality, with No. 5. One of its main difficulties consists in the even control of the persistent broken-chord figures in the left hand. A free arm technique is another requirement.

No. 11, in D-flat Major
(Harmonies du soir)
(Evening harmonies)

Not difficult for a player with a good hand and accurate weight control. The climax requires some power.

No. 12, in B-flat Minor
(Chasse-neige)
(Snow plough)

An étude with the same technical requirements— melody and tremolando accompaniment in the same hand—as the first Paganini étude, and calling for even more physical endurance.

Sonata in B Minor

Liszt's crowning achievement as a composer for the piano—a landmark in musical history. When the time of its production is remembered (1853-1854) it appears more than ever an extraordinary achievement, combining as it does with so much success the elements of a complete sonata in a single continuous design. This work has not only influenced much subsequent creative activity, but still holds its position as one of the most severe interpretative tests. On the technical side its demands are heavy—brilliant finger technique, glittering octaves at a high speed, accurate staccato in the central fugato, warm singing tone in its cantilena, and full power in chord playing.

Transcriptions from the Organ

Liszt's transcriptions from Bach's organ works deserve mention and some selection.

Six organ preludes and fugues were formerly published by Peters. Of these, that in A minor is also issued by Schirmer. The well known Fantasia and Fugue in G minor is published by the same firm.

Prelude and Fugue in A Minor	An effective piece on the piano—in the Fugue, special attention should be given to the various countersubjects, and their function in maintaining interest and building the climax. Wide range of tone and good octaves are demanded.
Fantasia and Fugue in G Minor	The Fantasia is one of Bach's greatest and most dramatic utterances—in a class with the Chromatic Fantasia for clavier. Liszt has not always presented Bach's text faithfully, and comparison should be made with a reliable organ version. With the exhilarating and brilliant Fugue, it challenges the piano to vie with the organ's sonority.

Transcriptions from the literature of the voice

From a long list of song transcriptions the following may be chosen:

Chopin:

The Maiden's Wish, Op. 74 No. 1	The melody is presented with effective variations; good finger technique is required. (Schirmer).
My Joys, Op. 74, No. 5	Expressive cantabile, and two characteristically Lisztian cadenzas. (Schirmer).

Schubert:

Hark, hark, the lark	The soft repeated chords in the accompaniment need good control, and Liszt's additional elaboration asks for digital dexterity. (Schirmer).
Erlking	The rapid and powerful repeated octaves and chords require strong wrists, though in this respect the transcription is perhaps less taxing than the original accompaniment. (Schirmer).

Schumann:

Widmung (Dedication)	Demands emotional warmth and singing tone, with careful balance of the tonal strands of the texture. (Schirmer).
Frühlingsnacht (Spring Night)	Rapid and delicate chord repetitions are the main technical problem. (Schirmer).

Schubert Waltzes:

Soirées de Vienne

Arrangements and elaborations of Schubert waltzes.
(Schirmer).

No. 6 in A Major

A rhythmic opening subject leads to two expressive waltz themes, the second of which is treated with effective florid variations requiring neat finger work.

EDWARD MacDOWELL (1861-1908)

First Modern Suite

In this early work there is an imposing Prelude largely consisting of left-hand cantabile with right-hand accompanying figuration; a Presto which is a good staccato étude; and a pleasant but not specially distinctive Andantino and Allegretto. The remaining two movements have less character.
(Breitkopf and Härtel).

Six Poems (after Heine), Op. 31

No. 2, Scotch Poem, has most appeal.
(Schirmer).

Four Little Poems, Op. 32

No. 1, The Eagle, and No. 4, Winter, have imagination and present no serious technical problems. Nos. 2 and 3 are less interesting.
(Breitkopf and Härtel).

Twelve Etudes, Op. 39

These serve various technical purposes, and have decided value for the student of moderate advancement, especially Nos. 1, 2, 3, 5, 6 and 7, which are quite simple. No. 8, Shadow Dance, is slightly more exacting; No. 11, Scherzino, is a useful double note study for the right hand; No. 12, Hungarian, might help to encourage a bravura quality.
(Schmidt).

Twelve Virtuoso Etudes, Op. 46

More advanced technically than Opus 39. Best are those requiring lightness and speed (No. 2—Moto Perpetuo; No. 3—Wild Chase; No. 5—Elfin Dance; No. 10—March Wind. The Polonaise, No. 12, may be used for developing bigness of style without making too great technical demands.
(Breitkopf and Härtel).

Ten Woodland Sketches, Op. 51

No. 1, To a Wild Rose, is the simplest of MacDowell's pieces, and one of the most characteristic. No. 6, To a Water Lily, is also easy. No. 2, Will o' the Wisp, and No. 7, From Uncle Remus, are not really difficult.
(Schmidt).

Eight Sea Pieces, Op. 55	One may select No. 1, <u>To the Sea</u>, No. 2, <u>From a Wandering Iceberg</u>, and No. 5, <u>Song</u>, as having most character. (Elkin)
Six Fireside Tales, Op. 61	The best is <u>Brer Rabbit</u>, with its humor and vigorous rhythm. <u>Salamander</u> is interesting, but the others have less distinction. (Schmidt).
Ten New England Idylls, Op. 62	These have imagination, though the actual thematic material is not always striking or individual.
Eight Marionettes	These are short and simple. (Schmidt).
Four Sonatas	Of these the best are the "Tragic" and "Keltic" sonatas. The other two, "Norse" and "Eroica," have less sustained interest.

GIUSEPPE MARTUCCI (1856-1909)

Martucci wrote numerous effective pianoforte pieces showing influences as diverse as Scarlatti and Brahms. They often have charm without very strong individuality. The workmanship is always impeccable. From a volume published by Ricordi the following may be mentioned:

Giga in F Major, Op. 61, No. 3 Scherzo in E Major, Op, 53, No. 2	Lively pieces of Scarlatti-like character.
Romanza in F Major, Op. 49, No. 3 Notturno in F-sharp Minor, Op. 70, No. 2	Here the resemblance is rather to Brahms.

NICHOLAS MEDTNER (1879-1951)

Medtner has written, in a somewhat conservative idiom, numerous short pieces with the title "Conte" (Fairy Tale), displaying a finished technique and decided individuality. Among the best are the following:

Op. 14, No. 1, in F Minor (Ophelia's Song)	A plaintive little piece, with individual character—not difficult.
Op. 14, No. 2, in E Minor (The Ride of the Knights)	This displays Medtner's contrapuntal gift to great advantage; it is an immensely effective piece, demanding a good mental grasp, and rather taxing—well written for the instrument.
Op. 20, No. 1, in B-flat Minor	Has a central emotional climax, with heavy chords reminding one of Rachmaninoff.
Op. 20, No. 2, in B Minor	A little austere—characterized by a reiterated five-note figure in the left hand which is cumulatively impressive.

| Op. 26, No. 3, in F Minor | A charming lyrical piece—comparatively easy, with subtle harmonic treatment. |
| Op. 34, No. 2, in E Minor | Also very effective—lyrical right-hand melody against running bass. |

All the above are listed by J. & W. Chester, as agents for the Edition Russe de Musique. All except Opus 20, No. 2 are also reprinted by E. B. Marks, New York.

Medtner's larger compositions, including several sonatas, are as a rule more involved and abstruse, and do not make the immediate appeal of his shorter works.

ÉTIENNE HENRI MÉHUL (1763-1817)

| Sonata in A Major, Op. 1, No. 3 | Flowing Allegro, lyric Minuet with Trio, bright, concluding Rondo. In Alte Meister, Vol. I (Pauer). |

FELIX MENDELSSOHN-BARTHOLDY (1809-1847)

The qualities that account for Mendelssohn's great popularity in the middle of the nineteenth century still justify his being assigned an honored and important place in the history of his art. They are—mastery of form, invariable effectiveness due to a thorough knowledge of the technique of any instrument for which he writes, and a great deal of melodic charm and harmonic ingenuity together with imagination of a peculiar fancifulness. His weaknesses—frequent commonplaceness in his material, a facile and exaggerated sentiment, and the trick of repetition of phrases, so that he at times appears to be saying everything twice—were for a while allowed to loom too large and obscure his real greatness.

Editions

A number of publishers who formerly issued complete editions of Mendelssohn's pianoforte works have apparently not yet (1951) recovered from war shortages, so that much that was available is now out of print and only accessible in libraries. It is particularly regrettable that the excellent five-volume editions of Schirmer, Peters and Breitkopf and Härtel are now discontinued.

Editions of Easier pieces

While Mendelssohn's pianoforte writing invariably lies well for the hand, the amount of elementary material is not very great. The following may be suggested, as having no severe exactions:

Six Children's Pieces, Op. 72 (discussed below)
Songs without Words, Nos. 6, 9, 12 and 28 (sustained cantabile)
Songs without Words, Nos. 45 and 47 (useful staccato studies)

| Capriccio in F-sharp Minor, Op. 5 | This long piece, composed at the age of sixteen, contains a wide variety of technical material, well divided between the two hands— passages involving finger technique, forearm rotation and hand staccato—and there is sufficient interest to recommend it as an exacting test for the advanced player. |

Characteristic Pieces, Op. 7

No. 3, in D Major—Kräftig und feurig (With power and fire)	Starting with a Bach-like fugal exposition, this continues with persistent vitality in a texture that exercises both fingers and wrists— a lively and effective piece.
No. 5, in A Major—Ernst, und mit steigender Lebhaftigkeit (Seriously, and with increasing animation)	A lengthy fugue, featuring smooth legato; there is a considerable display of contrapuntal device—augmentation, diminution, inversion, etc.
No. 7, in E Major—Leicht und luftig (Light and airy)	A delicate scherzo—sempre pianissimo—with Mendelssohn's characteristic hand staccato the constant technical feature. An original touch is the surprising minor ending.
Andante and Rondo Capriccioso, Op. 14	The familiarity of this should not cause us to underestimate it. The introductory Andante and the lively Presto with its wide technical variety are both in Mendelssohn's best style.

Three Fantasies or Caprices, Op. 16

No. 2 - Scherzo in E Minor	One of Mendelssohn's most effective pieces— an excellent staccato study as well.
Andante cantabile and Presto agitato (without opus number)	This deserves occasional revival. The Andante starting with a reminiscence of the Andante of Opus 14, has suave melodic charm, and the Presto, in spite of some mannerisms, has real vitality and effectiveness—its passage work, too, has decided technical value.
Fantasia in F-sharp Minor, Op. 28	This fine composition is little played. The first of its three movements, in two alternating tempi—con moto and andante—has a dramatic central climax leading to the fortissimo return of the main theme, and the coda ends with a pedal effect like that of the recitative in Beethoven's Sonata in D minor. The second movement is a placid Allegro con moto, with some interesting features in its phrase structure; and the concluding Presto is brilliant and fiery, making varied technical demands (rapid finger work, broken thirds, fourths and sixths, staccato octaves and chords).
Prelude and Fugue in E Minor, Op. 35, No. 1	Deservedly the best known of the six in this series. The simple Prelude, with its melody laid out in the instrument's most effective register, has great warmth of feeling. The Fugue, starting with a subject and development that are reminiscent of Bach's in D-sharp minor from Book 2 of the Well-tempered Clavier, takes an original turn with an acceler-

ando leading, through an inversion of the subject and the substitution of staccato for the initial legato, to a climax with mounting excitement, culminating in the statement (full chords in the right hand against a steadily moving bass) of a condensed version of the chorale "Ein' feste Burg."

Prelude in B Minor, Op. 35, No. 3

None of the other fugues approaches the first in sustained interest; but the Prelude of No. 3 in B minor is one more of Mendelssohn's staccato studies—mainly single notes for each hand—and it might be played separately.

Variations Sérieuses, Op. 54 in D Minor

By far the most important of Mendelssohn's sets of variations, and worthy of a place near the great sets of Beethoven and Brahms. These display a high degree of imagination in their material; and while they do not surpass in technical usefulness the thirty-two in C minor of Beethoven, they do foreshadow certain later developments—e.g., in Variation 12, where the pairs of repeated chords for alternating hands hint at the achievements of Liszt.

Andante con variazioni, Op. 82 in E-flat Major

This, the better of two smaller sets published posthumously, deserves mention; the gently expressive and poetic coda is a notable feature.

Three Etudes, Op. 104

No. 1, in B-flat Minor

Presents the problem of achieving a continuous cantabile in a melody divided between the two hands, the right hand meanwhile accompanying above with an arpeggio figure.

No. 2, in F Major

An attractive finger study.

No. 3, in A Minor

This uses ingeniously the two thumbs in alternation to help in the formation of a figure of accompaniment to a melody which appears in the second eighth note of each quarter of a 4/4 measure.

Scherzo, in B Minor (without opus number)

A useful and quite easy staccato étude.

Scherzo a capriccio, in F-sharp Minor (without opus number)

An important and elaborately developed composition in an approximation to sonata form; it makes demands upon the player's ability to produce a delicate staccato in either single notes or chords, with powerful octaves at the other end of the dynamic scale.

Children's Pieces, Op. 72

No. 1, in G Major
Allegro non troppo

Simple chords, staccato and tenuto.

No. 2, in E-flat Major
Andante sostenuto

Legato melody for right hand, with easy
accompanying figure for the left.

No. 3, in G Major
Allegretto

Technically like No. 1.

No. 4, in D Major
Andante con moto

Lyrical in character, with melody carried
generally in the upper notes of chords.

No. 5, in G Minor
Allegro assai

Rhythmical staccato chords and single
notes.

No. 6 in F Major
Vivace

An interesting staccato study; it has rhythmic
vitality and some contrapuntal features.

Songs without Words

In addition to the six Songs without Words already recommended among
Mendelssohn's simpler pieces the following, embodying somewhat more
advanced material, may be selected from the total of forty-eight.

Nos. 1, 18, 22, 25 and 17 (requiring control of smooth legato).
Nos. 14, 17 and 20 (which have a more passionate sentiment).
Nos. 23 and 27 (chord passages in march rhythm).
Nos. 30 and 36 (a lighter and more graceful lyricism).
No. 3 (Hunting Song), which has rather more than average technical
demands.
No. 34 (Spinning Song), a really difficult piece, requiring accurate rota-
tional control.
No. 10, a masterly composition—good wrists are needed for the repeated
notes of the accompaniment.

MORITZ MOSZKOWSKI (1854-1925)

Moszkowski wrote many effective pieces of a superior salon type, from
which the following may be selected.

Scherzino in F Major,
Op. 18, No. 2
Melodie Italienne, Op. 38
No. 4

These are useful staccato studies.
(Schirmer)

Melody in G-flat Major,
Op. 10, No. 1

Not difficult, with a pleasing climax.
(Schirmer)

Étincelles, Op. 36, No. 6
(Sparks)

Combines light staccato and brilliant finger
passages.
(Schirmer)

La Jongleuse, Op. 52, No. 4
(The Juggler)

Quite perfect within its limits; a staccato
study that is a clever counterpart, in sound,
of the juggler's dexterity, with every note
making the utmost effect.
(Boston Music Co.)

Valse in A-flat Major	Well written and easily effective. (Schirmer).
Valse in E Major	Also very effective, with more complicated technique. (Schirmer).
Tarantelle in G-flat Major, Op. 27, No. 2	Another brilliant show-piece. (Schirmer).
Étude de Concert in G-flat Major, Op. 24, No. 1	A fine and difficult left-hand study, making demands similar to those of Chopin's Étude, Op. 10, No. 12. (Schirmer).
Caprice espagnol, Op. 37	A brilliantly effective virtuoso piece. (Schirmer).

WOLFGANG AMADEUS MOZART (1756-1791)

While the greatest examples of Moazrt's genius as a composer for the piano are to be found in the concertos, the list of works for pianoforte alone nevertheless contains so many with his characteristic charm and apparent effortlessness that the survey of them has to be almost complete.

Editions of the Sonatas

The Breitkopf and Härtel Urtext, reprinted in America by Kalmus, contains seventeen sonatas, and is useful for its identification of the individual sonatas through the numbering in the Köchel catalogue, as well as for the absence of editorial interference.

The Peters edition contains eighteen sonatas (omitting K. 498 and 570), with editing that commands respect.

The current Schirmer edition of Richard Epstein is also a careful production, perhaps rather fussy and overdetailed in its markings. Kalmus has issued the most complete collection of the Mozart sonatas—twenty in number—with pedaling and dynamic indications by Bela Bartók. The editing seems to be partly by that distinguished musician and partly an inheritance from the German edition which he used in his teaching.

The English firm of Augener prints a good edition containing the same number as Bartók's, edited by Franklin Taylor. Nineteen sonatas in these two are identical; Bartók's prints one (K. 498) which is partly spurious, and Taylor's gives a doubtful one in C minor which is disowned by Köchel.

Breitkopf and Härtel, the Universal Edition and Durand also issue the Mozart sonatas; the scholarship is generally competent.

Twenty Sonatas

Sonata in C Major, K. 279	A little-known and not very significant sonata. The first movement is rather conventional in its passage work; the Andante is gently expressive; the finale is rather more enterprising than the first movement.
Sonata in F Major, K. 280	This sonata has a moving little Adagio and a spirited finale; the technical difficulties are not great.

Sonata in B-flat Major, K. 281	The most characteristic movement of this rarely played work is the final <u>Rondo</u>; it is not one of the most interesting of the series.
Sonata in E-flat Major, K. 282	This work has an unusual plan: a first movement in slow tempo; two alternating minuets; and a final <u>Allegro</u>. The first and third movements are in a terse sonata form; the material is not very striking.
Sonata in G Major, K. 283	An unpretentious but very charming sonata, with attractive material in all three movements. The simple, but most expressive, <u>Andante</u> is particularly delightful.
Sonata in D Major, K. 284	Here Mozart works on a larger scale. The first movement is vigorous and imposing; the slow movement is a graceful <u>Rondo</u>; and the variations which end the work show unusual inventiveness of treatment—it is easy to make a claim for them as Mozart's finest set of solo variations.
Sonata in C Major, K. 309	A fine work, with the spaciousness of design that now characterizes the sonatas. There is an impressive first movement; an expressive <u>Andante,</u> with interesting elaboration of the material on its recurrence; and a large-scaled <u>Rondo</u>.
Sonata in A Minor, K. 310	Another outstanding composition. The first movement has a touch of sternness in its dotted rhythms; the fine slow movement (in full sonata form) is most satisfactorily succeeded by a wistful <u>Presto</u> of uniform texture from beginning to end, making the whole movement out of a minimum amount of material.
Sonata in D Major, K. 311	In this sonata the only movement equaling in largness of design the two preceding works is the <u>Rondo,</u> which can stand comparison with any similar structure in the sonatas of Mozart. The first movement has a special interest for its unconventional treatment of the classical sonata form—the opening subject is by-passed at the recapitulation (which starts with the original thirteenth bar) and it has its only recurrence toward the end of the movement. The <u>Andante</u>, compared with the middle movements of the two preceding sonatas, is of extreme and charming simplicity.
Sonata in C Major, K. 330	A delightful work, with both first and last movements in sonata form, each with a development of a simply episodic character.

The first movement has a tiny coda (an unusual feature), using a phrase from the opening of the development section. A similar process may be noted in the concluding four bars of the <u>Andante</u>, which develop most effectively, in the major, the opening phrase of the central minor section of the movement.

Sonata in A Major, K. 331

The popularity of this is easily accounted for. It opens with a set of variations, on a most attractive theme, which are of the simplest construction and very easy to follow. And after a charming minuet, there is for finale a brilliant and vivacious "Turkish March." The whole scheme is a delight to the ear and is extremely grateful to the performer.

Sonata in F Major, K. 332

Another popular and effective sonata, with a notably brilliant finale. The slow movement has a very simple structure (sonata form minus the development), but is elaborately ornamented.

Sonata in B-flat Major, K. 333

This worthily completes a group of four sonatas in Mozart's mature style. Special attention may be directed to the large Rondo, which may be compared with the similarly spacious one in K. 311. The tiny cadenza in the latter, introducing an important recapitulation of the main theme, now becomes a full-sized "cadenza in tempo," occupying the position of the customary cadenza for the soloist in the classical concerto, a feature that is unique in the piano sonatas of Mozart.

Fantasia (K. 475), and Sonata (K. 457) in C Minor

Though this <u>Fantasia in C minor</u> and the sonata in the same key were written at different times and can be played separately, they were associated by the composer and have a spiritual affinity. Each of them has a kind of grandeur that is rarely met with in Mozart's compositions for solo piano. The astonishing freedom and range of tonality in the fantasia would alone make it noteworthy. The sonata is a worthy counterpart. It is hardly fanciful to notice in some of the passages of the first and last movements a kinship with the great concerto (K. 491) in the same key. The slow movement is perhaps the finest in the solo sonatas.

Sonata in C Major, K. 545

The familiar "easy" sonata, actually a very late work but serving as an ideal introduction to Mozart's style, the slow movement in particular having a theme that invites the player to develop his cantabile.

Sonata in B-flat Major, K. 570	This charming work is not much more difficult than K. 545. The design is more spacious, and there is some additional contrapuntal interest.
Sonata in D Major, K. 576	Technically the most difficult of the series, the close canons in the first movement presenting a real problem in control, and the final Allegretto also being by no means easy. There is a slow movement of exceptional charm. This, the latest of the sonatas, has an unusual amount of contrapuntal interest and seriousness of workmanship; the development section of the first movement is specially remarkable.
Sonata in F Major, K. 547	This, arranged by Mozart from a sonata for piano and violin, is not printed in the Urtext, but is issued by Schirmer, Peters, Durand, Augener and in the Bartók edition of Kalmus. The first of its two movements is perhaps less interesting in its material and treatment than most of its companions. The second is, almost note for note, transposed from the Rondo of K. 545.
Sonata in B-flat Major, K. 498	Printed by Schirmer, Augener and Kalmus (Bartók). Partly spurious, the Andante being a tabloid version (not by Mozart) of the slow movement of the Concerto in B-flat (K. 450), and the Rondo compiled from material in that and other concertos.
Sonata in F Major, K. 533 and 494	Assembled from an Allegro and Andante written in 1788, with a Rondo which dates from 1786, this sonata is one of Mozart's finest and (in the Allegro and Andante at least) weightiest. The first movement is on a big scale and extremely elaborate; the Andante has great nobility of feeling; and the added Allegretto, while lighter in texture, rounds off the scheme quite satisfactorily. (This sonata does not appear in the Kalmus reprint of the Urtext. The Rondo is printed by Kalmus in the separate volume of shorter pieces; and the whole sonata is in the Schirmer, Peters, Durand, Augener and Kalmus-Bartók editions).

Variations

Editions: Urtext (Kalmus) - 17 sets
          Patelson - 17 sets
          International Music Co. - 15 sets

Most of the separate sets of variations by Mozart for piano are of comparatively slight interest, and mainly concerned with repetition and embroidery of the melodic line of the theme so that the latter is easily recognizable. The original fifteen sets listed by Köchel are increased to seventeen by the inclusion of Mozart's arrangements of the variations in F from a sonata for piano and violin and the variations from the clarinet quintet in A.

Ah, vous dirais-je Salve tu, Domine	These two sets may be recommended as combining useful technical material of a not-too-advanced kind with simple musical attractiveness.
Unser dummer Pöbel meint	These variations, on the other hand (listed in the edition of the International Music Company merely as on "an air by Gluck"), are musically important and may be classed with the variations in the Sonata in D, K. 284. They have almost as much inventive ingenuity as the latter, and the finale has an exceptional humor and structural expansion.

Miscellaneous Pieces

Editions: Urtext (Kalmus)
          Peters, Schirmer, etc.

The small volume of Mozart's miscellaneous pieces has a musical value quite out of proportion to its size. The outstanding masterpieces are the Fantasia in C minor (K. 396), the Fantasia in D minor (K. 397), the Rondo in A minor (K. 511), the Adagio in B minor (K. 540) and the tiny but perfectly finished Gigue in G major (K. 574).

Fantasia in C Minor, K. 396	This is actually an adagio in regular sonata form, a piece of fine dignity that tests severely the player's rhythmic control and sense of continuity. From Köchel we learn that only the exposition—up to the double bar—was written by Mozart; his understudy was a very competent musical craftsman.
Fantasia in D Minor, K. 397	The Fantasia in D minor, comparatively simple technically but much less so interpretatively, exhibits the contrasts and alternations of mood that are associated with the title, starting with an introductory andante chord passage in arpeggio, followed by an expressive adagio, some interspersed cadenzas, and a final cheerful allegretto in the tonic major.
Rondo in A Minor, K. 511	Among Mozart's pianoforte compositions there is nothing more beautiful than the Rondo in A minor, nor any more finished example of his art. As usual, the apparent simplicity is deceptive, even from the purely technical point of view. For example, the achievement of a satisfactory legato in the first episode (starting at the thirty-first measure) is by no means easy.

Adagio in B Minor, K. 540	Another piece in sonata form, with a texture which strongly suggests the string quartet, and the deep emotional expressiveness which we find in the great slow movements of Mozart's full maturity.
Gigue in G Major, K. 574	This short gigue is a delicate staccato study, with a contrapuntal technique in its exposition that recalls similar examples by J. S. Bach, together with some characteristic Mozartean chromaticism.
Minuet in D Major, K. 355 Fantasia in C Major, K. 394 Rondo in D Major, K. 485 Overture in the style of Handel, K. 399 Andante (Rondo) in F Major, K. 616	The remaining pieces in this volume (published by Kalmus in a reprint of the Urtext, and also by Peters, etc.) include a charming <u>Minuet in D</u>; the <u>Fantasia in C</u>, consisting of an introductory Bach-like section followed by an elaborately worked out fugue; a so-called <u>Rondo in D</u>— really a movement in sonata form founded, after the manner of Haydn, on only one main subject; a less important "suite" consisting of an <u>Overture in the style of Handel</u>, in C, followed by an <u>Allemande</u> in C minor and a <u>Courante</u> in E-flat major; and a piece in rondo form, in F major, which exists in two versions —one, with a limited compass in the upper half of the keyboard, intended apparently for some kind of mechanical instrument, and another which makes use of the full range of Mozart's bass. The former, merely described as "Andante," appears in the Kalmus reprint; the latter is in the Peters volume, entitled "Rondo."
Rondo in F Major, K. 494	As has already been stated, Kalmus also in-cludes the <u>Rondo in F</u> which is used as the finale for the <u>Allegro</u> and <u>Andante</u>, K. 533.

Easier Pieces

Among publications that offer more elementary technical material by Mozart the following may be mentioned:

Peters - Volume of easiest original pieces
Augener - Twelve easy original pieces (Beringer)
Universal Edition - Twelve Waltzes
Schott - Six Viennese Sonatinas

MODEST MUSSORGSKY (1839-1881)

Gopak	A lively dance, with popular appeal. (Augener)
Pictures from an Ex- hibition	This series of pieces is Mussorgsky's most important contribution to the pianoforte literature. They display extraordinary

originality and vividness of imagination. Unfortunately, the pianoforte writing is sometimes
clumsy and unnecessarily awkward. The various editions should be compared, including the
revision by Harold Bauer published by Schirmer.
(Augener; Schott; International Music Co.
(edited by Philipp); Schirmer)

Augener and Schott each publish an additional volume of short pieces.

JEAN NICODÉ (1853-1919)

Tarantelle in G-sharp
Minor

Straightforward and uncomplicated. It lies
well and is an effective piece for a fairly advanced student.

IGNACE JAN PADEREWSKI (1860-1941)

Minuet in G Major,
  Op. 14, No. 1
Melodie in B Major,
  Op. 8, No. 3
Nocturne in B-flat Major,
  Op. 16, No. 4

Easy and attractive pieces of the salon type,
admirably suited to the instrument.
(Schirmer)

Legende in A-flat Major,
  Op. 16, No. 1

This also has a frank melodic appeal, and has
an imposing climax, with octaves in both
hands, that requires some power.
(Schirmer)

Caprice in G Major (after
  Scarlatti), Op. 14, No. 3

A good finger study for both hands.
(Oliver Ditson)

Cracovienne fantastique,
  Op. 14, No. 6

This is effective and attractive, with a rhythmic
main subject in thirds and one or two passages
that require agility.
(Oliver Ditson)

Thème varié in A Major

This set of six variations and finale have
achieved popularity that is warranted by their
musical and grateful quality and the skillful
pianoforte writing, with no excessive technical
hazards.
(Schirmer)

Variations and Fugue in
  A Minor, Op. 11

Have varied requirements, technically, and a
good deal of imagination. There is an amusing
glissando variation. The Fugue is rather lengthy
(and not particularly fugal).
(Bote & Bock)

Variations and Fugue in
  E-flat Minor, Op. 23

A very serious work based on a somewhat dry
theme. It has a great deal of imposing and
brilliant technical display. The Fugue is not
entirely successful in spite of high aims.
(Bote & Bock)

SELIM PALMGREN (1878-   )

May Night	An easy piece of a pleasant impressionist character. (Boston Music Co.)
Aria in C Minor Cradle Song in B-flat Major	These are pleasing and not difficult. (Boston Music Co.)
Legend, Op. 28, No. 3	Easy, except for a passage in legato sixths that might tax a small hand. (Boston Music Co.)
Humorous Dance, Op. 35, No. 4	Moderately difficult. (Hansen, Boston Music Co.).
The Dragon Fly	A good study in light broken octaves. (Boston Music Co.)
The Sea	Useful as a moderately easy left-hand study. (Boston Music Co.)
En Route	A good right hand finger study. (J. & W. Chester, E. B. Marks)

C. HUBERT H. PARRY (1848-1918)

Shulbrede Tunes	This is a series of ten charming and intimate pieces, by one of the leaders of the English Renaissance of the nineteenth century, suggested by the daughter and son-in-law of the composer and their children, who are individually pictured. The final movement (Father Playmate) is more weighty than the others; it is a skillfully constructed passacaglia. (Augener)
Hands across the Centuries	A suite on eighteenth-century lines; though the conventional names of the movements only serve as points of departure for structures that have individual character and (notably in the Quasi Sarabande) expressive dignity. (Augener)

ISIDORE PHILIPP (1863-   )

Feux Follets	A brilliant piece with few severe technical demands—very effective. (Schirmer)

SERGEI RACHMANINOFF (1873-1943)

The list of Rachmaninoff's pianoforte compositions starts with a number of light items which have the keyboard effectiveness to be expected of so eminent a virtuoso.

Prelude in C-sharp Minor, Op. 3, No. 2	It should be recognized that the popularity of this is based on genuine musical merit and originality. (Schirmer, etc.)

Elegie, Op. 3, No. 1
Serenade, Op. 3, No. 5   These lyric pieces have great charm.
Barcarolle, Op. 10, No. 3   (Schirmer)
Melodie, Op. 10, No. 4

Polichinelle, Op. 3, No. 4   Well written and brilliant.
Humoreske, Op. 10, No. 5   (Schirmer)

Ten Preludes, Op. 23

No. 1, in F-sharp Minor   This owes something to Chopin; it has a fine
                                emotional sweep.

No. 2, in B-flat Major   Brilliant and sonorous—difficult, especially
                                for a small hand.

No. 3, in D Minor   One of the best, full of rhythmic vitality and
                                contrapuntal interest.

No. 5, in G Minor   The most popular, requiring large range of
                                tone in its repeated chords.

No. 6, in E-flat Major   A little sweet; it has great melodic charm—
                                requires careful pedaling and skillful balancing
                                of tone.

No. 9, in E-flat Minor   A difficult double-note study.
                                (Schirmer)

Thirteen Preludes, Op. 32

No. 5, in G Major   This exploits most effectively the upper half
                                of the piano's compass. Requires delicacy.

No. 10, in B Minor   A composition of great nobility and grandeur—
                                perhaps the finest of all the preludes. Demands
                                power and fullness of tone.

No. 12, in G-sharp Minor   Has a texture somewhat similar to that of No. 5,
                                and similar ingratiating qualities.
                                (Schirmer).

Etudes Tableaux,   These make effective use of the resources of
   Op. 33 and Op. 39   the piano, but have less musical substance than
                                the preludes.
                                (International Music Co.)

Variations on a theme by   This long set is elaborate and ingenious; the
   Chopin, Op. 22   pianoforte writing is difficult though effective;
                                the variations are unlike those of many Russian
                                composers in not being tied to the melodic out-
                                line of the theme.
                                (International Music Co.)

Variations on a theme   These are less complicated than the earlier set,
   (La Folia) of Corelli,   though they still make considerable technical
   Op. 42   demands. Rachmaninoff's harmonic treatment
                                has become more sophisticated.
                                (Carl Fischer)

Sonata in D Minor, Op. 28	An imposing and serious work—taxing for the interpreter. (International Music Co.)
Sonata in B-flat Minor, Op. 36 (revised by the composer)	Also a complicated work, difficult for player and listener, but repaying study. (International Music Co.)

JOACHIM RAFF (1822-1882)

La Fileuse	Has a suave melody with accompanying rotation passages—not difficult. (Schirmer)
Rigaudon in D Major	A useful staccato study, with some exercise in octaves. (Theodore Presser)
Tarantelle in A Minor	From a sonatina in A minor, Op. 99, formerly published by Peters. Without being difficult, this has an effectiveness that will encourage pupils in early stages. (Carl Fischer)
Giga con Variazioni	This is at present hard to obtain; it is from a suite in D Minor, has a great deal of distinction, and makes greater technical demands. than the pieces above-mentioned. (Peters)

HENRI RAVINA (1818-1906)

Etudes harmonieuses, Op. 50	Twenty-five useful études, each confined to one technical problem. (Schirmer)

VLADIMIR REBIKOV (1866-1920)

Pictures for Children, Op. 37	Most of Rebikov's "teaching pieces" are easy, and these are further revised and facilitated by Gretchaninoff. (International Music Co.)

MAX REGER (1873-1916) Germany

Reger's enormous output for the piano is not well known in this country. The music covers a wide variety of genres built upon an imposing and sometimes majestic polyphony that operates within a curiously unstable, chromatic harmony evolved from Schumann and Brahms. The "characteristic" piano piece abounds. These are loosely assembled into sheaves (Aus meinen Tagebuch, Episoden, Traüme am Kamin, etc.). They include both lyric and dramatic essays, often modeled on specific pieces of Schumann, Brahms or Chopin. Most interesting are the humorous types "à la burlesca." They often constitute fascinating studies in skillful handling of the keyboard. The two large sets of variations (on themes of Bach and Telemann) are among the mammoth works of the piano literature demanding the highest degree of pianistic virtuosity and musical insight.

Reger's significance in the cultural heritage of German piano music lies in his intermediate position between Brahms and contemporary masters. The pianism is demanding. Thick textures, leaps, intricate polyphony, wide dynamic range, bravura playing, delicate balance of the parts; in short, all the problems of first-class keyboard control are here present. The style is often crowded with details, the more extended works herculean in concept. To mention that Reger deserves the attention of the serious student is the very least one can say of this musician, so greatly esteemed by his contemporaries.

Lose Blätter (1895)	Fourteen pieces in salon style partly à la Schumann. (Schott)
Aus der Jugendzeit, Op. 17 (1895)	Twenty children's pieces in three books in the tradition of the Schumann Kinderscenen.
Improvisationen (1895)	See especially Nos. 1, 2, 3 and 7. (Augener)
5 Humoresken, Op. 20 (1898)	Strongly rhythmic. See especially No. 2 (in magyar style) and No. 6 (vivace). (Universal Edition)
Six Pieces, Op. 24 (1898)	
Valse-Impromptu Menuet Rêverie fantastique Un moment musical Chant de la Nuit Rhapsodie	Strongly Chopinesque. No. 6 in Brahmsian style. (Forberg)
Aquarellen, Op. 25	Five little tone pictures. (Schott)
7 Fantasiestücke, Op. 26	See especially the Scherzo, Humoresque and Capriccio (on Reger's humorous side). (Forberg)
7 Characterstücke, Op. 32	Oriented toward Brahms. More stable harmonically than many of Reger's other pieces. In two books: I—Improvisation, Capriccio, Burlesque, Intermezzo; II—Intermezzo, Humoresque, Impromptu. (Universal Edition)
Bunte Blätter, Op. 36	Nine little pieces in two books. Good "house music." (Universal Edition)
Ten Pieces, Op. 44	For instructional purposes. (Universal Edition)
Six Intermezzi, Op. 45	Nos. 2, 4 and 6 virtuoso pieces. Nos. 3 and 5 tragic in mood. (Universal Edition)

Silhouetten, Op. 53	Seven pieces. Difficult. Reminiscences of Grieg and Chopin. See especially No. 6.
Variationen und Doppelfuge über ein Thema von Bach, Op. 81	Fourteen variations and fugue on a theme from Cantata No. 128, <u>Auf Christi Himmelfahrt allein</u>. Massive, noble work for mature musicians and accomplished pianists, calling for great stamina and concentration. Involved textures, difficult chord techniques, large skips, repeated chords, bravura passages, double notes. Long, taxing fugue, mountainous conclusion. (Bote & Bock)
Aus meinem Tagebuch, Op. 82 Vol. 1 - 12 pieces Vol. 2 - 10 pieces Vol. 3 - 6 pieces Vol. 4 - 7 pieces	Short piano pieces in the tradition of Schubert and Brahms. Generally homophonic with occasional contrapuntal essays. The demands are not superficial, involving a sensitive musicianship, a command of widely spaced sonorities and a versatile pianism. (Bote & Bock)
Four Sonatinas, Op. 89 No. 1 in E Minor No. 2 in D Major No. 3 in F Major No. 4 in A Minor	All in three movements except for No. 2 (four). Rather extended in length. Demand sensitivity and facility. No. 2 easiest. (Universal Edition)
Six Preludes and Fugues, Op. 99	Of the difficulty of the Bach "48." (Universal Edition)
Variationen und Fuge über ein Thema von Telemann, Op. 134 (1914)	From Telemann's "Hamburger Tafelkonfekt." Comparable in scope to the Bach variations but more diatonic and classic in structure. Demands virtuoso equipment. (Simrock)
Träume am Kamin, Op. 143 (1916)	Twelve pieces. Reger's last piano work. No. 8 recalls Chopin's <u>Étude</u>, Op. 10, No. 7. No. 12 is a study modelled after Chopin's <u>Berceuse</u>. (Simrock).
· Six Burlesken, Op. 58	Humorous studies on "Ach du lieber Augustin." (Simrock)
Four Special Studies for the Left Hand Alone	See especially No. 4, an impressive <u>Praeludium and Fugue</u>. (Universal Edition)

ALEXANDER REINAGLE (1756-1809)

An American musician of Scottish-German descent, active in Philadelphia for most of his life. His friendship with C.P.E. Bach influenced his style.

Sonata in E Major	Has a light, clear, fluent Allegro; a long, florid, improvisatory <u>Adagio</u>; and a gay, Haydnesque <u>Rondo</u>.

(This appears, shortened, in an album of Early American Piano Music published by J. Fischer & Bro.) Three other sonatas, in manuscript, are in the Library of Congress.

CARL REINECKE (1824-1910)

Sonatina No. 1 in C Major	One of six, providing easy material for the young student.
	Reinecke's numerous and valuable cadenzas to classical concertos should be noted. (Schirmer)

OTTORINO RESPIGHI (1879-1936)

Nocturne in G-flat Major	A pleasing salon piece. (Bongiovanni; Schirmer)
Study in A-flat Major	Asks for good double note technique, with interlocking hands. (Bongiovanni)
Three Preludes on Gregorian Melodies	These have a more complicated texture. (Universal Edition)

JOSEF RHEINBERGER (1839-1901)

The Chase, Op. 5, No. 1	A good exercise for staccato chords. (Schirmer)
Prelude and Toccata in G Minor	This might well be reprinted—it is musicianly and effective.

JEAN JULES ROGER-DUCASSE (1873-   )

Six Preludes	The first three are easy, the others more complicated. (Durand)
Four Etudes	More exacting than the above—a musicianly series. (Durand)

MORITZ ROSENTHAL (1862-1946)

Papillons	A pleasant, effective staccato study, with alternating hands. (Fürstner. Reprinted by E. B. Marks)

ANTON RUBINSTEIN (1830-1894)

Melody in F Major, Op. 3, No. 1 Romance in E-flat Major, Op. 44, No. 1	Easy pieces with characteristically suave melody. (Schirmer)

Barcarolle in F Minor, Op. 30, No. 1 Barcarolle in G Minor, Op. 50, No. 3	Of these, the less familiar piece in F.minor is perhaps the better. (Schirmer)
Six Études, Op. 23	These are for the virtuoso; the second is the famous staccato étude in C. (Schirmer)
Turkish March, from Beethoven's "Ruins of Athens"	This not-too-easy arrangement is a good test for rhythm and for control of gradual crescendo and diminuendo. (Schirmer)

FRIEDRICH WILHELM RUST (1739-1796)

The 12 Sonatas of Rust published by Rouart, Lerolle et Cie (edited by d'Indy) and available through Salabert are of interest for several reasons. This contemporary of Haydn, Mozart and Beethoven exhibits a varied pianism which, if it does not often sustain interest throughout an entire work, offers many moments of charm and beauty. The 11th Sonata in G ("....imitating the Timpanum, Psaltery and Luth") anticipates some contemporary twentieth century devices. Among others, Rust calls for harmonic tones to be produced by touching the string at a nodal point with the right hand while depressing the keys with the left. The sonatas are mostly in three movements of ample length, recalling the pianism of Clementi.

Sonata No. 12 in F-sharp Minor	Three movements (Allegro non troppo, Larghetto, Allegretto) based on a single germinal motive. In d'Indy's opinion superior to many of the Haydn and Mozart sonatas in originality and musical interest. Eminently worth playing.

CAMILLE SAINT-SAENS (1835-1921)

Valse Nonchalante, Op. 110	Easy and graceful, with neat workmanship; of the type of Liszt's "Valse oubliée." (Durand).
Six Études for the left hand, Op. 135	All of these are excellent and practical, with tuneful and not excessively difficult material. The Bourrée, No. 4, may be specially recommended. (Durand).
Six Études, Op. 52	These contain advanced technical material. No. 3, the Prelude and Fugue in F minor, should be noted; it has been edited separately by Philipp for Schirmer—the Prelude is a good wrist study. No. 6, Etude en forme de valse, is a brilliant show piece. (Durand).
Six Études, Op. 111	Another set with difficult material; the Toccata, No. 6, is again a virtuoso piece, the thematic

substance of which is derived from the last movement of the fifth piano concerto. (Durand)

Caprice on airs from Gluck's "Alcestis"

This brilliant composition, requiring mature technique, is the most popular of Saint-Saens's piano solos; the central theme and variation, in 3/8 time, is often played separately. (Fürstner; Schirmer)

PHILIP SCHARWENKA (1847-1917)

In a Gondola

This, requiring a good cantabile, is a fair example of this composer's not very distinctive style; it is not hard.

XAVER SCHARWENKA (1850-1924)

Polish Dance in E-flat Minor, Op. 3, No. 1

A popular piece with a lively rhythm. (Schirmer)

Staccato Etude in E-flat Major, Op. 27, No. 3

Well written and rather difficult. (Schirmer).

Separate numbers from the Album for Young Pianists are obtainable from Schirmer, and two books of Polish dances from Augener.

ERNEST SCHELLING (1876-1939)

Tempo di Valse (No. 3 of "Silhouettes")

An easy study in syncopated rhythm. (Carl Fischer)

Nocturne ("Ragusa")

This needs more maturity—it has imagination. (Carl Fischer)

FRANZ SCHUBERT (1797-1828)

If Schubert had not the structural power of the very greatest composers, he had a wealth of melodic invention and a natural harmonic sense that were unsurpassed. The essentially lyric quality of his genius that makes him so great a song writer is felt also in his pianoforte compositions, so that in his larger works—e.g., the sonatas—even when the first and last movements seem diffuse, the slow movements are invariably moving and full of charm, with magical modulations that are breathtaking.

Editions

The Sonatas, Impromptus, Moments musicaux, and Fantasias are published by Schirmer, Peters, Kalmus etc. The dances are published complete by Peters; Schirmer has a selection edited by Bauer. Peters also offers a volume of easy pieces edited by Alec Rowley.

Easier Pieces

A large number of short dances (waltzes, ländler, etc.) provide technically simple material, generally quite artless harmonically but always full of a childlike charm and sometimes (as in No. 8 of the Twelve Ländler, Opus 171) showing surprising subtlety. Other simple pieces are: the Scherzo in B-flat (Schirmer, etc.); Nos. 1, 2 and 6 of Moments Musicaux—

and the Impromptu in A-flat, Opus 142, No. 2.

Sonatas

The opus numbers attached to the ten sonatas usually listed do not indicate the order of their composition. The earliest were those in B major, Opus 147; A minor, Opus 164; and E-flat major, Opus 122, composed in 1817. Then came another in A minor, Opus 143 (1823); and two years later (1825) the three in A minor, Opus 42, D major, Opus 53, and A major, Opus 120. The three without opus number, in C minor, A and B-flat major, were written a few weeks before Schubert's death in 1828.

Sonata in B Major, Op. 147

Has a rather poorly organized first movement; the Andante has great beauty, and the Scherzo is also charming. The finale opens promisingly, but does not maintain its interest—the material is overworked.

Sonata in A Minor, Op. 164

The first movement is less capricious than that of Opus 147, but the material is not particularly distinctive. The Allegretto quasi Andantino which occupies the central position does not equal in interest the Andante of Opus 147; its main subject deserves notice for its near identity with that of the finale of the late sonata in A major. The third movement starts with an interesting whimsical idea, but is repetitious and rather trivial.

Sonata in E-flat Major, Op. 122

Has a larger and more successful first movement than either of the two preceding sonatas. The material is still not uniformly distinguished —e.g., the opening of the second subject. The Andante has some well-contrasted material, less appealing, however, than in Opus 147. The Minuet and Trio are simpler than the Scherzo and Trio of Opus 147, and have considerable charm. The finale is, like the first movement, more successful than in the other two early sonatas; again, it is somewhat repetitious.

Sonata in A Minor, Op. 143

This opens with an original and imaginative movement, distinctive and characteristic. The short slow movement is less striking, and the final Allegro vivace is somewhat garrulous—it has an octave passage at the end which is hardly practicable at the required speed and invites some modification.

Sonata in A Minor, Op. 42

A work on a large scale. The opening movement has a consistency and certainty that Schubert had not before attained in the piano sonatas; the coda is notably striking. A fine set of variations follows, with considerable variety of pianoforte effect. There is a delightful Scherzo, contrasted with a simple and beautiful Trio. The Rondo is apt to be monotonous if not skillfully handled; it makes a great deal of somewhat slight material.

Sonata in D Major, Op. 53

Another fine sonata; the first movement is a little more conventional in structure than the first of Opus 42. The slow movement is one of the finest in all the sonatas; it has remarkable rhythmic and harmonic interest added to the characteristic melodic beauty. There is a vigorous Scherzo, calling for accurate and powerful chord playing, with a quiet contrasting Trio. The naive rondo theme has two charming variations at its reappearances; like the Rondo of Op. 42, this requires skillfully varied and affectionate treatment.

Sonata in A Major, Op. 120

This, the easiest sonata to present, is a short work with little technical difficulty except in the third movement. The first is prevailingly lyrical in character except for an octave passage in the development, and lacks the dramatic contrasts that generally accompany sonata form. The Andante is simple, and ends with one of Schubert's happiest effects of minor-to-major transition. The finale, in sonata form, has more variety than the first movement and is more taxing.

The posthumous sonatas

Sonata in C Minor

Has a fine majestic opening movement, with exceptionally firm structural organization, which is maintained in the expressive Adagio. The Minuet and Trio are short and unpretentious, but the finale stretches out in repetitious treatment of its material, so that a cut invites consideration.

Sonata in A Major

The first movement starts imposingly and has some fine later ideas, but does not hold together so well as in the preceding sonata. The wistful quality of the main theme of the Andantino, contrasted with the wild outburst of its central section, is a notable feature. The Scherzo is more extended than the Minuet of the C-minor sonata, and has a capricious humor. The Rondo has actually only two distinct subjects, which are treated at considerable length; both are lyrical in character, and the first is almost exactly identical with the principal melody of the Allegretto in Opus 164.

Sonata in B-flat Major

By far the greatest of the Schubert sonatas, with a noble opening movement, where any attempt to lessen its diffuseness by cuts, or even more presumptuous liberties, is to be deprecated. A just tempo—with particular care to observe the "moderato"—and a constant search for the essential "melos" are the prime requisites. The Andante has, especially in the imaginative recapitulation of its first section, some of Schubert's most striking harmonic effects and a most moving emotional quality. The Scherzo has a Beethovenish character—note the progression which signalizes the return to the main subject, from the diminished triad on B to the tonic of B-flat. The influence of later Beethoven is again evident in the finale; its start, on the dominant of C minor, is an exact parallel with the start of the last movement of Beethoven's string quartet, Opus 130.

Fantasia in C Major, Op. 15

Here one has to overlook the structural weakness of the final Allegro (where Schubert, after a brave fugal exposition, is reduced to a vain beating of the air) for the sake of the sheer inspiration and dramatic power of the preceding three sections. The whole work is technically more spectacular than is usual with Schubert. Liszt's suggestions in his edition for the revision of the finale do something to improve the effect, and are perhaps worth trying.

Fantaisie, Andante, Menuetto and Allegretto, Op. 78

This long piece might really be included with the sonatas, its beautiful and very leisurely first movement, in spite of its lack of rhythmic contrast, having the characteristic key distribution of sonata form, and the remaining movements carrying out the usual scheme. The leisureliness which has been noted in the Fantaisie is also present in the Andante and final Allegretto, so that the whole composition is a searching test of the player's tonal resourcefulness and interpretative sympathy. The Menuetto, on the other hand, is immediately effective and might be played separately.

Four Impromptus, Op. 90

No. 1, in C Minor

An impressive piece, consisting of varied statements and development of a single theme, avoiding monotony and maintaining interest through changes in the figures of accompaniment, and skillful modulations. The repeated chords for the left hand may become a little tiring; otherwise there is no mechanical difficulty.

No. 2 in E-flat Major	Has brilliant, not very difficult, finger passages in its main section, calling for a wide tonal range, with a vigorous contrasting central part and coda.
No. 3, in G (G-flat) Major	Most frequently printed in G, though originally written and now often played in G-flat, this is, by reason of its melodic inspiration and harmonic magic, a supreme test of the player's power to sing on his instrument. Sensitive phrasing and nice balance of tone are prime requirements.
No. 4, in A-flat Major	A good rotation study for the right hand, with a passionately expressive lyric central episode.

Moments musicaux, Op. 94

No. 1, in C Major	Simple, and offering good practice in rhythmic control of triplets and even pairs of eighth notes, in succession and combination.
No. 2, in A-flat Major	A poetical piece of sustained lyric character; it requires an accurate time sense.
No. 3, in F Minor	Asks for delicate staccato and sensitive phrasing.
No. 4, in C-sharp Minor	Here the passage work, mostly in broken chords and broken thirds, needs careful fingering and a free rotational technique. Any exaggerated accent on the constant syncopations of the contrasting section has to be avoided if the rhythm is to be clear.
No. 5, in F Minor	Requires vigorous chord playing.
No. 6, in A-flat Major	An expressively lyric piece, in legato chords throughout.

Four Impromptus, Op. 142

No. 1, in F Minor	A fairly long piece, in sonata form minus the development section, having much interesting and varied material, and ending in a very brief, rather perfunctory coda. An arresting feature is the dialogue, played by the left hand crossing back and forth, the broken-chord accompaniment of the right, and constituting the latter part of the second subject group.
No. 2, in A-flat Major	Has a lyrical quality and texture resembling Opus 94, No. 6, but with a Trio which conceals its melodic line in triplet figuration.
No. 3, in B-flat Major	A popular piece consisting of a theme and five variations, with a great deal of technical variety; only moderately difficult, and very effective.

No. 4, in F Minor	Calls for delicate hand staccato and even scale playing. Three short passages in double thirds for the right hand are difficult at the required speed.

A volume of various pieces, mostly without opus number, has been issued by Kalmus. Among these may be mentioned three "Clavierstücke," of the apparent date 1828; also, of particular interest, the single variation which (as one of fifty contemporary composers) Schubert wrote on the waltz by Diabelli which inspired Beethoven's monumental set of thirty-three, Opus 120.

<u>Drei Clavierstücke</u>

No. 1, in E-flat Minor	A vigorous, somewhat humorous "allegro assai" alternates with the two andante sections which are expressive without having outstanding quality.
No. 2, in E-flat Major	An allegretto with less distinction than No. 1.
No. 3, in C Major	An allegro with lively syncopations is contrasted with a middle section in a persistent slow rhythm, interestingly harmonized.
Variation on a Waltz by Diabelli	Has Schubert's personal quality and harmonic resourcefulness.

ARTUR SCHULZ-EVLER (1854-1905)

Arabesques on Johann Strauss's "Blue Danube" Waltz	This single virtuoso piece entitles the composer to mention because of its dazzling effectiveness in sufficiently accomplished hands. (Schirmer).

ROBERT SCHUMANN (1810-1856)

Schumann's importance for the pianist almost approaches Chopin's. As a composer he is equally original, so that a comprehensive survey of his work is called for. Most of the compositions of his early life were pianoforte pieces, and almost from the start they have an astonishing romantic warmth and imagination, quite unlike anything that had appeared before. These qualities compensate for frequent formal defects in his larger works; he is at his best in short movements like those of the <u>Carnaval</u>, Opus 9, <u>Kinderszenen</u>, Opus 15, etc.

<u>Editions</u>

Mme. Schumann's edition of her husband's works is generally trustworthy. It has been subjected to revision by various hands, and one of these editions is reprinted in the U.S.A. by Kalmus. The Peters edition is also excellent. The edition of Vogrich issued by Schirmer takes some unwarrantable liberties with both text and original expression marks. Harold Bauer's editions, now published by Schirmer, contain some practical suggestions for redistribution of hands to facilitate performance, and also occasional alterations of the text, which should be compared with the original.

Easier Compositions

Album for the Young, Op. 68	
Bunte Blätter, Op. 99 (Colored Leaves)	All of these contain much charming material, suitable for beginners.
Three Sonatas for the Young, Op. 118	
Album Leaves, Op. 124	
Arabeske, Op. 18	A more extended piece, very poetical in character, and not much more difficult than those previously mentioned.
Blumenstück, Op. 19 (Flower Piece)	Also an extended piece, in several short sections, with material of uniform cantabile character throughout.

Kinderszenen, Op. 15, (Scenes of Childhood)

Only slightly more taxing than the above, and full of imaginative variety and charm.

Von fremden Ländern und Menschen (From foreign lands and people)	Cantabile melody, with accompaniment in middle voice, divided between right and left hand.
Curiose Geschichte (Curious story)	Rhythmic chord passages, with moderate span for the hand, encouraging free arm condition in their phrasing.
Hasche-Mann (Catch me)	Rapid finger staccato; a good study.
Bittendes Kind (Child at prayer)	Cantabile, with simultaneous accompanying notes in same hand.
Glückes genug (Perfect happiness)	Right-hand cantabile with imitations in the left; it needs careful phrasing.
Wichtige Begebenheit (Important event)	Heavy tenuto chord playing.
Träumerei (Dreaming)	Expressive legato; it asks for some flexibility in the phrasing.
Am Camin (By the fireside)	Flowing cantabile; some rearrangement of the original distribution is recommended for small hands.
Ritter vom Steckenpferd (Knight of the hobby-horse)	The syncopated rhythm provides good material for cultivation of a free arm condition.
Fast zu ernst (Almost too serious)	Requires a nice balance between the tone of the syncopated melody and the bass with its definition of the rhythm.
Fürchtenmachen (Frightening)	Imaginative treatment of the sharply contrasted phrases and careful attention to dynamic indica-

tions, including details like the accents at the end of measures 2 and 4 of the "Schneller," are required.

Der Dichter spricht (The poet speaks)	A test for rhythmic control, especially in the final ritardando.

Waldszenen, Op. 82 (Forest Scenes)

Technically on a par with Opus 15. Of the nine pieces, only No. 2 and No. 8 are of more than moderate difficulty.

Eintritt (Entrance)	Opening with a freedom in bar-rhythm $(2 - 1\frac{1}{2} - 2\frac{1}{2} - 1\frac{1}{2})$ that is unusual in Schumann, this presents some problems in tonal balance, e. g., in measures 9 - 13 and 12 - 22.
Jäger auf der Lauer (Hunter in ambush)	Technically quite difficult, especially in getting rhythmic accuracy from measure 10 onward.
Einsame Blumen (Solitary flowers)	A nice balance of two voices in the same hand (e.g., in bar 2) has to be carefully considered.
Verrufene Stelle (Haunted spot)	Exact treatment of the double dots and a well-controlled pianissimo are requisites in this eerie piece.
Freundliche Landschaft (Friendly landscape)	Requires good fingers and sensitiveness to details like the rubatos suggested in bars $12\frac{1}{2} - 13\frac{1}{2}$ and $20\frac{1}{2} - 21\frac{1}{2}$.
Herberge (At the Inn)	Needs, like No. 1, care for balance of tone.
Vogel als Prophet (The prophet bird)	Extreme delicacy is called for. The dot of the first note, as with Bach in similar cases, takes the value of a thirty-second—i.e., the following thirty-second notes are not a triplet. (Cf. the conclusion of the Humoreske, Opus 20, and No. 8 of Symphonic Etudes, Opus 13.)
Jagdlied (Hunting song)	A good wrist and arm study, with a test of rhythmic accuracy in the middle section.
Abschied (Farewell)	Balance of melody and accompaniment in the same hand, and control of rhythmical details (two against three) are the main technical problems.

Sonatas

Schumann's mastery of design is not equal to his inventive originality and warmth of feeling. In the piano sonatas there are structural weaknesses and redundancies that are nevertheless generally compensated for by the sheer inspiration of the musical ideas.

Sonata in F-sharp Minor, Op. 11

On the whole the greatest of the three sonatas. The first movement requires a powerful hand technique for its persistent staccato chords; the short slow movement (entitled <u>Aria</u>) is charged with romantic feeling; the main section of the energetic <u>Scherzo</u> alternates with two contrasting subjects, the second containing a striking passage of recitative. The finale suffers from a superabundance of material, so loosely organized that only a good deal of adroitness in the management of tempo can save the situation. Its excessive length makes a cut, sacrificing none of the material, desirable. The whole work demands considerable physical endurance.

Sonata in F Minor, Op. 14

In spite of the opus number, this is described, in addition to its first title—"Concerto without orchestra"—as the third sonata. It was subjected to much revision, some of it at a time when Schumann's powers were failing. Of the three sonatas this is decidedly the least satisfactory—the material is least inspired, and the whole piece (with the exception of some not too distinguished variations on a theme of Clara Wieck) is discursive and painfully repetitious.

Sonata in G Minor, Op. 22

The most concise of the sonatas. The first movement has fine rhythmic drive and spontaneity throughout (a good rotation technique is required); the <u>Andantino</u> has great lyrical beauty; the <u>Scherzo</u> is a short movement with lively persistent two-bar rhythms; in the final <u>Rondo</u> the broken-octave passages ask for some endurance. Both in the first and in the fourth movement care in the presentation is needed to prevent the continual "squareness" of the rhythmic structure from becoming tiresome.

Fantasia in C Major, Op. 17

Schumann's greatest composition on a large scale. Its three movements —the first a modification of sonata form, the second an exhilarating march, and the third a poetical <u>Adagio</u> —show him at the height of his inspiration. On the technical side there are severe demands on the player's range and variety of tone, and on his digital dexterity. The first movement needs exceptional interpretative sensitiveness together with a firm grasp and projection of its unusual design. The march calls for powerful chord playing, imaginative treatment of the central section, and a technique that can face the notorious hazards of the skips in the coda. The dreamy poetical opening of the third movement sets the general tone, with only two fortissimo climaxes by way of contrast.

Faschingsschwank aus Wien, Op. 26 (Carnival prank from Vienna)

A more loosely constructed piece, in five movements: A long opening movement consisting of a principal recurring idea which alternates with half a dozen contrasting ones, all in somewhat monotonous 3/4 rhythm; a brief Romanze, with wistful repetitions of a two-bar lyrical motive; a Scherzino which for much of its short career again harps on two-bar rhythm; an Intermezzo, full of warm feeling, the finest movement, which invites separate performance; and a finale in sonata form which presents somewhat greater difficulty than the moderate ones of the preceding movements.

Variations

Schumann's three separate sets of variations range from the early and not specially characteristic Opus 1 to the outstanding masterpiece, Opus 13. All ask for a well-developed technique.

Variations on the name "Abegg," Op. 1

These exploit a brilliant and effective Hummel-like type of technique, in four variations and an extended finale; the most representative of the real Schumann is Variation 2.

Impromptus on a theme of Clara Wieck, Op. 5

These variations exist in two versions, of which the second is decidedly superior. Nine variations containing much that is ingenious and imaginative lead to a final tenth which expands into a rather labored fugal section.

Symphonic Etudes, Op. 13

Subtitled "Etudes in form of variations," these have a less strict relation to their theme ("by an amateur") than do the classical sets of variations. They make severe demands, especially on a brilliant staccato chord technique, and are dazzlingly effective. Schumann's inventive genius and instrumental resource are nowhere more fully displayed.

Four sets of short pieces, so intimately connected as to make their performance in sequence desirable, are contained in Opus 2, Opus 4, Opus 6 and Opus 9.

Papillons, Op. 2

Six introductory bars are followed by twelve fanciful sketches of highly imaginative character. The finale introduces the Grossvaterlied, which is also quoted in the finale of Opus 9, and combines it contrapuntally with a recurrence of the first of the Papillons, in a descriptive "ball scene." Some of these little pieces are by no means easy.

Intermezzi, Op. 4	Six unfamiliar pieces, with original qualities that would justify more frequent performance. Most of them are of moderate difficulty, the most taxing being No. 2 (depicting Faust and Mephistopheles's journey through the air, with a plaintive "Meine Ruh' ist hin" from Gretchen in the middle).
Davidsbündlertänze, Op. 6	There are two slightly different versions of these eighteen pieces, the second representing Schumann's final decisions. In the freshness of their inspiration they anticipate the better known and more mature <u>Carnaval</u>, and they are similarly grateful and appealing. Four or five are of more than average difficulty—we may note the left hand skips of No. 3 and No. 9, the tricky left hand of No. 6 and the rapid chords of No. 13. It is possible to make more than one effective selection; e.g., the first six make a quite satisfactory group.
Carnaval, Op. 9	One of Schumann's most successful compositions, the simple rhythmic structure of the short pieces which occupy the greater part of the work being ideally suited to the material, and the whole displaying inexhaustible inventiveness and imagination. Most of the pieces are of about the same length as those of the Davidsbündler, but there is an extended introductory movement, and also a finale of similar proportions, both requiring mature technique and musicianship. The separate movements are provided with descriptive titles, referring not only to carnival characters such as Pierrot, Harlequin, etc., but also to Schumann himself and his friends. Of these only <u>Papillons,</u> <u>Reconnaissance</u> (with its rapid thumb repetitions), <u>Pantalon et Columbine</u> (finger staccato) and <u>Paganini</u> (left hand skips) present serious technical difficulties. The subtitle, "Scènes mignonnes sur quatre notes," is due to the fact that at the start of almost all of the movements the notes A, E-flat, C and B (German - A, Es, C and H) or alternatively A-flat, C, and B (As, C and H) appear. These are the "musical" letters of Schumann's name, Asch also being a town in Bohemia where one of his friends lived.

Three important groups of pieces, with more individual independence than those of the <u>Papillons,</u> <u>Davidsbündlertänze</u> or <u>Carnaval,</u> are contained in Opus 12, Opus 16 and Opus 21.

<u>Fantasiestücke</u>, Op. 12

Des Abends (In the Evening)	The phrasing of the melody, and the definition, through the fourth note of the left hand in each bar, of the cross-rhythm are of prime importance.

Aufschwung (Rapture)	Calls for rhythmic incisiveness, rotational freedom at the entry of the theme in D-flat, and a good cantabile at the modulation to B-flat.
Warum? (Why?)	Singing tone is the main requisite, with nice balance of the two-voice contrapuntal passages.
Grillen (Whims)	Requires a rhythmic drive like that of No. 2.
In der Nacht (In the Night)	Perhaps the finest of all Schumann's shorter pieces. It combines formal mastery and the highest emotional inspiration. Its technical difficulties are considerable, with the need for an independence of finger which can balance in the same hand simultaneous melodic lines, and for great power in the climax leading to the recapitulation of the opening.
Fabel (Fable)	A whimsical and imaginative little piece, with passages of delicate staccato and a vigorous central climax.
Traumes Wirren (Restless Dreams)	A difficult piece, calling for a good right-hand rotation technique and strong outer fingers.
Ende vom Lied (The Song's End)	Comparatively easy—simple chord passages, with hand and arm technique prevailing.

<u>Kreisleriana</u>, Op. 16

Aüsserst bewegt (Agitato assai)	Clear enunciation of the melody indicated by the two-note slurs, through a strong rotation technique, is essential. In the middle section the arm will take part more evidently, through the breaking of contact after every third note.
Sehr innig und nicht zu rasch (Molto espressivo e non troppo vivace)	(With two <u>Intermezzi</u>). The main sections of this piece ask for a good octave and double-note legato. The <u>Intermezzi</u> are in faster tempo; the first entering with a vigorous theme in slurred eighths accompanied by left-hand staccato sixteenths, and the second a smooth cantabile with arpeggio accompaniment in the same hand. The principal section needs careful pedaling.
Sehr aufgeregt (Molto agitato)	This consists mainly of persistent four-note figures, played with hand or arm touch, which drive to an energetic climax. The middle section presents a cantilena of a familiar type, the same hand also supplying part of the ac-companiment.
Sehr langsam (Molto lento)	An expressive adagio calling for warm tonal quality.

Sehr lebhaft
(Molto vivace)

The pianissimo of the opening subject, with its light staccato and two-note slurs, invites a delicate hand touch. The many repetitions of similar two- and four-bar rhythms in the contrasting sections are a test of the player's tonal and interpretative variety.

Sehr langsam
(Molto lento)

The requirements are similar to those of No. 4.

Sehr rasch
(Allegro assai)

This demands a strong finger technique.

Schnell und spielend
(Allegro scherzando)

For the delicate staccato of the opening the same approach as at the start of No. 5 is desirable. The first contrasting section adds a full-toned octave cantilena for the left hand; the powerful chord passages that occur later (marked, "Mit aller Kraft") require a free release of arm weight.

Novelletten, Op. 21

No. 1, in F Major

Detached full chords; flowing legato in alternating sections. Careful and flexible phrasing in the opening can avoid an impression of rhythmic "squareness."

No. 2, in D Major

This needs much practice to acquire the necessary endurance for the constant thumb repetitions; the piece is effective and grateful.

No. 3, in D Major

In its main section, a good staccato chord study.

No. 4, in D Major

In waltz rhythm, with some intriguing cross-rhythms and syncopations—lively and effective.

No. 5, in D Major

Has a liveliness similar to that of No. 4, but in polonaise rhythm; there is good technical practice for the wrists in the staccato chord passages.

No. 6, in A Major

Starting with staccato chords like No. 3, the piece moves lightheartedly through successive cantabile sections, the speed gradually increasing, until pulled up by a short coda, in the first tempo, based on preceding material.

No. 7, in E Major

Perhaps the most immediately appealing of the series, with its brilliant flying octaves and charming central cantilena.

No. 8, in F-sharp Minor

Characteristically discursive, but containing some of Schumann's most inspired music, and challenging the imaginative interpreter. This novellette is in two parts, one in 2/4 and the other in 3/4 time. They have a connecting link

in the striking episode entitled "Voice from
afar," a long-drawn melody appearing near
the end of the first half, and restated, fortissimo, in a powerful climax of the scherzo-like
second part.

The next four sets of pieces are less important as a whole but contain
much interesting material.

Nachtstücke, Op. 23

No. 1, in C Major

A marchlike subject in detached chords alternates with legato contrasting passages which
call for smooth phrasing. Not difficult.

No. 2, in F Major

Gives good practice in rapid, and not too difficult, chord playing. There is some of Schumann's favorite harping on similar repeated
rhythms, which has to be relieved by variations of tone.

No. 3, in D-flat Major

In the first measure the left hand states a
figure which is used to unify the whole composition (with the exception of a brief chord
passage near the end). A melody played by
the thumb of the right hand, which is occupied
at the same time with the aforementioned
unifying figure, offers a useful study in
phrasing.

No. 4, in F Major

The most popular of the set, with a familiar
melody stated generally at the top of detached
arpeggiated chords; there are some interesting problems in balance and control of tone.

Romanzen, Op. 28

No. 1, in B-flat Minor

A good étude, with a persistent figure, divided
between the hands, supporting a melody which
is a little dry.

No. 2, in F-sharp Major

This beautiful piece has always been popular
by reason of its charming melody—given out
first, in the piano's most effective register,
as a duet mainly between right and left
thumbs. Phrasing and pedaling are important concerns.

No. 3, in B Major

A piece with interesting ideas which are somewhat overworked, and too numerous.

Scherzo, Gigue, Romanze and Fughetta, Op. 32

Scherzo in B-flat Major

A piece somewhat reminiscent of the fifth of
the Kreisleriana, but shorter and simpler.

Gigue in G Minor

A useful hand-touch study, apart from its
musical and contrapuntal interest.

Romanze in D Minor	A short, effective composition with a subject in the main section stated in a uniform staccato supported by a brilliant accompaniment divided between right and left hand. In a contrasting middle section the same distribution continues in a uniform legato. The piece has value, as an étude, like Opus 28, No. 1, with more musical interest.
Fughette in G Minor	This so-called "fughette" has as subject a short four-bar phrase which is passed from right hand to left with accompanying chords and some simple development. It has unpretentious charm, and makes a useful and easy staccato étude.

Three Fantasiestücke, Op. 111

These short pieces were intended to be played in sequence; but this does not seem absolutely essential.

No. 1, in C Minor	This has a fine passionate sweep and displays much of Schumann's old power and inspiration; it is, technically, fairly taxing.
No. 2, in A-flat Major	Lyrically beautiful and technically simple.
No. 3, in C Minor	An energetic marchlike tune, with contrasting middle section and coda featuring graceful arabesques.
Toccata, Op. 7	This is in a class by itself. It presents difficult technical problems, and its double-note passages, etc., provide excellent material for the training of a student whose mechanical equipment has advanced to the necessary point.
Humoreske, Op. 20	A long, rather rambling piece in several sections that follow one another in a capricious manner that to some extent justifies the title. Some of the material has an affinity with light-hearted pieces like the third and sixth of the Novelletten; elsewhere, e.g., in the section with the general direction "Innig," there is a typically warm flow of sentiment. But on the whole this cannot be regarded as one of Schumann's most successful compositions.
Etudes on Caprices of Paganini, Op. 3 and Op. 10	Of these, Opus 3, No. 2, and Opus 10, No. 2 have also been set by Liszt. Schumann's versions are worth playing, even if they are without Liszt's virtuoso glitter. Opus 3, No. 3, a simple lyrical piece, might also be occasionally revived.
Six Studies for Pedal Piano, Op. 56	Four of these have been arranged by Madame Schumann and published by the English firm of

Novello. Those in A-flat major and B minor may be specially recommended for their skillful canonic treatment and melodic charm.

Four Sketches for Pedal Piano, Op. 58 — Less significant and interesting than Opus 56.

Four Fugues, Op. 76
Seven Pieces in the form of Fughettas, Op. 126 — In spite of a good deal of contrapuntal skill these become monotonous in effect through insistence on similar rhythms and types of movement.

Four Marches, Op. 76
Gesänge der Frühe, Op. 133 (Songs of the dawn) — These short pieces are rather dull and unrepresentative.

Allegro, Op. 8 — Influenced by Hummel; quite uncharacteristic.

EDOUARD SCHÜTT (1856-1933)

Étude Mignonne, Op. 16, No. 1 — This is a useful study, with the melody's accompanying figuration divided between the hands.
(Schirmer)

Rêverie, Op. 34, No. 5 — Also pedagogically useful. A good exercise in tonal balance (left hand crossing over right).
(Boston Music Co.)

Pizzicato-Valse, Op. 38, No. 1 — Has more distinction than most of Schütt's work.
(Schirmer)

LUDWIG SCHYTTE (1848-1909)

Scenes of Childhood — Separate numbers of these twelve comparatively easy pieces are available.
(Schmidt).

Etude in B Minor, Op. 15, No. 12 — A study in repeated notes.
(Schirmer)

GIOVANNI SGAMBATI (1843-1914)

Vecchio Minuetto — A graceful dance with popular appeal.
(Schott; Schirmer)

Gavotte in A-flat Minor — Also effective when played with the right rhythmic vitality.
(Schott; Presser)

Toccata in A-flat Major — A good finger study.
(Schott; Schirmer)

Melody (from Gluck's "Orpheus") — An effective transcription.
(Schirmer)

JAN SIBELIUS (1865-   )

Romance in D-flat Major — An effective piece, with a pleasing romanticism which does not quite represent its
composer.
(Boston Music Co., etc.)

Valse triste — Also popular but unrepresentative.
(Schirmer)

Sonatina in B-flat Minor, — This is more cryptic than the above-mentioned
Op. 67, No. 3 — popular pieces. Its three sections are founded
on rhythmical variations of one main short
motive.
(Breitkopf and Härtel)

CHRISTIAN SINDING (1856-1918)

Marche grotesque, — Popular, with an incisive rhythm that is en-
Op. 32, No. 1 — hanced by the alternating-hand technique.
(Peters; Schirmer)

Rustle of Spring, Op. 32, — Another popular composition that makes an
No. 3 — easy effect with its conveniently placed ar-
peggio figures.
(Peters; Schirmer)

EMIL SJÖGREN (1853-1918)

Erotikon, Op. 10 — Five pieces showing some individuality without
presenting any interpretative problems. All
are lyrical in feeling, with the exception of
No. 3, in A-flat, a lively piece with double-
note passages requiring agility and finger
independence.
(Boston Music Co.; No. 3 also Schirmer).

BEDŘICH SMETANA (1824-1884)

Three Polkas — Of moderate technical difficulty; they are
contained in an album of twelve pieces.
(Schirmer).

Polka poétique — Pleasing and moderately easy.
(Heugel, ed. Philipp)

Polka de Bohème — Exploits double-note staccato, and is more
difficult than its companion.
(Heugel, ed. Philipp)

Czech Dances — These are technically difficult; they have
strong national flavor.
(Urbanek a Synové)

By the Seashore — A fine virtuoso study.
(Schirmer)

CHARLES VILLIERS STANFORD (1852-1924)

Four Irish Dances

These are based on Irish folk melodies, were originally composed for orchestra, and are arranged for piano most effectively by Percy Grainger. No. 1, "March-Jig," requires some technical brilliance for its adequate performance; No. 2, "A Slow Dance," demands a strong rhythmic sense; No. 3, "The Leprechaun's Dance," has extreme delicacy; No. 4, "A Reel," tests, more than the others, the pianist's finger dexterity. All reveal the composer in his most ingratiating aspect.
(Stainer & Bell—J. Fischer)

SIGISMOND STOJOWSKI (1870-1946)

Chant d'amour, Op. 26, No. 3

The best known of a large number of musicianly and idiomatic compositions—its warm and genuinely felt lyricism has made it deservedly popular.
(Schirmer)

RICHARD STRAUSS (1864-1949)

Stimmungsbilder, Op. 9

Strauss's early romantic feeling is well exhibited here. These "Mood Pictures" have, perhaps, greater value than most of his few pianoforte compositions.
(Universal Edition)

No. 1, Along the silent forest path, and No. 4, Rêverie, have been reprinted also by Schirmer.

PETER ILICH TSCHAIKOWSKY (1840-1893)

Album for the Young, Op. 39

The twenty-four pieces in this collection are simple and admirably adapted to their purpose.
(Schirmer)

The Seasons, Op. 37

Somewhat more exacting technically than Opus 39. From the twelve pieces, each bearing the name of one of the months, the Barcarolle in G minor (June), which has some contrapuntal interest, and the pleasing En Troika (November) may be specially noted.
(Schirmer)

Songs without Words, in F Minor, Op. 2, No. 3
Romance in F Minor, Op. 5
Humoresque in G Major, Op. 10, No. 2
Chanson triste, in G Minor, Op. 40, No. 2

These four also present little or no technical difficulty, and are all likable.
(Schirmer)

Scherzo humoristique, Op. 19, No. 2 Nocturne in C-sharp Minor, Op. 19, No. 4	Two pieces which need rather more keyboard command. The Nocturne has, at the recapitulation, some characteristic counterpoint in the right hand against the melody in the left. (Schirmer)
Eighteen pieces, Op. 72	Of these late compositions of Tschaikowski, only No. 5, Meditation, is at present easily available. That, however, can be regarded as perhaps the most successful of the series, with marked poetical quality. (Schirmer)
Theme and Variations in F Major, Op. 19	This set of variations, in spite of a rather weak coda, is quite charming and might be played more often. (Augener; also Carl Fischer, edited by Siloti, who has altered the original here and there).
Sonata in G Major	The largest of Tschaikowsky's compositions for piano solo. It has not proved strong enough to survive. (Rahter)

CARL MARIA von WEBER (1786-1826)

Most of the representative pianoforte compositions of Weber are at least comparatively difficult, and they often require a large hand to do them justice. They are not often heard now, with the exception of one or two with virtuoso features, but the best of them have a romantic quality that can still exert its charm.

Editions

As with Mendelssohn, wartime shortages have interfered with the publication of complete editions, and Weber's piano compositions have temporarily disappeared from the catalogues of some important publishers. At the time of writing, the firm of Schirmer lists only two (C major and D minor) of the four sonatas; but they publish a volume containing the five principal shorter pieces (Opus 12, Opus 21, Opus 62, Opus 65 and Opus 72) with three others of less importance. The four sonatas (edited by Liszt) are published by Augener (American agents—Broude Bros.).

Four Sonatas

No. 1, in C Major, (Op. 24)	This has a cumulative effectiveness. A rather barren first movement, containing passages of considerable technical difficulty, is followed by a slow movement with a dramatic central section; the Minuet is full of vitality, and the final Rondo is the famous dazzling moto perpetuo—a show piece for anyone with good fingers.
No. 2, in A-flat Major, Op. 39	The finest of the sonatas. It has a noble opening movement, an Andante which gives a foretaste of Brahms's Opus 1, a brilliant

Minuet, and a rather naive Rondo which needs sympathetic playing to make it thoroughly acceptable.

The third and fourth sonatas are less interesting.

Momento capriccioso, Op. 12	An excellent and taxing staccato study, anticipating some of Mendelssohn's similar pieces.
Rondo brillante, Op. 62	This has an old-fashioned elegance, and varied technical material that is not without value.
Invitation to the Dance, Op. 65	Perhaps the best of Weber's shorter pieces, with a lively charm that has not yet faded, in spite of the unenterprising persistent alternations of tonic and dominant harmony. The difficulty is moderate.
Polacca brillante, Op. 72	Similar in quality to the Rondo, Op. 62, but with less technical variety.
Introduction and Polonaise in E-flat, Op. 21	Have little distinction.
Variations, Op. 7, Op. 40	The Schirmer volume of shorter pieces includes two of Weber's sets of variations, which are not very rewarding musically, but which contain a large variety of passages of considerable technical difficulty and might be substituted for some of the conventional material of the Czerny and Clementi études.

Part III
Piano Music of the Twentieth Century

Piano Music of the Twentieth Century

Although it cannot be maintained that the piano in this century plays a role equivalent to its position in the eighteenth and nineteenth centuries (when it often occupied a central position in the musical thinking of the foremost composers) still there are many major works bequeathed to the repertoire in our era that demand the attention of the serious student of keyboard music. And, it might be added, there are a host of minor works that make welcome additions to the main body of the literature (along with many others of completely problematic intent and quality).

The diversity of styles is the most apparent characteristic of our contemporary repertoire: the French Impressionism of Debussy along with his followers in countries outside France, the Neo-classicism of Hindemith with its expanded concepts of tonality and its emphasis on linear writing, the Nationalist tendencies of the Latin-Americans as manifested in composers such as Villa-Lobos, the complex pianism of the twelve-tone composers rooted in the completely new and characteristic keyboard style of Schönberg, the strong Primitivism of Bartók built on a solid core of folk music, the varied approaches of the Americans, at times leaning heavily on European models, at times emphasizing national traits or, like Ives, creating something quite individual and characteristic, the post-romanticism of a Rachmaninoff, the current change in style in the Soviet Union and so on ad infinitum. For the pianist the problems are manifold if he wishes to master the major styles of the period, and yet, with all the difficulties involved, no one can consider himself thoroughly acquainted with twentieth-century piano music without at least casual acquaintance with such diversified pieces as, let us say, the Ludus Tonalis of Hindemith, the Études and Preludes of Debussy, Gaspard de la Nuit and the Miroirs of Ravel, Trois Mouvements de Petrouchka by Stravinsky, Three Piano Pieces, Op. 11, of Schönberg, the Sonatas of Scriabin and Prokofieff, the Outdoors Suite and folksong settings of Bartók, to name but a few of the highlights.

The task of selection among such varied styles is hazardous, to say the very least. Every major figure in the modern repertoire is included here, with the minor figures perhaps weighted on the side of the younger composers. The main intent has been to present the well-established works of the modern repertoire and to fill in the most glaring gaps in the hypothetical reader's general knowledge. Consequently the composers in the United States and Latin-America receive much space, in the hope that the attention of students of the keyboard will be drawn to those creative figures who are working within our own hemisphere but who have been perhaps unjustly neglected and overlooked.

The dislocations effected by World War II have made necessary the inclusion of some European-born composers in the sections on American piano music. This has been done where many years of creative endeavor in the United States or Latin-America seem to warrant inclusion among composers born in these areas. Nevertheless the birth country of foreign-born composers is noted in the body of the material.

The reason for not listing European composers in national groupings is simply that an attempt to convey adequately a well-rounded account of national contributions to the piano repertoire is beyond the scope of this volume and, in view of the present international situation, frankly impossible.

Some short biographical statements on Latin-American composers, are included because, of all contemporary composers represented in this volume, they are least known to the American public.

Collections:

Con Tempo , E. B. Marks. An album compiled and edited by Erno Balogh. Twelve compositions by Albeniz, Bartók, Cowell, Debussy, Granados, Lopatnikoff, Mignone, Ravel, Shostakovitch, Szymanowski, Turina, Villa-Lobos. On the difficult side.

Fifty-one Pieces from the Modern Repertoire, G. Schirmer. Representing composers of thirteen nationalities. Includes Farwell's Sourwood Mountain; Griffes's White Peacock; Little Suite by Harris; Jeux d'Eau by Ravel; Étude in F-sharp Major by Stravinsky.

Masters of Our Day, Carl Fischer. Series of graded piano pieces for young players by such diverse contemporary composers as Jacobi, Milhaud, Paz, J. J. Castro, Cowell, Elwell, Sessions, Goossens, Pisk, Rathaus, Revueltas, Caturla, etc.

Meet Modern Music, Mercury Music. Two books of easy original compositions by contemporary composers. For less advanced players.

The New Piano Book, Associated Music. Three volumes of short pieces by Bartók, Copland, Gretchaninoff, Hindemith, Korngold, Toch, Stravinsky, etc. Excellent collections for students.

Composers in the Continent of Europe, in Great Britain, Israel and Russia

HAIM ALEXANDER (1915-) Israel

Alexander is a graduate of the Israeli Conservatory of Music and is at present teaching piano and composition at the New Jerusalem Conservatory and Academy. He is the winner of several important competitions.

Six Israeli Dances (1949-1950, revised 1951)	"....written in the spirit of various folk dances but not based on any folk material." Suite of six pieces, short, of moderate difficulty, cleanly and clearly written with characteristic Israeli rhythmic and melodic features. Could be played as a group. Strong, rhythmic ending. (Israeli Music Publications, through Leeds Music.)

ANATOL ALEXANDROW (1888-) U.S.S.R.

Alexandrow is a composer of individuality whose style leads from early Scriabinesque essays to a recent preoccupation with folk materials in a more diatonic context.

Sonata No. 5 in G-sharp Minor, Op. 22 (1922)	In two movements: (1) free, Scriabinesque style, (2) ten variations leading to a fugue and conclusion. (Universal Edition)
Sonata No. 6, Op. 26 (1925)	Predominantly lyric. Idyllic opening followed by an Adagio and a strong rhythmic Foxtrot to close. (Through Leeds Music)
Eight Pieces on Folk Songs of the U. S. S. R., Op. 46 (pub. 1938)	Clear, short, simple settings of Russian, Tchouvach, Kirghiz and Armenian tunes. (Through Leeds Music)
Sonata No. 8, Op. 50 (pub. 1946)	Clear, transparent piece: joyous Allegretto giocoso, pensive Andante cantabile, energetic finale combining various jubilant dance and march tunes. Uses many melodies from Opus 46 (see above). (Through Leeds Music)
Sonata No. 9, Op. 61 (pub. 1946)	Flowing Allegro moderato, lyric Andante, tarantella-like Allegro with quiet interlude. Moderate difficulty. (Through Leeds Music)
Six Pieces of Medium Difficulty	Short, unhackneyed character pieces for youthful players. (Through Leeds Music)

GEORGES AURIC (1899-) France

Sonatine (1922)	A crisp work of moderate difficulty in three movements: thin, clear, rhythmic Allegro;

flowing <u>Andante</u>; brisk <u>Presto</u> finale requiring some facility and endurance.
(Salabert)

Petite Suite (1927)	Clear, neat qualities throughout. Mostly two- and three-part writing: brilliant opening <u>Prelude</u>; light, staccato <u>Danse</u>; processional <u>Vilanelle et Entrée</u>; expressive <u>Sarabande</u> in dotted rhythms; <u>Voltes,</u> a concluding rondo, exploiting the drone and the higher reaches of the piano. (Heugel, through Mercury Music)
Sonata in F Major (1931)	Large, uninhibited work, virtuoso style. An improvisatory quality pervades the entire piece. Demands an energetic pianism, power, brilliance and vitality. (Salabert)
La Seine, au Matin.... (1937)	Short piece for the album <u>A l'Exposition</u>. Light, jazz quality. (Salabert)
Adieu, New York! (1919)	Lengthy foxtrot, not difficult, ragtime bass, spirited. (Edition de la Sirène)
Trois Pastorales	Short. The end pieces dancelike, spirited and somewhat rough; the middle one calm and quiet. (Salabert)

HENRI BARRAUD (1900-) France

Six Impromptus

Souple et Calme	Short, expressive, chordal.
Rapide	Melody in long tones supported by rapid, broken chord figuration, flowing eighths in 9/8.
Lent et Grave	Sombre opening, animated, difficult middle section in fast sixteenths, dissonant double notes. Big climax, quiet return.
Modéré	Short. Supple figuration over melody in tenor.
Sans trainer	Dirgelike, ostinato rhythms in bass.
Cursif	Two voices in flowing sixteenths. One of the best of the set. (Amphion, through Elkan-Vogel)
Histoires pour les Enfants	Four easy pieces. (Durand)
Premiers Pas	Five children's pieces. (Eschig)

BÉLA BARTÓK (1881-1945) Hungary

It will be some years before it is possible justly to evaluate Bartók's entire musical output. Since it would be presumptuous to attempt a definitive evaluation and selection from the work of a composer so important and as yet so incompletely known, a more or less complete listing of his piano works follows. Though not the most significant of his contributions, the piano pieces are fascinating and rewarding. They range in difficulty from the most modest to the most demanding musical and pianistic problems.

The piano music of Bartók exhibits a variety of styles. The early Rhapsody takes its point of departure from Liszt. The Bagatelles show a preoccupation with the treatment of various characteristic sonorities and musical ideas in miniature. The mass of folk-song arrangements often use block chordal accompaniments, other homophonic settings or occasional light contrapuntal textures. The drone bass is frequent, especially in "bagpipe" effects. Octaves and chords are often heavy, demanding and unorthodox. Stretches become a technical problem of importance (Musettes, Etude No. 1) and the treatment of characteristic sonorities achieves prominence (Night's Music). Wide skips also abound (Sonata, Improvisations) and the clever balancing of harsh sounds is important to proper projection of the music (Diary of a Fly). Irregular meters are plentiful (Dances in Bulgarian Style) and rapid ostinato figures offer problems in endurance and control (The Chase, Suite Op. 14, third movement). Asymmetrical phrase groupings constantly add to the interest and vitality of the music.

Since Bartók's music is built primarily on the melodic, harmonic and rhythmic vocabulary of Central and Eastern European folk music (on which he was an outstanding authority), it is well to begin study of his piano works with some of the folk-tune and folk-dance arrangements that occupied much of his attention. Although pedalings, phrasings, fingerings and metronome marks are almost too finicky (he uses subdivisions applicable only to the electric metronome), they are all authentic and, if carefully considered, will lead to greater comprehension of his musical intent.

The piano music is published by Boosey & Hawkes. There are some duplications by other firms among which must be mentioned a very good one-volume collection by G. Schirmer. It contains, among other things, all the bagatelles.

Four Pieces (1903)	Study for the Left Hand (sonata-rondo), wistful First Phantasy, Second Phantasy, exuberant Scherzo.
Rhapsody, Op. 1 (1904)	Lisztian piano style. Later version for piano and orchestra.
Three Popular Hungarian Songs (1907)	Simple, unadorned statements.
Fourteen Bagatelles, Op. 6 (1908)	Short pianistic essays in the handling of characteristic sonorous materials. See especially No. 12 for its free improvisational treatment, originality and ingenious unity.
Ten Easy Piano Pieces (1908)	Short, simple sketches including Evening in the Country and Bear Dance.
Two Elegies, Op. 8b (1908-1909)	Heavy, florid piano style. Lengthy, sombre, not easy.
For Children, 85 Pieces for Piano (1908-1909) revised 1945 (79 pieces)	Subtle, discreet treatment of various folk melodies: simple chordal accompaniments, two- and three-part linear writing, broken-

Vol. 1 Based on Hungarian Folk Tunes Vol. 2 Based on Slovakian Folk Tunes	chord patterns in close position.
Three Burlesques, Op. 8c (1908-1910)	Rushing <u>Presto</u> ("Querelle"); sardonic, wry <u>Allegretto</u> ("Un peu gris"); witty <u>Molto vivo, capriccioso</u>. No folk elements.
Seven Sketches, Op. 9 (1908-1910)	Short, tenuous ideas. Not difficult except for No. 4. Could be played as a unit. (E. B. Marks)
Two Rumanian Dances, Op. 8a (1909-1910)	Difficult bravura settings of folklike dance tunes. Octaves, chords, double notes, large skips.
Four Nénies (Dirges) (1910)	Short laments, bare in outline, deceptively simple, demanding skillful pedaling, musicianly understanding of phrase relationships. Primarily harmonic, melodies doubled or tripled. (Leeds Music)
Allegro Barbaro (1911)	Sonorous, boisterous, dancelike piece. Demands power and bravura. Moderate difficulty.
Fifteen Hungarian Peasant Songs (1914-1917)	Connected cycle of short folk-tune settings. Simple harmonizations. The <u>Ballad</u> especially interesting. Rousing "bagpipe" finale to the entire set: <u>Four Old Tunes, Scherzo, Ballad, Old Dance Tunes</u>.
Sonatine (1915)	Miniature, not difficult. Sonorous, driving <u>Bagpipe</u>, clumsy <u>Bear Dance</u>, rapid, dancelike <u>Finale</u>.
Rumanian Folk Dances (1915)	Six short pieces (see especially No. 3 with its peasant pipe whistling above a simple drone).
Rumanian Christmas Songs, Two Series (10 each) (1915)	Subtle, pianistic handling of some highly flexible asymmetrical modal tunes. See especially second series.
Suite, Op. 14 (1916)	Playful <u>Allegretto</u>, folk style; robust <u>Scherzo</u> demanding agility; driving <u>Allegro molto</u> with running unison passages and reiterated motives; short sensitive <u>Sostenuto</u> to close.
Three Etudes, Op. 18 (1918)	Virtuoso concert pieces exploiting new sonorities in pianistic figures of great originality. Highly dissonant.
Allegro molto	Constant stretches of broken ninths and tenths. Demands endurance, quick expansion and contraction of the hand.
Andante sostenuto	Impressionist study in sonority. Rolling arpeggios in irregular groupings. Cadenza in double notes.

Tempo giusto	Constant left-hand figuration against lightly plucked chords. Irregular meters and rhythms. Demands quick shifts of the hand.
Improvisations, Op. 20 (1920)	High point in Bartók's treatment of folk materials. Eight tunes handled in improvisational style in a connected cycle. Highly dissonant, individual and marked in character. No. 7 in memory of Debussy.
Sonata (1926)	Bartók's most extended work for piano solo. Folk materials molded into a classic structure. Driving rhythmic Allegro moderato; cryptic, short, angular Sostenuto e pesante; spirited variation-rondo Allegro molto. Entire work difficult. Demands power, rhythmic drive, clear, dry sound.
Out of Doors (1926)	Cycle of five descriptive pieces.
With Drums and Pipes	Short, rhythmic, percussive.
Barcarolla	Exploits the sound of lapping water against a swaying barcarolle figure.
Musettes	Dissonant drone embellished with trills. Melodic interludes. Problems in mixing major-minor sonorities.
Night's Music	Tour de force in catching the hum of a summer's night: croaking frogs, the sound of crickets, distant melodies.
The Chase	Wild, ostinato bass working perpetually against pounding, asymmetrical phrases. Very wide, quick skips. Fast octaves and parallel ninths. Highly dissonant.
Nine Little Pieces in 3 Bks. (1926)	Four short studies in two- and three-part counterpoint, wry Menuetto, Air, satiric Marcia della Bestie, sonorous Tambour de Basque, lengthy Preludio-All'Ungharese.
Three Rondos on Folk Tunes (1916-1927)	Light, witty. No. I easiest and most popular.
Little Suite (1936)	Six adaptations from Forty-four Duos for Two Violins: Slow Melody, Walachian Dance, Whirling Dance, Quasi pizzicato, Ukrainian Song, Bagpipe.

Mikrokosmos, 153 progressive piano pieces in 6 vols. (1926-1937)

Beginning in the tradition of the Bach Notenbücher (as teaching pieces for his son Peter), Bartók proceeded to compile a series of short musical essays on compact musical and technical problems.

Vol. I, 1-36	Hands in unison. Independence developed by simple two-part counterpoint, including canon. Modal melodies almost immediately.
Vol. 2, 37-66	Two-part writing, various homophonic accompaniments, legato and staccato, dynamics,

	pieces for two pianos, some chromaticisms, more difficult key signatures. Technical exercises.
Vol. 3, 67-96	Double notes, chord studies, irregular rhythmic groupings, inventions, changing meters, technical exercises.
Vol. 4, 97-121	More complicated problems, studies in clashing dissonances, Bulgarian rhythms.
Vol. 5, 122-139	Double notes, chord studies, thirds, fourths, major and minor seconds, whole tone scales, syncopations, changing meters.
Vol. 6, 140-153	More extended treatment of the foregoing problems, culminating in six dances in Bulgarian rhythms (irregular groupings of 5/8, 7/8, 8/8, 9/8).

The following may be recommended as especially interesting:

40—In Jugoslav Mode	Easy melody and accompaniment, drone bass.
43—In Hungarian Style 44—Contrary Motion 55—Triplets in Lydian Mode	Simple pieces for two pianos.
59—Major and Minor	Two voices, one in either mode.
63—Buzzing	A miniature Diary of a Fly (see 142).
68—Hungarian Dance	For two pianos.
79—Hommage a J.S.B.	In the style of a broken-chord prelude.
94—Tale	Simple melodic dialogue, changing meters.
102—Harmonics	Overtone effects, brusque chords.
108—Wrestling	Brutal, grunting effects, irregular rhythms, unison melodic fragments against sustained tones.
109—From the Island of Bali	Short three-part piece, flowing melody, unison passages risoluto, some imitation.
113—Bulgarian Rhythms	Irregular 7/8. Good preparation for dances in volume six.
116—Melody	March.
122—Chords Together and Opposed	Rhythmic study.
124—Staccato	Two voices, repeated notes, short interjected figures.
128—Peasant Dance	Easy three-part writing, including a canon.
138—Bagpipe	Particularly engaging piece in a genre that seems to have fascinated the composer.
142—From the Diary of a Fly	Tour de force. Modern counterpart of Couperin's Le Moucheron. Buzzing effects in realistic style.

146—Ostinato	Sonorous, driving chords. Short melodic interjections.
147—March	Plodding, heavy octaves.
148-153—Dances in Bulgarian Rhythm	All six may be recommended for study.
Transcriptions of XVII and XVIII Century Italian Cembalo and Organ Music	Pieces by Marcello, M. Rossi, della Ciaja, Frescobaldi and Zipoli. See under these composers. (Carl Fischer)
Two Preludes by Purcell	From the suites in G Major and C Major. (Leeds Music)

STANLEY BATE (1912-   ) Great Britain

Seven Pieces
 	
  Prelude
  Romance
  Chanson Populaire
  Moment Musical
  Polka
  Valse
	Short essays of moderate difficulty with a few bows in the direction of the Shostakovitch Preludes. (Associated Music)

Six Pieces for an Infant Prodigy, Op. 13	Short, light sketches, rhythmically simple. (Mercury Music)
Sonatina No. 6 in E-flat Major (1943)	Clear, facile pianistic writing. Chord structures in fourths and fifths. Three movements: Moderato, Andante, Allegro. (Associated Music)
Sonatina No. 7 in C Major	Slighter than No. 6, easy, bright in quality. (Associated Music)
Sonatina No. 8 in C Major	Prelude, Valentine, Toccata: all short movements, the first and last posing moderate technical problems in fast tremolos, scales, repeated notes, alternating hands. (Associated Music)

ARNOLD BAX (1883-   ) Great Britain

This gifted composer has written extensively for the piano, always showing great facility and a warmly imaginative and romantic temperament. Various influences have contributed to his productivity - among them, an early visit to Russia, and a strong sympathy for Celtic (Irish) literature and folk music.

Two Russian Tone Pictures

Nocturne (May Night in the Ukraine) Gopak (National Dance)	Romantic and poetical—its elaborate figuration asks for a good deal of keyboard facility. Needs a strong rhythmic impetus. Its brilliant, non legato passages are well written and effective. (Joseph Williams)

Country Tune	An easy piece, with opportunity for skillful balance of tone. (Murdoch, Murdoch & Co.)
Lullaby	Has a simple melody, subjected to varied harmonic treatment. Apart from a few bars, where the left hand, with the theme, is accompanied by right-hand florid passage-work, the technical requirements are quite elementary. (Murdoch, Murdoch & Co.)
Toccata	Brilliant, with much rapid double-note technique for the right hand. It requires a wide range of tone. (Murdoch, Murdoch & Co.)
Nereid	A poetical piece, with flowing cantabile and persistent rhythmic figure—needs delicate treatment—of moderate difficulty. (J. & W. Chester)
Winter Waters	With a subtitle, "Tragic Landscape," this achieves a sinister atmosphere with a menacing ground-bass of four notes that continues throughout. Not very difficult, in spite of some complication of harmony and texture, and decidedly effective. (J. & W. Chester)
Whirligig	Here again is the device of a persistent ostinato figure, this time in spirited sixteenth-notes handed back and forth between right and left hand. Considerable finger dexterity is needed for this brilliant and clever piece. (J. & W. Chester)
Sonata No. 1, in F-sharp Minor	An early work, later revised, this has a single movement, in various tempi, and full of romantic feeling. Its frequently thick texture requires much power, a wide range of tone, and well-developed technique. (Murdoch, Murdoch & Co.)
Sonata No. 2, in G Major	A rhapsodical work in one movement of imaginative character, using five separate themes in varying tempi. Some of the material suggests folk-song influence. Much of the writing is thick and is not easy except for a large hand. (Murdoch, Murdoch & Co.)
Sonata No. 3, in G-sharp Minor	Unlike the preceding sonatas, this is in three separate movements. The first has a principal subject in broken rhythm, with a brooding atmosphere and dissonant accompanying chords. A second theme has a more continuous melodic line, with extreme chromatic

harmony. The structure is not easily followed
by the listener, and needs a skilled interpreter.
The second movement starts more simply, and
has a central theme with a strong "Irish folk
song" flavor; later there is some complicated
pianoforte writing, though it is always idiomatic. The finale is more straightforward than
the first movement, with some vigorous rhythmic material; it ends with an imaginative
reference to the opening subject of the whole
work.
(Murdoch, Murdoch & Co.)

VICTOR BELYI (1904-) U.S.S.R.

Three Miniatures (1939)

Two lyric pieces, one dancelike. Moderate
difficulty.
(Leeds Music)

Third Sonata (pub. 1945)

One movement, vigorous, energetic, dissonant.
Leeds Music)

Fourth Sonata (pub. 1947)

More consonant than the third sonata. Requires
all-round pianism. Allegretto semplice with
strongly contrasting ideas; sombre, impassioned Moderato sostenuto; vigorous finale
Andante con moto and Allegro appassionato.
(Leeds Music)

ALBAN BERG (1885-1935) Austria

Sonata, Op. 1 (1908)

Berg's unique work for solo piano was written
in his student days with Schönberg. Although
not a twelve-tone work, it is highly chromatic,
intense in expressive content and dense in
texture. Demands a high level of musicianship and pianism.
(Associated Music)

LENNOX BERKELEY (1903-)

Five Short Pieces (1937)

Technically fairly easy; Nos. 1 and 5 have
some rhythmic sophistications.
(J. & W. Chester)

Six Preludes (1948)

Nos. 1 and 3 require an agile finger technique;
2, 4 and 6 have legato cantilena with some contemporary dissonance; No. 5 is an attractive
little piece, not difficult, which owes much of
its piquancy to 7/8 rhythm.
(J. & W. Chester)

Scherzo (1950)

This shows a confident creative talent and
command of contemporary idiom. The technical difficulties are considerable; they present rapid alternations of repeated-note,
double-note, staccato-chord and finger
passages, etc.
(J. & W. Chester)

LORD GERALD TYRWHITT BERNERS (1883-   ) Great Britain

Trois Petites Marches Funèbres	Three satirical funeral marches: <u>Pour un Homme d'Etat</u> (slow and pompous); <u>Pour un Canari</u> (whimsical); <u>Pour une Tante à Héritage</u> (<u>Allegro giocoso</u>!) Not really difficult. (J. & W. Chester)
Trois Fragments psychologiques	Each piece characterises a psychological stage of mind: hate, laughter, sighing. (J. & W. Chester)
Poissons d'or	An impressionist study. Not easy. (J. & W. Chester)

BORIS BLACHER (1903-   ) Germany

Blacher is one of the leading figures in contemporary German music. His influence, especially since World War II, has been pronounced. Little is known of him in this country but the following works are available and represent his most recent activity in the field of "the new rhythm." Compare these pieces with the variable metrics of Paul Juon's <u>Tanzrytmen</u> (for four hands).

Ornamente, Op. 37 (1950)	Seven contrasting studies on variable meters. Each measure is in a different meter, the meters following a preconceived arithmetic plan; e.g., 2/8, 3/8, 4/8....9/8, 8/8, 7/8.... 2/8 etc. Bare, dry textures. Short, not difficult, varied in pace and character. (Bote & Bock)
Sonate, Op. 39	The above viewpoint worked out in a sonata structure of moderate length. Bare, taut qualities. Not difficult technically, requires sensitive musicianship. Two sections: <u>Allegro ma non troppo</u> leading to quiet <u>Andante</u>; inversion of the <u>Andante</u> leading to a light, scherzando-like <u>Vivace</u> with stringendo ending. (Bote & Bock)

B. BOGDANOV-BEREZOVSKY, U.S.S.R.

Sonata, Op. 24 (pub. 1946)	In two movements. Diatonic, organlike sonorities. Clear, strong qualities. Problems in octaves and passage playing. (Leeds Music)

ALEXANDER URIAH BOSCOVICH, Israel

Semitic Suite	Six pieces, national in character: strongly rhythmic <u>Allegretto</u> in dance style; short singing <u>Andantino</u>, <u>rubato</u>, <u>teneramente</u>; light, lively <u>Folk Dance</u> with strong syncopated rhythms; curious <u>Andantino</u> with phrases suggesting recitatives; fairly long <u>Pastorale</u>, melody over drumlike basses; concluding <u>Dance</u>, vigorous and sonorous. (Israeli Music Publications, through Leeds Music)

FRANK BRIDGE (1879-1941) Great Britain

Bridge's output includes a considerable number of short piano pieces, all of them written effectively for the instrument. There are at least three recognizable styles.

Early compositions of a romantic type:

Three Sketches

April	A brilliant piece, for the most part requiring delicate and rapid double-note technique, and with one passage of fortissimo octaves.
Rosemary	Has charm in its expressive legato phrases; not difficult.
Valse Capricieuse	A graceful and easy trifle, with effective alternations of legato and finger staccato. (Schirmer)
Capriccio in F-sharp Minor	A brilliant and clever show piece, requiring both a good finger technique and, in its central section, warm singing tone. (Augener)

Middle period of impressionism, more recondite harmonically:

Three Poems

Solitude	Slow and expressive, somewhat dissonant in its harmony—technically easy.
Ecstasy	Rapid and brilliant double-note passages, requiring powerful fingers, but lying well for the hand.
Sunset	Easy technically; the main requisite is sensitiveness to tonal balance. (Augener)

The Hour Glass

Dusk	A sensitive and delicate piece, requiring smooth legato and accurate balance of tone.
The Dew Fairy	The rapid figuration needs a fine pianissimo. One of the most effective of Bridge's compositions.
The Midnight Tide	A slow piece, in which the surge of the sea is imaginatively suggested by rocking phrases and thick harmonies. Full power is required at the climax, but there is no great difficulty. (Augener)

Compositions in a dissonant contemporary technique:

In Autumn

Retrospect	A solemn, somewhat austere composition, with harsh, slow-moving harmonies; the chromatic steps of much of the bass give a sense of direction and help to make the structure clear.
Through the Eaves	A short piece, almost entirely in the upper half of the keyboard, with an effective texture con-

sisting of a left-hand melodic line accompanied
by "twittering" figures in the right—all lying
easily.
(Augener)

Sonata

A long, very serious work in three movements,
in uncompromising dissonant idiom, showing
imagination and deep feeling. It presents
formidable technical and interpretative
problems.
(Augener)

BENJAMIN BRITTEN (1913-   ) Great Britain

Holiday Diary (1934)

Suite for piano

Early Morning Bathe

Vivacious, fast 6/8, triplet sixteenth-note
figuration. Requires some stamina.

Sailing

Swaying melody, sonorous accompaniment.
Animated, agitato middle section.

Fun-Fair

Very brilliant rondo, requiring bravura, command of chords and octaves, sharp rhythmic
accentuation.

Night

Tranquil finale, melody in the midst of widely
separated intervallic sonorities.
(Boosey & Hawkes)

ROBERT CASADESUS (1899-   ) France

Twenty-four Preludes

In four books. Essays in a variety of genres:
melodic, energetic, brusque, flowing, dans le
goût espagnol, atmospheric, tender, intimate,
marcia funèbre, dans le style ancien (with
musette), Bourrée, etc. A useful collection
worth exploring for concertizing or teaching.
Oriented toward Ravel (to whom they are
dedicated).
(Eschig)

Eight Etudes

Accent on facility. Fairly difficult pieces exploring the following pianistic problems:
thirds, octaves, resonance, fourths and fifths,
two against three, left hand, chords, lightness
of touch.
(Schirmer)

Toccata (1950)

Lengthy essay in double notes and octaves.
Requires virtuosity, endurance, precision and
power.
(Durand, through Elkan-Vogel)

ALFREDO CASELLA (1883-1947) Italy

The changing character of Casella's piano style gives evidence of a restless, agitated mind constantly exploring new avenues of expression. Both
the whimsical character of his shorter pieces and the broad, expansive
qualities of his more extended works display a wide variety of musical and

technical elements: love of the grotesque (<u>Deux Contrastes</u>), a bold pianism (<u>Toccata</u>), a complete immersion in Ravel (<u>A notte Alta</u>), simplicity of means (<u>Inezie</u>), harmonic and contrapuntal complexity when the issue demands it (<u>Sinfonia</u>, <u>Arioso</u> and <u>Toccata</u>), or an original solution to an old problem (<u>Due Ricercari sul nome B.A.C.H.</u>). He is little played in this country and, for several purposes and uses, worth exploring.

Toccata (1904)	Lengthy, bravura <u>Allegro</u>. Demands stamina and brilliance in broken octaves, chords and broken chords. Difficult. (Ricordi)
Sarabande (1908)	Long, lyric piece, sonorous, modal, chromatic. Florid figuration. Not easy. (Salabert)
A la Manière de....	Short pieces "in the style of...," Excellent fun.
Vol. I	
R. Wagner	<u>Einleitung des 3 Aufzuges</u> (Prelude to a "3rd Act").
G. Fauré	Lyric <u>Romance sans Paroles</u>.
J. Brahms	Agitated <u>Intermezzo</u>.
C. Debussy	<u>Entr'acte pour un drame en preparation</u>. Atmospheric, parallel harmonies.
R. Strauss	<u>Symphonia molestica</u>, a symphonic transcription.
C. Franck	<u>Aria</u>, chromatic, walking chords in quarters. (Salabert)
Vol. II	
V. d'Indy	<u>Prélude à l'après-midi d'un Ascète</u>. Symphonic style.
M. Ravel	<u>Almanzor ou le mariage d'Adelaïde</u>. Clever potpourri in waltz style.
	The other two pieces in this volume are imitations of Borodine and Chabrier by Ravel. (Salabert)
Deux Contrastes (1916-1918)	Short, not difficult.
Grazioso	<u>Hommage à Chopin</u>. Distorted version of the A-major prelude.
Anti-grazioso	Grotesque dance, rough harmonies. (J. & W. Chester)
Inezie (1918)	Three "trifles."
Preludio	Languid, expressive melody over an ostinato.
Serenata	Capricious tune over staccato, ostinato broken-chord figures. Brilliant climax.
Berceuse	Pentatonic melody over a tonal ostinato. Requires sensitivity. (J. & W. Chester)
A notte alta (1917)	An impressionist poem. Music of the night. Deep bell-like sonorities, lush polychords, distant, melancholy tunes. Big climax, quiet ending. One of his most significant pieces. (Ricordi)

11 Pièces Enfantines (1920)	Prelude, Waltz, Canon, Bolero, Hommage to Clementi, Siciliana, Giga, Minuetto, Carillon (especially interesting), Berceuse and Galop. Simple textures, in a modern vein. Only moderate facility required. (Universal Edition)
Due Ricercari sul nome B.A.C.H. (1932)	
Funèbre	Sombre, three and four voices. Not long or difficult. Intense and effective.
Ostinato	Quick marchlike motion, percussive, sempre accelerando, finally breaking into a run. Fairly difficult. (Ricordi)
Sinfonia, Arioso and Toccata, Op. 59 (1936)	Large-scale work requiring full pianistic command.
	Sonorous, propulsive Sinfonia opening with big, declamatory phrases.
	Tender Arioso supported with multiple accompanying parts and full harmonies.
	Vigorous, closing Toccata with passage playing, alternating double notes, octaves, chords. Jubilant ending pesante and festoso. (Carisch)
Sonatina (1916)	
Allegro con spirito Minuetto	Ironic, grotesque. Traditional minuet in modern dress. Melancholy.
Finale	Lengthy, capricious, difficult. Rapid figuration, staccato chords, left-hand passage playing, widespread chords. Luminous, sonorous ending. (Ricordi)
Nove Pezzi (1914)	Nine pieces in various "modes": funereal, barbaric, elegiac, burlesque, exotic, in the style of a nenia, minuet, tango, in rustic vein. Polychordal harmonies requiring large hand. Fairly difficult both musically and pianistically. (Ricordi)

MARIO CASTELNUOVO-TEDESCO (1895-   ) Italy

The piano music of Castelnuovo-Tedesco consists primarily of single pieces or cycles of pieces in descriptive genre employing a broad piano style over the entire register of the keyboard and inclined toward a romantic sonority. The texture is primarily though not exclusively homophonic with some emphasis on atmospheric figuration. The difficulties, though mainly conventional, are likely to be considerable, especially in the more extended pieces which often require bravura octaves and brilliant chord techniques.

I Naviganti (1919)	Long, florid poem. Gentle beginning working to a great climax. (Forlivesi)
Cipressi (1920)	Large canvas, sombre, swaying rhythms, sonorous climax, quiet ending. (Forlivesi)
Cantico (1920)	Luminous, extended climax, heavy octaves and chords. (Forlivesi)
Il Raggio verde (1916)	Light, rapid, vivacious, lengthy, difficult. (Forlivesi)
Epigraphe (1922)	An extended lament. Flowing, liquid, florid figuration surrounding the melody. Climactic. Quiet ending. (Forlivesi)
La Sirenetta et il Pesce turchino (1920)	Long, brilliant, colorful. Requires full equipment. Impressionist water effects. (Forlivesi)
Alghe (1919)	Not difficult. Melodic, atmospheric, gentle. (Forlivesi)
Alt Wien (1923)	A Viennese rhapsody, one of his best pieces.
Walzer	Piquant, brilliant, dissonant, capricious waltz, Viennese style.
Nachtmusik	Atmospheric nocturne quasi Barcarolla. Melody between pedal point and surrounding figuration.
ˆMemento mori	"Fox-trot tragico." Wild, heavy textures, difficult octaves, double notes, skips. (Forlivesi)
Piedigrotta (1924)	A Neapolitan rhapsody. Quite difficult.
Tarentella scura	Bravura skips, repeated notes, cross rhythms.
Notte 'e luna	Nocturne. Melody over lush, evocative figuration.
Calasciunata	Guitar-like piece, freely changing moods, dancelike, Spanish qualities.
Voce luntana	Nostalgic lento, phrases interrupted by distant echoes, supple dance tunes. Evocative, atmospheric.
Lariulà!	Short transition to a lengthy Alla marcia paesana in gay, popular style with fife effects. Climactic ending. (Ricordi)
Tre Corali su Melodie ebraiche (1926)	A cycle of three extended pieces on Hebrew melodies to be played without pause. Difficult.
Grave e meditavo	Sombre, choral-prelude style. Quiet organ-like sonorities.
Con ritmo rude e ostinato di danza	Rough dance, double sixths, some contrapuntal interludes.

Vivo e scalpitante	A "stamping" dance. Requires stamina, precision, brilliance. (Universal Edition)
Candide (1944)	Six musical illustrations for the novel by Voltaire. A light, good-natured program suite with conventional difficulties.
The Castle in Westphalia	Tempo di minuetto.
March of the Bulgarian Soldiers	Slavic march.
March of the Inquisitors and Earthquake (Lisbon (1755)	Improvisations on the Dies Irae.
The Young Girls and the Monkeys (South America)	Scherzando, à la rhumba.
The Carnival of Venice	Five variations on a well-known theme, and coda.
The Garden on the Bosphorus (Epilogue)	Atmospheric andante using the theme from the Rondo alla Turca of Mozart. (Leeds Music)
Passatempi (1928)	Cycle of five little waltzes: elegant, burlesque, melancholy, serene, à la Viennese and coda recalling the earlier pieces. (Forlivesi)
Le Danze del Re David (1925)	Hebrew rhapsody on traditional themes. (Forlivesi)
Two Film Studies (1931) Charlie Mickey Mouse	Program pieces on two famous film comedians: the first in rapidly changing moods, the second in the style of a fox trot. (Ricordi)
Tre Preludi Alpestri (1935)	
Die singende Wiese	Lively, light texture, close broken-chord and interval figuration.
Glocken im Thale	Atmospheric, impressionist lento. Quiet bell effects.
Rauschen im Walde	Tumultuous, rapid. Forest sounds. Climactic. (Ricordi)

CLAUDE DEBUSSY (1862-1918)

Claude Debussy, the most original composer for the piano since Liszt, brought to its repertoire a delicate feeling for simultaneous "layers" of tone, producing effects that are comparable to those of the French impressionist painters, with new uses of the pedals that enhance the atmospheric quality of the best of his creations. His style, it is true, sometimes displays mannerisms that lend themselves easily to caricature; but it cannot be denied that he has enlarged the expressive range of the piano through the imaginativeness of his mature work.

Editions

Copyright restrictions confine at present the printing of Debussy's compositions mainly to the French publishing houses of Durand and Fromont (American agents—the Elkan-Vogel Co.). Some early pieces have been reprinted in America.

Easier Pieces

A good deal of Debussy's output is of not more than moderate difficulty, but there is not much that is definitely easy. The qualities called for include a sensitive feeling for tone, extreme delicacy of touch, and really imaginative pedaling. Among simpler compositions that would serve as a good introduction to this style are:

Arabesques in E Major and G Major
Valse - La plus que lente
Suite Bergamasque (four pieces)
Suite - "Children's Corner" (Nos. 1, 2, 3, 5, & 6)
Sarabande (from suite - Pour le piano)
"Des pas sur la neige" and "La fille aux cheveux de lin" (from Preludes, Book I)

There are four clearly marked periods. First, some early compositions, not fully characteristic, from which the following selection will suffice:

Arabesque in E Major	A pleasant salon piece; its smooth legato triplet figures lie easily for the hand, and it has a graceful melodic line.
Arabesque in G Major (1888)	Also a light and pleasing piece, consisting mainly of persistent four-note figures and staccato passages employing hand technique.
Rêverie	Legato cantabile of similar character to the material in the first Arabesque.
Valse—La plus que lente	A comparatively late piece (1910) which yet has the marks of Debussy's early style. It has a graceful rhythm.
Danse	One of the best of the early pieces, with lively cross-rhythms and a climax with brilliant repeated chords.
Suite Bergamasque (1890)	
Prelude	Contains easy finger passages and legato double thirds.
Menuet	Has material similar to the Prelude, and some simple staccato chord passages.
Clair de lune	Has popular appeal, with flowing melodic lines, requiring good legato in double notes and chords.
Passepied	Over a staccato broken-chord figure for left hand, the right has a melody in single notes, legato thirds, staccato chords, etc., embodying techniques already found in the other numbers of this suite.

Next come some compositions in a transitional style.

Suite pour le piano (1901)

Prelude — A brilliant, not particularly difficult piece; it is a little superficial, has ear-tickling glissandos, and culminates in an effective cadenza.

Sarabande — This invites imaginative treatment of its tonal contrasts, and calls for a fine rhythmic sense.

Toccata — An effective moto perpetuo, technically exacting.

Masques — Published in 1904, this has material recalling the earlier <u>Danse</u>, at somewhat greater length.

L'Isle joyeuse (1904) — Has the characteristics of the group now being discussed, though published later. It is an exacting piece which almost seems to call for choreographic interpretation. Its effect depends upon an unremitting rhythmic drive and the necessary reserve of power for the brilliant coda.

The third group consists of compositions that show Debussy at the height of his power.

Estampes (1903)

Pagodes — Conveys the sounds and atmosphere of an Oriental temple; the clanging of bells is suggested, using the pentatonic scale and washes of pedal. The sweeping right-hand accompaniment figures of the coda require a fine pianissimo.

La soirée dans Grenade (Evening in Granada) — This is extraordinarily successful in communicating a genuine Spanish quality. The rhythm of the habañera accompanies five distinct short themes of varied character. There are two guitar-like interruptions, and the piece ends with a return to the plaintive melody of the opening. The main difficulty lies in the control of some rapid soft staccato chord passages.

Jardins sous la pluie (Gardens in the rain) — The opening measures present the main technical problem in the rapid sixteenth-note figures (alla breve, and pianissimo); the stormy climax, leading to the central episode with its dripping raindrops, lies well under the hand and is very effective. The whole piece requires a wide tonal range and considerable power.

Images (1st set) (1905)

Reflets dan l'eau (Reflections in the water) — One of the outstanding compositions of Debussy's maturity. A rhythmic control that allows only the slight rubato required, for example, in measures 3 and 4 without losing continuity is a main essential. There are some of the glissando-like sweeping accompaniment figures already met with in "Pagodes," and in general extreme delicacy of touch is needed.

| Hommage à Rameau | Has similar character to the sarabande in the suite—"Pour le piano." It is more complicated in its structure, and on the whole less successful than the earlier piece. As in that, a firm rhythm is necessary. |
| Mouvement | An étude-like piece—musically a little unsubstantial. |

Images (2nd set) (1907)

Cloches à travers les feuilles (Bells heard through the leaves)	Requires a sensitive balance of the various strands of the texture. It seems to anticipate the quality of some of the later preludes.
Et la lune descends sur le temple qui fut (The moon goes down on the ruined temple)	This has less musical substance and more of Debussy's mannerisms than its companions. Even with delicate and sympathetic playing it is hard to make it convincing.
Poissons d'or (Goldfish)	Another notably successful piece of tonepainting. As in "Jardins sous la pluie," there is the technical problem of playing a rapid accompanying figure in a delicate pianissimo; the two pieces are of approximately equal difficulty.

Children's Corner (1908)

A charming suite that suggests a comparison with Schumann's Kinderscenen. Only one of the six members—"The snow is dancing"—presents any serious mechanical problem, but they all demand accurate judgment of tonal values.

Doctor Gradus ad Parnassum	An amusing caricature of a child's technical practice, with some mild sophistication through touch-variations of the opening finger passages.
Jimbo's Lullaby	Another humorous little piece requiring delicate treatment and careful relating of the two tempi.
Serenade for the doll	Here, exact observance of Debussy's careful instructions regarding dynamics, etc. (with use of una corda pedal throughout), is all that is necessary for a successful performance.
The snow is dancing	The most subtly conceived of the set, with some technical difficulty. Measures 14-21 may, for any but large hands, be justifiably rearranged to make tonal control easier. The expressive little phrase entering at measure 34 poses a small interpretative problem in its delivery. The utmost delicacy of touch is needed.
The little shepherd	Extremely simple, but a test for expressive legato and sympathetic imagination.
Golliwog's cake walk	A humorous and somewhat boisterous finish to the suite, requiring a good rhythmic sense. The ingenious quotation from Wagner's Tristan und Isolde should not be overlooked.

Préludes—Book I (1910)

Danseuses de Delphes (Delphic Dancers	A firm flowing rhythm and fine balance of simultaneous tonal lines are the obvious requirements.
Voiles (Sails)	Accurate balance of tone is again needed, with smooth legato for the whole-tone series of double thirds.
Le vent dans la plaine (Wind in the plain)	A whispering pianissimo represents the wind, the dominating figure of six notes requiring fine technical control.
Les sons et le parfums tournent dans l'air du soir (Sounds and scents mingle in the evening air)	Easy, so far as the mere playing of the notes is concerned, but making demands on the pianist's imagination and sensitiveness to tonal balance.
Les collines d'Anacapri (The hills of Anacapri)	A brilliant piece, largely in tarantella rhythm, also employing folk-song-like material—more difficult than most of the preludes.
Des pas sur la neige (Footsteps in the snow)	Technically simple—requires sustained and expressive legato.
Ce qu'a vu le vent d'Ouest (What the West Wind has seen)	The most exacting technically of the twelve preludes in this set. Powerful chords and broken octaves, and control of rapid tremolando passages played by alternating hands, are requisites.
La fille aux cheveux de lin (The girl with flaxen hair)	Requires flexible phrasing and smooth legato.
La sérénade interrompue (The interrupted serenade)	Light staccato, sometimes accompanying sustained cantabile. The humor of the piece, with the need for sharp tonal contrasts, is easily conveyed.
La cathédrale engloutie (The submerged cathedral)	Technically easy. Calls for a wide range of tone and feeling for rhythmic continuity.
La danse de Puck (Puck's dance)	Asks for delicacy of touch, rhythmic vitality and accuracy - comparatively difficult.
Minstrels	Incisive rhythm and humorous alternations of mood characterize this prelude. The direction to place the grace notes "on the beat" must be carefully observed, particularly when they are in the middle or on the lowest note of a chord.

Préludes—Book II (1913)

Brouillards (Mists)	Delicate figuration accompanies what is hardly more than the suggestion of a melodic line, conveying the impression of the title; fine control is needed.
Feuilles mortes (Dead leaves)	Has something in common with "Les sons et les parfums" of the first set of preludes, and asks for similar care for tonal balance.

La puerta del Vino	This prelude, calling up the picture of a Spanish cabaret dancer, is one of the most successful of the set. Sharp contrasts and wide range of tone, with continuous rhythmic vitality, are the salient characteristics.
"Les fées sont d'exquises danseuses" (The fairies are exquisite dancers)	The difficulty of this consists in a delicacy similar to that of "Brouillards," with greater speed.
Bruyères (Heaths)	The gentle sentiment of this recalls "La fille aux cheveux de lin"; it requires a similar flexibility and smooth legato. It is one of the easier preludes.
"General Lavine," eccentric	Here the affinity is with "Minstrels" of the first book. There is a similar rhythmic incisiveness, and not more technical difficulty.
La terrasse des audiences du clair de lune (The moon holds her court)	One of the most delicate and imaginative of Debussy's compositions; the player needs, besides a fine tonal control, an appreciation of, and a power to communicate, the subtle changes of mood.
Ondine	Another delicate piece, giving a perfect representation in tone of the gambols of the capricious waternymph; as in the preceding prelude, there are fluctuations of sentiment which challenge the imaginative interpreter.
Hommage à S. Pickwick, P.P.M.P.C.	This has little technical difficulty; its success in characterization is questionable, in spite of its quotation of the British national anthem and the clever suggestion of Sam Weller's whistling.
Canope	A mournful little piece, technically easy, with an atmosphere, and even some of its material, like "Et la lune descends sur le temple qui fut" in the second set of Images.
Tierces alternées (Alternating thirds)	Devoted to the technical problem stated in the title, and anticipating the type exemplified in the études of Debussy's latest period. The two hands play in continuous rapid alternation, hardly ever rising to a forte, and making their effect through slight rise and fall of soft tone.
Feux d'artifice (Fireworks)	A difficult and very brilliant display of musical fireworks, consisting on the technical side largely of alternations of right and left hand in sweeping arpeggio and allied figures. This and the seventh prelude of the first set are the most spectacular of the twenty-four.

The fourth group of compositions—twelve études—shows Debussy concentrating upon a number of advanced technical and tonal problems. This attitude had already been displayed in pieces like "Tierces alternées," in the second set of preludes. It now produces results that at best have a certain dry humor, but which do not achieve the poetry and imagination of Debussy's greatest creative period.

Twelve Études (1915)

Five-finger Exercise	The description—"after Czerny"—indicates the humorous intention of this somewhat lengthy étude, in which five-finger passages are presented in spasmodic fashion, with grotesque interruptions.
Study in Thirds	Contains a few passages of a novel type, with unusual finger positions.
Study in Fourths	Ingenious exploitation of the interval. There is a wide variety of tonal combinations.
Study in Sixths	Less interesting than No. 3.
Study in Octaves	Has a brilliance that is effective from the purely pianistic angle.
Study for Eight Fingers	To be played without thumbs—it consists of rapidly alternating groups of notes, each lying within the span of the four fingers of one hand.
Study in Chromatic Steps	A good finger study.
Study in Ornaments	The description is only a partial one, and there is a tonal variety similar to that of No. 3.
Study in Repeated Notes	A grotesque scherzo, making use of rapid finger alternations on repeated notes, mainly piano and pianissimo.
Study in Opposed Sonorities	Exploits subtle contrasts and combinations of touch.
For Composite Arpeggios	I.e., arpeggios consisting of broken chords with the addition of auxiliary notes. One of the most musical of the set.
For Chords	Useful for the practice of prompt and accurate grasp of chord positions.

BERNARD VAN DIEREN (1884-1936) Holland

Six Sketches, Op. 4a (1911)	An atonal cycle. Difficult.
Moderato assai	Complex prelude, interlacing figuration, atmospheric, lyric.
Quasi andante	Fleeting figures, sustained tones against repeated note motives, harmonies in fourths.
Allegro, rullante— Gracile ma distinto	Flowing sixteenth-note triplets over sustained tones, atmospheric, contrasting passages.
Allegro momente	A scherzo, staccato eighths and sixteenths, double notes, octaves, legato cantando phrases for contrast.

Poco lento	Flowing opening builds to intense, sonorous climaxes, vigorous, declamatory.
Poco piu lento che Pezza I	Summation of the cycle, formed by combining elements from the five previous pieces. Quiet, evanescent close. (Universal Edition)

PAUL DUKAS (1865-1935) France

Sonata in E-flat Minor (1899-1900)	An austere work, somewhat Franckian in places, with complicated pianoforte writing that requires mature technique and musicianship to do it justice. It has a concise and well-constructed first movement; a slow movement with a flowing cantabile given out first in simple chords and later with elaborate figuration; a scherzo whose main section is characterized by brilliant toccata-like passages in alternating-hand technique; and a finale which is less inspired in material and development, but has an imposing tonal climax. (Durand)
Variations, Interlude et Finale sur un thème de Rameau	An extended piece exploiting a many-sided virtuoso pianism. Eleven variations (contrapuntal playing, passages, double notes, etc.), improvisatory interlude in free style interspersed with runs, leading to a bright, clear, unencumbered finale, moderately animated. (Durand)
La plainte, au loin, du faune....	Lament for Debussy. Lento in 3/4. Plaintive oboe-like melody over pedal tones and sustained inner harmonies. In Le Tombeau de Claude Debussy (Album-Editions de la Sirène).

LOUIS DUREY (1888-) France

Première Sonatine in C Major	Cool, intimate Modérément animé gathering sonority as it proceeds; Lent with chord-supported melodies over an ostinato bass; busy, bright rondo Très animé, the hands chasing one another with five-finger figures. Not easy. (Heugel, through Mercury Music)
Dix Inventions	Mostly in two voices, mixing free contrapuntal and homophonic textures. A graceful collection, largely intimate. See especially No. 4 (slow, serious), No. 7 (whimsical) and No. 10 (animated gigue-like finale). (Heugel, through Mercury Music)

HANNS EISLER (1898-) Germany

Petits Morceaux pour les enfants	An outstanding collection, interesting, full of tenderness and humor. Not one note too many.
(In two collections)	
1) Eighteen little pieces	No more than a page apiece. The first eleven are simple variations on a march melody, mostly two voices, occasional chords or passages. The others are little canons, accompanied melody, two <u>Preludes</u>, two-voice <u>Fughetta</u> and a <u>Scherzo</u>.
2) Seven pieces	More extended and more difficult: <u>Invention</u> (two voices), rhythmic <u>Allegretto</u>, a kind of Bach <u>Prelude</u>, <u>Chaconne</u>, short <u>Scherzando</u>, a mirror canon and a good-humored <u>Rondo</u>. (Heugel, through Mercury Music)
Sonata, Op. 1	Serious work in the Central European tradition.
Allegro	Scherzando material alternating with an <u>espressivo</u> Tempo II.
Intermezzo	Melody over detached ostinato octaves, <u>Andante con moto</u>, short sustained middle section.
Finale	An extended complicated <u>Scherzo</u>. Entire sonata demands greatest precision in touch and accentuation, sensitivity to tempo changes, control of legato against staccato, rapidly moving staccato double notes. (Universal Edition)

GEORGES ENESCO (1881-) Rumania

Third Sonata in D Major, Op. 24, No. 3 (1933-1935)	A serious, extended work (with Rumanian elements), mostly delicate, extremely flexible in tempo, melodic movement and texture. Only climactic point is ending to last movement, triple-forte, vibrante. Difficult, interesting and provocative. Requires command of the instrument and an imaginative musicianship. The edition is a reproduction in the composer's own hand. (Salabert)
Vivace con brio	
Andantino cantabile	
Allegro con spirito	

MANUEL DE FALLA (1876-1946) Spain

Homenaje	Inscribed - "For the death of Debussy," this is a guitar piece arranged by the composer. It has a pleasant rhythmic swing in its easy staccato passages. (J. & W. Chester)
Pièces espagnoles	
Aragonesa	Has lively Spanish rhythms resembling those of Chabrier's "España."

Cubana	Has intriguing 3/4 and 6/8 cross-rhythms and considerable melodic interest.
Montanesa	This has a folk-song-like cantilena, recalling Albeniz.
Andalusa	Completes an effective set, with its staccato dance rhythms; not very difficult. (Durand)
Fantasia Baetica	The most ambitious of de Falla's piano solos. It features primitive repetitions of rhythmic motives; has brilliant and difficult pianoforte writing, but fundamentally simple harmonic treatment. (J. & W. Chester)
Ritual Fire Dance	This poor arrangement by the composer claims mention because of its familiarity, but does not fairly represent him.

SAMUEL FEINBERG (1890-   ) U.S.S.R.

Feinberg takes his point of departure from Scriabin. Within a complicated, widespread pianistic fabric he unfolds a generally restless melodic content using irregular rhythmic groups and sonorities that demand the binding use of the pedal. It is interesting to see how much more diatonic the style becomes in later works such as the <u>Ninth Sonata</u>.

Sonata No. 2, Op. 2 (1916)	In one movement, moderate length. Scriabin-esque, flowing, dramatic, ingenious treatment of the piano. Difficult. (Leeds Music)
Fantasy in E-flat Major, Op. 5 (1917)	Impassioned, nervous qualities. In one movement. (Leeds Music)
Fantasy in E Minor, Op. 9 (1919)	Generally melancholy, disconsolate in character. (Leeds Music)
Sonata in A Minor, Op. 10 (1921)	In one movement. Complicated pianism. (Leeds Music)
Suite, Op. 11	Four short pieces in the form of études. Predominantly lyric. (Leeds Music)
Two Tchouvash Melodies, Op. 24a	Two folk tunes set within a widespread pianistic figuration.
Sonata No. 9	In one movement. Predominantly lyric, strong ending, sonorous climaxes. Not easy. (Leeds Music)

HOWARD FERGUSON (1908-   ) Great Britain

Sonata in F Minor	Large-scale work in post-romantic piano style demanding full pianistic equipment.

Lento	Declamatory introduction leading to a restless
Allegro inquieto	opening movement.
Poco adagio	Florid slow movement leading to a
Allegro non troppo	broadly swinging finale moving through a
	scurrying allegro molto to a reprise of the
	introductory lento. Maestoso conclusion.
	(Boosey & Hawkes)
Five Bagatelles	Contrasting sketches around motives contrib-
	uted by a friend of the composer. To be
	played as a connected cycle. Moderately
	difficult.
	(Boosey & Hawkes)

JERZY FITELBERG (1903-1951) Poland

Sonate No. 1	In one movement, primarily two- and three-
	part writing, in propulsive sixteenth-note
	figuration. Problems in staccato parallel
	chords, fast repeated chords, passage playing,
	broken octaves and sevenths. Tonal only in a
	very free sense. Difficult.
	(Eschig)

MARKIAN FROLOV (1892-1944) U.S.S.R.

Sonata, Op. 20	Large-scale work in three movements. Pro-
(1942-1943)	grammatic qualities. Impassioned, romantic.
	Requires full pianistic equipment.
	(Leeds Music)

EUGENE GOOSSENS (1893-   ) Great Britain

Concert Study, Op. 10	Brilliant broken-chord study, staccato six-
	teenths both hands. Problems in touch, facility,
	sonority. Difficult.
	(J. & W. Chester)
Kaleidoscope, Op. 18	Album of twelve short pieces on children's
	themes. Chromatic harmony. Requires some
	facility.
	(J. & W. Chester)
Four Conceits, Op. 20	Short pieces of moderate difficulty; the first
(1917)	three in grotesque vein, the fourth a block
Gargoyle	chordal treatment of a melody.
Dance Memories	(J. & W. Chester)
Marionette Show	
Walking Tune	
Nature Poems, Op. 25	Rather extended pieces partly impressionist
(1919)	in style, sonorous, improvisatory, utilizing
Awakening	very full chromatic harmonies with strong
Pastoral	climactic points. Elaborate chordal techniques.
Bacchanal	Not easy.
	(J. & W. Chester)

Two Studies, Op. 38	Tranquil <u>Folk Tune</u> harmonized with chromatic chords and a rhythmic <u>Scherzo</u> in 6/8 with melodic interlude. Fairly difficult. (J. & W. Chester)

Ships
  The Tug
  The Tramp
  The Liner
	Suggestive sketches of moderate length. See especially No. 2. (J. Curwen and Sons)

PAUL BEN-HAIM (1897-) Israel

Ben-Haim is one of the outstanding figures in the "Eastern Mediterranean School" in Israel. His music is warm, lyric, colorful and filled with exotic traits derived from Oriental music. He also displays a real flair for the keyboard.

Nocturne (from Op. 20b)	Folklike melody, atmospheric, short. Not difficult. (Edition Negen, Leeds Music)
Five Pieces for Piano, Op. 34	Short essays that can be played as a long group or separately: exotic, improvisational <u>Pastorale</u> on a "shepherd's pipe" melody; quiet, atmospheric <u>Intermezzo</u> with siciliano rhythms; bravura <u>Capriccio agitato</u> with arpeggiando figuration and a powerful ending; quiet <u>Canzonetta</u> with warm melodic contours; brilliant, effective <u>Toccata</u> built on insistent repeated note figuration. (Edition Negen, Leeds Music)
Sonatina in A Minor, Op. 38 (1946)	Rather lengthy work requiring flexible rhythmic approach, color and drive: whimsical, delicate, capricious <u>Allegretto grazioso</u>; free, rubato <u>Improvisazione</u> on a "shepherd's pipe" melody; driving <u>Molto vivo</u> with insistent passage playing culminating in a finale on rhythms derived from the national dance, the "Hora." (Israeli Music Publications, Leeds Music)

There is also a <u>Melody with Variations</u> which will shortly be available through Leeds Music.

ERNESTO HALFFTER (1905-) Spain

Dance of the Shepherdess (1927)	Good encore or student piece. Broken chords over tenths and broken tenths, moderate sixteenth-note motion. (Associated Music)
Sonata (1926-1932)	In one movement. Fresh, triadic harmonies, at times bitonal. Short fugal section. Mostly eighth- and sixteenth-note motion in broken-chord figuration. Full, sonorous timbres, straightforward and clear. Fusion of French and Spanish elements. (Eschig)

Dance of the Gypsy	Energetic moderato, exotic qualities. Double thirds, broken chords, florid melodies. Fairly difficult. Good encore. (Eschig)

ARTHUR HONEGGER (1892-) Switzerland

Although Honegger is Swiss-born, his music belongs with that of his French confrères. One gets the impression of a certain musical weight and substance that is missing from much of the piano music of his contemporaries among "Les Six."

Toccata and Variations (1916)	Large work. Toccata demands facility, sensitivity. Variations are on a choral-like theme, serious and intense. Quiet close. Difficulties in double notes, balance of sound. (Salabert)
Trois Pièces (1915-1919)	Serious, weighty Prélude with dry sonorities, big climax, intense. Hommage à Ravel, a sensitive lyric tribute in flowing 2/4. Rapid, brilliant Danse requiring stamina in fast repeated intervals over long sections. (Salabert)
Sept Pièces Breves (1919-1920)	Short sketches, a page or two in length: Souplement (flowing, melodic), Vif (fleeting), Très lent (processional, thick in texture), Legèrement (playful), Lent (florid melodies, habanera rhythms), Rhythmique (staccato double notes), Violent (brusque, percussive scherzando, sharp dissonances). (Eschig)
Le Cahier Romand (1921-1923)	Five short pieces, all lyric except No. 4, a brusque, rhythmic dance movement. The entire set requires sensitivity. (Salabert)
Hommage à Albert Roussel (1928)	Short chordal piece in striding quarter notes. Ingenious, syncopated melody. Not difficult. (Salabert)
Prelude, Arioso et Fughetta (on the name Bach) (1932)	Broken-chord Prelude, improvisatory Arioso over an ostinato bass, cadenza and three-voice fugue in non-legato sixteenth notes. All material is derived from the tones B A C H. Not long, moderate difficulty. (Salabert)
Deux Esquisses (1943)	Broad, rhapsodic piece and melancholy Allegretto. (Elkan-Vogel)

JACQUES IBERT (1890-) France

Histoires	Ten light, descriptive pieces: La Meneuse de tortues d'Or (tender, melancholy), Le petit

âne blanc (humorous), Le vieux mendiant
(sombre), A giddy girl ("in the style of a sentimental English romance"), Dans la maison
triste (plaintive, slowly moving), Le palais
abandonné (sustained, serious), Bajo la mesa
(strong, rhythmic, dancelike), Le Cage de
Cristal (light, bantering), La marchande d'eau
fraiche (gay, humorous), Le Cortège de Balkis
(dancelike, dotted rhythms, "free and brilliant,"
light, piquant ending).
(Alphonse Leduc)

MANUEL INFANTE (1883-) Spain

Gitanerias

Virtuoso Spanish Gypsy dance style. Many
different moods, from moderately moving to
sonorous recitatives, brusque 6/8 staccato
motion, exuberant conclusion.
(Salabert)

Sevillana

Impressions of the Fête at Seville, a fantasy
exploiting a sonorous piano style in a variety
of virtuoso problems. Conventional harmonically. Bravura ending. Difficult.
(Salabert)

El Vito

Six variations on a popular theme (virtuoso
style) and a closing brilliant Danse Andalouse.
(A. Z. Mathot, through E. B. Marks)

D. E. INGELBRECHT (1880-) France

La Nursery

Six collections (six pieces in each) of French
nursery tunes in moderate to rather difficult
pianistic settings, tastefully and clearly written. Also published in an excellent four-hand
version for teacher and pupil.
(Salabert)

JOHN IRELAND (1879-) Great Britain

Ireland's contributions to the literature of the piano, during his entire
productive period, while generally modern in feeling, have avoided stylistic extremes and have shown from first to last little change in technical
method. The pianoforte writing is idiomatic, with a sympathetic approach
to the instrument; the short pieces all have distinctive titles that appeal
to the imagination and are often strikingly apposite.

Decorations

  The Island Spell

A bell-like motive, in detached notes, with
accompanying figures divided between the
hands, constitutes the main material of the
piece, which has a fortissimo carillon effect
in the middle, then dies away in a delicate
pianissimo.

Moon-glade	Soft arpeggio figures accompany a short lyrical phrase that is developed briefly; adroit pedaling is required, but there are no other technical difficulties.
The Scarlet Ceremonies	Brilliant and rather difficult; the right hand is called upon, in the main section, for continuous double-note trills and tremolos, against the rhythmically vigorous left hand. (Augener)

Preludes

The Undertone	A two-bar figure in even eighth notes and in 5/8 rhythm persists throughout this prelude and accompanies the gently expressive upper voice. Sensitive feeling for tonal balance is needed.
Obsession	A constantly repeated three-note rhythmic figure justifies the title of this restless and somewhat dissonant piece. The moderate tempo and comfortably lying arpeggio figures present only medium difficulty.
The Holy Boy	Deliberately simple and naive; smooth legato and expressive treatment are requisites.
Fire of Spring	Again a piece of moderate technical demands for the average hand. A good rhythmic drive for its urgent phrases and irregular groupings is necessary. (Boosey & Hawkes)

London Pieces

Chelsea Reach	Slow moving legato chords, suggesting the motion of the water of a large river approaching the sea.
Ragamuffin	A rollicking rhythmical tune, straightforward technically and musically.
Soho Forenoons	Melodious, but more sophisticated harmonically than No. 1 and No. 2. It has double-note passages that require some digital skill. (Augener)
Equinox	Has an effective étude-like character, with continuous five-note rotational figures. (Augener)

Green Ways

The Cherry Tree	A graceful piece with lyrical quality; its rippling incidental figuration lies easily for the hand.
Cypress	A small motive that has been used in "The Cherry Tree" reappears here, in a slower tempo, associated with a wistful bass figure.
The Palm and May	The "tree motive" is heard again, in livelier guise, in a bright, rhythmically vital final

number, with some brilliant passages requiring
good finger technique.
(Boosey & Hawkes)

Sonata

This, which dates from 1920, has been almost
entirely neglected in recent years. It is,
however, a skillfully constructed and imaginative work that might well bear re-examination
and would stand comparison with most compositions of similar aims produced in the past
thirty years. It has a vigorous first movement,
a lyrically expressive slow movement and an
imposing finale requiring a great deal of
power. The technical demands are considerable—a good double-note technique, brilliant
staccato octaves and chords, and sensitive
tonal discrimination.
(Augener)

Sonatina

This has shared the neglect of the sonata, but
is much lighter in texture and much easier of
access, technically and musically. The opening Moderato is given much of its character
by a little six-note triplet figure which appears
constantly throughout, during the prevailing
legato flow. A short slow movement, the
legato double-note passages of which suggest
instruments, leads directly to a final Rondo,
with perpetual rhythmic (gigue-like) triplets
that need good fingers and bring the little
work to a brilliant conclusion.
(Oxford University Press)

PHILIP JARNACH (1892-   ) French-born Spaniard

Sonatina, Op. 18
(Romancero I)

An intense work demanding concentration and
musicianship. Freely chromatic. Constantly
changing textures; Allegretto vivace, Concitato,
Sostenuto assai quasi largo e con summa
espressione.
(Schott)

Drei Klavierstücke
  Ballabile
  Sarabande
  Burlesca

Three dance pieces, the last one a lengthy,
animated grotesque, strongly rhythmic in
emphasis. Difficult.
(Schott)

Kleine Klavierstücke

Ten miniatures, mostly two- and three-part
writing. Not for children. Could be used as
a group.
(Schott)

Das Amrumer Tagebuch

Three pieces: majestic chordal Hymnus,
atmospheric Elegie with strong, climactic
middle section, wild Sturmreigen with quiet
ending.
(Schott)

VALERY JELOBINSKY (1912-1946) U.S.S.R.

Six Short Etudes, Op. 19 (1933)	To be played as a group.
Toccata	Brilliant, perpetual motion.
Nocturne	Widespread sonorities à la Rachmaninoff.
Valse	Brilliant. Difficult skips, bravura.
Reminiscence	Florid, chromatic melody.
Danse	Bravura 6/8, difficult octaves.
Recitatif	Quiet improvisation. (Leeds Music)

ANDRÉ JOLIVET (1905-) France

Cinq Danses Rituelles (1947)	An exotic, dynamic group. Difficult.
Danse initiatique	Irregular meters. Florid melodic line over atmospheric chords and syncopated rhythms. Big climax, quiet close.
Danse du Héros	Wild, furious, hammered leit-motif, bold figuration.
Danse nuptiale	Flexible, lyric, irregular phrases. Big climax, quiet ending.
Danse du rapt	Simulated drum basses, muttering effects, rapid passages, steady 4/4.
Danse funéraire	Processional. Irregular meters, intense outbursts. (Durand)

DMITRI KABALEVSKY (1904-) U.S.S.R.

Although many Soviet composers take pleasure in writing for children, Kabalevsky seems to be outstanding in his flair for meeting the problems of young players. There is a vividness to the style that catches the attention of young students and the pianistic settings are always interesting and colorful without being too demanding. The sonatas and preludes are, of course, on a completely different level requiring a developed pianism and musical maturity. The difference between the second and the third sonata is striking, indicating a complete change in musical orientation.

Fifteen Children's Pieces, Op. 27 Ten Children's Pieces, Op. 27 Twenty-four Little Pieces, Op. 39 Four Little Pieces, Op. 14	Mostly in the lower middle grades except for the pieces in Opus 39, which are for first- and second-grade students. (Leeds Music)
Sonatina in C Major, Op. 13, No. 1	Bright, clear piece, not difficult: <u>Allegro assai</u>, <u>Andantino</u>, <u>Presto</u>. End movements brilliant. (Leeds Music)
Sonatina in G Major, Op. 13, No. 2	Less well known than the above and more serious in content. Longer than No. 1:

marchlike <u>Allegro moderato, risoluto;</u> processional <u>Sostenuto</u> in dotted rhythms; transitional <u>Moderato</u> leading to a busy two- and three-voice finale, étude style with charming three-voice fugato inserted into the rondo.

Variations, Op. 40	Two sets of easy variations for young players; the first set (twelve variations and coda) in a light, pointed style, thin in texture; the second (five variations) more serious in character. (Leeds Music)
Twenty-four Preludes, Op. 38	Great variety of pianistic styles. Requires capable pianism, easy to very difficult. (Leeds Music)
Sonata No. 2 in E-flat Major, Op. 45 (1945)	Three ample movements requiring some virtuosity: assertive <u>Allegro moderato</u>, <u>Festivamente</u> (vigorous rhythmically, with strong middle section <u>Allegro molto</u>), sonorous <u>Andante sostenuto</u> working to a broad climax; propulsive <u>Presto assai</u> as finale, spirited, rhythmic, brilliant. (Leeds Music)
Sonata No. 3 in F Major, Op. 46	Shorter than No. 2, more conventional in harmonic and melodic vocabulary: <u>Allegro con moto</u> with flowing, suave melodies interrupted by agitated middle section; short <u>Andante cantabile</u> with melody in inner voice; dancelike finale <u>Allegro giocoso</u> with brilliant climaxes. (Leeds Music)

ZOLTÁN KODÁLY (1882-) Hungary

Nine Piano Pieces, Op. 3	Exploration of various musical ideas (somewhat akin to the Bartók Bagatelles). Essentially improvisatory in style, demanding rubato, flexibility in rhythm, imagination, humor, facility in chord and interval playing. See especially No. 2 (<u>Andante poco rubato</u>), No. 5 (<u>Furioso</u>), No. 8 (<u>Allegro Comodo</u>, <u>burlesco</u>). Reprinted by Leeds Music with an additional <u>Valsette</u> as <u>Zongora Musica</u>, Ten Pieces for Piano Solo.
Seven Piano Pieces, Op. 11 (1910-1918)	Folklike, partly impressionist. See especially No. 3, <u>Il pleut dans la ville.</u> (Universal Edition)
Méditation sur un motif de Claude Debussy (1907)	Improvisational, sombre, sonorous. (Associated Music)
Gyermektáncok (1945)	Twelve children's dances all on the black keys, moderately difficult. Include a <u>Hornpipe</u> and a <u>Friska</u> in the Hungarian style of 1790. (Boosey & Hawkes)

ARAM KHATCHATURIAN (1903-) U.S.S.R.

The music of Khatchaturian is strongly conditioned by his background as a Soviet Armenian. The stimulus of Armenian folklore accounts for the rhapsodic freedom and colorful timbres that are to be found in his piano pieces.

Two Characteristic Pieces (1942, 1947)	Short pieces in two-part counterpoint: A Glimpse of the Ballet (melancholy adagio, expressive and rubato); Fughetta (flowing allegro moderato, chromatic and intense. (Leeds Music)
Two Pieces	Short, moderately difficult: the first a Valse-Caprice "a tempo rubato"; the second an emphatic, rhythmic Danse, strongly marked and, at times, capricious. (Leeds Music)
Adventures of Ivan	Eight pieces for students. 'A fairly long set of moderate difficulty, on the melodic, good-humored side: Ivan sings, can't go out today, is ill, goes to a party (Waltz), is very busy (Etude), is with Natasha, rides on a hobby horse and hears an exotic tale of strange lands. (Leeds Music)
Toccata	Brilliant, sonorous, driving piece of moderate difficulty with short nostalgic middle section. Requires bravura. (Leeds Music)
Poem	Good companion piece to precede the Toccata. Fairly long Allegro ma non troppo in free style, changing textures, exotic colorings. Quiet close. (Leeds Music)

CHARLES KOECHLIN (1867-1950) France

The miniature, lyric essays that constitute Koechlin's contribution to the piano repertoire have much to commend them to student, professional and amateur. Koechlin's fresh linear and harmonic qualities have the melodic freedom of plain chant and the clear, open sonorities reminiscent of the parallel movements of early organum. At times the pianistic writing attains a complexity of texture in the use of multiple chord structures but, even in these instances, there is a quality to the sonorities that is completely refreshing.

Douze Esquisses, Op. 41, Nos. 1 and 2	Two series, twelve pieces in each. Songs without words in a variety of styles: melodic writing over spread-out harmonies, chordal essays, flowing contrapuntal pieces, quasi-counterpoint within broad, sonorous chord movements, organ style, a few pieces in the style of popular songs. (Oxford University Press)

Douze Petites Pièces, Op. 41 bis	Tiny essays in program music: <u>Return of Spring</u>, <u>Garden Roses</u>, <u>Cross Country</u>, <u>Fisherman's Song</u> etc. Neatly written in light harmonic or contrapuntal style. No time signatures, only occasional bar lines. Require musicality and musicianship. Easy. (Oxford University Press)
Cinq Sonatines, Op. 59	Three- and four-movement works with irregular phrase structures, clean transparent qualities, supple flowing counterpoint, some bitonality. See especially No. 3. No. 5 is the longest and most difficult. (Oxford University Press)
Nouvelles Sonatines, Op. 87	Four pieces each in four movements: Nos. 1 and II contain folk-song elements, Nos. III and IV are more complicated in texture. (Salabert)
Paysages et Marines, Op. 63	Two collections, six pieces in each. Landscape and marine sketches, mostly lyric. Often crammed with notes (as many as ten different tones in a single chord) but the sonorities are clear and spacious. Fairly difficult musically. (Oxford University Press)

JULIAN KREIN (1913-   ) U.S.S.R.

Six Pieces, Op. 40 (pub. 1938)	Poetic pieces in free style harmonically oriented toward the French. Not easy. (Leeds Music)
Suite on Uzbek Folk Themes (1942)	Ten spirited pieces on folk material. Quite long. See especially No. 1. (Leeds Music)

CONSTANT LAMBERT (1905-1951) Great Britain

Sonata	Lengthy work based on jazz idioms. Difficult.
Allegro molto marcato	Vigorous, strongly syncopated rhythms in modern vein.
Nocturne	Blues melody set off by two contrasting sections in rapid ragtime style.
Finale	Brilliant, lengthy movement, dramatic ending. (Oxford University Press)
Elegy (1938)	Short, improvisational <u>Lento</u>, <u>molto rubato</u>. Impassioned, energetic. (Oxford University Press)

G. FRANCESCO MALIPIERO (1882-   ) Italy

Malipiero leans heavily on impressionist methods. His piano pieces are suggestive or descriptive, sometimes restricting themselves to mere sketches which he assembles into cycles or short collections. Of these

the Preludi autunnali and Barlumi may be singled out as especially interesting. Longer works such as the Pasqua di Resurrezione are held together
by essentially programmatic devices. The difficulties are not excessive.

Poemetti Lunari (1909-1910)	Seven pieces. See especially No. IV (Presto scherzando) and No. VII (an extended grotesque, agitated and impulsive). (Salabert)

Preludi autunnali
(1914)

Lento, ma carrezzevole	An impressionist nocturne. Flowing, chromatic figuration, rudimentary melodies.
Ritenuto, ma spigliato	Distant horn calls. Variety of walking, flowing and running figures. Short, atmospheric.
Lento, triste	Sombre dirge, ostinato harmonies.
Veloce	Rapid scherzo, transparent textures, brilliant and gay. (Salabert)

Poemi Asolani (1916)

La Notte dei morti	Macabre, sullen, chordal, atmospheric.
Dittico	Wry, whimsical. Fragmentary melodies, impressionist sonorities.
I Partenti	Improvisatory. Flexible, flowing phrases and figuration leading to fast, short dance and quiet Lento ending. (J. & W. Chester)

Barlumi (1917)	One of his best sets.
Non lento troppo	Atmospheric.
Lento	Sombre, melodic, chordal, widely separated sonorities in parallel open fifths.
Vivace	Busily moving double notes, opposed sonorities, changing meters. Strong ending.
Lento, misterioso	Hushed chords and melodies, chordal and broken chordal sonorities.
Molto vivace	Brisk dance, vigorous, guttural bass patterns, fast repeated and parallel chords.

Armenia (1917)	"Armenian songs treated symphonically." Sequence of songs each treated in different textures and connected into a single piece. Not long. Medium difficulty. No climactic point. Good encore. (Salabert)

Maschere che passano (1918)	Five suggestive sketches. Not too easy.
Allegro vivace	Grotesque, capricious.
Lento, ma non troppo	Melodic, chordal, processional, con una certa goffaggione (with a certain awkwardness).
Mosso, spiritato	Fleeting sketch, rumbling, guttural.
Un poco ritenuto	Grotesque.

Vivacissimo	Furious finale. Chords, quick leaps, passage playing. (J. & W. Chester)
Hommage à Claude Debussy	Short. Diatonic, parallel triadic harmonies leading to a drumlike accompaniment. Quiet close. In Le Tombeau de Claude Debussy (Album-Edition de la Sirène).
Cavalcate (1921)	Three modes of four-legged locomotion.
Somaro	Recalcitrant donkey. Humorous. Broken rhythms, chords and octaves.
Camello	Swaying camel. Lyric Lento. Melodic-block chords and easily flowing figuration.
Destriero	Fiery steed. Rhythmic sketch. Fast, parallel, detached triadic chords. Climactic. (Salabert)
Il Tarlo (1922)	Four short sketches, generally impressionist in character. See especially No. 3 (interesting use of parallel harmonies) and No. 4 (gay beginning, rapid parallel organum-like harmonies, quiet end). (Salabert)
Pasqua di Resurrezione (1924)	An extended piece, partly impressionist. Parallel harmonies, broken-chord figuration, octaves, trills, alternating hands. Atmospheric throughout. Fairly difficult. (Salabert)
3 Preludi a una Fuga (1926)	Three connected preludes (tranquilly flowing, melodic-chordal Lento, brisk Scherzando) moving to a legato three-voiced Fugue with climactic ending. (Universal Edition)
Hortus Conclusus (1946)	Cycle of eight pieces in varying styles: flowing Prelude, stately Lento, scherzando Allegro, quiet Andante, subdued Tranquillo, fluid Lentamente, organ-like Allegro moderato, extended finale (quasi variazioni in eight short sections). (Ricordi)
Risonanze (1918)	Four short impressionist preludes, each exploiting a different problem in sonority.

OLIVIER MESSIAEN (1908-) France

The stylistic characteristics of Messiaen's piano music have strong roots in his beliefs as a Catholic mystic. The following works are program pieces whose rhythmic, melodic, contrapuntal and general sonorous organization serve to project moods and ideas clearly religious in inspiration. The pianistic textures include repeated harmonies that achieve an enveloping, swimming sonority; contrapuntal devices that utilize great changes of register to mask imitative phrases (carefully pointed out by the composer's own remarks in the score); and, in some cases, a play with those intricate rhythmic theories for which Messiaen seems to be at least partially indebted to early Hindu theoreticians (retrograde rhythms, rhythmic canons, chromatic rhythms, rhythmic modes, etc.). His own book, <u>Technique de mon langage musical</u> (Paris, 1944), is indispensable for a thorough understanding of his procedures. The chordal complexities, the mere multiplicity of notes and the simultaneous planes of sound in which he often indulges make for considerable pianistic difficulties.

Préludes

La Colombe	Short, expressive, lazy sonorities.
Chant d'Extase dans un Paysage triste	Slow, sad, subdued.
Le Nombre Léger	Light, rapid figuration supporting a spun out melodic line.
Instants Défunts	Distant, atmospheric, short.
Les Sons Impalpables du Rêve	Extended piece, climactic moments.
Cloches d'Angoisse et Larmes d'Adieu	Very slow, extended piece, complex figuration.
Plainte calme	Short, melodic essay.
Un Reflet dan le Vent	Flowing pianism, long and climactic. (Durand)
Vingt Regards sur l'Enfant Jésus	A very lengthy cycle dealing with contemplation of the infant Jesus by twenty different personages: the Father, the Star, the Virgin, the Angels, etc. Leit motifs represent God, the Star, the Cross and the heavenly arch. Rhythmic canons, polymodality, wide variety of complex pianistic sonorities. "More than in all my preceding works, I have sought a language of mystic love, at once varied, powerful and tender, sometimes brutal, in a multi-colored ordering." (Durand)

NIKOLAI MIASKOVSKY (1881-1951) U.S.S.R.

Miaskovsky is an example of a prolific composer with a large number of piano works to his credit written in a not very modern manner but nonethe-less characteristic and individual in content. They range from pieces of moderate difficulty and length to extended large-scale sonatas requiring a full virtuoso equipment. His works are not sufficiently known; but, judging from what is at present available, seem to merit further exploration.

Fourth Sonata, Op. 27 (pub. 1947)	Large-scale work demanding complete pianism. Declamatory opening <u>Allegro moderato</u>; variations on a theme quasi-sarabanda; lengthy toccata-like finale with many problems in double notes. (Leeds Music)

Yellowed Pages,
Op. 31 (pub. 1948)

Seven contrasting pieces. See especially No. 1 (sombre, declamatory melody), No. 4 (elfin-like scherzo), No. 6 (sharply opposed wildness and melancholy), No. 7 (modal, processional). (Leeds Music)

Stylisations, Op. 73 (1946)

Nine pieces derived from classic dance styles. Conservative harmonies. Moderate difficulty. (Leeds Music)

Six Improvisations, Op. 74

Short pieces in a post-romantic chromatic idiom: broad, chordal Prélude, impetuous Élan, quiet Berceuse, sonorous Carillons, sombre Nocturne, Last Story as conclusion. (Leeds Music)

Sonata in D Minor, Op. 83 (1949)

Three movements. Easy, conventional both melodically and harmonically. (Leeds Music)

MARCEL MIHALOVICI (1898-   ) Rumania

Ricercari, Op. 46

Free variations on an eight-bar passacaglia theme, the variations grouped into eleven movements. Large-scale, serious work, freely chromatic. Requires grasp of large masses of sound, big style, virtuosity, variety of touch. Quiet ending. (Heugel, through Mercury Music)

DARIUS MILHAUD (1892-   ) France

The following works for solo piano are characterised by the same easy-going, casual, sensitive quality that pervades Milhaud's recent informal autobiography, Notes sans Musique (René Julliard, Paris, 1949). Except for parts of the two sonatas, the pieces have an informal, conversational quality marked by a certain intimacy and restraint. The difficulties are moderate in this music which is, by and large, for the home, the study or the enjoyment of a few friends and, only in some cases, for the concert hall. Suavity, sensitivity and polish are its main requirements. Milhaud's dealings with polytonality find frequent expression in his piano pieces and, where this preoccupation is joined with a factor such as exotic Brazilian elements, the result is unique.

Printemps (1915-1920)

Two sets of three pieces each; intimate, relaxed, evocative, quiet, short. Require suave legato. (La Sirène Musicale, through Associated Music)

Sonata No. 1 (1916)

Décidé
Pastoral
Rhythmé

Clear, sonorous work, uninhibited qualities. Folklike melodies, chords in superimposed fifths, parallel open sonorities, bitonal structures, interesting changes in texture. Difficulties not excessive but require full use of the keyboard, especially chord techniques. (A. Z. Mathot)

Saudades do Brazil (1920)
  Vol. I
    Sorocaba
    Botafogo
    Leme
    Copacabana
    Ipanema
    Gavea

Suite of dances in sophisticated popular Brazilian style, each dance two pages long. The titles refer to various sections of Rio de Janeiro. Ingenious use of bitonality, all sorts of interesting piano styles and sonorities: tango and habanera rhythms, ostinato basses, chord and double-note techniques, large stretches. Problems in mixing sonorities with the pedal.

  Vol. II
    Corcovado
    Tijuca
    Paineras
    Sumaré
    Laranjeiras
    Paysandu

Especially to be noted are the dances in the second volume.
(Eschig)

L'Automne (1932)

  Septembre

A propulsive movement ("allant"), sixteenth-note scale and broken-chord figuration. Some double notes.

  Alfama

Lively sixteenth-note figuration in both hands, some octaves.

  Adieu

Intimate, relaxed song, quasi-contrapuntal.
(Salabert)

Quatre Romances sans Paroles (1933)

Four short, easy, lyrical sketches.
(Salabert)

L'Album de Madame Bovary (1933)

Series of seventeen pieces extracted from the film music for <u>Madame Bovary</u>. For amateurs. Real "Album Blätter," short, sensitive, easy, Schumannesque.
(Elkan-Vogel)

Trois Valses

Also from <u>Madame Bovary</u>.
(Elkan-Vogel)

Le Tour de l'Exposition (1933 revised 1937)

Animated 6/8. Some double notes and stretches. Fresh, open quality.
In "<u>A l'Exposition</u>" (album published by Salabert).

Four Sketches (1941)

Pieces of moderate length.

  Eglogue
  Madrigal

Pastoral 6/8, lyrical.
Melody in 4/4, three- and four-part accompaniment. Short contrasting middle section, more florid.

  Alameda
  Sobre la Loma

Melancholy habanera, atmospheric.
Rhumba rhythms, some florid pianism, most difficult of the set.
(Mercury Music)

The Household Muse (1914)

Fifteen short genre pieces in three volumes treating such diverse household activities as: <u>The Awakening</u>, <u>Poetry</u>, <u>Cooking</u>, <u>Laundry</u>, <u>The Son Who Paints</u>, <u>Flowers</u>, <u>Reading at Night</u>, etc.

Sensitive lyric sketches, restrained and
polished, avoiding triteness. Require imagination. Not difficult.
(Elkan-Vogel)

Une Journée (1946)

L'Aube
La Matinée
Midi
L'Après Midi
Le Crépuscule

Set of lyrical miniatures, technically easy,
requiring sensitivity. Generally subdued in
character.
(Mercury Music)

L'Enfant Aime (1948)

Five short children's pieces. Chromatics.
Require some sophistication and facility.
(Leeds Music)

Sonata No. 2 (1949)

More intimate than the first sonata (except for
the last movement). Mostly two- or three-
voiced textures with emphasis on a flowing,
supple, linear motion. Passage playing, some
octaves. Requires sensitive phrase articulation and legato.
(Heugel, through Mercury Music)

**Le Candélabre à Sept
Branches (The Seven-
Branched Candelabrum)
(1951)**

Suite of seven pieces on the seven festivals
that make up the Jewish Calendar: New
Year (quiet, dignified good spirits); Day
of Atonement (short, sombre); Feast of the
Tabernacles (joyous); Resistance of the
Maccabeans (vigorous, marcato); Feast of
Esther (stately-moving 5/4); Passover (short,
quiet); Feast of Weeks (expressive, quiet).
(Israeli Music Publications, through Leeds
Music)

ERNEST J. MOERAN (1894-1951) Great Britain

Stalham River

A poetical piece, with flowing legato chord and
double-note passages requiring good tonal
control. A central section with rotational figuration and a fortissimo climax is effective and
less difficult.
(J. & W. Chester)

Toccata

Brilliant, with rotation figures that for the
most part lie easily under the hand. A pleasing
contrast comes from a short cantilena of folk-
song type.
(J. & W. Chester)

Summer Valley

Dedicated to Delius and having much of his
characteristic quality, this is a gently expressive piece with siciliano-like rhythm—not
difficult.
(Oxford University Press)

| Bank Holiday | Rhythmical chord and double-note technique is the main technical feature of this cheerful piece, with occasional spice in the harmonies. (Oxford University Press) |

FEDERICO MOMPOU (1893-   ) Spain

Mompou is a miniaturist. His tiny pieces have the fleeting quality of quick, casual sketches. Each piece is confined to a few ideas similar in many ways to Satie. The very look of the page, with its only occasional bar lines, French slurs ("laisser vibrer") and personal remarks to the player ("répétez, je vous prie") shows his affinity to the Frenchman. A dash of Spanish song and dance adds a flavorful quality to these predominantly descriptive genre essays.

Scènes d'Enfants (1915)	Five genre pieces, not difficult. Quickly-changing descriptive phrases. Popular quality, especially No. 5. (Salabert)
Suburbis (1916-17)	Five suburban scenes of moderate length and difficulty: street airs and dances, descriptive passages. (Salabert)
Canco y Dansa	Four pieces in popular Spanish style, polished, simple, suave, unpretentious. See especially No. 1. (Salabert)
Fêtes lointaines (1920)	Cycle of six pieces, mostly dancelike. See especially Nos. 3, 5 and 6. (Salabert)
Trois Variations	Unaccompanied melody, march (les soldats), waltz (courtoisie), "in the silence of the night" (le crapaud). Short, easy, quiet. (Associated Music)
Dialogues	Two atmospheric sketches, quiet conversations, the melodies dialoguing with one another. Widely spaced Scriabinesque figuration, relaxed, sonorous. (Associated Music)
Charmes	"....forme primitive d'incantation": six tiny coloristic sketches invoking fleeting moods. (Associated Music)

JOAQUIN NIN (1883-   ) Spain

The same Nin who succeeded in unearthing and publishing the rich two-volume collection of Spanish successors to Scarlatti has contributed some original pieces well worth playing. The style is basically romantic and thoroughly impregnated with indigenous Spanish harmonic procedures, guitar effects and flamenco stylistic elements (vocal cadenzas, rhythmic accompaniments, etc.). Especially rewarding are the three Danses Espagnoles.

Cadeña de Valses (1927)	A lengthy chain of waltzes (Spanish dance style) with a short musical <u>comentario</u> (commentary) between each of the first six. A romantic evocation of masters of the waltz with <u>Messages</u> to Schubert, Ravel, Chopin and a <u>Homenaje à la Jota</u> (Spanish national dance). Not easy. (Eschig)
Mensaje à Claudio Debussy (1929)	Message to Debussy, a "symphonic sketch." An extended, melancholy <u>Tempo di Habanera</u>, lush, free, climactic. (Eschig)
Trois Danses Espagnoles (1938)	
Danza Murciana	Extended piece. Not easy. Alternating 6/8 and 3/4. Improvisatory cadenzas.
Danza Andaluza	Rapid rhythmic dance on <u>El Vito</u>. Repeated notes, percussive guitar effects, brilliant.
Secunda Danza Iberica	Melancholy dance in 3/8. Full of guitar intonations, free vocal cadenzas. (Eschig)
Canto de cuña para los Huerfanos d'España (1938)	Lengthy, florid, modal berceuse for the orphans of Spain. (Eschig)
Iberian Dance (1925)	Spirited, percussive <u>Allegro vivace</u>, expressive, sonorous <u>Lento</u>, free recitatives, spirited conclusion. Long, not easy. (Eschig)

RICARDO PICK-MANGIAGALLI (1882-   ) Italy

Danse d'Olaf	From <u>Deux Lunaires</u>. Virtuoso, scherzando dance, traditional concert style. Brilliant, scintillating, long, difficult. (Ricordi)

GABRIEL PIERNE (1863-1937) France

Variations in C Minor, Op. 42 (1918)	Large-scale work (thirty-six pages) exploiting the coloristic and bravura resources of the piano, sometimes requiring four staves for its notation. Demands a developed octave equipment. Cortot considers this one of the peaks of the twentieth-century French school of pianism. (J. Hamelle)

WILLEM PIJPER (1894-1947) Holland

Sonatina No. 2 (1925)	Short one-movement work, constantly changing irregular meters and tempi. Flexible, asymmetrical phrases. On the scherzando side with atmospheric contrasts. Not easy. (Oxford University Press)

Sonatina No. 3 (1925)	Short, capricious. Touches of impressionism and jazz. Irregular meters. Requires facility and precision in touch. (Oxford University Press)
Sonata (1930)	Asymmetrical meters throughout. Short, rhythmic <u>Allegro</u>; sombre, impressionist <u>Adagio molto</u>; brilliant, energetic <u>Allegro volante</u>. (Oxford University Press)

LEONID POLOVINKIN (1894-) U.S.S.R.

Fourth Sonata, Op. 18 (1926)	Large-scale work in three movements. Strong qualities, somewhat bare in sonority. Spirited <u>Presto</u>, pensive <u>Lento</u>, final <u>Allegro con brio</u>. (Leeds Music)
Five Dances (pub. 1945)	Dainty <u>Sarabande</u> and <u>Gavotte</u> and three South American dances (<u>Rumba</u>, <u>Tango</u> and a lengthy <u>Paso Doble</u>).
Second Divertimento (pub. 1947)	Four lyric pieces in salon style. Not difficult. Includes a waltz and a set of variations.

FRANCIS POULENC (1899-) France

Poulenc has written extensively for the piano. Although there are no works that are weighty or essentially serious in character, there is a wide variety of pieces characteristically witty, gay, intimate or, on occasion, brilliant and bravura in style. His unashamedly sentimental melodic writing is basically "music hall" in character. Harmonically speaking, an over-ripe sonority prevails. The pianistic figuration is generally salon style. Perhaps the <u>Napoli</u> suite and <u>Les Soirées de Nazelles</u> may be considered his most important works for piano solo. They both require considerable pianistic achievement for a convincing projection.

Mouvement Perpetuels (1918)	Not difficult, short.
Assez modéré	Best known of the three. Ostinato bass, "sans nuances."
Très modéré	Short melody, walking eighth notes. "indifferent."
Alerte	Bright, more sonorous than the previous two, quiet ending. (J. & W. Chester)
Trois Pièces (1918-1928)	
Pastorale	Short, atmospheric, "calme et mystérieux."
Toccata	Bravura perpetual motion. Alternating hands, passage playing, broken-chord figures, swinging melodies.
Hymne	Processional chordal opening, florid melody leading to some elaboration and a return double forte. Quiet ending. (Heugel, through Mercury Music)
Suite (1920)	A light work, predominantly on the white keys.

Presto Andante Vif	Folk and popular quality to the melodies. Ambulatory qualities to the end movements, constantly busy and propulsive. Moderate difficulty. (J. & W. Chester)
Five Impromptus (1920-21)	Short characteristic pieces: 1-agitated perpetual motion. 2-brusque, vivacious waltz. 3-satirical, jazzlike. 4-"violent." 5-sombre <u>Andante,</u> funereal quality. Entire set is interesting. (J. & W. Chester)
Intermezzo in A-flat Major	Salon style, fluid, widely spaced figuration supporting the melody. (Associated Music)
Valse	From the <u>Album des Six</u>. Short rapid caricature. (Associated Music)
Presto in B-flat Major	Staccato passage playing, melody over broken-chord figuration, legato middle section. Light, pointed style. Good short encore. (Salabert)

Feuillets d'Album
 	
  Ariette
 	
  Rêve
  Gigue
	
	Mostly two voices, middle section in a popular sentimental style.
	Melody over repeated chords.
	Prestissimo 6/8, double notes, staccato.
	(Salabert)

Napoli (1922-1925)
 	
  Barcarolle
 	
  Nocturne
 	
  Caprice Italien
	
	Short lyric piece, melody with accompaniment, crossed meters, piquant harmonies.
	Atmospheric, lush, short. Brusque middle section.
	An "all out" <u>Presto;</u> brilliant, pianistic tarantella, recitative-like cadenza leading to popular Neapolitan melodies broken by pianistic flourishes and dance tunes. Long and difficult. Brilliant close.
	(Salabert)

Huit Nocturnes (1929-1938)	More twilight than nocturnal! A cycle assembled from various creative periods. No. 8 serves as coda. Melodically the style is strongly popular, sentimental in flavor, supported by lush harmonies and widely-spaced sonorous figuration. See especially No. 3 in F major (simple and effective), No. 4 in C minor (slow, short waltz), No. 6 in G major (calm and spacious) and the relaxed coda. (Heugel, through Mercury Music)

Villageoises (1933)

Five little children's pieces and a coda ("résumé). Easy waltz, march, lively melody, polka and a round. Everything melodic. Attractive group for young students. (Salabert)

Improvisations (1934)

Vol. I (1-6)
Vol. II (7-10)

Informal pieces of moderate length, salon style; in turn suave, tongue-in-cheek, gavotte-like, marchlike, lyric and brilliant. (Salabert)

Suite Francaise (1935)
(after Claude Gervaise, sixteenth century)

Bransle de Bourgogne
.Pavane
Petite marche militaire
Complainte
Bransle de Champagne
Sicilienne
Carillon

Seven pieces in quasi-archaic style with added modernisms. Completely diatonic, modal. Fairly easy. (Durand)

Les Soirées de Nazelles

Préambule
Variations (8)
Cadence
Final

"The variations which form the center of this work were improvised at Nazelles during the course of long soirées in the country when the author played at "portraits" with friends grouped around the piano. We hope today that, presented between a Préambule and a Finale they will evoke the memory of this game played in the setting of a Touraine salon, a window opening on to the night." (Composer's note.) Requires an all-round pianism. Can be played with omissions. (Elkan-Vogel)

Bourrée au Pavillon d'Auvergne

Excellent for young players. Melody over drone in the bass, drum effects. Short. In A l'Exposition (album published by Salabert)

SERGE PROKOFIEFF (1891-1953) U.S.S.R.

Prokofieff is one of the most prolific composers of contemporary piano music. The earlier works are in a post-romantic idiom whose over-ripe qualities reach over into an opus as recent as the second movement of the seventh sonata. Beginning with Opus 4 the piano writing assumes a more dissonant, percussive character with emphasis on the grotesque (Sarcasms, Suggestion diabolique, Toccata). This tendency also invades the lyricism of the Visions Fugitives. The most difficult segment of his piano music seems to date from the time of Prokofieff's stay in Paris (1922-1933): Fifth Sonata, Things in Themselves, Two Sonatinas, Piano Pieces, Opus 59 and Thoughts, Opus 62. Here the abstruse nature of the writing, the harmonic vocabulary, the general texture and the organization of the phrases all present the player with searching problems in projection. The sonatas culminate in the sprawling, massive sixth; the biting, compact seventh and the lyrical eighth.

Pianistically the demands vary. There is music at all levels of difficulty since Prokofieff has addressed himself to children as well as to virtuosi. The early Toccata is still a formidable study in double notes, chords and skips. Octaves as well as demanding passage playing are predominant features of the more extended works, with the passages asking for a high degree of articulation and bite. A good staccato is an asset. The same for a large hand, strength and power. On the other hand, the children's pieces are very moderate in their demands but still ask for some agility in lateral movements since no one of them remains in a five-finger position.

It must also be mentioned that Prokofieff has transcribed much of his ballet, theatre and film music for the piano. In this category are Opus 75 (Romeo and Juliet); Opus 77 (Hamlet); Opus 95 (Cinderella); Opus 96 (War and Peace, Lermontov) and Opus 97 (Cinderella). It is also obvious that much of the composer's preoccupation with dance genres in the piano works comes from his interest in stage and theatre music.

The music is handled by Leeds Music Corporation and Boosey & Hawkes (Edition Gutheil and Edition Russe), the latter especially for works of the Paris period. For a full discussion of his life, works and music consult Israel Nestyev: Serge Prokofieff, His Musical Life, Knopf, 1946 (includes a complete list of works up to Opus 100).

Sonata No. 1, Op. 1, in F Minor (1909)	One movement, youthful, romantic qualities, broad pianistic style.
Four Etudes, Op. 2 (1909)	Difficult studies in double notes, chords, octaves, running passage playing, chromatics, broken octaves.
Four Pieces, Op. 4 (1910-1912)	Reminiscence (pensive melody, chromatic harmony), Élan (vigorous, short, double notes), Despair (agitated andante, chromatic ostinato throughout), Suggestion diabolique (grotesque, bravura, demands endurance).
Toccata, Op. 11 (1912)	Perpetual motion. Leaps, double notes, fast chromatic-chord passages in contrary motion. Very difficult. Demands endurance.
Ten Pieces, Op. 12 (1913)	Crisp March, Gavotte, catchy Rigaudon, capricious Mazurka built completely on interval of the fourth, Caprice, Legend, broken-chord Prélude, Allemande, wry, staccato Scherzo humoristique, Scherzo.
Sonata No. 2, Op. 14, in D Minor (1912)	Lyric Allegro ma non troppo, effective Scherzo with staccato double-note figuration punctuated by motives crossing the hands, melodic Andante (melody surrounded by chromatic double note figuration), concluding tarantella, Vivace in 6/8.
Sarcasms, Op. 17 (1912-1914)	Cycle of five pieces, ironic, brusque, percussive: Tempestoso (sharply accented non-legato, marcato), Allegro rubato (improvisational, plucked chords, arpeggio flourishes), Allegro precipitato (bitonal), No title (dotted, jerky rhythms), Precipitosissimo (loud, fast repeated chords, contrasting melancholy middle section).

Visions fugitives, Op. 22 (1915-1917)	Twenty pieces. Short, fleeting, poetic sketches, mostly lyrical with contrasting movements interspersed. Demand sensitivity, variety of sound, imagination.
Sonata No. 3, Op. 28, in A Minor (1917)	The most popular of the sonatas. In one movement (Allegro tempestoso). Brilliant, driving, bravura. Demands agility, power and vitality.
Sonata No. 4, Op. 29, in C Minor (1917)	Entire sonata not as demanding as those to follow: Allegro molto sostenuto (predominantly lyric, lugubrious), Andante assai (melody surrounded by rich, widely spaced figuration), Allegro con brio, ma non troppo (an engaging rondo requiring some facility).
Tales of the Old Grandmother, Op. 31 (1918)	Four short, simple melodic pieces. Could be used for moderately advanced student.
Four Pieces, Op. 32 (1918)	Dance, Minuet, Gavotte, Waltz. Of these four the Gavotte (F-sharp minor) is superior, easy, witty and short.
Sonata No. 5, Op. 38 in C Major (1923)	Relatively short: Allegro tranquillo (fresh, square melodies, parallel triadic harmonizations), Andante (dancelike, miniature, grotesque), Un poco allegretto (straightforward, open quality, takes large hand).
Things in Themselves, Op. 45 (1928) Allegro moderato Moderato scherzando	Two rather long, cryptic pieces demanding a high degree of musicianship and pianism. Abstruse and involved: the first having a certain rhythmic and melodic propulsion, the second more lyric in quality. Problems in pedaling.
Six Transcriptions, Op. 52 (1931) Intermezzo Rondo Etude Scherzino Andante Scherzo	From the ballet The Prodigal Son, a song, Opus 35; the Andante from the Quartet Opus 50 and the Scherzo from a Sinfonietta. Difficult, the Scherzo especially effective; dry, staccato, bravura.
Two Sonatinas, Op. 54	Short, sophisticated works each in three movements. See especially No. 1 in E minor: Allegro moderato (abrupt, laconic motives set off by lyric phrases), Adagietto (arioso) Allegretto (gentle dance, light in texture).
Thoughts, Op. 62 (1933-34)	Introspective, bare, abstruse: Adagio penseroso, Moderato (melody doubled two octaves apart, treated heterophonically with florid variations in right hand), Lento (three-voice choral-like setting of a melody), Andante (most extended of the set, melody and countermelodies, varied textures, mostly chromatic).

Music for Children, Op. 65 (1935)	Twelve easy pieces covering a variety of problems. Excellent introduction to Prokofieff. In the tradition of the Kinderscenen, in the spirit of Peter and the Wolf.
Ten Pieces from Romeo and Juliet, Op. 75 (1937)	Short, characteristic sketches: Mercutio, Friar Lawrence, Juliet, etc. Can be played separately or as group.
Gavotte, Op. 77, in E-flat Major from music to Hamlet	Crisp, incisive, effective, not difficult.
Sonata No. 6, Op. 82, in A Major (1939-1940)	Massive work demanding resourceful virtuoso equipment and grasp of large structural masses.
Allegro moderato	Biting, dissonant sonata-allegro. Long, energetic development, shortened recapitulation. Double notes, arpeggio sweeps, interlocking thumbs, repeated notes, quick skips, percussive chords ("col pugno"—with the fist), screaming passages in extreme upper register.
Allegretto	Marchlike. Quiet staccato chords, melodic middle section.
Tempo di valzer lentissimo	Slow waltz, romantic, lengthy.
Vivace	Brilliant closing rondo. Clear, fresh melodies, effective return of material from opening movement. Thunderous coda.
Sonata No. 7, Op. 83	Best known after No. 3, shorter than No. 6. Allegro inquieto (percussive, bare, laconic), Andante caloroso (unexpectedly romantic in viewpoint), Precipitato (perpetual motion, toccata-like in 7/8 building to imposing climax).
Sonata No. 8, Op. 84, in B-flat Major (1939-1940)	Longest and most lyrical of the sonatas, more gentle and less harsh than the sixth or seventh. Songful, Schumannesque Andante dolce with powerful climax; minuet-like Andante sognando becoming more and more florid in figuration; long Vivace (fast-moving rondo) set off by a scherzo Allegro ben marcato, the whole being completely joyous and spirited.
Three Pieces, Op. 95 (1942)	Intermezzo, Gavotte, Valse Lente from the ballet Cinderella. The Gavotte comes off best, piquant and charming.

NIKOLAS RAKOV (1908-   ) U.S.S.R.

Water Colours	Nine easy pieces. Light, salon style. (Leeds Music)
Classical Suite (1943)	Prelude, Menuet, Gavotte, Air, Gigue. (Leeds Music)

Eight Pieces on a Russian Folk Theme (pub. 1950)	Short, diatonic, not difficult. Theme treated in a variety of dance styles. See especially Nos. 2, 6 and 8. Can be played as a group. (Leeds Music)
Variations in B Minor (pub. 1950)	Folklike theme, five variations and finale. Moderate difficulty. (Leeds Music)

MAURICE RAVEL (1875-1937) France

Ravel's name is inevitably linked with Debussy's. While the latter had some undoubted influence, there is however to be noted in Ravel's work a special technical finish that reminds one of his master Fauré, and even of Saint-Saens. This fastidious workmanship is allied at times with an almost romantic lyrical quality—e.g., in "Ondine," the "Menuet" of Le Tombeau de Couperin, etc.

Editions

As with Debussy, the laws of copyright still operate (1951), and most of Ravel's compositions are printed by Durand (U.S. agents, Elkan-Vogel Co.). Some of the earlier works, originally issued by Demets, etc., are now reprinted in America—Jeux d'eau and Miroirs by Schirmer; Pavane pour une Infante defunte by Boston Music Co.

Easier pieces

There is in the work of Ravel hardly anything that can be described as technically simple, but the following are without any serious difficulty:

> Pavane pour une Infante defunte
> Minuet - on the name of Haydn
> Minuet - from Sonatine
> Menuet - from Le Tombeau de Couperin
> Forlane - from Le Tombeau de Couperin

Pavane, pour une Infante defunte (Pavan, for a dead Infanta) (1899)	A simple diatonic piece, requiring a steady rhythmic flow. One or two wide chord positions may tax a small hand. It is worth while to note that the original edition prescribed the very slow metronome speed—$\rho = 54$.
Jeux d'eau (1901)	This early composition, at first disapproved by Ravel's teacher Fauré, finally conquered the latter through its beauty and startling originality. It has no great problems for a mature pianist with a good rotational technique, and its passages lie easily under the hand. It has a permanent place in the literature similar to that of Debussy's "Reflets dan l'eau."
Sonatine (1905)	This work is in three short movements. Its themes are unified through the prevailing intervals of the fourth and its inversion, the fifth, and through some further devices of thematic rhythmical variation. Throughout there is a notable avoidance of thickness of texture,

and a fondness for the upper half of the keyboard. The first movement, in sonata form, has Ravel's usual neatness and finish; neither here nor in the second movement - a charming minuet - is there any special digital difficulty, though there is opportunity for nice tonal judgment and balance. The third movement, in modified sonata form, is more exacting, and there is here special need for careful pedaling.

Miroirs (1905)

Noctuelles (Night moths)	Delicate flickering figures and brief fragments of melody combine in a somewhat elusive piece which tests the interpreter. The pianoforte writing is idiomatic and effective.
Oiseaux tristes (Mournful birds)	Another imaginative piece, requiring accurate tonal balance and beauty of touch—otherwise not difficult.
Une barque sur l'ocean (A ship on the ocean)	Sweeping arpeggios suggest the title. The main difficulty lies in the maintenance of continuity throughout the fluctuating rhythms.
Alborado del gracioso (Aubade of the jester)	Spanish rhythms are exploited very effectively. This is much the most exacting of the set, with its rapid repeated notes and double glissandos, and the necessity for a driving energy.
La vallée des cloches (The valley of bells)	Has technical and tonal requirements similar to those of "Oiseaux tristes," though here there is an additional feature in a middle section with an extended melodic line.

Gaspard de la nuit (1908)

Ondine	This poses two main problems—the technical control of the unusual opening accompaniment figure with the prescribed pianissimo, and the avoidance of rhythmic rigidity in the expressive cantabile, mostly in the left hand.
Le gibet (The gibbet)	This eerie piece, the least difficult of the three, still has its problems of tonal balance and requires a fairly large hand.
Scarbo	One of Ravel's most difficult compositions, interpretatively and technically, picturing an impish phantom dwarf in passages that demand both great delicacy together with high speed and sharp tonal contrasts with incisive and accurate rhythm.

Minuet—on the name of Haydn (1909)	Simpler than most of Ravel's piano pieces - has unpretentious charm.
Valses nobles et sentimentales (1911)	These delightful waltzes, eight in number, occasionally reminiscent of Johann Strauss, are prophetic of Ravel's own "La Valse" (see, in particular, No. 7). They are clearly intended as a connected series, and the mournful little

theme of No. 2, together with hints of others of the set (Nos. 3, 4 and 6), appears again in the epilogue (No. 8). There are no great technical severities; except in the vigorous and forceful first waltz, delicacy rather than power is required. Ravel's harmonic technique, always logical but highly individual, has here a notably clear exposition.

Le Tombeau de Couperin (1917)

Prelude	Characterized by rapid finger passages founded mainly on a recurring six-note figure. The level of tone is generally piano or pianissimo, with only two fortissimo climaxes.
Fugue	Built on a short subject with a rather elusive rhythm, this shows Ravel's contrapuntal mastery, and repays study.
Forlane	Of the three dance movements in the suite, this is particularly original and charming. It is comparatively easy.
Rigaudon	A straightforward piece with sharply incisive rhythm and an oboe-like cantabile in the contrasting middle section.
Menuet	Technically simple, but most finished in workmanship and extremely charming in both melody and harmony.
Toccata	In a different class from the rest of the suite. A brilliant virtuoso piece; its repeated-note technique demands extreme accuracy in judgment of the key's action. For its proper effect it also requires most careful pedaling.

ALAN RAWSTHORNE (1905-   ) Great Britain

Bagatelles (1938)	Cycle of four short pieces: a scherzando _Allegro_; _Allegretto_ in siciliano vein; a scurrying _Presto non assai_; short, concluding, serious _Lento_. (Oxford University Press)
Sonatina Allegro sostenuto e misterioso Lento ma con movimento Allegretto con malinconia Allegro con brio	Serious work. First three movements on the subdued, melancholy side. Last movement stands in vivid contrast—a vigorous, brusque finale. The entire work has individuality and an earnest quality of musicianship. Requires moderate facility. (Oxford University Press)

ALBERT ROUSSEL (1869-   ) France

Suite, Op. 14 Prélude Sicilienne Bourrée Ronde	An extended work requiring complete pianistic equipment. Full, thick textures, broken-chord sonorities, large spacings, double notes, chords, passage playing. Strong, climactic ending. (Salabert)

Sonatine, Op. 16 (1912)	In two big sections, each subdivided.
Modéré - Vif et très leger	Lyric, interspersed with energetic moments (double notes) leading to a staccato scherzo (octave problems).
Très lent - très animé	Sombre chordal textures in 5/8 leading to dance-like animated finale, also in 5/8. Difficult. Requires bravura and stamina. (Salabert)
Trois Pièces, Op. 49 (1946)	
Allegro con brio	Spirited, rhythmic. Octaves and passage playing. Requires facility and drive.
Allegro grazioso	Light <u>Tempo di Valz</u>, two- and three-voiced textures.
Allegro con spirito	Longest of the set. Requires neatness, brilliance and, in the lyric middle section, an intense, heavy climax. (Durand)
Petit Canon Perpetuel (1948)	Short, lyric canon, free middle voice. Not easy. "....go back to the da capo, transposing the three voices up an octave and continue thus as far as the range of the keyboard will permit." (Durand)
Rustiques, Op. 5 (1904)	Three pieces. (Durand)
Segovia Op. 29	Originally for guitar. (Durand)
L'Accueil des Muses	Lament for Debussy, thick-textured, block chord and broken harmonies, full climax. (Editions de la Sirène)

KAREL SALOMON (1897-   ) Israel

Bagatelles on a popular theme (1947)	Eight programmatic variations on the popular Jewish tune "Am Israel Hai" (Israel Lives), depicting the sons of a newly-born nation in various surroundings; in the diaspora (agitato), in the nursery (scherzino), at school (canon), marching along (lydian mode), at sea (barcarolle), at the factory (perpetuum mobile), in Jerusalem (solemn), in Tel Aviv (energetic). Not difficult. Good for moderately advanced students. (Israeli Music Publications, through Leeds Music)

ERIK SATIE (1866-1925) France

The legend of Satie's influence on modern French composers, his friendship with Debussy, his position as forerunner and champion of "Les Six" (Auric, Tailleferre, Durey, Poulenc, Milhaud, Honegger), has consistently drawn attention away from actual knowledge and performance of his music. The piano pieces are a large segment of his small output and bear all the essential traits of his style; the satirical lampooning with which his name is invariably associated, a transparent texture, simple melodies, fresh harmonies, a complete avoidance of histrionics or involved complexities, in short, a type of music that the pianist can take or leave at his pleasure, just as he would the armchair in his living room. Satie even coined the phrase "musique d'ameublement" (furniture music) to characterize his aesthetic conception at one period in his life.

Curiously enough, the piano pieces are grouped in threes (just as the eighteenth-century composers favored groups of six, twelve, or twenty-four), a mystical Trinitarian idea that seems to have been something of an obsession with him. There is much two- and three-part writing in a pianistic style of moderate difficulty. The running commentaries in French, Latin, or words of his own fabrication add to the general amiable confusion, for they sometimes have musical counterparts in the accompanying phrase or, at other times, simply exist independently of it. In any case if, as someone has said, Satie is Satire without the r, there is much to be enjoyed in his music by those in search of whimsical, sophisticated jokery or sensitive lyricism on a small scale.

Salabert, Carl Fischer and Associated Music Publishers handle most of the music. For a full account of his work cf. Rollo Meyers: <u>Erik Satie</u>, London, 1948, and Alfred Cortot's article on the piano music of Satie in the <u>Revue Musicale</u> for April, 1938.

Trois Sarabandes (1887)	Delicate, serious pieces, melancholy and graceful.
Trois Gymnopédies (1888)	The title is a coined word probably meaning to suggest "the tracing of some graceful arabesque by naked boys dancing under an early morning Grecian sky." (Meyers). Thin melodic line over gently dissonant basses.
Trois Gnossiènnes (1890)	The title may be an allusion to the palace of Knossos in Crete. In barless notation without time signature, slight Oriental flavor, containing satiric indications foreign to the music, later to become a component of all his piano pieces.
Prélude de la Porte Héroique du Ciel (1894)	One of the most successful pieces stemming from his religious, mystical period.

Pièces Froides (1897)
  Airs à faire fuir
  Danses de travers
	Fluid, supple motion, clear texture; the <u>Airs</u> somewhat in the style of the <u>Gnossiennes</u>, the <u>Danses</u> built on gigue rhythms.

Véritables Préludes Flasques (1912)	"Flabby Preludes," No. 2 especially appealing (lyric piece in two voices). Mock Latin directions throughout.
Descriptions Automatiques (1913)	Contains allusions to various popular songs.
Embryons Desséchés (1913)	Portraits of three imaginary crustaceans invented by Satie accompanied by nonsensical

descriptions. Parody of Chopin's Funeral March in No. 2 labelled "quotation from the celebrated Mazurka of Schubert."

Croquis et Agaceries d'un Gros Bonhomme en Bois (1913)

Three witty sketches with allusions to Mozart's Rondo à la Turca and satirical thrusts at Chabrier and Debussy.

Chapitres Tournés en Tous Sens (1913)

No. 1, a parody on a wife who talks too much, No. 2, about a porter who carries heavy stones, No. 3 uses the air "Nous n'irons plus au bois" (cf. "Jardins sous la pluie" of Debussy).

Vieux Sequins at Vielles Cuirasses (1914)

Allusions to Gounod, King Dagobert and "Malbrouck s'en va-t-en guerre."

Menus Propos Enfantins (1913)

Simple children's pieces, easy to play—for small hands, no thumb crossings.

Heures Séculaires et Instantanées (1914)

Running verbal commentary, grotesque narratives for all three pieces. Satie, in a footnote, expressly forbids the player from reading the text aloud during performance promising "ma juste indignation" to every transgressor.

Trois Valses Distinguées du Précieux Dégoûté (1914)

A surrealist montage of 1) quotations from La Bruyère, Cicero and Cato, 2) incongruous running verbal comments by Satie, 3) clear cut, ingenious, transparent miniature waltzes. Some use of bitonality.

Sports et Divertissements (1914)

The Swing
Hunting
Italian Comedy
The Bride
Blind Man's Buff
Fishing
Yachting
Bathing
Carnival
Golf
The Octopus
Racing
Puss in the Corner
Picnic
Water Slide
Tango
The Sledge
Flirt
Fireworks
Tennis

Twenty tiny sketches of outdoor sports and diversions written to accompany an album of drawings by Charles Martin. "Turn the pages of this book with an amiable and smiling hand; for this is a work of fantasy and does not pretend to be anything else. For those who are dried up and stultified I have written a Chorale which is serious and respectable. This Chorale is a sort of bitter preamble, a kind of austere and unfrivolous introduction. I have put into it everything I know about Boredom. I dedicate this choral to those who do not like me— and withdraw." (From the Preface.)
The original de luxe edition contains the drawings of Martin on pages complementary to the music.
Milhaud considers this work one of the most characteristic products of the modern French School.

Sonatine Bureaucratique (1917)

Neo-classic work in the pianistic style of Clementi.

| Cinq Nocturnes (1919) | Final works for piano, each a page long, all built on the plan of the Aria da Capo. |

FLORENT SCHMITT (1879-   ) France

Soirs (Ten Preludes)	These have no serious technical problems, and are imaginative, with modern feeling. (Durand)
Enfants, Op. 94	Eight short pieces, with varied technical requirements. (Durand)
Clavecin obtempérant, Op. 107	These four pieces are more exacting technically and rhythmically. (Durand)

CYRIL SCOTT (1879-   ) Great Britain

Three Little Waltzes	Simple, short. (Elkin, through Ricordi)
Pastorale Suite	Courante, Pastorale, Rigaudon, Rondo, Passacaglia. See especially the last piece (the passacaglia idea built on a folklike tune). (Galaxy Music Corp.)
Chimes, Op. 40, No. 3	Chordal, sonorous, striding quarter notes.
Lotus Land, Op. 47, No. 1	Atmospheric, sonorous, exotic. Pentatonic harmonies and melodies. (Galaxy Music Corp.)
Sonata, Op. 66	In one movement, with final fugue. Improvisatory, impassioned. (Schott)
Old English Dances	Three pieces of moderate difficulty. (Schott)

ALEXANDER SCRIABIN (1872-1915) Russia

The pianism of Scriabin has its roots in the pianism of Chopin. Valse, mazurka, nocturne, impromptu, prelude and étude are the vehicles for his early musical efforts. Harmonically he proceeds in the Liszt-Wagner tradition to develop a highly chromatic style. In the later works the style crystallizes into a highly individual vocabulary. The mystic, theosophic preoccupations of his later life provide the specific guiding impetus for its evolution. The enraptured, ecstatic quality, marked by curious indications for the performer ("avec une joie exaltée," "epanouissement de forces mystèrieuses," "ailé, tourbillonnant," "avec une celeste volupté"); these can best be understood and projected by the pianist who knows something of Scriabin's life and thinking.

The short pieces are of varying difficulty. Often they are no more than fleeting sketches, the best of them retaining an enigmatic, aphoristic quality anticipating the Opus 19 of Schönberg. The larger single pieces are virtuoso in style, very full in texture and thoroughly romantic in concept.

However, the core of his efforts resides in the ten sonatas covering the period 1893-1913. They are all difficult, demanding a highly developed pianism, imagination, flexibility of phrase and sensitivity to timbre.

In a special category are the Etudes Opus 8, 42 and 65. Scriabin here explores new facets of modern pianism, knotty problems demanding a developed sense of piano sonority and sure control of polyrhythms.

Technically the piano music of Scriabin is generally characterised by a pedaling that binds sonorities over an extended keyboard range, widely spaced figuration, flexible irregular rhythmic groupings, octave and chord passages that benefit from a large hand, the use of the trill as coloristic effect (especially in the later works) and a rich, luxuriant, over-ripe sonority.

The original publishers were M. P. Belaieff, Leipzig, and Jurgenson, Moscow. Two volumes of a complete edition of the piano works have already appeared in this country published by the State Publishing House, U. S.S.R. (Prof. Egumnov): Vol. I (Opus 1-11 and twelve youthful compositions), Vol. II (Opus 12-42). These are available through Leeds Music. Leeds also prints the Ten Sonatas in one volume (Howard Sheldon), an excellent buy. Other publishers include Boston Music Co., Universal, International Music Co., G. Schirmer, etc. A complete listing of the works may be found in Grove.

Shorter Pieces

Ten Mazurkas, Op. 3	See especially No. 9 (G-sharp minor).
Two Impromptus à la Mazur, Op. 7	Rambling, chromatic salon pieces.
Prelude and Nocturne, Op. 9	For the left hand alone. Good for control and balance of tone. Nocturne difficult.
Twenty-four Preludes, Op. 11	Outstanding among the early works. Strongly Chopinesque. Demand bravura, sensitivity, careful sonority. Easy to difficult. See especially No. 2 (A minor), No. 3 (D major), No. 6 (B minor), No. 8 (F-sharp minor), No. 14 (E- flat minor), No. 15 (D-flat major), No. 16 (B-flat minor), No. 18 (F minor) No. 24 (D minor).
Six Preludes, Op. 13	Generally diatonic, not too difficult, some finger passages, double sixths, chords.
Seven Preludes, Op. 17	Include an octave study, romantic salon improvisation, sombre Lento, brilliant Prestissimo, quiet Andante doloroso and a concluding Agitato piece.
Four Preludes, Op. 22	Completely lyrical, not difficult.
Four Preludes, Op. 31	Brief, interesting sketches.
Two Poems, Op. 32	No. 1—flexible, nervous, lyric. No. 2—declamatory, chordal.
Four Preludes, Op. 37	Simple, direct, expressive Mesto; fiery, short, chordal Maestoso; lyric Andante; short Irato impetuoso with explosive phrases.

Three Pieces, Op. 45	Fleeting miniatures, salon style: <u>Feuillet</u> <u>d'Album</u>, <u>Poème</u> <u>Fantasque</u>, <u>Prelude</u>.
Three Pieces, Op. 49	Agitated <u>Etude</u>, spasmodic motives; brusque, epigrammatic <u>Prelude</u>; fragile, piquant <u>Rêverie</u>.
Four Pieces, Op. 51	See especially No. 4, <u>Danse languide</u>.
Three Pieces, Op. 52	Veiled, languorous, chromatic <u>Poème</u>; capricious, fleeting <u>Enigme</u> (prototype for Schönberg's Opus 19?); improvisational <u>Poème</u> <u>languide</u>.
Four Pieces, Op. 56	Declamatory, violent <u>Prelude</u>; grotesque <u>Ironies</u>; veiled, melting <u>Nuances</u> "like velvet"; light, quick, short <u>Etude</u> to end.
Two Pieces, Op. 57	Voluptuous <u>Désir</u>, tour de force in augmented sonorities. Fragile, delicate, undulating <u>Caresse dansée</u> in 3/8.

Two Dances, Op. 73
 	
  Guirlandes
  Flammes sombres
	See especially <u>Flammes sombres</u>, a graceful <u>dolente</u> contrasting with a <u>Presto</u>, <u>tres dansant</u>. Rhythmic swing and sonority main problems.

Five Preludes, Op. 74
 	
  Douloureux déchirant
  Très lent, contemplatif
  Allegro drammatico
  Lent, vague, indécis
  Fier, belliqueux
	Highly intense, characteristic, late-Scriabinesque harmonies, everything dependent on the initial sonorities.

More extended single pieces

The following are generally characterized by a virtuoso, bravura, post-romantic pianism on a large scale, featured by a sonorous octave and chord technique and widely spaced figuration supporting a melody and almost invariably leading to heavy climaxes.

Polonaise, Op. 21	On the scale of the Chopin polonaises in F-sharp minor and A-flat major.
Tragic Poem, Op. 34	Somewhat in the style of the famous <u>Étude in D-sharp minor</u>, Op. 8.
Satanic Poem, Op. 36	Ironic. Forerunner of Prokofieff's <u>Suggestion diabolique</u>.
Poème, Op. 41	Melody with increasingly complex figuration. Lyrical nocturne.
Vers la Flamme, Op. 72	Ecstatic. Great closing climax. One chord generates the entire piece. Atmospheric, intense.

Sonatas

Sonata No. 1, Op. 6, in F Minor (1893)	Sonorous, chordal, Brahmsian <u>Allegro con fuoco</u>. Slow, improvisational movement in 4/4. Agitated <u>Presto</u> leading to concluding funeral march.

Sonata-Fantasy No. 2, Op. 19, in G-sharp Minor (1892-1897)	Brooding, introspective <u>Andante</u> with the melody emerging from the midst of widely spaced figuration. <u>Presto</u> in perpetually moving triplets, broad melodies. Entire sonata not especially chromatic and eminently worth playing. Good introduction to the sonatas.
Sonata No. 3, Op. 23, in F- sharp Minor	Four movements. Entire sonata seems to lack invention.
Sonata No. 4, Op. 30, in F-sharp Major (1903)	Tender, delicate, atmospheric <u>Andante</u> leading into a <u>Prestissimo volando</u> of great élan and drive culminating in a grand climax that transforms the opening <u>Andante</u> melody into a brilliant paean. One of the shortest of the sonatas.
Sonata No. 5, Op. 53 (1907)	This and the fourth sonata mark a departure from the earlier style into a mystical, fantastic manner. In one movement. Impetuous, constant change of mood, quasi fantasia. Furious closing section. Demands good staccato chord technique in skips, supple rhythmic sense, elastic cantabile.

The last five sonatas fall into one group. They are mystical poems, one movement in length. The veiled outlines stem from an impressionist technique grafted on to Scriabin's individual harmonic system. The sonorities require four staves for their notation. All the last five sonatas are very difficult.

Sonata No. 6, Op. 62 (1911-1912)	
Sonata No. 7, Op. 64 (1911-1912)	Called the "White Mass"(by the composer.
Sonata No. 8, Op. 66 (1913)	
Sonata No. 9, Op. 68 (1913)	Called the "Black Mass" by the composer.
Sonata No. 10, Op. 70 (1912-1913)	

<u>Etudes</u>

Twelve Etudes, Op. 8	Moderate to great difficulty. See especially No. 2 in F-sharp minor (declamatory, capricious, five against three); No. 3 in B minor (tempestuous, octaves and chords, three against two); No. 5 in E Major (a favorite. Octaves and chords, quick lateral displacements, sonorous); No. 6 in A Major (double sixths); No. 9 in C-sharp minor (<u>Alla ballata</u>, fine octave study); No. 10 (famous study in major double thirds, left hand skips); No. 11 in B-flat minor (melody with accompaniment); No. 12 in D-sharp minor (<u>Patetico</u>, broad declamatory style, octaves, repeated chords, demands bravura and elan).

Eight Etudes, Op. 42	Difficult. All these studies feature problems in irregular cross meters: 9/8 against 5/4, five against three, three against two, four against three. No. 3 in F-sharp major is a short trill study.
Three Etudes, Op. 65	In fifths, sevenths and ninths.

DEODAT DE SÉVÉRAC (1873-1921) France

The piano music of de Sévérac is mostly in descriptive genres, casual in style, employing a conventional pianism, euphonious harmonies and some elements of improvisation. All have titles indicating the program in mind.

Cerdana	Five Etudes pittoresques, rather extended in length.
En Vacances	Short romantic pieces of middle difficulty. Two collections (seven and three pieces respectively).
En Languedoc	Suite of five pieces.
Baigneuses au Soleil	Rather difficult extended piece. (All published by Salabert)
Chant de la Terre (1900) (Poème Georgique)	Impressionistic. See especially the Intermezzo and the lively Epilog. (Salabert)

VISSARION SHEBALIN (1902-   ) U.S.S.R.

Three Sonatinas, Op. 12	Vivacious pieces, fairly difficult, skillfully made.
No. 1	Flowing, lyric Moderato, short Canzona, vigorous scherzo-like Fughetta.
No. 2	Short, lively Prelude in perpetual motion. Aria in two-part writing, frisky March, brilliant, closing Rondo.
No. 3	Festive opening Sinfonia, Burlesca in 5/8, short, sombre Meditation, boisterous Finale. (Leeds Music)

DMITRI SHOSTAKOVITCH (1906-   ) U.S.S.R.

Shostakovitch has not written any extended serious works for piano solo outside the two sonatas listed below. They represent completely different stylistic premises; the first a dashing "modern" idiom, the second more conservative from every angle, relatively easy to play and listen to, although somewhat repetitious in its working out.

Three Fantastic Dances	Early student work. Easy. (Various publishers)
Twenty-four Preludes (1932-33)	Especially to be noted are: No. 2 (A minor)—short dance; No. 5 (D major)—breathless perpetual motion, over in a moment; No. 6 (B minor)—satiric polka; No. 9 (E major)—running

étude-style; No. 10 (C-sharp minor)—lyric, processional; No. 13 (F-sharp major)—tiny march, fife and drum effects; No. 14 (E-flat minor)—weighty, sombre, orchestral, best of the set; No. 15 (D-flat major)—waltz; No. 16 (B-flat minor)—march; No. 24 (D minor)—satiric gavotte.
(Various publishers)

Sonata No. 1, Op. 12
Stormy one-movement work, biting dissonances, virtuoso style.
(Kalmus)

Sonata No. 2 in B Minor, Op. 64
Simple, clear textures, moderate difficulty: Allegretto with running figuration over simple, triadic melody—march-like sections; Largo, atmospheric melody with simple accompaniment; Moderato, thirty-bar theme and nine variations, with quiet ending.
(State Music Publishers, through Leeds Music)

Six Children's Pieces
Easy miniatures, mostly in two voices. Some chromatic tones but simple rhythmically. Written for his daughter.
(Leeds Music)

ERICH-WALTER STERNBERG (1898-) Israel

Sternberg is a musician who does not stress the oriental aspects of his present musical environment but seems to be more rooted in the musical milieu of Germany, the land that gave him birth.

Toccata (1943)
Lengthy, driving, rhythmic piece demanding power, agility, endurance and virtuosity.
(Israeli Music Publications, through Leeds Music)

KAROL SZYMANOWSKI (1883-1937) Poland

The piano music of Poland's best-known contemporary keyboard composer is based upon the idioms of Brahms, Reger, and (in his later works) Debussy, Scriabin and Schönberg. All of Szymanowski is quite difficult with a major portion of the works demanding virtuoso equipment. The piano style exploits not only the sonorous fabric of late romantic pianism, but also explores the effervescent, shimmering colors of Impressionism within a harmonic framework that becomes increasingly chromatic and dissonant as the style matures.

Although his music is at present difficult to obtain (Universal, through Associated Music) Szymanowski deserves at least cursory exploration by serious students of the piano for he is a provocative figure and one not widely played in this country.

Four Preludes, Op. 1
Lyric and dramatic in turn. Broad, post-romantic piano style. See especially No. 4 (tender) and No. 5 (dramatic, impetuous).
(Albert Stahl)

Four Etudes, Op. 4	Romantic essays exploiting three against two, double notes, octaves, broken-chord and broken octave figuration etc. (Universal Edition)
Variations on a Polish Folk Theme, Op. 10	Ten variations in an elegant, post-romantic, virtuoso piano style. Brilliant ending. (Universal Edition)
Sonata No. 2, Op. 21 (1912)	Strong influence of Reger. Opening movement Appassionato, followed by variations on a gavotte-like theme capped by a powerful fugue. (Universal Edition)
Métopes, Op. 29 The Isle of the Sirens Calypso Nausicaa	Three extended, florid, highly coloristic poems demanding great virtuosity. Oriented toward Scriabin. The pieces explore fleeting, evanescent, fluttering qualities of sound. Improvisatory in character. (Universal Edition)
Masques, Op. 34 (1919)	Scheherezade, Tantris der Narr and a Don Juan - Serenade. (Universal Edition)
Twelve Etudes, Op. 33	Short pieces meant to be played as a connected set. Difficult both musically and pianistically. (Universal Edition)
Sonata No. 3, Op. 36	In one movement. Oriented toward Scriabin. Covers a wide variety of unorthodox pianistic problems. Requires complete equipment. Light, delicate opening growing in agitation, intensity and pianistic complexity toward a culminating Fuga, scherzando e buffo. Energetic conclusion. (Universal Edition)
Mazurkas, Op. 50 (1926-1931)	In five volumes, four mazurkas in each. Rhythmically, harmonically and melodically subtle. Require skillful, sensitive pianism. (Universal Edition)

GERMAINE TAILLEFERRE (1892-) France

Pastorale in A-flat Major (1928)	Flowing, ambling melody supported by smooth figuration interrupted by agitated middle section. Cool. Serene qualities. Moderate length and difficulty. (Heugel, through Mercury Music)

ALEXANDRE TANSMAN (1897-) Poland

The piano music of Tansman is not widely known in this country. It falls roughly into several distinct categories: music for instructive purposes (pieces for children based upon traditional harmonic and pianistic procedures), music based on distinctly Polish traits (Mazurkas, various dances) music based predominantly on American jazz idioms (Sonatine Transatlantique, Preludes in "blues" style) and works more extended and serious in nature displaying a more universal approach and couched in a more dissonant, daring harmonic vocabulary (Ballads, Fourth Sonata, Intermezzi). Tansman knows the keyboard intimately. The music lies well in the hand and even the most difficult passages reveal a penetrating knowledge of idiomatic keyboard writing.

Pour les Enfants	Four graded collections of children's pieces, twelve in a set (except No. 4, which has ten). Conventional harmonic, melodic and pianistic idioms. (Eschig)
Ten Diversions for the Young Pianist	See especially those that require facility (Nos. 3, 6 and 9). (Associated Music)

Novelettes
  Caprice
  Etude
  Exotique (danse javanaise)
  Danse Tzigane
  Obertas (danse polonaise)
  Blues
  Prélude et Fugue
  Improvisation
	Two- or three-page pieces in an easily accessible idiom. Moderate difficulty. See especially No. 2 (for facility), No. 6 (chordal, chromatic, stylized), No. 7 (Aria and scherzando, chromatic fugue). (Eschig)

Cinq Impressions (1934)	Short sketches of moderate difficulty: Calme (cantabile, chromatic, chordal), Burlesque (brilliant grotesque, buffo style), Triste (melancholy sketch), Animé (jazzy, dissonant), Nocturne (tiny, distant, atmospheric). (Eschig)
Petite Suite (1919)	Seven easy short pieces, mostly lyric. No. 7 (Scherzino) requires some facility in double notes. (Eschig)
Trois Préludes en forme de Blues	Easy, chordal, relaxed. See especially Nos. 1 and 2. (Eschig)

Sonatine Transatlantique (1930)
  Fox-trot
  Spiritual and Blues
  Charleston
	"This work does not propose to realize an 'American Music,' but simply to put down the 'reaction' of a European musician to contact with the dance rhythms from across the sea." (Composer's note.) Moderately difficult, amusing. (Alphonse Leduc)

Four Preludes	Short, difficult chromatic essays: Lent (blues), Lent (homage to Ravel, bell sonorities), Andante (dramatic, rhapsodic, Scriabinesque), Moderato (deciso then grazioso). (Demets)

Mazurkas

Collection I (1918-28)

Collection II (1932)

Ten pieces, easy to difficult. See especially
Nos. 1 and 3 (vigorous Oberek), No. 6 (chroma-
tic dolente), No. 10 (berceuse).
Nine pieces, fairly difficult. See especially
No. 1 (vigorous), No. 2 (melancholy), No. 6
(unusual scale features), No. 8 (vigorous,
rough).
(Eschig)

Intermezzi (1939-40)

Series I (1-6)
Series II (7-12)
Series III (13-18)
Series IV (19-24)

Pieces in more dissonant style of moderate
length, fairly to very difficult. See especially
No. 1 (lyric, flexible), No. 3 (graceful Allegretto), No. 6 (vigorous, marcato, perpetually
moving sixteenths, big octave climax), No. 16
(vigorous double-note étude), No. 18 (agitated,
heavy octaves, chords, double notes), No. 19
("To Charlie Chaplin," florid melody), No. 20
(dry, rhythmic, hammered), No. 21 (used as the
slow movement of Sonata No. 4), No. 24
(lyric).
(Eschig)

Troisième Sonatine
(1933)

Supple, animated Pastorale; short, chordal
Hymne; concluding Rondo, constant eighths
and sixteenths in furious perpetual motion.
(Eschig)

Sonata No. 4 (1941)

Extended, serious work, difficult. Intense
Andante sostenuto, sliding chromatic harmonies
leading to scherzando section. Chromatic
Adagio lamentoso leading to recapitulation of
opening Andante. Transition to Allegro deciso,
rhythmic finale, strong ending.
(Eschig)

Suite dans le Style
Ancien

Rhythmic, processional Entrée. Romantic
Sarabande, intense climax. Graceful Gavotte
with piquant, biting dissonances. Four-part
Choral Fugue. Aria in Bach style. Vigorous
closing Toccata, perpetual motion in double
notes. Requires strength.
(Eschig)

Three Ballads (1941)

No. 1

No. 2

No. 3

Extended, serious pieces. Acrid dissonances,
intense, demanding an all-round pianism.

Sombre, chromatic-chord movements, rapid
extended middle section with alternating
hands, double notes, broken chords. Quiet
ending.
Improvisational, subdued opening leading to a
propulsive middle section, Lento interlude and
brilliant Presto close. Requires stamina.
Longest of the set. Bold, declamatory opening.
Light Allegro scherzando. Quiet, atmospheric

chordal <u>Andante</u>. Long, bravura closing section <u>Presto mecanico</u>, brilliant and effective.
(Eschig)

MICHAEL TIPPETT (1905-) Great Britain

Piano Sonata (in G Major)	Large-scale work, essentially diatonic. Clean, firm lines. Difficult pianism.
Allegro	Twenty-five-bar theme, five variations (brilliant, vigorous, poco maestoso, scherzando, toccata in alternating octaves) and theme da capo.
Andante molto tranquillo	Simple melody, some contrapuntal elaboration in flowing lines, quiet coda.
Presto	Brilliant 6/8, octaves, unison passages, cross rhythms, mostly thin texture in two voices, quiet ending.
Rondo giocoso con moto	Elaborate rondo, passage playing, broken chord and arpeggio figuration. Difficult. (Schott)

JOAQUIN TURINA (1882-) Spain

Turina has written voluminously for the piano in a facile, semipopular
style. The demands are more pianistic than musical, and even the musical
problems are more or less conventional, offering, in most instances, only
moderate interpretative difficulties.

Danzas Gitanas	Spanish gypsy dances, two series (five in each). Pieces of moderate difficulty, rather conventional in treatment, moderate in length. See especially No. 5 in Series I (<u>Sacro-monte</u>). (Salabert)
Ninerias (1919)	
First Series, Op. 21	A little suite of eight descriptive pieces, each moderately long, except for the tongue-in-cheek <u>Prelude and Fugue.</u> On the casual side. (Salabert)
Second Series, Op. 55	Another set of eight. (Salabert)
Silhouettes, Op. 70	Five descriptive pieces. See especially No. 2 (a light <u>Allegretto</u> dance), No. 3 (<u>La Puerta del sol</u>—two moods juxtaposed), and No. 5 (<u>El Faro de Cadiz</u>—a sonorous brilliant piece). (Salabert)
Sonata romantique sur un thème espagnol	An extended work, all movements built on the <u>El Vito</u> theme. Difficult. Requires all-round facility. (Eschig)
Thème et Variations Scherzo (Vif) Finale (Lent-Allegro)	
Contes d'Espagne	Story in seven tableaux.

| Jardins d'Andalousie | Suite of three pieces. |
| Femmes d'Espagne | Three portraits of Spanish women. |

FARTEIN VALEN (1887-   ) Norway

The Norwegian composer, Valen, is not a strict twelve-tonalist but takes his point of departure from Schönberg, emphasising linear writing within a freely used chromatic scale without adhering to a rigid use of the tone rows.

| Variations, Op. 23 | Ten-bar melodic theme (unaccompanied) on a twelve-tone row and its retrograde form, twelve variations with increasingly complex polyphony; short, relaxed, quiet coda. (Peters) |
| Prelude and Fugue, Op. 28 | Prelude in two voices, moderato, invention style, invertible counterpoint. Fairly long Fugue in three voices, 12/8, allegro, sixteenth-note triplet motion, gigue style, fortissimo ending. (Peters) |

ALEX VOORMOLEN (1895-   ) Holland

| Kinderbuek (1923-1925) | Twenty-four little pieces in two books. Tiny sketches covering a wide variety of descriptive and stylistic problems. Not too easy. Plenty of chromatics. Requires some sophistication. (Salabert) |

Tableaux des Pays-Bas

Series 1:

Night in an Ancient City	Lush, chromatic chords, atmospheric ending.
Autumn Landscape	Slow chordal phrases, square in structure, chromatic harmony.
The Haven	Rolling figuration over single ostinato bass supporting a melody. Most interesting of the three. Strong ending.

Series 2:

Homage to Valerius	Siciliano style, chordal throughout.
At Jan Steen's	Allegretto dance in 3/4, moving eighths and quarters.
Twilight at Delft	Four-part harmony, wandering effects.
The Wind and the Wind Mills	Bouncing Scherzo in 3/8 on a Dutch children's song.
Veere in Zeeland	Slow mystic, triadic harmonies (for the city of Veere "having a Gothic Cathedral and situated on an arm of the sea.") Some references to previous pieces in the cycle. (Salabert)

Salabert also publishes: Première Suite pour Piano, Sonnet, Scène et Danse Érotique, Berceuse.

ANTON VON WEBERN (1883-1945) Austria

Variations, Op. 27 (1936)	Twelve-tone work, extreme in every respect. Bare, dry sonorities, huge skips, spasmodic rhythms and dynamics. For a detailed analysis cf. Rene Leibowitz's Schönberg and his School, Chapter XI. (Universal, through Associated Music)

JEAN WIENER (1896-   ) France

Wiener's piano works are interesting in relationship to the impact of Negro jazz bands in France in the early 1920's. Their sophisticated stylizations are fluent, facile and, at times, demanding.

Sonatine Syncopée Lourd Blues Brillant	Difficult, extended work using a dissonant, varied pianism within the context of stylized jazz. Author's prefatory note thanks the Negro musicians to whom he owed the stimulus for his development. (Eschig, through Associated Music)
Sonate (1925)	Light work in three movements. Difficult. Requires a fluent pianism, relaxed and, at times, sonorous. (Eschig, through Associated Music)
Deuxième Sonatine (1928)	Not easy. Flowing, relaxed, chordal style, popular flavor. Bouncing, rhythmic finale. (Eschig; through Associated Music)

Composers in the United States

(Including Foreign-born Residents)

Piano music written by composers in the United States presents a very uneven quality of achievement. Until very recent times composers born in this country have been, in most cases, a pale reflection of European trends. Especially is this so with composers steeped in the tradition of German Romanticism. It has been a battle for the American composer to come out from under the shadow of powerful, long-established traditions to create an individual, national school built on the best world-wide traditions but nonetheless characteristically American in style and content. The situation in the field of piano music is but one phase of the musical situation in general.

However, there are a number of works that begin to form the body of a repertoire for pianists interested in exploring and presenting the efforts of native contemporary composers. The following list must be accepted as a selection that merely suggests the growing extent of the field and undoubtedly has many gaps both in composers and individual works.

No mention of American music is complete without reference to the American Music Center, 250 West 57th Street, New York City. This organization retains on its premises a lending library of not only published works by American composers but also many items in manuscript or blueprint form. In addition they serve as agents for New Music and Arrow Music Press, two pioneer organizations in publishing contemporary works.

Among other publishers who are daily adding to their catalogues piano works by American composers, the following must be singled out: G. Schirmer, Inc., Carl Fischer, J. Fischer, Mercury Music, Southern Music Publishing Co., Elkan-Vogel, Leeds Music Corporation.

It must also be mentioned that the American Composer's Alliance maintains a reference and rental library at 580 Fifth Avenue, New York City (Broadcast Music, Inc.). This organization also projects the publication of new works by American composers in its Composer's Facsimile Edition. A catalogue of the piano works in this series may be obtained by writing to the above address.

Collections:

U.S.A., Vol. I, Vol. II, Leeds Music. Anthologies of nineteen short pieces by American composers (Antheil, Bowles, Chanler, Diamond, Mason, Maxwell, Read, Scott, Wolpe, Bacon, Creston, Fuleihan, Jacobi, Josten, McKay, Piston, Still, Vaughan).

ERNST BACON (1898-   )

Sombrero

Moderately fast dance in 5/8. Humorous, light, short, not difficult.
In U.S.A. 1946 (album published by Leeds Music).

SAMUEL BARBER (1910-   )

Excursions

"These are 'Excursions' in small classical forms into regional American idioms. Their rhythmic characteristics, as well as their source in folk material and their scoring,

reminiscent of local instruments, are easily recognized": <u>Un poco Allegro</u> in "boogie-woogie" style, <u>In slow blues tempo</u>, <u>Allegretto</u> (cowboy song with variations over ostinato harmonies), concluding square dance <u>Allegro molto</u>.
(Schirmer)

Sonata in E-flat Minor, Op. 26 (1949)

Allegro energico
Allegro vivace e
  leggiero
Adagio mesto
Allegro con spirito
  (Fuga)

Energetic, sonorous, large-scale work with a great variety of textures. Middle two movements short, fugue very effective and demanding. Strong conclusion. Requires complete pianism.
(Schirmer)

MARION BAUER (1887-   )

From the New Hampshire Wood, Op. 12

Lyric pieces in the MacDowell tradition: <u>White Birches</u>, <u>Indian Pipes</u>, <u>Pine Trees</u>.

Turbulence, Op. 17, No. 2

Prelude-like, vigorous, broad piano style. Octaves, chords punctuated with short motivic outbursts.
(E. B. Marks)

A Fancy

Short, impressionist, atmospheric.
(Axelrod)

Four Piano Pieces, Op. 21

Chromaticon
Ostinato
Toccata
Syncope

Short studies in various compositional problems. Chord structures in fourths and fifths, broken-chord figuration, block chords, alternating hands, wide keyboard scope, dissonant.
(Arrow Music Press)

Dance Sonata, Op. 24

Graceful work in three movements: chromatic <u>Allegro Appassionata</u> with quiet side theme; stately <u>Sarabande</u> with five variations, concluding scherzo; <u>Allegretto giocoso</u> with lyric interlude. Moderate difficulty.
(A.C.A. Library)

Patterns, Op. 41 (1946)

Five twelve-tone pieces; flowing <u>Allegretto</u> in two voices, fast waltz, scherzo, expressive slow movement, concluding <u>Toccata</u> ("fast and ferociously"). Moderately difficult.
(A.C.A. Library)

JEANNE BEHREND (1911-   )

Quiet Piece (1932)

Warm, lyric qualities, unhackneyed, intimate, short.
(Axelrod)

Dance into Space (1933)

Capricious, lengthy, sonorous piano style.
(Axelrod)

From Dawn until Dusk
(A Child's Day)

Suite of seven genre pieces. An extended
cycle. Sensitive, unpretentious. Nos. 3 and 5
difficult.
(Elkan-Vogel)

ARTHUR BERGER (1912-   )

Three Bagatelles (19 6)

Risoluto con moto
Poco andante
Allegro brillante

Moderate length, dry timbres, interrupted
rhythms. Require neat articulation.
(E. B. Marks)

Suite for Piano (1946)

Graceful Capriccio, expressive Intermezzo in
two voices andante, graceful Rondo with woodwind qualities. Problems in precision of
touch.
(A.C.A. Library) The Rondo is published
separately by Mercury Music.

Partita (1947)
Intonazione
Aria
Capriccio
Intermezzo
Serenade

All moderately short movements. Oriented
toward Stravinsky.
(A.C.A. Library)

Fantasy

Moderato beginning, graceful scherzo, short
meno mosso section leading to a rapid close.
(A.C.A. Library)

WILLIAM BERGSMA (1921-   )

Three Fantasies (1943)

Impetuous opening with declamatory pianistic
figures over sonorous pedal tones in the bass.
Quiet melody over pizzicato basses. Vigorous
rondo in fast perpetually moving sixteenth
notes. Moderately difficult, the last piece demands some bravura.
(Hargail)

Tangents

"Although the pieces can be played separately,
Tangents is planned as a contrasting set and
specifically for the second half of a program"
(composer's note).

Prologue
Prophecies

Short fanfare
Broad, declamatory, assertive First Prophecy;
cantabile Second Prophecy with florid melodic
figuration within a free polyphony.

De Rerum Natura

Unicorns (jaunty, rhythmic scherzo), Fishes
(short, quiet, melodic), Mr. Darwin's Serenade
(satiric "wrong note" burlesque).

Masques
Pieces for Nickie
Epilogue

Two pieces to balance the first two prophecies.
For Nickie happy, angry and asleep.
Reworking of the Prologue with additional
material.
(Carl Fischer)

LEONARD BERNSTEIN (1918-   )

Four Anniversaries (1948)	For Felicia Montealegre (lyric, flowing), For Johnny Mehegan (tiny, jazzy scherzo), For David Diamond (tender, flowing), For Helen Coates (in high spirits, cocky, boisterous). (Schirmer)
Seven Anniversaries	For Aaron Copland (quiet, smooth), For my sister Shirley (light, bouncing), In Memoriam: Alfred Eisner (serious, somber elegy), For Paul Bowles (eight-measure ground bass, four variations and coda), In Memoriam: Nathalie Koussevitsky (slow elegy), For Serge Koussevitsky (declamatory melody in striding quarter notes, noble, severe), For William Schuman (impetuous, agitato, fleeting, energetic). (M. Witmark)

ERNEST BLOCH (1880-   )

The piano music of Bloch (Swiss-born naturalized American) is character-ized by an impressionistic use of melody and harmony. It exploits the damper pedal fully to bind together rich sonorities that unfold with breadth and character. Mysticism pervades his style. The melodies are often ir-regular in construction, modal and, on occasion, full of a rhapsodic declamation.

Poems of the Sea (1922)	Descriptive cycle (prefaced by verses of Walt Whitman): Waves (modal melodies over ostinato figures), Chanty (short folklike melody), At Sea (perpetually undulating motion, melody suggest-ing a hornpipe). (Schirmer)
Five Sketches in Sepia (1923)	An impressionistic cycle of brief sketches: Prélude, Fumées sur la ville, Lucioles, Incer-titude, Epilogue. The last piece serves as summary, recalling and quoting from the previous pieces. Demands delicately mixed sonorities, sensitive subdued colors. (Schirmer)
In the Night (1923)	"A love-poem." Atmospheric. (Schirmer)
Sonata (1935)	Bloch's most extended work for solo piano, con-ceived as a cyclic work on a large scale in three connected movements: bold, declamatory Maestoso ed energico set off by a quiet, atmos-pheric Pastorale leading into a Moderato alla Marcia, rough, assertive and colorful. Quiet conclusion. Demands bravura pianism, power, color and drive. (Carisch and Co., Milan)

Visions et Prophécies (1940)	Five short declamatory statements; rhapsodic, mystic, intense and effective.
Enfantines	Ten children's pieces, somewhat on the sophisticated side. Minimum demands on facility.
Nirvana	Short, exotic, mystic poem. Eerie, distant timbres over ostinato harmonies. Not difficult.

PAUL BOWLES (1911-)

Extensive travels have provided Bowles with the exotic dance styles that mark his music, strongly Latin-American in flavor.

El Indio El Bejuco (1943)	Two short dances using Mexican Indian material; the first is an arrangement from his ballet Pastorelas, the second is based on a popular song. (Mercury Music)
Huapango No. 1 (1937) Huapango No. 2 (El Sol)	Mexican dance style. Irregular meters, fast repeated chords. Short. (Axelrod)
Sayula	Popular dance-hall flavor, moderato. (Hargail)
Six Preludes (1933-1944)	Short, easygoing, casual pieces popular in style, mostly lyric. (Mercury Music)
Two Portraits	Short, not difficult. (Axelrod)
Sonatina	No exotic elements: clear, melodic Allegro ritmico with transparent texture often in two voices; lush Andante cantabile; rhythmic Allegro with problems in octaves, skips and double. notes. (Elkan-Vogel)
Carretera de Estepona (Highway to Estepona)	Moderately long, rhythmic Allegretto with propulsive sixteenth notes, repeated chords, syncopations, octaves. (E. B. Marks)

GEORGE BOYLE (1886-1948)

The pianoforte pieces of this Australian-born composer deserve mention and exploration for their musicianly and imaginative qualities, though not all those that have been published (by Schirmer and Elkan-Vogel) are still in print. He was never converted to contemporary anti-romanticism, but he had genuine musical invention.

Suite de ballet	This contains three pieces with moderate technical demands. (Schirmer)

More exacting are the Berceuse, Serenade, Waltz and Romance, which are very effectively written for the instrument and have individual musical quality. Published by Schirmer.

JOHN ALDEN CARPENTER (1876-1951)

Danza	Vigorous staccato dance in irregular meters, bare, accented sonorities. Requires energy and variety of touch. (Schirmer)
Little Dancer	Easy, brisk, staccato.
Little Indian	Melodic <u>Lento</u>, sombre.
Polonaise Americaine	Moderate length and difficulty.
Tango Americaine	Not easy. <u>Moderato</u>, rhythmic.
Diversions	Five pieces individual in style, casual in content. Moderate length and difficulty. (Schirmer)

ELLIOTT CARTER (1908-   )

Sonata (1945-1946)	Large-scale work (written during tenure of a Guggenheim fellowship) consisting of two long, elaborately planned movements. The first movement alternates a maestoso introductory tempo with rapid scurrying sections marked by consistently irregular meters with a sixteenth-note constant. A third flowing legato section is also incorporated into the scheme. The second movement opens with a sonorous <u>Andante misterioso</u> leading to a final <u>Allegro giusto</u> in 6/8 in fugal style. The climax is big, demanding bravura octaves and power; the ending is atmospheric and quiet. Demands a high level of pianism and musicianship. (Mercury Music)

GEORGE W. CHADWICK (1854-1931)

Six Characteristic Pieces, Op. 7	See especially the <u>Scherzino</u>, an <u>Allegro con fuoco</u> in the Mendelssohn tradition. (Arthur P. Schmidt)

THEODORE CHANLER (1902-   )

Toccata (1939)	Perpetual motion in two voices (à la Paradisi <u>Toccata</u>, but longer). Conventional in style. Good study in passage playing for both hands. Square-dance flavor. (Mercury Music)
Three Short Pieces	Slight lyric essays, sensitive, tonal.
Andante sciolto	Chordal, modal, three-part harmony, legato.
Andante con moto	Singing, weaving three-part counterpoint.
Allegramente	Bouncing eighths in 2/4, light texture, <u>giocoso</u>. (Arrow Music Press)

ULRIC COLE (1905-   )

Three Vignettes — See especially the first two. Demand good staccato, sonorous chords and octaves. Moderate difficulty. (J. Fischer)

AARON COPLAND (1900-   )

The two early pieces are avowedly French in idiom, but both the Variations and the Sonata are completely modern in conception and constitute solid additions to the pianist's repertoire. Above all they demand power, rhythmic energy and an incisive piano sonority.

Scherzo Humoristique (1920) (The Cat and the Mouse) — Descriptive piece, pianistic joking. (Durand)

Passacaglia (1922) — Eight-bar theme treated to a variety of textures: lyric playing, chord work, passage playing, big climax in octaves. (Senart)

Piano Variations (1930) — Theme, twenty variations and coda. Bare, dissonant work, the entire fabric depending upon the initial tones that form the theme. Harsh, uncompromising, original. Difficult. (Arrow Music Press)

Two Children's Pieces (1936) — Sunday Afternoon Music and The Young Pioneers. Easy. (Carl Fischer)

Sonata (1939-1941) — Bare, sonorous Molto moderato with nervous middle section. Jerky, spasmodic Vivace with irregular meters, jazz qualities. Declamatory Andante sostenuto, sustained harmonies over sonorous organ points. Quiet ending. (Boosey & Hawkes)

Four Piano Blues — Pieces of moderate length and difficulty in jazz styles: Freely poetic (1947), Soft and Languid (1942), Muted and sensuous (1948), With Bounce (1926). (Boosey & Hawkes)

HENRY COWELL (1897-   )

Henry Cowell's special interest in developing novel tonal resources led him to develop techniques of manipulating the keyboard with the fist, flat hand or the entire forearm. Cowell also has the pianist reach into the piano to strum or pluck the strings. The inventiveness and daring of his approach to piano timbres, unorthodox as it may appear, is often put at the service of a music based upon folk melodies, usually Celtic or American in origin. The result is a preoccupation with novel color while the underlying melodies, harmonies and forms are generally simple, regular and conventional. The following is a short selection of his many piano pieces.

Dynamic Motion	Clusters from three semitones to those demanding the forearm. Vigorous, jagged rhythms. (Associated Music)
Exultation	Forearm clusters. Folk tune, diatonic style. (Associated Music)
The Harp of Life	Forearm clusters both arms. Diatonic tune, triadic harmonization. Overtone effects, sonorous climax. (Associated Music)
The Snows of Fuji-Yama	Quiet piece built on pentatonic scale. (Associated Music)
The Irishman Dances The Irish Minstrel Sings	Two easy pieces. (Carl Fischer)
Maestoso	Sonorous piece, simple melody treated with parallel seconds, octave and chord passages. (New Music)
Aeolian Harp	Simple triads played internally by sweeping and plucking the strings. Short and simple. (Shilkret)
The Banshee	Two players necessary: one to hold down the right pedal, the other to sweep or pluck the open strings. (Shilkret)

RUTH CRAWFORD (1901-   )

Four Preludes	Nos. 1, 2 and 4 are atmospheric, Scriabinesque, characterized by predominance of major sevenths. No. 3 is a scherzo in alternating open fifths—grazioso. Short, not tonal. New Music, Vol. 2, No. 1.

PAUL CRESTON (1906-   )

Five Two-Part Inventions, Op. 14 (1937)	Rather lengthy essays in two-part, free, dissonant counterpoint. (Schirmer)
Five Little Dances, Op. 24 (1940)	Short, easy: heavy Rustic Dance, Languid Dance, dainty Toy Dance, lyric Pastoral Dance, rhythmically strong Festive Dance. (Schirmer)
Six Preludes, Op. 38	Studies in various metric and rhythmic problems. Not easy. Require agility and some maturity. (Leeds Music)
Seven Theses	Complicated studies in counterpoint and various metric and harmonic problems. Sophisticated, abstruse, difficult. In New Music, January, 1935.

| Prelude and Dance | Moderate length and difficulty.
(Mercury Music) |

R. NATHANIEL DETT (1882-1943)

| Eight Bible Vignettes | Descriptive pieces in a romantic piano style accompanied with program notes by the composer. Moderate difficulty.
(Mills Music) |
| In the Bottoms | Suite for piano containing the well-known <u>Juba Dance</u>.
(Clayton F. Summy) |

DAVID DIAMOND (1915-   )

Sonatina (1935)	Three short movements: sombre <u>Largo assai</u>, flowing <u>Allegretto</u>, scherzo-like <u>Allegro vivace</u>. (Mercury Music)
Eight Piano Pieces	For very young children, illustrating familiar nursery rhymes. (Schirmer)
The Tomb of Melville (1949)	An extended lament. Ample, sonorous treatment of a motive. Requires intensity and some maturity. (Leeds Music)

HERBERT ELWELL (1898-   )

| Sonata
  Allegro
  Andante espressivo
  Allegro con brio | A smooth, engaging work, not difficult. Requires cantabile, legato, good balance of parts and, in the last movement, some facility in passage playing.
(Oxford University Press) |

ARTHUR FARWELL (1872-1952)

A pioneer in exploring the possibilities of a national music for America. Farwell is most interesting when handling American Indian material.

Navajo War Dance No. 2	American Indian melodies used ingeniously in a driving piece built largely on ostinato figures over pedal basses. Demands bravura octaves and chords. (Mercury Music)
Pawnee Horses	Short, characteristic piece using an Omaha melody treated with a "galloping" figuration. (Schirmer)
Sourwood Mountain	In Farwell's words, a "rip-snorting development of a good old American tune." Takes heavy chord and octave technique, power and élan. Virtuoso style. In <u>Fifty-one Pieces from the Modern Repertoire</u>, Schirmer.

IRVING FINE (1914-   )

Music for Piano (1947)	Oriented toward Stravinsky.
Prelude	Rhythmic, trumpet-like motives, bouncing, carefree.
Waltz Gavotte	Grazioso waltz, elegant, with gavotte in irregular meters as trio.
Variations	Theme and three variations, mostly lyric and flowing, leading from a
Interlude-Finale	Short transition to a gay two- sometimes three-voiced finale <u>sempre staccato</u> in irregular meters. (Schirmer)

VIVIAN FINE (1913-   )

Suite in E-flat Major	Warm, lyric <u>Prelude</u>; stately <u>Sarabande</u> with florid melody; dainty <u>Gavotte</u>; quiet <u>Air</u>; short, crisp <u>Gigue</u> to close. (A.C.A. Library)

ROSS LEE FINNEY (1906-   )

The piano music of Finney exhibits warm, simple, human qualities in a style that might be characterized as conservatively modern. The following works are extended efforts to contribute to the piano literature; they command respect for their craftsmanship and directness of expression.

Sonata in D Minor (1933)	Three movements: bleak <u>Adagio</u> alternating with a rough <u>Allegro,</u> short <u>Aria</u> (<u>molto adagio</u>), and a <u>Toccata</u> in perpetual motion style interrupted by a short lyrical section. In <u>New Music</u>, Oct., 1937.
Sonata No. 3 in E Major	
Allegro giusto	An assertive opening motive serves as basic material for the movement. Unison passage playing, chordal and broken-chord techniques.
Lento	Chorale-like piece with solo melody as middle section. Simple.
Prestissimo	Fast repeated-note motive in 7/8. Brilliant driving close. (Valley Music Press)
Sonata No. 4 in E Major (Christmastime 1945)	Clear, unpretentious qualities. Thoroughly tonal.
Hymn	Short choral-like <u>Adagio</u>.
Invention	Two and three voices, running sixteenths, <u>giocoso</u>.
Nocturne	Thoughtful, homophonic <u>Andante</u>, very mildly dissonant.
Toccata	Energetic <u>Presto</u> in 6/8. Passage playing, chords, octaves, double notes leading back to
Hymn	the opening majestic <u>Hymn</u>. Quiet close. (Mercury Music)

| Fantasy (1939) | An extended work juxtaposing a variety of homophonic textures: impetuous unison passages, quiet arias, rhythmically propulsive sections, atmospheric <u>Andante</u> leading to a vivacious toccata-like finale with fast repeated notes and unison passages. Quiet, melodic close. Demands a broad pianistic style. (Arrow Music Press) |

ARTHUR FOOTE (1853-1937)

Five Poems after Omar Khayyam, Op. 41	Programmatic essays prefaced by quotations from the poem. See especially No. II, a decisive, vigorous piece with contrasting middle section. (Arthur P. Schmidt)
Five Silhouettes, Op. 73	See especially No. 4 (<u>Flying Cloud</u>), a rhythmic allegro with étude-like figures divided between the hands. (Arthur P. Schmidt)
Two Prelude-Etudes, Op. 37	No. 1 for the left hand alone, No. 2 for the right hand alone. (Arthur P. Schmidt)
Twenty Preludes, Op. 52	In the form of short technical studies. (Arthur P. Schmidt)

LUKAS FOSS (1922-   )

Four Two-Voiced Inventions (1938)	The first serves as introduction to the set which can be performed as a unit. Fairly extended pieces demanding musicianship and sensitivity. (Schirmer)
Grotesque Dance (1938)	Difficult, bravura pianism. (Schirmer)
Fantasy-Rondo	An extended piece demanding variety of touch and stamina. Irregular meters, cross rhythms, broken-chord figuration. (Schirmer)
Passacaglia	Four-bar bass, twenty-two variations. Some rhythmic problems. Increasing activity to a sonorous climax. Quiet ending. Medium difficulty. (Schirmer)

ISADORE FREED (1908-   )

| Sonata (1933) | <u>Allegro non troppo e ardente</u> in irregular meters; <u>Andante sostenuto</u> with cool, open, triadic harmonies and an intense climax; closing <u>Allegro e ben ritmato</u> in rapid 6/8, |

shifting accents, fast octaves and repeated
tones. Requires stamina. Quiet ending.
(Associated Music)

Pastorales	Eight little pieces for children. Moderate facility required. Mildly modern. (Associated Music)
Sonorités Rhythmiques (1931)	Six studies in rhythmic problems and opposing sonorities. Freely chromatic. (Salabert)
Prelude, Canzonet and Caprice	Suite for piano of moderate length and difficulty. See especially the Caprice, an étude-like essay in running passage playing. (Elkan-Vogel)
Five Pieces for Piano (1928-1930)	Sophisticated pieces of moderate length. See especially No. 2 (quiet, supple melody over a chromatic, ostinato bass) and No. 3 (fast, vigorous march, martial and weighty). (La Sirène Musicale)
Intrada and Fugue	Majestic, sonorous, organ-like prelude with noble, lyric declamation. Expressive three-voice Fugue, smoothly flowing. Moderate difficulty. (Axelrod)

ANIS FULEIHAN (1900-   )

Cypriana	Set of pieces employing exotic coloristic, melodic and harmonic resources from the island of Cyprus: The Girl from Paphos (simple staccato dance in 3/4 alternating with a florid rhapsodic song treated to a kind of cembalom or guitar accompaniment), Syrtos (rhythmic dance, cross accents), Kyrenia (slow folklike melody with broken-chord figuration), Serenade (tango or habanera style, short Presto middle section, great verve and freedom), Café Dancer (a kind of jota in fast 3/8, drum and guitar effects).
Sonatina No. 1	In three movements: the first featuring open textures and modal scales; the second is a short marchlike 5/4; the third is a light rondo, modal with folklike melody. (Leeds Music)
Sonatina No. 2	Short three-movement work: Limpid, flowing figuration around simple melody; short, slow section in two voices; animated finale, quasi-fugal. Moderate difficulty. (Leeds Music)
Sonata No. 1	Two long movements: Allegro con brio e energico, Molto moderato, the second being

	an extended theme with variations. Demands full command of traditional piano techniques. (Schirmer)
Harvest Chant	Folklike tune set to pealing, bell-like harmonies, crescendo and diminuendo to a quiet close. Short. (Schirmer)
Fifteen Short Pieces for the Piano	Series of sketches a page or two in length. See especially No. 1 (Madrigal), No. 3 (Motet), No. 10 (Conversation), No. 13 (Toccatina). Problems in linear clarity, irregular meters, timbre, variety of tone, octaves, double notes, passage playing. (Carl Fischer)

GEORGE GERSHWIN (1898-1937)

Preludes	Three short essays based on jazz materials.
Allegro ben ritmato e deciso	Primarily rhythmic. Demands energy, command of syncopated rhythms, bravura.
Andante con moto e poco rubato	Lyric "blues."
Allegro ben ritmato e deciso	Rough rhythms, catchy syncopations, brilliant, effective. (New World Music Corp.)

VITTORIO GIANNINI (1903-   )

Variations on a Cantus Firmus	Large-scale work in post-romantic piano style demanding a variety of pianistic accomplishments including virtuosity and bravura. Each group can be played separately or the entire set can be played as a complete unit. (Elkan-Vogel)
Moderato, Var. 1-10	
Aria, Var. 11-12	
Toccata, Var. 13-22	
Interlude, Var. 23-24	

MIRIAM GIDEON (1906-   )

Canzona (1945)	One-movement piece written in a two-voiced texture featuring wide skips, crisp piano style, animated restless motion, staccato timbres. Demands musicianship and keyboard skill. Not tonal. In New Music, Jan., 1947.

ROGER GOEB (1914-   )

Fuga Contraria (1950)	Five twelve-tone fugues posing knotty problems in clarity of texture. See especially No. 5; a light, staccato piece, scherzando in quality. (A. C.A. Library)

Fantasia (1950)	A work conceived on a broad scale; dissonant, percussive, bold. (A.C.A. Library)
Dance Suite (1950)	Set of moderately long pieces, not easy. (A.C.A. Library)

RICHARD FRANKO GOLDMAN (1910-   )

Nine Bagatelles	Tiny pieces for children. Illustrations by Alexandra Rienzi. (Axelrod)
Sonatina (1942)	Vigorous opening movement <u>Moderately Fast</u> with lyric theme contrasting; quiet slow movement with rich, thick harmonies; very fast finale in 5/8 having the qualities of a hornpipe. Requires a large hand, incisiveness, sensitivity. (Mercury Music)
Etude on the White Keys	Brilliant piece in double notes, chords, some cantabile melody, asymmetrical rhythms. Not easy. (Mercury Music)
Aubades	Four short pieces of contrasting character: one and three are melodic, two and four have running figuration. (Mercury Music)

MORTON GOULD (1913-   )

Prologue—1945	Jubilant, dramatic piece heralding the birth of the United Nations. Sonorous, dissonant and chordal. (Mills Music)
Boogie-Woogie Etude	Vigorous, brilliant, bravura, percussive piece on an ostinato bass. Takes stamina and drive. (Mills Music)
Sonatina (1939)	
Moderately fast— spirited	Driving, rhythmic movement, non legato eighths in alla breve.
Spiritual	Lazy, relaxed melody, simple homophonic accompaniments.
Minuet	Bright, crisp caricature.
Finale	Fast, vigorous, satirical. Requires strong fingers, verve and brilliance. (Mills Music)
	Carl Fischer and Mills also publish a large number of other piano pieces by Gould.

PERCY GRAINGER (1882-   )

Percy Grainger's compositions have an individuality like that of his pianoforte playing.

Country Gardens	This has an uninhibited quality that, together with its lack of technical difficulty, has made it popular. (Schirmer)
Shepherd's Hey	Needs considerable technical power to achieve its full brilliance of effect. (Schirmer)
Londonderry Air	This arrangement shows great feeling for tonal beauty and much harmonic ingenuity. (Schirmer) (See also under C. V. Stanford)

RAY GREEN (1908-)

Sonatina
 	
  Introduction
  Vigorously
  Slowly
  Vivace
  Coda
	No bar lines, special effects with the middle pedal, declamatory qualities.
	Last movement in toccata style leading back to introduction and coda. Short, energetic, musically difficult.
	In New Music, April, 1934.

Festival Fugues (An American Toccata)	A good-natured collection flavored with American folk materials: ambling Prelude Promenade, bouncing Holiday Fugue, Fugal Song, modal Prelude Pastorale, jazzy Jubilant Fugue as finale. (Arrow Music Press)
An American Agon	Sonata in three sections: hard, energetic introduction; light, imitative fugato; rhapsodic summation. Difficult, dissonant. (American Music Center)
Preludes Four	Short sketches: one and three intense and lyric, two and four full of nervous, energetic vigor. (American Music Center)
Short Sonata in F Major	Brisk, good-natured Opening Movement; melodic Pastorale; short, chordal Chorale; lively Ending Movement recalling the opening. (American Music Center)
Suite (1931)	Theme and variations: Ritmico-con fuoco on an ostinato bass, sombre Nocturne with sudden explosive comments, tiny Interlude leading to Spinich Tanzer (satiric habanera) and Fugato ("starts with imitation and ends with technic"—including "Pop Goes the Weasel"). (American Music Center)
Dance Set	An American Rigaudon in fast square-dance style, Pastoral Nocturne in the style of a saxophone or clarinet tune with florid improvisa-

tion on reiterated accompanying figure, and
An American Bourrée (easy, short).
(American Music Center) The Bourrée is
published separately by Axelrod.

Pieces for Children	Four pieces "to introduce contemporary music materials to children—and to adults who hear or play them." Not difficult, attractive rhythmically and melodically. (American Music Edition, through American Music Center)

CHARLES TOMLINSON GRIFFES (1884-1920)

The earlier pieces are strongly derivative in idiom but the Sonata is more
original in treatment and perhaps constitutes a landmark in American
piano music. It displays an energy and a sense of large design that make
it a work to reckon with. It may well be true that it is underestimated and
not played as often as its content merits. All the music below is published
by Schirmer.

Three Tone Poems, Op. 5

The Lake at Evening Night Winds The Vale of Dreams	Atmospheric essays rooted in French Impressionism. See especially No. 2 with its fluent pianistic qualities.
Fantasy Pieces, Op. 6 Barcarolle Nocturne Scherzo	Extended piano pieces in a post-romantic style. Lush, widespread, broken-chord sonorities. Occasional exotic chromaticisms. The first two are atmospheric, demanding sensitivity and color. The third requires verve and bravura.
Four Roman Sketches, Op. 7	Impressionist studies, atmospheric, evocative. Not difficult.
The White Peacock (1915) Nightfall (1916) The Fountain of the Acqua Paola (1916) Clouds (1916)	Predominantly chordal, some passage playing. Requires sensitivity and flexibility of phrase. Lento misterioso, floating sonorities. Liquid figuration. Problems in double notes, cross-rhythms. Processional chord movements, generally quiet, polytonal.
Sonata (1917-1918)	Large-scale, serious work. Energetic, vigorous, bold. In two large sections with subdivisions.
Feroce—Allegretto con Moto	Fast, impulsive 12/8. Great variety of textures, agitated. Lyric contrasts leading to a Molto tranquillo with quiet melody in a bare, stately 4/4 with agitated moments.
Allegro vivace	Rapid 6/8 predominantly rhythmic in emphasis. Interruptions by previous material from the slow movement. Impassioned presto ending.
	Demands complete equipment.

LOUIS GRUENBERG (1884-   )

Polychromatics, Op. 16

A miscellany of piano pieces.

Instead of a Prolog

Rhythmic prelude, brilliant octaves, double notes, passages.

Out of the Mist

Tranquil, atmospheric lento, big climax, quiet close.

The Lady with the Damask Mantle

Capricious, light scherzo.

The Knight of the Black Pool

Robust, energetic, short.

Festivities

Free allegro, changing moods.

A Rag-Time Fragment

"Tempo di Jazz"

Invocation

Majestic, quasi-improvisato.

Instead of an Epilog

(Universal Edition)

Jazzberries, Op. 25 (1924)

Foxtrot
Blues
Waltz
Syncopep

Imitation of various jazz styles of the 1920's. Requires sharp rhythmic sense and some facility.

(Associated Music)

ALEXEI HAIEFF (1914-   )

Five Pieces (1946)

Energetic, propulsive _Allegro_ with irregular meters and bold skips. Quiet, free-voiced _Andantino_ in imitative counterpoint. Light, lively _Vivace scherzando_ demanding agility. Quiet, relaxed _Lento molto_. Bravura, dance-like _Allegro molto_ with fast octaves, skips and irregular accentuation.
(Boosey & Hawkes)

HOWARD HANSON (1896-   )

Dance of the Warriors
Enchantment

Two pieces for children: the first spirited and assertive; the second songlike and smooth in quality.
(Carl Fischer)

ROY HARRIS (1898-   )

Sonata, Op. 1 (1928)

Prelude
Andante Ostinato
Scherzo (leading through a short cadenza to)
Coda

Majestic opening, chordal textures.
Quiet slow movement, homophonic.
Rhythmic, busy movement, imitative figures, mostly in two voices.
Sonorous close, maestoso, recapturing the texture of the opening movement.
(Arrow Music Press)

Little Suite for Piano (1938)

Bells	Four tiny pieces, irregular meters, problems
Sad News	in sonority and rhythm, chords in fourths and
Children at Play	fifths.
Slumber	(Schirmer)

American Ballads (1946) Paraphrases of American folk songs. Such tunes as Wayfaring Stranger, Cod Liver Ile, Black is the Color of My True Love's Hair, etc., are treated to a variety of pianistic settings, mostly homophonic. Independent piano pieces, not merely arrangements. (Carl Fischer)

Toccata (1949) An improvisatory piece. Sustained chords and bass tones, over which the melodies move in octaves or double octaves. Chordal textures, two-voice fugato, cadenza finale. Open sonorities. (Carl Fischer)

Suite for Piano Moderate difficulty.

Occupation Ringing, hammered octaves, irregular meters, sonorous throughout.

Contemplation Folklike tunes treated to a variety of textures and figurations. Slow 3/4.

Recreation Crisp 6/8 in bouncing gigue-like motion. Requires energy and drive. (Mills Music)

LOU HARRISON (1917-   )

Six Sonatas For cembalo or pianoforte. Modern essays in the one-movement form and predominantly two-voiced texture of Domenico Scarlatti. Modest, craftsmanlike music, chamber style. In New Music, Oct. 1943.

FREDERIC HART (1898-   )

Three Preludes Melodic essays of moderate length and difficulty. No. 2 a contrasting Allegro vivace. (American Music Center)

CHARLES HAUBIEL (1894-   )

Elves Spinning Delicate scherzo requiring fine finger work and lightness of touch. (Composer's Press)

HERBERT HAUFRECHT (1909-   )

Sicilian Suite

Preludio Bright, rapid figuration, étude style.

Siciliana Graceful Allegretto. Irregular meters opposing traditional siciliano rhythms.

Tarantella	Short, brilliant. Requires facility and energy. (A.C.A. Library) The <u>Tarantella</u> is also available at E. B. Marks.
Passacaglia and Fugue (1947)	Large-scale work on six-bar theme. Sixteen variations, big climax, maestoso ending. Requires all-round equipment. (A.C.A. Library)
Whoa, Little Horses and other pieces	Eight short, easy pieces in descriptive vein: <u>Horses</u>, <u>Bees</u>, <u>Fish</u>, <u>Birds</u>, <u>Gorillas</u>, <u>Cats</u>, <u>Frogs</u>, <u>Children</u>. (American Music Center)

PAUL HINDEMITH (1895-   ) Germany

Hindemith has given the pianist some significant works to consider. The same carefully constructed devices that characterise his style at large form the basis of his piano music, i.e., a painstaking linear writing based on a clear, firm, but expanded concept of tonality. The works repay study. The initial reaction of dryness makes way, upon closer acquaintance, for an awareness of a musician of stature at work. A key to his musical outlook can be obtained from <u>The Craft of Musical Composition</u>, Hindemith's own theoretical writings in two books (Associated Music). Schott originally published all the piano music which is now handled by Associated Music Publishers.

Tanzstücke, Op. 19	Eight dance pieces, the last five grouped under the heading <u>Pantomime</u>. A vigorous set requiring strong octaves and chords.
Suite "1922," Op. 26 Marsch Schimmy Nachtstück Boston Ragtime	Witty, ironic treatment of dance styles of the Twenties. Demands an uninhibited approach. The note to Ragtime is characteristic: "Forget everything you have learned in your piano lessons. Don't worry whether you must play D sharp with the fourth or the sixth finger. Play this piece wildly but in strict rhythm, like a machine. Use the piano as an interesting kind of percussion instrument and treat it accordingly." The <u>Nachtstück</u> is a lyrical nocturne that can be played separately. The <u>Boston</u> demands an imaginative rubato.
Sonata No. 1 (1936)	Large-scale work in five movements inspired by the poem <u>Der Main</u> of Friedrich Hölderlin. Demands mostly a good chord technique and clear part playing. Difficult. For mature players.
Sonata No. 2 (1936)	In the spirit of a large sonatina. Three movements with short slow introduction to the final rondo. Ingratiating, graceful qualities. Easiest of the sonatas.

Sonata No. 3 (1936)	Large-scale work in four movements closing with a huge double fugue. Orchestral sonorities at the close. Takes power and a resourceful command of the piano.
Übung in drei stücken Op. 37 Pt. 1 (Exercise in three pieces)	1—robust, marcato two-part writing, irregular meters, light, jazzy middle section. 2—quiet melody within difficult figuration leading to prestissimo close over a prolonged ostinato bass. 3—brilliant rondo, rhythmic problems.
Reihe kleine stücke Op. 37 Pt. 2 (Set of little pieces)	Thirteen pieces of moderate length: two- and three-part inventions, light waltz, bravura pieces, scherzi, etc. Quite difficult. See especially Einleitung und Lied. Entire set requires some maturity and dexterity.
Kleine klavier musik	Twelve easy five-tone pieces in various moods. Middle grade.
Wir bauen eine Stadt (Let's build a city)	Piano music for children (from the play cantata of the same name).
Ludus Tonalis (1943) ("Studies in Counterpoint Tonal Organization and Piano Playing")	"Twelve Fugues, in as many keys, connected by Interludes in free lyric and dance forms, old and new, and framed by a Prelude and Postlude that have more in common than meets the casual ear." A modern Well-tempered Clavier using a richly assorted array of contrapuntal devices within the framework of Hindemith's expanded concepts of tonality. The Interludes are bravura, pastoral, scherzando, étude-like, lyric, march, waltz, etc. The Fugues are three and four voices, quietly moving, scherzando (5/8), energetic, giguelike, assertive, graceful, etc. The pieces vary from moderate to great difficulty.

ANDREW IMBRIE (1921-)

Sonata (1947)	Compact work, serious in intent. Requires maturity and all-round pianism. Propulsive, linear, dynamic Allegro nervoso. Intense Adagio quasi elegiaco with strong central climax. Harsh, biting Presto con brio with strong marcatissimo ending. (Valley Music Press)

CHARLES IVES (1874-)

The piano music of Ives is a tough nut to crack, whether in actual performance or by way of evaluation. The style (or styles) most often presents a page crowded with notes, apparently aimless or chaotic in structure, bristling with chromatics and complicated polyrhythms, sometimes impossible to play without the cooperation of another performer (which he often recommends!). Or, on the contrary, the music will lapse into simple triadic hymnlike passages disconcertingly but often touchingly juxtaposed with strongly dissonant sections. With all the diffuseness there are moments when one feels that Ives is imbued with deeply national American traits matched by no other composer. The Concord Sonata is a document to prove this point. Ives's Essays Before a Sonata (partially reprinted in the Arrow Music Press edition of the sonata) and the composer's own notes on·performance (included in the same edition) provide, more than anything else, an insight into the mind of the man who created this mountainous set of four pieces. After John Kirkpatrick's historic first performance in 1939, the late Lawrence Gilman wrote: "This sonata is exceptionally great music—it is, indeed, the greatest music composed by an American in impulse and implication." Certainly only posterity can provide final judgment on such a point. Meanwhile only pianists with complete equipments and musicians interested in exploring problematical music will grapple with Ives's piano pieces.

So far the following have been published:

Second Pianoforte Sonata "Concord, Mass., 1840-1860" Emerson Hawthorne The Alcotts Thoreau	"....a group of four pieces called a sonata for want of a more exact name. The whole is an attempt to present one person's impression of the spirit of transcendentalism that is associated in the minds of many with Concord, Mass. of over a half century ago....impressionistic pictures of Emerson and Thoreau, a sketch of the Alcotts, and a scherzo supposed to reflect a lighter quality which is often found in the fantastic side of Hawthorne." (Composer's note.) Demands a complete command of the instrument. Very difficult problems in unorthodox figurations and sonorities. (Arrow Music Press)
Three-Page Sonata	Original manuscript three pages long. Pokes fun at traditional sonata form. Problems in polyrhythms. (Mercury Music)
The Anti-Abolitionist Riots in Boston in the 1850's	Adagio maestoso, no bar lines. Heavy thick chordal textures, fff climax, quiet ending. Short. (Mercury Music)
Some Southpaw Pitching	Chromatic figuration in left hand, melody with triadic harmonies in the right. (Mercury Music)
Three Protests 22	Very tiny sketches, completely problematical. In New Music

FREDERICK JACOBI (1891-1952)

Introduction and Toccata	Improvisational introduction, free declamation, brilliant alternating octaves, solo melody. Fast dancelike Toccata in 2/4. Close passage playing in running sixteenths, crossed hands.

	Frequent interjection of the introductory material. Brilliant close. Demands facility. (Axelrod)
Moods	Moderately long, moderately difficult. Assertive, declamatory phrases opposed to gentle and then impassioned lyric statements. In U.S.A. 1946 (album published by Leeds Music)
Prelude and Toccata in E Minor	Gently flowing, lyric Prelude with the Toccata in perpetually-moving sixteenth-note figuration for the right hand. Moderate difficulty. (Axelrod)

HUNTER JOHNSON (1906-   )

Sonata (1933-1934, rewritten 1936, revised 1947-1948) Allegro molto e dinamico Andante cantabile Allegro giusto	Large-scale, serious work demanding mature musicianship and pianism. "....my spirit was teeming defiantly with America....It is an intense expression of the South....the nostalgia, dark brooding, frenzied gaiety, high rhetoric and brutal realism are all intermingled." Varied, spacious textures, sonorous, lyric and dramatic by turns, driving rhythms, asymmetrical meters. Strong declamatory conclusion, using fragments from the previous movements. (Mercury Music)

NORMAN DELLO JOIO (1913-   )

The piano music of Dello Joio is characterized by facility, clarity, polish and drive. Although harmonically indebted to Hindemith, Dello Joio often turns to Gregorian tunes for inspiration and, in more effervescent moods, to the rhythms of American jazz. The difficulties are not excessive even though some of his movements call for a brilliant bravura. In his best moments his music is modern in style, meaningful in content, energetic and, at the same time, readily accessible to average music-loving audiences.

Prelude: To a Young Musician (1944)	Lyric moderato, homophonic, not difficult, quiet. (Schirmer)
Prelude: To a Young Dancer (1945)	More extended and more difficult than the above. Climactic. (Schirmer)
Suite for Piano (1940)	Four short pieces: lyric, rhythmic (jazzlike), atmospheric, vigorous. Demands good legato, color, incisiveness, some bravura. (Schirmer)
Sonata No. 1 (1943)	Intense Chorale Prelude (broad chorale tune over pedal point), Canon in four-voice lyric counterpoint, exuberant Capriccio as finale with problems in octaves, chords, double notes. (Hargail)

Sonata No. 2 (1943)
 	
  Presto martellato
  Adagio
  Vivace spiritoso
	Dissonant, driving work demanding power and stamina. Fast repeated octaves and chords. Each movement has powerful climactic points. (Schirmer)

Sonata No. 3 (1948)	Five variations and coda on a Gregorian tune: short scherzo (Presto e leggiero); clear, melodic Adagio; vivacious finale (Allegro vivo e ritmico). (Carl Fischer)
Nocturne in E Major	Florid four-part writing with contrasting solo melody in middle section. (Carl Fischer)
Nocturne in F-sharp Minor	Quiet opening. Delicate, bouncing, rhythmic middle section. Large stretches. (Carl Fischer)

ULYSSES KAY (1917-   )

Eight Inventions (1946)	A large group, not easy: breezy Allegro, lyric three-voice Moderato, plaintive Andantino, Scherzando in 5/8, Grave in free declamatory style, flowing Moderato in three voices, atmospheric Larghetto in four voices, breathless Presto with fast-running passages bravura—strong ending. (A.C.A. Library)

LEON KIRCHNER (1919-   )

This young composer from California has shown a vitality, intensity and seriousness of purpose that merits the attention of musicians. The following pieces (his only piano works thus far published) reveal a kinship with the music of Bartók.

Sonata	Demanding in every sense: emotionally, rhythmically, technically. Requires virtuosity, an ability to hold together large sections, a sense of color, an impulsive, vital accentuation and stamina. Slow introduction (Lento - poco a poco doppio movimento) leads to an energetic, rhythmic allegro which connects to an atmospheric slow movement (Adagio). Closing movement intense (Allegro Barbaro) with reprise of material from first movement. (Bomart)

Little Suite
 	
  Prelude
  Song
  Toccata
  Fantasy
  Epilogue
	Short, intense sketches each about a page in length. Require musicianship rather than facility. For serious young students. (Mercury Music)

ELLIS B. KOHS (1916-   )

Kohs has written a series of piano pieces that are eminently playable. The piano sonority is incisive, unencumbered and direct; the writing controlled and the structure clear. He uses medieval (L'Homme Armé), baroque (Toccata) and contemporary sources for inspiration with equal facility.

Toccata	For harpsichord or piano. An extended work modeled after the toccatas of the baroque era; free passages, recitative, fugato sections, cadenzas, canon, chordal sections and a chorale. Both dramatic and lyric qualities. Difficult and largely not tonal. (Mercury Music)
Piano Variations (1946)	Built on a basic set of four chords from which the ideas unfold. Some counterpoint, many types of broken-chord textures. The variations lead into one another without break. Climactic end. Fairly difficult. (Mercury Music)
Étude (1946) (In Memory of Bartók)	Short, bold, rough timbres featuring the interval of the ninth. Requires assertiveness and a large hand. (A.C.A. Library)
Variations on "L'Homme Armé" (1946-1947)	Eighteen variations and theme da capo on the famous medieval song. Requires full command of the piano, bravura, precision in touch. Quiet, elegiac ending after brilliant climax. (A.C.A. Library)
Ten Inventions (1949-1950)	An elaborately worked-out set of contrapuntal problems involving two voices. Require mature musicianship and pianism. Kohs explores monotonality, polymodality, polytonality, a six-tone scale, simultaneous use of both whole-tone scales, motivic elaboration, canon, inversion, retrograde, harmonics, etc. Nos. 2 and 9 are for left hand alone. Nos. 3 and 8 are for right hand alone. The entire work has a symmetrical structural plan. (A. C.A. Library)

BORIS KOUTZEN (1901-   )

Sonatine (1931)	Three movements, connected and related. Dissonant Vivo in marcato sixteenth notes, linear, two to four voices. Transition to quiet fugal movement with some energetic elaboration. Dancelike finale; light, clear textures. Coda serves as résumé of previous material. Climactic ending. Freely chromatic, difficult. (La Sirène Musicale)

ERNST KRENEK (1900-   ) Austria

Those piano pieces of Krenek written in the twelve-tone manner exhibit a compromise between a ruthless, linear writing (with minimum consideration for the traditional vertical aspects of sound) and the conventional tonal organization of music. Both the rhythms, melodies and musical textures are less jagged and abrupt than is usual, for example, with Schönberg. By contrast, the pianistic style is softer in contour, the figuration along more traditional lines and, in some cases, "the harmonic processes are controlled by the desire of creating a lively and expressive alternation of tension and release through proper manipulation of interval combinations of higher and lower tension (less exactly known as 'dissonances' and 'consonances')." (Composer's notes to Eight Piano Pieces, 1946.)

Toccata and Chaconne, Op. 13 on the choral "Ja, Ich glaub' an Jesum Christum"	Large, complicated Toccata in baroque style (free fugatos, shifting moods, big emotional canvas). Extended Chaconne on a fourteen-bar bass leading to a weighty, bravura elaboration requiring power and stamina. Quiet, chordal close after the climax. Freely chromatic. Demands complete pianistic equipment. (Universal Edition)
Little Suite, Op. 13a (on the above choral) **Allemande** Sarabande Gavotte Waltz Fugue Fox Trot	A tour de force. Tiny movements retaining the texture of the old dances within a modern idiom making free use of tonality (except for the atonal fugue). All movements linked thematically. Moderate difficulty. To be played with the good humor in which it is written.
Two Suites, Op. 26 (1924)	Five short movements in each suite. Fairly difficult, dissonant. Require mature musicianship. (Universal Edition)
Five Piano Pieces, Op. 39 (1925)	Short, expressive, intimate mood pieces, not difficult. Freely tonal, mildly dissonant. A useful group for study or performance. (Universal Edition)
Sonata No. 2, Op. 59 (1928) Allegretto Alla marcia, energico Allegro giocoso	Buoyant, spirited work. Demands rhythmic vigor and vitality. Mostly chordal techniques. Dry, martellato passage work. Free use of all chromatic tones with a tonal basis to the entire structure. Fairly difficult. (Associated Music)
12 Short Piano Pieces, Op. 83 (1938)	Descriptive pieces with programmatic titles, all written in the twelve-tone method on the same basic row. Very moderate pianistic difficulty. A good introduction for inexperienced pianists. (Schirmer)

Sonata No. 3 (1943)	Twelve-tone work, not excessively difficult.
Allegretto piacevole	Smoothly flowing, lyrical.
Theme, Canons and Variations	Variety of textures and moods; expressive, dramatic, graceful, vigorous.
Scherzo	Violent motives alternating with graceful and tranquil ideas. Martellato climax double forte.
Adagio	Thick-textured, expressive movement leading to climax and then an ending pppp. (Associated Music)

Eight Piano Pieces (1946)	Twelve-tone pieces built on a single row ac-
Etude	companied by Krenek's analysis and sugges-
Invention	tions for interpretation. Demand careful
Scherzo	phrasing, independent voice leading, sensitive
Toccata	balance, moderate facility.
Nocturne	(Mercury Music)
Waltz	
Air	
Rondo	

Sonata No. 4	Large-scale, serious work demanding mature musicianship and pianism (twelve-tone).
Sostenuto—Allegro ma non troppo—Allegro assai	Introspective, diffuse opening leading to more and more vigorous and decisive conclusion.
Andante sostenuto, con passione	Sharply contrasting phrases and timbres. Opposition of sostenuto and staccato phrases.
Rondo-vivace	Scherzando, staccato opening, alternating with a furious rhythmic section culminating in vio-lent unison passages and concluding with rolling ostinato figures and an abrupt ending double forte.
Tempo di minuetto, molto lento	Ten-bar theme (reminiscent of the Tempo di minuetto in Beethoven's Diabelli Variations), several short variations, leading to a quiet, evanescent ending. (Bomart)

GAIL KUBIK (1914-   )

Sonata	Lengthy work based on American idioms.
Moderately fast, gracefully	Ambling qualities, chordal textures, octaves, irregular meters.
Gaily	Wry humor, strongly contrasting textures, at times percussive.
Slowly, expressively	Quiet, hymnlike opening leading to sharply percussive middle section. Heavy climax, quiet ending.
Fairly fast, hard, bright, mechanical	Driving rhythms, strongly accented, percus-sive. Strong ending. (Southern Music Publishing Co.)

Sonatina (1941)

Moderately fast	Smooth, graceful, irregular meters.
Lively	Sharp, biting outbursts, spirited.
Very slowly	Some canonic writing, solo melody, interweaving parts.
Toccata	"Fast, hard and brittle," changing meters. (Mercury Music)

ROBERT KURKA (1921-   )

For the Piano (1949)
An extended piece, moderato sixteenth notes, no bar lines, the quarter note serving as unit. Improvisational in general character, elaborating a variety of ideas and textures in a style requiring full command of the piano and a discerning musicianship.
(Mercury Music)

Sonata, Op. 20
Fresh, vigorous work exploring American folk materials: fast, dynamic opening movement with quiet side theme; simple, euphonious, lyric movement, relaxed and tender; bravura finale, <u>Very Fast</u>, on a tune that might be a sea chanty.
(American Music Center)

DAI-KEONG LEE (1915-   )

Sonatina
   Allegro moderato
   Andante sostenuto
   Scherzo
A genial work of modest proportions. Ingratiating qualities, especially the rhythmic bounce of the final <u>Scherzo</u>.
(Mills Music)

Three Preludes for Piano
Short pieces exploiting characteristic ideas using many chords built in fourths. The second piece is a spirited rondo.
(Arrow Music Press)

JOHN LESSARD (1920-   )

Mask (1946)
Lively allegretto, dissonant, clear textures, dancelike, moderate length and difficulty. Requires sharp accentuation, precision and neatness. Some octaves and skips.
(Mercury Music)

ERNST LEVY (1895-   ) Switzerland

Five Pieces (1945)
Free pieces in irregular meters: Smoothly-flowing three voices in 7/8; vigorous, rhythmic scherzo in 7/8, 9/8, 11/8; short unbarred prelude in three voices, striding quarter notes; agitated, rough lamentation leading to long, quiet melodic section with parallel ostinato harmonies; singing, modal, four-voice

fugue driving to an effective climactic
ending.
(Associated Music)

NIKOLAI LOPATNIKOFF (1903-   ) Russia

Five Contrasts, Op. 16   Effective treatment of five moods: impassioned, tender, agitated, expressive, ener-
getic. Dissonant but tonal. Demands bravura
and variety of touch.
(Associated Music)

Dialogues, Op. 18 (1932)   Five essays in two-part writing, freely tonal;
Moderato, Allegro molto, Vivace, Grave,
Epilog (moderato). Interesting and varied
pianism. Demands musicianship and moder-
ate facility.
(Schott, through Associated Music)

Sonata, Op. 29 (1943)   Virtuoso work, the end movements requiring
an energetic drive; toccata-like Allegro
risoluto with bold melodies, martellato passage work and suave, quiet middle section;
relaxed Andantino at a walking pace, folklike
melodies working to a central climax; bravura
Allegro molto vivace with quiet interlude.
A challenging work.
(Associated Music)

Toccata   From a sonatina. Fugal texture, perpetually
hammered sixteenth notes, double notes,
octaves, chords in fourths, heavy climax.
Effective, not too long.
In Con Tempo (album published by E. B.
Marks).

BOHUSLAV MARTINU (1890-   ) Czechoslovakia

Three Czech Dances   Exuberant, bravura. Various chord tech-
    Okračák   niques, broken chords, octaves and double
    Dupák   notes.
    Polka   (Eschig)

Études and Polkas (1945)   Sixteen pieces in three books, each Étude
alternating with a Polka. The Etudes demand
bravura and endurance, the Polkas require a
sensitive, rhythmic bounce and precision in
touch. See especially the last Polka in Bk. III.
(Boosey & Hawkes)

Fantaisie et Toccata   Large-scale, bravura work exploiting a wide
variety of textures. Requires all-round
pianism.
(Associated Music)

DANIEL GREGORY MASON (1873-   )

Country Pictures, Op. 9

Bk. I	Set of descriptive pieces in the Brahmsian
Cloud Pageant	tradition, but individual in profile. Post-
Chimney Swallow	romantic piano style. The second and sixth
Bk. II	demand facility.
At Sunset	(Associated Music)
The Quiet Hour	
The Whippoorwill	
Night Wind	

JACQUES DE MENASCE (1905-   )

Perpetuum Mobile

A bravura piece, broken-chord figures in left hand, double thirds, sixths and sevenths in the right. Fast moving 6/8, effective and breath-taking.
(Elkan-Vogel)

Five Fingerprints

Page-length bagatelles of moderate difficulty. Characteristic sketches.
(Elkan-Vogel)

Sonatina No. 2

Requires facility and adroitness: sly, grotesque Allegro leading without pause to a Scherzo, molto vivace with a light waltz as trio; short, expressive Adagio in four voices; animated Finale.
(Mercury Music)

Sonatina No. 3

A good-natured work: short, rhythmic Allegro scherzando with contrasting lyric section; cantabile theme and four variations (three on the brilliant side) with lyric coda; bright, rhythmic Rondo - Allegro assai alternating with a scherzando Tempo II, meno mosso.
(Mercury Music)

Danse Champêtre

Requires agility, clarity, neatness. Lively sixteenths in 4/4.
(E. B. Marks)

Romantic Suite

Five short pieces in intimate vein: light Rondino, flowing Berceuse, Moment Musical, sustained Romanza, perpetually moving Toccatina.
(American Music Center)

PETER MENNIN (1923-   )

Five Piano Pieces (1951)

To be played separately or as a group. Irregular meters throughout. Require facility, rhythmic intensity, power and sensitivity.

Prelude	Short, light, perpetual motion.
Aria	Sustained, tranquil adagio, climactic.

Variation-Canzona	Contrapuntal transformations of a rhythmic idea in 5/8.
Canto	Lengthy andante, flowing cantabile style.
Toccata	Vigorous rhythms strongly accented. Perpetual motion. Difficult. (Carl Fischer)

DOUGLAS MOORE (1893-   )

Suite for Piano

Prelude	Bouncing tune over two light accompanying voices, con brio. Changing meters.
Reel	Tricky 6/8, becoming quite florid,
Dancing School	Light buoyant rhythms and textures. Melody in unison octaves. Bare harmonies. Quite extended.
Barn Dance	Rollicking bit of Americana. Unhackneyed, not easy. Requires agility in general execution. Skips.
Air	Sustained melody, clear transparent treatment. Open, direct qualities.
Procession	Marchlike allegro moderato. Requires precise staccato octaves, clear accentuation, energy. (Carl Fischer)

ROBERT PALMER (1915-   )

Three Preludes (1941)	In irregular meters, quite difficult.
Vivace con grazia	Unusual lyric essay with a fine working out of ideas. Constantly changing meters.
Molto tranquillo e cantabile	Flowing song without words in 17/16.
Molto pesante-Allegro con energia	Heavy, dissonant. Requires strength in left-hand broken figuration. In 11/4. (Valley Music Press, Northampton, Mass.)
Toccata Ostinato	Rough, energetic, fast, brittle, percussive. Ostinato bass. Requires rhythmic vitality and drive. (Elkan-Vogel)

VINCENT PERSICHETTI (1915-   )

Perhaps the clue to Vincent Persichetti's rapidly growing output for piano is the composer's own exceptional pianism. Although he has withdrawn many earlier works, Persichetti still has a large number of piano pieces to his credit. They display at least two marked characteristics: a sensitive lyricism (Poems for Piano, slow movements of the sonatas) and a genuine joy in playing the instrument (closing movements of the sonatas and sonatinas). Everything is in order, everything lies well in the hand. While some of the music is in a casual vein, a work like the Fourth Sonata is weighty and serious in intent, offering problems that are difficult but not excessive. The music is published by Elkan-Vogel.

First Piano Sonata (1939)	Jaunty opening movement; thick-textured Adagio; bright, crisp Vivace; lengthy, complex Passacaglia on an eight-bar theme. Climactic ending.
Second Piano Sonata (1939)	
Third Piano Sonata (1943)	Declaration in predominantly block-chordal textures; quiet, melodic Episode and a Psalm leading to triple forte conclusion.
Fourth Piano Sonata (1949)	Most extended of the sonatas. Large-scale, serious work. Great variety of problems: rhythmic accuracy, power, cantabile and fugato playing, octaves, fast repeated notes. Requires facility, stamina and energy.
Fifth Piano Sonata (1949)	Amiable, flowing opening; quiet Berceuse; brisk, non-legato finale with brilliant passage playing, exuberant cross accents and irregular meters. Requires some facility.
Sixth Piano Sonata (1950)	Graceful four-movement work with brilliant finale.
Seventh Piano Sonata (1950)	Graceful, ambling Moderato with folklike qualities; short, transparent, linear slow movement; fast, scherzo-like conclusion.
Eighth Piano Sonata (1950)	In three movements, generally light in texture.
Five Sonatinas No. 1 (1940) No. 2 (1949) No. 3 (1950) No. 4 (1950) No. 5 (1950)	Light-textured works of moderate difficulty. See especially No. 2 (In one movement: lyric canon in four voices leading to gay finale in the Haydn tradition—modern vein. Bright, rhythmic play. Clear, pointed style, "five-finger" figures).
Poems for Piano (1939)	Eleven short pieces in two volumes suggested by verses of Untermeyer, Fitzgerald, T. S. Eliot and others. Predominantly lyric except for No. 6 (a tiny scherzo) and No. 11 (brilliant Presto). Emphasis on tender, sensitive moods. Volume III (1941) in preparation.

BURRILL PHILLIPS (1907-   )

Three Divertimenti Fancy Dance Homage to Monteverdi Brag	Casual, very brief pieces, each exploiting a single idea. Not difficult. (Elkan-Vogel)
Toccata	Ostinato bass reminiscent of "boogie-woogie," eighth-note motion. Two voices throughout, passages distributed between the hands. Not difficult. (Elkan-Vogel)

A Set of Three Informalities

Blues	Melody with chords over octaves.
Scherzo	Rapid and short. Left hand on black keys, right hand on white. Fast passages for alternating hands. Parallel triads.
Sonatina	Lush melodic opening, rapid middle section in 6/8. Most difficult of the set. (Elkan-Vogel)

PAUL A. PISK (1893-   )Austria

Vier Klavierstücke, Op. 3	Short, prelude-like pieces, freely tonal. See especially No. 1. (Universal Edition)
Sechs Konzertstücke, Op. 7	Difficult, rhapsodic, chromatic. (Universal Edition)
Sonatina (Death Valley), Op. 49	Brusque Alla Marcia; light two-voiced Scherzino with lyric Trio; concluding Finale (alla marcia) recapturing some of the opening movement. (Editorial Cooperativa Interamericano; Southern Music Publishing Co.)
Engine Room	"Motor Study for Piano." Energetic perpetual motion, moderate difficulty. (Leeds Music)
Five Sketches	Short, genial pieces: lyric Andante, light Presto in scherzo vein; Menuetto, quasi habanera, Allegro piacevole (with brilliant ending). In New Music.
Five Piece Set	Short sketches of moderate difficulty. See especially No. 2 (Caprice) and No. 5 (Drollery). (Mills Music)

WALTER PISTON (1894-   )

Passacaglia	Four-bar bass in 5/8, andantino, gathering momentum with each variation to a noble chordal climax. Increasingly complex textures. Sonorous ending. Short. Demands careful phrasing. Moderately difficult. (Mercury Music)
Improvisation	Short lyric piece, relaxed, moderate climax, chord structures in fourths. Quiet ending. Not difficult. in U.S.A. 1946 (album published by Leeds Music)

KAROL RATHAUS (1895-   ) Austria

Five Pieces, Op. 9	Rhythmically strong, linear in emphasis. (Universal Edition)

Six Little Pieces, Op. 11 (1926)	Miniature grotesques. (Universal Edition)
Ballade, Op. 40	<u>Variations on a Hurdy-Gurdy Theme</u> (Bomart)
Three Polish Dances, Op. 47	Three lengthy dances demanding vigor and a fairly advanced pianism: spirited <u>Oberek</u> with quiet middle section and vigorous ending; sensitive, short, melancholy <u>Kujawiak</u>; lengthy and elaborate <u>Mazurka</u> exploiting a variety of textures, broad climax and ending. (Boosey & Hawkes)

GARDNER READ (1913-   )

American Circle	Music for a dance. Folk-song-like melody with several varied settings. Short, not difficult. (Clayton F. Summy)

WALLINGFORD RIEGGER (1885-   )

Four Tone Pictures	Four neatly written, fleeting sketches dealing with single ideas.
Prelude	Atmospheric.
Angles and Curves	Rhythmic scherzando figure opposed to a short melodic idea.
Wishful Thinking	Melody over a two-bar ostinato.
Grotesque	Rhythmic essay using tone clusters and pentatonic scale. Not difficult. (Arrow Music Press)
Finale from the New Dance	Brilliant virtuoso-type piece using Latin-American rhythms. Good closing piece to a group. Demands flexibility in left-hand skips. Fairly difficult. (Arrow Music Press)
New and Old	Twelve instructive pieces with an analysis and explanation of modern terms. (Boosey & Hawkes)
Blue Voyage	Free, improvisatory, rhapsodic piece after the poem by Conrad Aiken. Sharp contrasts; heavy, florid climaxes. Lush, impressionistic piano style. (Schirmer)

BERYL RUBINSTEIN (1898-1952)

Two Etudes (1929)	
Ignis Fatuus	<u>Will o' the Wisp</u>. Fast staccato double notes, short, fleet presto.
Whirligig	Perpetually running passages in the right hand. Light, articulate, brilliant. (Oxford University Press)

Sonatina in C-sharp Minor (1929)	Spirited, joyous opening movement, atmospheric Adagio leading to tarantella-like Allegro vivace, brilliant and effective. (Oxford University Press)
Three Dances for Piano	Moderate difficulty.
Gavotte (1930)	Light allegretto grazioso, some double notes.
Sarabande (1930)	Stately, sonorous. Contrapuntal middle section leading to double forte maestoso climax. Quiet close.
Gigue (1931)	Longest of the three. Brilliant, neat writing, quiet middle section, strong ending. (Riker, Brown and Wellington, Boston)
Twelve Definitions	Set of characteristic pieces defining the following moods: Gently Moving (flowing), Animated (vigorous, rhythmic essay in double notes), Lightly (gently flowing, caressing qualities), Decisive ("very marked, almost brutal," sharp dotted rhythms, heavy octave climax), Gay (perky, dancelike, light syncopated rhythms), Lyric (smooth, songlike), Serene (atmospheric), Spritely (crisp, decisive, fast march), Graceful (waltzlike), Agitated (fiery, impetuous, bravura), Expressive (flexible, freely dramatic and lyric), Spirited (brilliant concluding toccata, rapid alternating hands, fast repeated notes, forceful ending). (Schirmer)

DANE RUDHYAR (1895-   )

Prophetic Rite (1935)	Intense, rhapsodic, improvisatory. Reiterated harmonies, tumultuous, mystical. (Merrymount Music Press)
Granites	Set of improvisatory pieces. In New Music.

ARTUR SCHNABEL (1882-1951) Germany

Piece in Seven Movements Moderato semplice Vivace un poco resoluto Allegretto piacevole Allegretto agitato Vivacissimo Adagio (Variant of No. I)	An extended complicated work demanding a complete pianism and mature musicianship. Four, five and six very lengthy. In the Central European tradition. (E. B. Marks)

ARNOLD SCHÖNBERG (1874-1951) Austria

The piano works of the originator of the method of composing with twelve tones come from periods crucial to his general development. The musical and technical problems are more understandable if studied in relation to other works in his output: the Chamber Symphony, Opus 9 (transcription by Edward Steuermann for piano solo), the Serenade, Opus 24, and the string quartets. Several factors ask for special study: the melodies, characterized by wide intervals and apparent discontinuity; the rhythms, using a variety and subtlety of stress that serve to conceal the main beat; the sonorities, that ask for a perfect balance and a very discreet use of the damper pedal to achieve the utmost in clarity. Schönberg's markings are minute to a disconcerting degree. His own explanations of these markings precede several of the works. Metronome indications are often included but must not be followed mechanically. Their function is merely to assist in establishing a satisfactory tempo.

Perhaps least important in the performance of these works is an understanding of the twelve-tone method of composing. A clear delineation of the phrase, the proper adjustment of accompaniment to melody and the careful projection of the polyphony are more important considerations for the performer. All the pieces are difficult, calling for the utmost concentration and the achievement of great precision in pianism and musicianship. It is a humble but useful suggestion to play the melodic content of each piece from beginning to end before embarking on a detailed working out of pianistic problems.

For a general account of the twelve-tone school consult the studies of René Leibowitz, especially Schönberg and his School, New York, 1949 (English translation by Dika Newlin). Helpful for an understanding of the piano music is the article by Edward Steuermann in Schönberg, Merle Armitage, editor, G. Schirmer, 1937. Most of the piano music is available through Associated Music Co. unless otherwise indicated.

Three Piano Pieces, Op. 11 (1908)	Three epoch-making pieces in Schönberg's trend away from tonal music: the first two somewhat Brahmsian, using readily recognizable motivic material, the third retaining a psychological continuity but containing few repetitive elements comprehensible to the ear.
Six Little Piano Pieces, Op. 19 (1911)	Least difficult of his piano pieces. Fleeting sketches, subtle, sensitive, some only a few measures long.
Five Piano Pieces, Op. 23 (1923)	All pieces pose the most difficult problems in phrasing, touch and stress. The fifth piece (Walzer) is the first in which Schönberg generated the entire work from a row of twelve tones. (Hansen)
Suite for Piano, Op. 25 (1924)	More elaborate use of twelve-tone techniques with many traditional elements of the classic suite retained (the rhythms of the gavotte, the organ point of the musette, etc.): Präludium, Gavotte with Musette, Intermezzo, Minuet with Trio, Gigue.
Piano Piece, Op. 33a (1932)	Intensely expressive and concentrated in structure, elaborate use of the row. For an analysis cf. Leibowitz: Introduction à la Musique de Douze Sons, Paris, 1949.

Piano Piece, Op. 33b (1932)	Long-spun melodies supported by complex figuration. In New Music, April, 1932.

WILLIAM SCHUMAN (1910-   )

Three-Score Set (1945)	Three tiny pieces, each twenty measures long: 1—legato, smoothly flowing, 2—bitonal block chords in opposing motion, 3—fast scherzo in two voices, rapid staccato, tricky rhythms. (Schirmer)

ROGER SESSIONS (1896-   )

Roger Sessions is an American composer who is neither facile nor superficial. The seriousness of his intent and his wide grasp of the problems of music in general have stamped him as one of the most influential individuals in shaping the paths of many younger composers of this country. His few piano works are characterized by solidity, a certain problematical quality and a content that is a challenge to performer and listener alike. They demand the utmost concentration on the part of all concerned.

Sonata No. 1 Andante Allegro Andante Molto vivace	Complicated, knotty work in a series of connected movements employing a great variety of textures. Requires virtuosity and mature musicianship. (Schott)
Four Pieces for Children (1935)	Short, easy pieces, good for teaching material. (Carl Fischer)
From my Diary (1937-1940)	Four short pieces in contrasting moods.
Poco adagio	Sombre, melodic, predominantly three voices. Requires good legato, sensitivity.
Allegro con brio	Scurrying passage work, tranquil middle section, energetic climactic points. Quiet ending.
Larghissimo e misterioso	Brief, atmospheric, expressive.
Allegro pesante	Energetic. Clumps of chords, sharp rhythmic accentuation. (E. B. Marks)
Sonata No. 2 (1946) Allegro con fuoco Lento Misurato e pesante	Large-scale, serious work, completely chromatic in treatment. Harmonically, rhythmically and technically complex. Demands highest level of musicianship. A knotty problem for mature pianists. (E. B. Marks)

HAROLD SHAPERO (1920-   )

Three Sonatas (1944)	Moderate length essays in adapting the textures and formal procedures of the early classic

sonata (especially Haydn) to a modern idiom.
No. 3 is the most substantial in content and
most difficult in execution. All three sonatas
require facility and musicianship.
(Schirmer)

ARTHUR SHEPHERD (1880-)

Gay Promenade (1936)

For children. Rhythmic problems.
(Carl Fischer)

Autumn Fields (1936)

For children. Two-part melodic writing.
(Carl Fischer)

Second Sonata in F Minor
(1930)

Large-scale work.

Moderato, ma deciso

Clear, contrasting themes, incisive. Mostly
homophonic with some quasi-contrapuntal
problems.

Moderato cantabile ma
semplice

Lazy, swinging American folklike tune with
six variations (four-part counterpoint, unison
passage playing, melody in inner part, rhythmic
gigue, calm, sonorous end).

Enfatico ed affrettato
Toccata

Short declamatory transition to a
Lively exuberant finale in mixed meters (3/8-
4/8) demanding vitality, stamina, brilliance,
strong fingers.
(Oxford University Press)

Exotic Dance (1930)

Basis of the composer's later orchestral
Choreographic Suite. Short.
(Oxford University Press)

ELIE SIEGMEISTER (1909-)

An American Sonata
(1944)

Three movements based on popular American
idioms. End movements primarily rhythmic,
middle movement lyric. Fairly difficult.
(E. B. Marks)

Sunday in Brooklyn

Five extended tableaux from the American
scene.

Prospect Park
Sunday Driver
Family at Home
Children's Story
Coney Island

Blues.
Brilliant, perky scherzo.
Relaxed, melodic.
Short, simple, folklike.
Boisterous. Strong ending.
(E. B. Marks)

LEO SOWERBY (1895-)

Toccata

Energetic piece, chord structures in fourths.
Mostly detached martellato playing. Demands
drive and impact.
(Mercury Music)

Florida	Program suite.
River Night	Evocative, lush.
St. Augustine	Sonorous, martial. Octaves, chords, broke chords.
Cypress Swamp	Heavy, foreboding, big climax, quiet end.
Sun-Drenched Palms	Bright, majestic, clangorous sonorities, vigorous rhythms.
Pines at Dusk	Barren, nostalgic. Requires sensitive tonal qualities. (Oxford University Press)

ROBERT STARER (1924-   ) Israel

Five Caprices	Short musical essays of moderate difficulty: light scherzando, serious adagio, rhythmic two-part invention, lyric melody, rapid toccata in burlesque vein. (Peer International Corporation)
Seven Vignettes	Very short easy pieces for students. (Leeds Music)
Prelude and Toccata (1946)	Lyric, chordal Prelude. Rhythmic, perpetually moving Toccata in irregular meters. Moderate length and difficulty. (Leeds Music)
Sonata (1949)	Large-scale, energetic work. Vigorous Allegro; florid, melodic Andante; concluding Allegro frivole. Requires all-round equipment. (Leeds Music)

HALSEY STEVENS (1908-   )

Although it is out of fashion today to characterize a composer as "musical," the first reaction one has to the piano music of Stevens is the sense of a completely musical temperament at work. The singing quality of the lines, the complete clarity and immaculateness of structure and texture unencumbered by padding of any kind, the straightforwardness of his approach and the fine control over his medium create the impression of a composer worth exploring, serious in intent and skilled in craft.

Sonata No. 3 (1947-1948)	Large-scale, serious work in three movements: Allegro non troppo, assertive, bold lines, rhythms in constantly shifting meters; quiet Moderato con moto with one central climax; strong Molto vivace requiring agile passage playing and bravura. Entire sonata is linear in emphasis, clear and clean in its working out. (A.C.A. Library)
Piano Music, Vol. I	A collection of miscellaneous pieces of moderate length, easy to moderately difficult.
Toccata (1948)	Light Allegro capriccioso in irregular meters with sharply accented rhythms. Buoyant qualities.

Three Inventions (1948)	Short pieces in two voices to be played as a unit: rhythmic <u>Allegro</u> requiring neat accentuation; lyric, expressive, legato <u>Andante</u>; rhythmic <u>Allegretto</u> with sharp, dotted rhythms.
A Tune (1947)	Easy, sensitive, short.
Musette (1947)	In alternating 5/8 and 4/8. Oriented toward Bartók.
Improvisation (1949)	Deep, singing qualities, melodic throughout.
Scherzo (1949)	Boisterous, sharply accented caprice requiring agility and vitality. (A.C. A. Library)
Népdolszvit (1950) (Magyar Folk Songs)	Eight short settings in the Bartók manner on tunes collected by the Hungarian master. Skillfully worked out, sensitive, clean, interesting. (A.C.A. Library)

WILLIAM GRANT STILL (1895-   )

Three Visions	Short characteristic pieces.
Dark Horseman	Rapid, galloping figures.
Summerland	Tranquil, melodic sketch.
Radiant Pinnacle	Predominantly lyric moderato. (J. Fischer)
Bells	
Phantom Chapel	Exploits the deeper, sonorous and mystic qualities of bell tones.
Fairy Knoll	In the higher registers of the piano simulating tinkling timbres—a light scherzo. (Leeds Music)
Seven Traceries	Subdued, sensitive sketches in a quasi-impressionist vein, harmonically close to Bloch. Moderate difficulty. Only No. 6 and 7 have dynamic climaxes. (J. Fischer)
Cloud Cradles	
Mystic Pool	
Muted Laughter	
Out of the Silence	
Woven Silver	
Wailing Dawn	
A Bit of Wit	

IGOR STRAVINSKY (1882-   ) Russia

The piano music of Stravinsky varies in viewpoint from the early <u>Études</u> through the jazz-inspired <u>Piano Rag Music</u> to the brilliant virtuoso piano reduction of the orchestral <u>Petrouchka</u> and the more discreet chamber style of the <u>Sonata</u> and the <u>Sérénade</u>. Although a tradition of impersonality and objectivity has grown up in connection with Stravinsky's music, it may well be that movements in the last-named pieces are underedited and do not sufficiently indicate the full gamut of expressive nuances that seem more suitable for their proper realization. It may also be mentioned that

acquaintance with the <u>Octet for Winds</u> throws some light on both the
timbre, sonority and general spirit of the Sonata and <u>Sérénade</u>. Alfred
Cortot discusses the complete piano music of Stravinsky in <u>French Piano
Music</u>.

Four Etudes, Op. 7 (1908)	Nos. 1 (C minor), 2 (D major) and 4 (F-sharp major) deal with metrical problems. No. 3 (E minor) is shortest and simplest of the set. No. 4 is a brilliant and effective perpetual motion. Various reprints.
Piano Rag Music (1919)	Percussive, rhythmic piece based on early ragtime. Difficult, short. (J. & W. Chester)
Les cinq doigts (1921)	Eight easy pieces on five notes. For beginners. Very simple. (Mercury Music)
Trois Mouvements de Petrouchka (1921) Danse Russe Chez Petrouchka La Semaine grasse	Virtuoso version of three scenes from the ballet. Colorful, brilliant, demanding. It goes without saying that any pianist essaying this score should familiarize himself with the original ballet. (Edition Russe, Boosey & Hawkes)
Sonata (1924)	Chamber style. "I have used the term <u>Sonata</u> in its original sense, deriving from the word <u>sonare</u>...." Ambling opening movement in flowing eighth notes. Florid <u>Adagietto</u>, arioso with meandering arabesques. Toccata-like finale in perpetual motion, capricious, short. (Boosey & Hawkes)
Sérénade en la (1925)	In the spirit of the "nachtmusik" of the eighteenth century. No one movement longer than the side of a phonograph record (original contract!). Solemn, processional <u>Hymne</u>. Elegant, coquettish <u>Romanza</u>, solo melody with opening and closing cadenzas. Quiet <u>Cadenza finale</u> in flowing eighth notes. (Boosey & Hawkes)

HOWARD SWANSON (1909-   )

The Cuckoo	Short, characteristic scherzo built on the call of the cuckoo. Moderate difficulty. Excellent encore. (Leeds Music)
Sonata	In three movements: vigorous <u>Allegro risoluto</u>, flowing <u>Andante cantabile</u>, vigorous <u>Allegro vivo</u>. The writing is mostly in two- or three-part counterpoint and the entire sonata has a certain problematical quality. (Weintraub Music)

LOUISE TALMA (1906-   )

Sonata No. 1 (1943)	Serious, large-scale work. (Winner of the North American Prize, 1947, awarded by the E. Robert Schmitz School of Piano.)
Largo—Allegro molto vivace	Short declamatory homophonic introduction leading to a propulsive rhythmic movement in staccato 6/8, two-voiced texture, ostinato figures, sharp accentuation.
Larghetto	Quiet melody in quarters and eighths, four-part harmonic writing, chord structures in fourths and fifths, uniform textures and rhythms. Woodwind quality.
Presto	Rhythmic toccata-like finale, ostinato figures, repeated tones, irregular rhythms, staccato style, climactic ending. (Carl Fischer)
Alleluia in Form of Toccata	An extended piece, good-humored bouncing style, staccato figuration, clear melodies. Demands agility, lightness, neat rhythmic accentuation, stamina. (Carl Fischer)

VIRGIL THOMSON (1896-   )

This well-known critic has contributed a series of pieces for the piano calculated to divert and entertain both player and listener. Thomson must be approached on his own terms if he is to be enjoyed at all. His wry sophistication blends the outlook and methods of the modern French school (especially Erik Satie) with his own personal brand of Americanisms.

Five Two-Part Inventions	Essays in flowing and running two-part writing. A few allusions to J. S. Bach. See especially Nos. 1 and 5. Tonal, yet modern in flavor. (Elkan-Vogel)
Ten Etudes for Piano	Diverting set of ingenious pieces full of a good-humoured utilization of the keyboard: Repeating Tremolo, Tenor Lead, Fingered Fifths, Fingered Glissando, Double Glissando, For the Weaker Fingers, Oscillating Arm, Five Finger Exercise, Parallel Chords, Ragtime Bass. (Schirmer)
Portraits (in 3 albums)	From a hundred musical sketches of various people begun in 1928. "The subject sits for his likeness as he would for a painter. An effort has been made to catch in all cases a likeness recognisable to persons acquainted with the sitter." On the humorous side, not difficult. For more serious moments see Album 3, the neo-classic portrait of Nicolas de Chatelain. Also:

Album 1—<u>Tango Lullaby</u> (Mlle. Alvarez de Toledo).

Album 2—Portrait of R. Kirk Askew
<u>In a Bird Cage</u> (Lise Deharme).

(Mercury Music)

ERNST TOCH (1887-   ) Austria

The piano style of Toch, although not based on Schönberg's method of composing with twelve tones, makes free use of all the tones in the chromatic scale. The emphasis is a great deal on linear treatment and is perhaps in some ways more akin to Hindemith, not only in linear emphasis but also in chord structures and the frequent use of the triad as conclusion. The general character of the sound exploits the drier qualities of piano timbre, with little use of the damper pedal. Clarity, careful phrasing, precision in touch and rhythmic verve are essential to the proper projection of his music.

Burlesken, Op. 31

Three scherzi, of which No. 3 is the well-known <u>Der Jongleur.</u> All the pieces demand facility and rhythmic verve.
(Associated Music)

Three Piano Pieces, Op. 32

Quiet
Delicate, without haste
Allegro moderato

Short sketches requiring delicacy and, in the last one, a moderate bravura.
(Associated Music)

Five Capriccetti, Op. 36

Tender, reflective
Lively
Graceful, gay
Dolce e affetuoso
With exuberant humor

Short pieces requiring spirit, sensitivity and facility. Moderate difficulty.
(Associated Music)

Kleinstadtbilder, Op. 49
(From a small town)

Fourteen tiny pieces, a modern <u>Kinderscenen</u> demanding a variety of touch and subtlety in phrasing, minimizing the aspect of facility.
(Associated Music)

Five times ten Studies for Piano

10 Concert Studies, Op. 55
10 Recital Studies, Op. 56
10 Studies of Medium Difficulty, Op. 57
10 Easy Studies, Op. 58
10 Studies for Beginners, Op. 59

A collection exploring various facets of modern piano style. Non-tonal, for the most part, using the twelve tones of the chromatic scale freely. Cover a wide range of problems.
(Associated Music)

Profiles, Op. 68	Set of six pieces conceived as a cycle.
Calm	Lyric, dissonant counterpoint, scherzando middle section.
Moderato	Irregular meters. Melodic and motivic idea elaborated in free counterpoint.
Calm, fluent, tender	Folklike cradle song, simply treated.
Merry	Rhythmic scherzo in 5/4, dry staccato.
Slow, pensive, very tender	Mostly single melody, lightly accompanied.
Vigorous, hammered	Perpetually moving eighth notes in 3/4. Bold octaves and chords moving to an energetic climax <u>sempre marcatissimo</u>. (Associated Music)
Ideas	Short essays, uneven bar lengths.
Calm	Free lyric two- and three-part counterpoint.
A black dot dances in my closed eye	Flowing figuration, close position, simple melody.
Vivo	Variety of problems; legato, crispness, delicacy.
Allegro	Two-part counterpoint, "each note hammered." (Leeds Music)
Sonata, Op. 47	
Quasi Toccata	Assertive, bold, marcato quarters and eighths with humorous side theme, grazioso.
Intermezzo	Fluent two-part writing, gentle, delicate.
Allegro	Hammered two-part counterpoint, bold, marcato. Quiet catch ending after heavy climax. (Schott, through Associated Music)

GODFREY TURNER (1913-   )

Pianoforte Sonata No. 1 (1941)	In one movement, with basic harmonies in fourths. Broken-chord textures, sonorous climaxes, strong ending. (American Music Center)
Great Paul	Short piece exploiting bell sonorities suggested by Great Paul, one of the big bells of St. Paul's Cathedral, London. (Hargail)

BERNARD WAGENAAR (1894-   )

Ciacona	Four-bar chordal phrase, varied seven times. Florid melodies, chordal textures, some counterpoint, triple-forte close. Short, not difficult. Dissonant but tonal. (E. B. Marks)
Sonata (1920)	Large-scale, serious work along broad, ample lines, exploiting the full resources of the piano. Free, improvisatory style

predominates. Broad, declamatory opening
movement connected to a <u>Rondoletto</u> finale by
an atmospheric, lyric <u>Improvisation</u>. Demands
dramatic qualities, sensitive control of widely
spaced sonorities, facility and a mature
musicianship.
(American Music Center)

ROBERT WARD (1917-)

Lamentation

Sombre largo building to sonorous climax.
Chords in fourths. Some brilliant octaves.
Requires intensity. Fairly difficult.
(Merrymount Music Press)

BEN WEBER (1916-)

Ben Weber takes his point of departure from Schönberg. His piano pieces
display a sensitive musicality expressed in terms of a grateful lyricism,
the expert handling of linear elements and a keen sense of proportion. The
piano writing, although at times tricky, is accessible and rewarding.

Five Bagatelles (1939)

Short pieces using twelve-tone techniques:
playful essay in two-part counterpoint,
melancholy <u>Allegretto alla Canzonetta</u>,
rhythmic <u>Presto</u> in two voices, concentrated
<u>Adagio</u> with big climax, concluding <u>Moderato
non troppo</u> in marcato, three-part dissonant
counterpoint.
In <u>New Music</u>.

Piano Suite, Op. 27
(1948)

<u>Allegro spiritoso</u> in staccato three-part
writing; lyric <u>Lento moderato</u> delicate and
intense; grotesque <u>Affetuosamente</u>, <u>ma con
umore</u> with halting scherzando phrases; vigorous concluding <u>Presto</u> with large skips and
cross-rhythms.
(A.C.A. Library)

Fantasia, Op. 25 (1946)
(Variations)

Complex, large-scale, serious work requiring
mature musicianship and pianism. Warm, intense, broad piano style exploiting the full
range of the keyboard.
(A.C.A. Library)

EMERSON WHITHORNE (1884-

New York Days and
Nights

A descriptive suite with program notes by the
composer.

On the Ferry (1923)

Figures suggesting the paddle wheels of the
old ferries.

Chimes of Saint
Patrick's

Bell sonorities.

Pell Street (1920)

Pentatonic melodies and harmonies simulating
Chinese music.

A Greenwich Village
Tragedy (1922)

Impassioned lyric sections, dramatic
climax.

Times Square (1920)

Animated, rhythmic, busily moving. Includes
fragments of popular tunes of the day.
(Carl Fischer)

ESTHER WILLIAMSON (1915-   )

Sonatina (1941)

Smoothly flowing, linear opening movement;
legato Andante in free "blues" style; light,
scurrying two-voice Scherzo to close.
(A.C.A. Library)

STEFAN WOLPE (1902-   )

Dance (in form of a
chaconne)

Vigorous, rhythmic, percussive, short, not
easy.
(Arrow Music Press)

Passacaglia (1936)

Involved, large-scale work on an eight-bar
theme using all the intervals from minor
second to major seventh. Complex pianism.
In New Music.

Zemach Suite (1939)

Series of pieces based upon a dance suite.
(Hargail)

Pastorale

Two-part lyric counterpoint, improvisational
quality, gently singing. Requires sensitivity.
In U.S.A. Vol. II (album published by Leeds
Music)

Composers in Latin America

(Including Foreign-born Residents)

To think of Latin-American piano music in terms of Lecuona and Villa-Lobos (to mention two of the best-known figures) is not only to oversimplify the picture but to misconstrue the actual state of affairs. There are many interesting figures in the field, perhaps even those who may, in the final reckoning, make a lasting contribution to the literature for piano. And among these figures there are a sufficient number of diverse trends to force us in the northern part of the hemisphere to alter sharply our conceptions as to the pianistic activities of Latin-American musicians.

If it is true that national elements play a weighty role in matters of style, it is just as true that more individual traits are emerging among many composers and more universal concepts are being fused with indigenous materials. To study the music itself is to prove the point. Whereas the music of the dominant figure Villa-Lobos is primarily coloristic in style, influenced by folk material and perhaps fundamentally French in harmonic idiom, one can find numerous composers in completely different camps. The main difficulty in this country is our restricted means of access to sufficient music. But there are many works available that ought to be played and that make one ask for more. Guarnieri has contributed some interesting items; mostly single pieces, strongly individual but clearly national in character. The pieces by Graetzer and Bosmans are those of capable musicians bringing the stream of European tradition into their local musical scenes. The same may be said of Koellreutter and Eitler, both inclined toward twelve-tone writing. Paz, the leading indigenous twelve-tonalist, is known by only a small part of his output. The pieces of Villoud show a preoccupation with indigenous traits quite distinct from those displayed by Villa-Lobos. Morillo offers primitivist qualities that remind one of Stravinsky and, when he chooses, is able to give us works that are really bare and taut, eschewing all national idioms. The Castro brothers, Chavez, Luis Gianneo and Ginastera all offer interesting fare for pianists. While it is hazardous to judge on the basis of the limited avenues of knowledge at our disposal (represented by publications at present available either in libraries or on the market) it seems safe to say that there is more in Latin-American piano music than meets the ear (under present conditions) and that our pianists would do well to extend their repertoires by exploring many of the works listed below.

Abbreviations:

BLAM—Boletin Latino-Americano de Musica, official organ of the Instituto Interamericano de Musicologia. Four volumes with musical supplements.
EAM—Editorial Argentina de Musica, Carl Fischer.
ECIC—Editorial Cooperativa Interamericana de Compositores, Southern Music Publishing Co.
LAAM—Latin-American Art Music for the Piano, G. Schirmer.
An anthology by twelve contemporary composers selected, and provided with a preface and biographical data by Francisco Curt Lange.

The following publications of the Music Division of the Pan American Union are also useful in supplementing the material in this section:

Music in Latin-America 1942, Washington, D. C.

Partial List of Latin-American Music Obtainable in the United States, 1942, Washington, D. C.

L. HUMBERTO ALLENDE (1885-   ) Chile

Although the following pieces are brief, they exhibit, on the part of this Chilean composer, a sensitive joining of piquant harmonies and melodies with an irregular metric structure. The result is interesting and worth exploring, especially the specifically Chilean Tonadas and the Miniatures Grecques.

12 Tonadas	Short pieces of popular Chilean character, each consisting of an expressive Lento in 7/8 and a brisk dancelike vivo in 6/8. Moderately difficult. Problems in tonal balance, phrasing, and rhythmic precision. (Salabert)
6 Etudes	See especially No. 1 (a short, sensitive tranquillo). Moderately difficult. (Salabert)
Tempo di Minuetto	Chromatic, lyric intermezzo, free-voiced, lush, short. (Salabert)
6 Miniatures Grecques	A sensitive group, all on the white keys except No. 5. (Salabert)

JOSÉ ARDÉVOL (1911-   ) Cuba

Spanish-born composer Ardévol has been in Cuba since 1930. He has been extremely active in the Municipal Conservatory in Havana and is considered to be one of the guiding mentors of the younger generation of Cuban musicians. The leading members of the Grupo de Renovacion of Havana are his disciples. His is a music free of exoticisms although he often uses Spanish and Cuban folk themes.

Sonata No. 3	A serious work demanding competent musicianship.
Moderato	Alternating use of three contrasting textures (sixteenth-note toccata-like passages, block chords in dissonant canon, four-part dissonant, chromatic harmonization of folklike tune).
Invenciones en Rondo	An extended allegretto. Elaborate working out of two- and three-part counterpoint in a light rondo. Rhythmically tricky.
Diferencias sobre la cantiga "Entre Ave et Eva" del Rey Sabio	Theme and nine variations, theme da capo. Various homophonic and contrapuntal treatments of a modal tune. Mostly quiet and calm. ECIC, through Southern Music Publishing Co.
Sonatina (1934)	Two short movements: lyric, linear Larghetto, vigorous, non-legato Allegro in two and three voices. Dissonant. In New Music, July, 1934.

Other works listed include: <u>Capriccio</u> (1922), <u>Nocturnos</u> (1924),
<u>Invenciones a dos voces</u> (1926), <u>Sonata</u> (1927), <u>Preludios</u> (1927, 1928, 1931),
<u>Tres Sonatas</u> (1944), <u>Tres Pequenos Preludios</u> (1945).

ARTURO BOSMANS (1908-   )

Bosmans is a Belgian-born composer who emigrated to Portugal and then
to Brazil around 1940. He is Professor of Composition at the Conservatorio Brazileira de Musica and Director of the orchestra at Belo Horizonte.

Sonatina Lusitana	Sonatina on Portuguese folk tunes.
Allegro vivace	Ingenious, light treatment of two tunes sepa-rated by pianistic interludes.
Cantiga do Cêgo	"Ballad of the Blind." Heavy, sonorous, bare. Chord structures in fourths over pedal point.
Allegro non troppo	Rhythmic, gay. Fast double notes, spirited conclusion, chords and octaves. ECIC, through Southern Music Publishing Co.
Sonata en Colores (Sonata in Colors)	
Rojo (Red)	Exciting, agitated, propulsive broken-chord figuration, étude style.
Gris (Gray)	Melody in parallel fourths, neutral timbres, square phrases, calm.
Verde (Green)	Rhythmic, buoyant four-part writing, quasi-contrapuntal, fast parallel chords. Not too easy. ECIC, through Southern Music Publishing Co.
Lusitanas	Cycle of songs and dances of Portugal.
No. 1 - Ai a Menina	(Ed. Irmaos Vitale, Rio de Janeiro.)
Album de Anécdotas	<u>Anécdota</u> <u>No. I</u> in <u>Suplemento</u> <u>Musical</u> de la <u>Revista</u> <u>Resenha Musical</u>, <u>Sao Paulo</u>, Nos. 67-68, March-April, 1944.

Other listed works include:

<u>Epigramas</u>, <u>Tocata</u>, <u>Piezas liricas</u>, <u>Marcha fûnebre para un negro de jazz</u>.

JUAN JOSÉ CASTRO (1895-   ) Argentina

The three brothers Castro are among those Argentinian musicians to be
reckoned with. There is little by Juan José that is available.

Toccata (1940)	A large-scale piece exploiting a virtuoso piano style within a fairly traditional harmonic and technical idiom. On about the same scale as the toccatas of Prokofieff and Ravel. Demands bravura, stamina, boldness and clarity. EAM, through Carl Fischer.
Casi Polka (1946)	For children. Bizarre, partly polytonal. EAM, through Carl Fischer.

JOSÉ MARIA CASTRO (1892-   ) Argentina

Sonata de Primavera (1939) (Spring Sonata)	An extended, serious work that achieves its effects by sensitive, original manipulation of traditional triadic harmony. Essentially lyric and flowing.
Allegro moderato	Smooth, placid gentle motion. Full, warm sonority. Moving eighths and triplet eighths in moderate tempo.
Andante	Walking eighths in smooth 4/4. Effective dotted rhythms for contrast. Chorale-like coda, atmospheric ending.
Allegro	Prolonged perpetual motion in rapid sixteenths. Bright, jubilant. Alternating hands. EAM, through Carl Fischer.
Cuatra Piezas	From Diez Piezas breves. A simple Estudio (easy finger passages), a short lament, a humorous galop and a closing piece on bell sonorities. Clear, dissonant qualities. Not difficult. In LAAM, Schirmer.
Pequena Marcha	For children. Short, light, staccato march. Two clear voices. EAM, through Carl Fischer.
Vals Miniatura	For children. Piquant dissonances. Two voices. EAM , through Carl Fischer.
Sonata (1931) Allegro moderato Arietta con Variazioni (6) Finale	A quiet work, predominantly flowing in character. Clear, transparent throughout. Moderate difficulty. (Grupo Renovacion, Buenos Aires, through Ricordi)

Other listed works include: many sonatas, Des Canciones, Motivos infantiles, Cinco Piezas poeticas, Tres Piezas (BLAM, Vol. IV)

WASHINGTON CASTRO (1909-   ) Argentina

The few pieces available by Washington Castro reveal a musician of imagination with perhaps more important things to say in other works. One would like to know more of this composer's music.

Arrorro	For children. Quiet lyricism, sensitive, short. EAM, through Carl Fischer.
Campanitas de Fiesta	For children. Jubilant, energetic, festive. Ringing bell sonorities in fourths. Rhythmically energetic. EAM, through Carl Fischer.
Four Pieces on Children's Themes (1942)	Not for children to play!
Juegos	Jugglers. A clever, varied piece. Brilliantly descriptive. Not too easy.

Haciendo Nonito	A lullaby. Problems in three against two. Unhackneyed, touching.
Era un pajorita	
Ronda	Buoyant. Requires facility, clarity and verve. EAM, through Carl Fischer.

ALEJANDRO GARCIA CATURLA (1906-1940)

Cuban composer, specializing in the tunes and rhythms of the Cuban Negroes.

Comparsa	Negro dance from his Second Suite of Cuban Dances. Virtuoso piece exploiting the fullest sonorities of the piano. Demands good chord techniques, full resonance. Syncopated rhythms over ostinato basses. In New Music, Vol. 10, No. 3.
Sonata	Musicalia Edition, Havana.
Dos Danzas Cubanas	Two short, dissonant dances.
Danza del Tambour	Cross rhythms, drum figurations.
Danza Lucumi	Irregular phrase impulses, chords in fourths. (Salabert)
La Numero 3	Cuban dance, complex cross-rhythms. Vivacious, tricky, dissonant. (Arrow Press, Inc., Havana)
Un Canto de Cuna Campestre	Peasant lullaby, short, not difficult. (Carl Fischer)
Son in Fa Menor	(Carl Fischer)
Preludio Corta No. I	Unbarred, simple melody, open fifths. To the memory of Erik Satie. In New Music, July, 1934.
Sonata Corta	Short essay in two-part counterpoint, allegro con brio. In New Music, July, 1934.

CARLOS CHAVEZ (1899-   )

Mexico's most distinguished composer has written a few piano pieces characterized by a resilient, clear musicality and power, emphasizing, at times, an uncompromising sonorous scheme based fundamentally on the white keys of the piano. There is an attractive quality in the lean, biting sound. For the performer the demands are primarily on clarity in all directions; sonority, phrasing, voice leading and rhythmic accentuation.

Sonatina (1924)	Four-page piece moderato. Generally even textures, three and four voices in moving eighth notes. Dissonant, with some flavor of Ravel. Main problems are sonority and balance. (Arrow Music Press)

Sonata (1928)	Taut, lean work, uncomprisingly acid in harmony. Mostly on the white keys. Irregular meters, cross-rhythms, "open," clear, percussive texture.
Moderato	
Un poco mosso	
Lentamente	
Claro y conciso	In <u>New Music</u>.

Seven Pieces for Piano

Poligonos (1923)	Powerful, incisive. Broad declamation, impulsive and sonorous.
Solo (1926)	Simple diatonic melody with added voice in dissonant counterpoint. Short.
36 (1925)	Bravura piece, perpetually moving. Great rhythmic verve, percussive motives.
Blues (1928)	Two voices, wide intervals, bare suggestion of blues syncopation.
Fox (1928)	Jerky, syncopated rhythms, percussive two-voiced texture, large skips.
Paisaje (1930)	Tiny melodic interlude.
Unidad (1930)	Vigorous, bravura piece, longest of the set. Fast passage playing, repeated tones, broken octaves, cross-rhythms. Demands an extroverted pianism. In <u>New Music</u>.

| Ten Preludes (1937) | More modal than tonal. Only the last (a lengthy perpetual motion in A major) uses black keys to any extent. Pieces in lyrical two-, three- and four-part writing; busy two-part counterpoint; a dance tune simply set, Latin-American style; a piece in sustained, sonorous harmonies; several good-natured, bouncing movements. A very usable collection. Mildly dissonant, moderately difficult. Problems in cross-rhythms, touch, clarity and neatness. No sixteenth notes! (Schirmer) |

LUIZ COSME (1908-   ) Brazil

Cosme studied, among other places, at the Cincinnati Conservatory of Music under Bakaleinikoff. He is at present living in Rio de Janeiro.

From Tres Manchas

| Cançao do Tio Barnabé | Catchy, syncopated tune over samba rhythms. Excellent encore. Not difficult. ECIC, through Southern Music Publishing Co. |
| Dansa do Fogareiro | (Ed. by the author, Rio de Janeiro.) |

ESTABAN EITLER (1913-   )

Eitler is a Tyrol-born composer who has been in Buenos Aires since 1936. He is a member of Nueva Musica, an avant-garde group interested in the propagation of new music. His general orientation is toward twelve-tone writing.

Preludio y Capricho (1945)	Legato, cantabile <u>Preludio</u> in 6/8, three-part counterpoint. Rhythmic, fugal <u>Capricho</u> in bouncing two- and three-voices. Dissonant, twelve-tone piece. Not easy. ECIC, through Southern Music Publishing Co.
Acalanto para Paulo Antonio (1947)	Quietly-flowing twelve-tone lament with occasional climactic outbursts. (Ediciones Musicales Poletonia, Buenos Aires)

Other listed works include:

<u>Sonatina</u> (1943), <u>Anoranzas</u> (1943), <u>Pieza</u> (1944), <u>Variaciones</u> (1944), <u>Variaciones sobre un tema de Claudio Debussy</u> (1944).

JACOPO FICHER (1896-)

This Russian-born composer is one of the leaders of the Argentine musical scene. His piano works are more or less in traditional vein both harmonically and pianistically, although the Tres Danzas are thoroughly imbued with polytonal procedures.

Six Animal Fables	Short descriptive pieces of medium difficulty, Nos. 4, 5 and 6 most difficult. This musical barnyard includes an arrogant rooster, a humble hen, a pussy cat, a nanny goat, two sparrows and some bears. The finale is a grand march. (Elkan-Vogel)
Sonata, Op. 44 Lento-Allegro Andantino Allegro molto	Municipal Prize, City of Buenos Aires, in 1943. An extended work with conventional difficulties. (Carl Fischer)
Three Pieces for Children	Fairly easy.
El Desfile Polka Cancion triste	A march. Traditional harmonies. Chromatic. EAM, through Carl Fischer)
Tres Danzas (in popular Argentine style)	Moderate difficulty. Polytonal. Among his best pieces.
En Estilo de Zamba	Moderato 6/8, staccato chords, passage playing. Requires verve.
En Estilo de Vidalita	Sombre, linear, parallel triadic chords, rhythmic, drum ostinato.
En Estilo de Gato	Most difficult of the set. Energetic, syncopated. Fast staccato parallel chords, octaves, rapid passage playing. EAM, through Carl Fischer)

VIRGINIA FLEITES (1916-) Cuba

A pupil of Revueltas and Ardévol, Fleites has been active in the Municipal Conservatory in Havana and is one of the founding members of the Grupo de Renovacion Musical.

Pequena Suite (1943)	An easy suite. Miniature essays in two-part counterpoint; flowing, mildly dissonant, playful. Charmingly irregular phrases.
Preludio	
Siciliana	ECIC, through Southern Music Publishing Co.
Pastoral	
Canon	

Other listed works include: <u>Invenciones a 2, 3 y 4 voces</u> (1941), <u>Sonata en un Tempo</u> (1942), <u>Sonata en re</u> (1942), <u>Fugas a 3 y 4 voces</u> (1943), <u>Variaciones sobre un tema de Frescobaldi</u> (1944).

LUIS GIANNEO (1897-   )

Director of the State Conservatory and Symphony Orchestra in Tucumán, northern Argentina, Gianneo impresses by a certain grateful quality in his piano pieces. The writing is fluent and the general outlook serious and sensitive. He is looked upon as one of the leading Argentine composers.

Sonata in B-flat Minor	Grateful, idiomatic piano style. Lies well in the hand.
Allegro	Steady, running 6/8, cross-rhythms. Clear tonal motivic and melodic ideas. Some bitonal chord structures.
Romanża	Simple melody and accompaniment, contrasting textures, florid da capo, short.
Allegro molto	An extended rhythmic 6/8, dissonant but tonal. Brilliant, voluble. Climactic ending.
	Not an excessively difficult work. (Carl Fischer)
Sonatina	A lengthy work full of lightness, charm and gentleness.
Allegro	Fast 2/4 in running sixteenths. Passage playing, clear profiles, effective.
Tempo di Minuetto	In the tempo of the <u>Don Giovanni</u> Minuet. Harmonies in fourths.
Allegro vivo	Dancelike 6/8 (jota?). Rondo on a halting four-bar phrase. Light staccato textures, florid running passages. EAM, through Carl Fischer.
Villancico (1946)	For children. Melancholy, winsome, simple 3/4. Touching chromaticisms. Good encore. EAM, through Carl Fischer.
Caminito de Belen	Marchlike allegretto, folk-tune style. Simple staccato clusters. For children. Effective. EAM, through Carl Fischer.
Suite (1933)	
Vivo	Lively dance opposing 3/4 to 6/8. Sustained, propulsive motion.
Calmo	Atmospheric lento, full textures.
Allegro rustico	Lengthy dance using a variety of textures. Bravura ending. Requires stamina. (Grupo Renovacion, Buenos Aires, through Ricordi.)

Cinco Pequenas Piezas   Five short pieces of moderate difficulty: Coquetry, Cradle Song, March, Waltz, Perpetual Motion.
(Eschig, through Associated Music)

ALBERTO GINASTERA (1916-   ) Argentina

Piezas Infantiles   Three brief pieces: Antón Pirulero, gay gigue-like nursery rhyme in bouncing 6/16; Chacarerita, lively dance from the Argentine interior, chords in seconds and fourths; Arroz con Leche (Rice Pudding), marcato, dissonant treatment of diatonic nursery tune, triple forte ending.
In LAAM, Schirmer.

Twelve American Preludes (1944)

Volume I   For accents (étude style, broken chords, arpeggios, bitonal), Triste (simple melody, one accompanying voice), Creole Dance (rhythmic, rustic, violent, marked, dissonant), Vidala (short melody in smoothly dissonant 3/8), In the First Pentatonic Minor Mode (two-part counterpoint, Andante in 7/8), Tribute to Roberto Garcia Morillo (rapidly alternating hands, sixteenth-note motion, presto).

Volume II   Octaves (étude style, unison octaves, fast skips), Tribute to J. J. Castro (short Tempo di Tango, simple melody), Tribute to Aaron Copland (bravura passage playing, breathless), Pastorale (open fifths in bass, ostinato in alto, melody in soprano, lento), Tribute to Heitor Villa-Lobos (wild, sempre forte, unison passages, irregular intervals, syncopated rhythms), In the First Pentatonic Major Mode (bell-like sonorities over pedal point, quadruple forte ending.
(Carl Fischer)

Tres Piezas (1940)   Flowing, melodic, lyric Cuyana. Melancholy, atmospheric Nortena. Lively, propulsive, robust Criolla.
(Ricordi Americana)

Malambo (1940)   Driving dance in 6/8. Insistent rhythms, dissonant, ostinato harmonies. Requires energy.
(Ricordi Americana)

Danzas Argentinas   Danzas del viejo bayero, Danza de la moza donosa, Danza del gaucho matrero.
(Ricordi Americana)

HECTOR MELO GORIGOYTIA (1899-   )

Gorigoytia is an engineer born in Santiago, Chile. He is Professor of Industrial Technology in the School of Applied Arts, University of Chile. He is also founder of the Society of Chilean Composers, the National Association of Composers and other groups, and is the winner of many composition prizes.

Manchas de Color	Three short sketches, atmospheric, lush.
(Spots of Color)	ECIC, through Southern Music Publishing Co.

   Preludio
   Primavera
   Este era un Rey

Other listed works include: <u>Canciones y Tonadas</u>, <u>Latrilla</u>, <u>Sauces en el estero</u>, <u>El velorio</u>, <u>En un album infantil</u>, <u>Leah</u>, <u>Chalom</u>, <u>Romantica</u>.

GUILLERMO GRAETZER (1914-   )

Graetzer is a Viennese expatriate living in Buenos Aires since 1939. From perusal of the few pieces below one would like to know more of this composer. There is a vigor and tension to the toccatas that suggests a vital musical personality.

Tres Toccatas	Three extended pieces displaying an all-round pianism demanding bravura and mature musicianship. Modern harmonic and pianistic vocabulary. Difficult.
Allegro (1937)	Fast unison figuration, quiet melodies, syncopated rhythms, some three-part counterpoint, big climactic ending.
Con brio (1938)	Octaves, double notes, alternating hands, fast chordal passages, declamatory adagio section. Climactic ending.
Allegro ma non troppo (1938)	More lyric than the above, driving to a powerful close. ECIC, through Southern Music Publishing Co.
Rondo (1947)	For children. Light allegretto, moderate difficulty, mostly two voices, bouncing. A free C major. EAM, through Carl Fischer.

CAMARGO GUARNIERI (1907-   )

This Brazilian composer writes a varied, interesting and unhibited piano style. Native Brazilian melos and rhythmic elements lend his piano pieces a piquant and arresting character. He can be disarmingly simple (<u>Maria Lucia</u>) or display pianistic virtuosity and exuberance at will (<u>Toccata, Danza Brasiliera</u>). Although a solid core of popular elements pervades his style Guarnieri manages to retain a strong individuality, imagination and craftsmanship.

Toccata	Study in chromatic, perpetually moving double notes mostly in the right hand. (Associated Music)

Choro Torturado	An agitated, chromatic piece demanding a broad, extroverted pianism. Octaves, chords, cross-rhythms, passage playing. Strong climactic ending. (Associated Music)
Danza Brasiliera	Lusty <u>Tempo di Samba</u>, popular flavor, repeated octaves, chords, big sonorities. (Associated Music)
Little Horse with the Broken Leg (1932)	Limping figures, syncopated rhythms in three-voiced texture with a lament over a pedal point as middle section. Not difficult. (Associated Music)
Third Sonatina in the G Clef	Tour de force in the middle and upper registers of the piano: <u>Allegro</u> in constant eighth-note motion, three voices, grazioso; melancholy melody over broken-chord figuration <u>Con tenerezza</u>; <u>Two-Part Fugue</u> with rhythmic, busily moving sixteenth notes, forte ending. Moderately difficult. (Associated Music)
Maria Lucia	Quiet, short lyric sketch in smoothly moving eighth notes. (Mercury Music)
Lundú	Traditional Brazilian song-dance in rapid tempo, steadily moving eighth notes. Folk rhythms and scales patterns, exotic. Requires energy and crispness, command of four against three. (Mercury Music)
Ficarós Sosinha	Short, graceful, simple piece built around a Brazilian children's game. Quiet, utterly disarming, easy. (Mercury Music)
Toada Triste	Short, expressive lyric pieces demanding sensitive rubato, skillful pedaling. In <u>LAAM</u>, Schirmer.
Dansa Negra	Sombre lament, intense, sonorous middle section. "Blues" quality. Not short, moderately difficult, effective. (Associated Music)

RUDOLPH HOLZMAN (1910-   )

Holzman is a German-born composition student of Vladimir Vogel and Karol Rathaus who settled in Lima, Peru in 1938.

Pequena Suite (1942)	Little suite on Peruvian folk motives.
Preludio Pastoral	Quiet melodies in pastoral vein.
Bailan das Muchachas	Young girl's dance, light staccato, syncopated rhythms.

Melodia triste	Melancholy moderato
Fanfarria Campestre	"Country Fanfare." Horn calls.
Interludio Evocativo	Atmospheric, nocturnal.
Danza Final	Difficult, energetic 3/8. Fast double notes, octaves.
	ECIC, through Southern Music Publishing Co.

Other listed works include: 12 Variations in Romantic style on a theme of Mozart (1929), Pequena Suite (1941), Suite "In Memoriam" (1941).

FAUSTINO DEL HOYO (1909-   )

Preludio y Doble Fuga	Musical Courier prize for best work by Latin-American composer. Elaborate melodic broken-chord Prelude, flowing 6/8. Extended Double Fugue, three voices in concert style using the textures of the Bach-Busoni transcriptions. Traditional harmonic procedures. (E. B. Marks)

CARLOS ISAMITT (1885-   ) Chile

Estudio No. 3	Un poco allegro, grazioso 3/8, two and three flowing voices. Some polychords, double notes. Freely tonal, moderately long, fairly difficult. (E. B. Marks)

H.-J. KOELLREUTTER (1915-   )

This German-born composer was founder of the Arbeitskreis für Neue Musik in Berlin in 1935. In 1937 he took up residence in Brazil. Koellreutter has been active in forwarding new music and has participated in many events connected with the discussion of problems in contemporary composition. Since 1938 he has been Professor at the Conservatorio Brasileira de Musica in Rio de Janeiro and also Professor of Counterpoint and Composition in the Musical Institute at Sao Paulo.

Musica 1941	Three pieces oriented toward the twelve-tone method of composition.
Tranquilo	Essentially lyric, wide skips, angular melodies, phrases punctuated with rests.
Muy expressivo	Short, atmospheric, tender tribute to the memory of the composer's mother.
Muy ritmado y destacado	Extended rhythmic movement. Most difficult of the set. Light two and three voices. Angular skips and rhythms.
	ECIC, through Southern Music Publishing Co.
Tres Bagatelles	(Ed. Musica Viva, Rio de Janeiro.)

Other listed works include: Sonata (1939), Preludio, Coral y Fuga (1940).

ISIDRO B. MAIZTEGUI (1905-   )

Maiztegui has held many important musical posts in Argentina.

Escarceo Criolla	A free fantasy exploiting broken-chord and blocked-chord sonorities in fourths and fifths. Free unbarred sections, habanera rhythms, metric changes, cross accentuation, several climactic points, quiet close. Fairly difficult. ECIC, through Southern Music Publishing Co.

Other listed works include: 6 Sonatinas, 8 Preludios, 6 Milongas, 3 Vidalitas, 3 Gatos, 6 Huellas, 5 Zambas.

FRANCISCO MIGNONE (1897-   )

The following pieces by this Brazilian nationalist (all published by E. B. Marks) exhibit a lush, romantic piano style based on popular Brazilian elements and a late-nineteenth-century concept of piano sonority. The pieces entitled Lenda Brasileira are the most rewarding, especially Nos 2, 3 and 4.

Tango Brasileira	Some problems in double sixths.
Quasi Modinha	Samba rhythms, melodic.
Miudinho	Light, rhythmic, crisp.
Lenda Brasileira No. 1	Atmospheric, lazy, big climax, quiet ending.
Lenda Brasileira No. 2	Short, evocative, some arpeggio figuration.
Lenda Brasileira No. 3	Violent, improvisatory, sudden dynamic outbursts.
Lenda Brasileira No. 4	Smoothly flowing, brilliant climax, quiet close.
Crianças Brincando (Children at Play)	Different in style from any of the above. Percussive, brilliant, dissonant, primarily rhythmic. Alternating hands in presto 6/8. In Con Tempo, an album published by E. B. Marks.

ROBERTO GARCIA MORILLO (1911-   ) Argentina

One gets the impression from the Variations and Conjuros of Morillo that he is not a composer who wastes notes. The use of single sonorities over long sections and the careful husbanding of musical resources in general, coupled with a tendency toward acrid harmonies creates a lean, gaunt quality reminiscent of Chavez or even some of Aaron Copland. A blunt primitivist quality is also characteristic, manifesting itself in strongly reiterated bass figures and rudimentary melodies. Morillo is a professor at the Conservatorio Nacional de Musica y Arte Escenico.

Tres Piezas, Op. 2

Cortejo Barbaro	Wild, energetic. Sonorous climax on driving ostinato drum-like basses.
Poema	Lyric, chromatic introduction à la Scriabin, murmuring, indefinite pedal basses under long-drawn-out melody tones, improvisatory return to opening material.

Danza de los animales al salir del Arca de Noé	"Homage to Stravinsky." A driving grotesque. (Ricordi Americana, through Carl Fischer)
Conjuros (Incantations)	Primitivist suite, atmospheric, not very difficult.
Tchaka	Foreboding opening, building to driving climax over heavy ostinato basses. Rudimentary melodies.
El Genio de las Aguas	Primitive melodies, guttural basses, clear, crystalline second half.
Schango, el Genio del Trueno	Animated, incisive. Requires boldness and drive.
El Primogenito del Cielo y de la Tierra	Quiet trills over descending chromatic fourths leading to a "marcha funebre" with ostinato bass and piercing melody tones ornamented by dissonant acciacaturas. ECIC, through Southern Music Publishing Co.
Variaciones, Op. 10 (1942)	Six variations on four three-measure phrases (chordal, featuring parallel sevenths). Clean, dry, astringent. Big climax, great economy of means, finale "come una marcia funebre." Not long. Moderate difficulty. (Ricordi Americana, through Carl Fischer)
Variaciones, Op. 13 (1944)	Seventeen variations on a three-bar theme. Bleak, bare sonorities featuring the major seventh and minor ninth. A dry, tightly knit work reminiscent of the variations of Aaron Copland (to whom they are dedicated). ECIC, through Southern Music Publishing Co.
Malborough's Return	From Cuentos para Ninos traviesos (Tales for Noisy Children). A grotesque march heralding the return of the Marlborough who went to war (?). EAM, through Carl Fischer.
Cancion triste y Danza alegre	Short lento leading to lively staccato, percussive dance. In LAAM, Schirmer.

Other listed works include: Tres Piezas, Dos Sonatas, Op. 4.

SAMUEL NEGRETE (1892-   ) Chile

Negrete is Director of the Conservatoria Nacional de Musica and active in the Association of Chilean Composers.

Ritmica	Lively, flowing sixteenths. Augmented sonorities. Mostly in the middle and upper registers of the piano. ECIC, through Southern Music Publishing Co.
Paisajes	Ediciones de Musica Chilena del Conservatorio Nacional de Musica, 1932.

Armonias campestres

Portico	In the Musical Supplement to the Review Aulos, Vol. I, No. 1, Santiago, 1932.
Sendero	In the Musical Supplement to Revista de Arte, Santiago, Vol. II, No. 8, 1936.
Danza	In BLAM, Vol. IV.

JULIAN ORBON (1925-   )

Julian Orbon is a Spanish-born citizen of Cuba, a resident of Havana since 1940. He was a student of Ardévol in composition, active as a music critic and member of the Grupo de Renovacion Musical. The Tocata (sic) seems to take its point of departure from the later de Falla.

Tocata (1943)	In the broad sense of a keyboard piece.
Preludio	Simultaneously running eighths in both hands in 6/8. Voluble, flowing, diatonic.
Cantares	Smoothly flowing two-, three- and four-part counterpoint. Archaic quality, melancholy.
Sonata	Dissonant, jubilant Vivace in fast sixteenths recalling the texture of some of the sonatas of Soler. Difficult. Irregular meters. Requires energy, bravura, clarity. ECIC, through Southern Music Publishing Co.

Other listed works include: Sonata (Homenaje sobre la Tumbe del Padre Soler) (1942), Dos Danzas con un Interludio para "La Gitanilla" de Cervantes (1944).

JUAN ORREGO-SALAS (-   ) Chile

Variaciones y Fuga sobre el Tema de un Pregon	Eight variations and fugue on a street cry. Modal, diatonic, chords with open and parallel fifths. Requires good legato, facility in repeated notes, rhythmic verve, bravura. Fugue in three voices, cantabile, moderato. Bravura finale. Moderately long. (Hargail)

JUAN CARLOS PAZ (1897-   ) Argentina

A unique figure in Latin-American music, Paz has exerted a great influence through his independent activity as a twelve-tonalist. He founded the Grupo de Renovacion Musical and the Nueva Musica group. He is respected as a person of wide musicianship.

Sonatina No. 3, Op. 25 (1933)	A light work, slightly grotesque. Thin, crisp two-part writing, wide melodic skips, sharp accentuation. Sparing use of the pedal.
Allegro moderato Andante sin expression Allegro moderato	In ECIC, Southern Music Publishing Co.

Canciones y Baladas, Op. 31

Balada No. 1	In the review Musica Viva, No. 10, Rio de Janeiro, 1941.

Balada No. 2	Short twelve-tone piece in 6/8, eighth-note motion throughout. Staccato against legato lines. In LAAM, Schirmer.
Diez Piezas sobre una serie de doce tonos Op. 30	Short pieces, a page or two in length: Preludio, Cancion, Carol, Danza, Balada, Toccata, Passacaglia, Vals, Elegia, Leyenda. Paz employs the tone row within a conventional rhythmic framework. Moderately difficult. (Ediciones Musicales Politonia, Tucuman, Argentina)
Tres Movimentos de Jazz	Edition Grupo Renovacion, Buenos Aires, 1934.
Tres Invenciones a dos voces	Edition Grupo Renovacion, Buenos Aires, 1936. No. 1 of these inventions is in BLAM, Vol. I.
Pampeana	Carl Fischer
En la Casta del Parana	Variations on a tango theme. (Carl Fischer)

Also listed by Paz are: Preludio, Coral y Fuga, Tercera Sonata de los doce tonos, Fantasia y Fuga, Tres piezas liricas, Cinco piezas caracteristicas, Variaciones sobre un tema de la "Cumparsita."

OCTAVIO PINTO (1890-1950) Brazil

Danca Negreira (Negro Dance)	Rapid, vigorous, propulsive presto, constant sixteenth-note motion, strong syncopations. Requires rhythmic vitality and endurance. (Schirmer)
Marcha do Pequena Polegar (Tom Thumb's March)	Short, crisp. (Schirmer)
Scenas Infantis	Five descriptive scenes from childhood. Moderate difficulty. (Schirmer)
Festa de crianças (Children's Festival)	Five pieces. (Schirmer)

JUAN BAUTISTA PLAZA (1898-) Venezuela

Sonatina venezolana	In one movement. Built on native Venezuelan themes and rhythms in two-part Scarlattian form. Syncopated rhythms. In LAAM, Schirmer.

MANUEL M. PONCE (1886-) Mexico

Deux Etudes	1—Short, lyric study, crossed hands, bell-like sonorities. 2—Bravura double notes and octaves. In LAAM, Schirmer.

Four Pieces for Piano
(1929)

Preludio scherzoso
Arietta
Sarabande
Gigue

Short essays in the sonorous possibilities of
using one hand on the white keys, the other
on the black. See especially No. 1 (an ingenious scherzo) and No. 2 (an Arietta ending
scherzando).
(Salabert)

SYLVESTRE REVUELTAS (1899-1940) Mexico

Cancion
Allegro (1939)

Two pieces for young players, the first lyric,
the second a rhythmic essay using bitonality
and polyrhythms.
(Carl Fischer)

CARLOS RIESCO (1925-   ) Chile

Pupil of Humberto Allende, Aaron Copland and Curt Sachs. Riesco is
interested in the investigation of the music of indigenous Araucanian
groups in the south of Chile.

Semblanzas Chilenas
(Chilean Likenesses)

Chromatic, chord structures in fourths:
light, rhythmic, whimsical Zamacueca in
allegretto 6/8; slow Tonada, mostly chromatic
treatment of melody in four-part harmoniza-
tion; Resbalosa, light waltz leading to a bright
vivo mostly in the upper registers of the
instrument, brilliant end, not very difficult.
ECIC, through Southern Music Publishing Co.

ANDRÉS SAS (1900-   ) Peru

Himno y Danza

An evocation of Inca culture. Short, chordal,
processional Lento y grave leading to a
driving huayno (native Peruvian dance).
Ostinato rhythms.
In LAAM, Schirmer.

ENRIQUE SOLARES (1910-   )

Estudio en Forma de
Marcha

March in 2/4, percussive, polychordal,
staccato passage playing, arpeggio sweeps,
vigorous ending. Moderate length and
difficulty.
(E. B. Marks)

CARLOS SUFFERN (1905-   )

Suffern is Professor of Solfege and Theory at the Conservatorio National
de Musica y Arte Escenico in Buenos Aires, Argentina.

La Nostalgia

Flowing 6/8, romantic nocturne in salon
style.
(E. B. Marks)

Danza

On Argentine material. Eighth-note motion
in 6/8, moderato. Double notes, cross-
rhythms, lush texture.
In LAAM, Schirmer.

Other listed works include: <u>Cuentos de ninos</u> (Children's Tales), <u>Nynpheos</u>, <u>La Danzarina sagrada</u>, <u>Sonata</u> (one movement).

HECTOR TOSAR (ERRECART) (1923-) Uruguay

Tosar is a former Guggenheim Fellow who has been active in groups for the propagation of Latin-American music.

Improvisacion	Lengthy, ambling poco animado, constant four (right hand) against three (left hand). Broken-chord figuration throughout. Espressivo middle section. Fairly difficult. ECIC, through Southern Music Publishing Co.
Danza Criolla (1941)	Steadily moving eighths in a running 12/8. Long, not easy. Requires stamina, vigorous accentuation, good articulation. (Broude Bros.)

Other listed works include: <u>Sonatina</u>, <u>Dos Estudios</u>, <u>Sonata</u>, <u>Suite</u>.

THEODORO VALCARCEL (1900-1942) Peru

Valcarcel seems to have been a colorful musician of temperament whose career was cut off by premature death. His deep interest in Peruvian folklore is evident in the following piece.

Kachampa (Danza del Combate)	Angular, interrupted rhythms. Irregular, clipped phrases. Octaves, chords, dotted rhythms. Fairly long. ECIC, through Southern Music Publishing Co.

Other listed works include: <u>Berceuse</u>, Op. 15, No. 5; <u>Funeral March of a Pierrot</u>; <u>In senzo di fioritura</u>; <u>Gondola de media noche</u>; <u>Himno al sol</u>; <u>Preludio</u>, Op. 24, No. 7 (published in Lima, Peru); <u>Fiestas andinas</u>, <u>Cancion Colonial</u> (1940).

ROBERTO CARPIO VALDES (1900-) Peru

Valdes is mostly self-taught in Harmony, Composition and Counterpoint. He is staff pianist of Radio Nacional of Lima.

Suite (1934)	Euphonious, smoothly flowing piece, neither long nor difficult: <u>Allegretto</u> with flowing broken-chord figuration; simple, short, melodic <u>Andantino</u>; light, fast rondo <u>Allegro animato</u>, transparent in texture.

Other listed works include <u>Nocturno</u> (1921), <u>Tres Estampas de Arequipa</u> (1927), <u>Hospital</u> (suite), <u>Dos Piezas</u>, <u>Dos Impresiones aymaras</u> (1930), <u>Triptico</u>, <u>Cuatro Preludios</u> (1933).

HEITOR VILLA-LOBOS (1894-)

The enormous number of piano pieces that marks the output of Villa-Lobos is but one characteristic facet of his mountainous production in all fields of composition. Villa-Lobos is primarily a folklorist. His many transcriptions of Brazilian folk tunes and his use of folk inflections in the harmonic, melodic and rhythmic fabric of his music testify to his complete immersion in specifically Brazilian idioms. The pianism in which he clothes his national traits is an uninhibited one embodying a free coloristic treatment of the keyboard. Improvisatory sweeps, impressionist sonorities, intricate cross-rhythms and a compelling use of extreme dynamic levels all contribute to a certain rudimentary animal excitement. At the other end of the gamut the folk-song settings in Guia Pratico often use a conventional harmonic and pianistic idiom. Perhaps the most impressive of his piano pieces are to be found in Prole do Bébé, Series II. The pianist must bring to bear upon these surprisingly extended pieces a wealth of color, imagination and technical resourcefulness. The following list is by no means complete. Sampaio Arraujo and Co. (Casa Arthur Napoleão, 122 Avenida Rio Branco, Rio de Janeiro, Brazil) list many pieces which are not available in this country at present.

Ten Pieces on Popular Children's Folk Tunes of Brazil	Two volumes, five pieces in each. Simple, unpretentious settings in a traditional harmonic vocabulary. Short, easy. Good for students in the middle grades. (Mercury Music)
Guia Pratico (1932-1935)	A collection of at least nine albums with about half a dozen pieces in each. Casual settings of popular Brazilian children's songs. Not too easy for children to play. See especially Album I, No. 1 (Dawn), Album 8, No. 1 (Little Orange Tree) and No. 4 (The Old Woman that had Nine Daughters). Albums 1, 8 and 9 are published by Villa-Lobos Music Corporation; Albums 6 and 7 by Mercury Music.
Francette e Pia	Cycle of ten pieces using the story of a little Brazilian Indian who went to France and met a little French girl. Each combines a French and a Brazilian tune. Excellent for children. Demand imagination, but only moderate facility. (Eschig, through Associated Music)
The Three Maries	Charming set on a Brazilian folk story. Popular flavor, modal colorings. Short.
Alnitah	Requires facility and brilliance.
Alnilam	Lyric, with short contrasting staccato middle section.
Mintika	Requires facility, free pedaling and careful balance. (Carl Fischer)
Cirandas (1926)	Collection of sixteen fairly difficult pieces on popular Brazilian themes. The following seven are representative of the entire set:
Therezinha de Jesus	Syncopated rhythms in broken-chord textures, close position. Not difficult.

Fui no Tóróró	Warm, simple melody, constant figuration. Difficult middle section (three against eight). Requires good control in left hand.
Olha O Passarinho, Domine	Extended, brilliant piece with busy staccato figuration in a four-measure ostinato pattern. Big climax, quiet ending.
A' procura de uma agulha	Chordal, tune in alto, two contrasting sections, repeated chord techniques.
A canôa virou	Syncopated and cross-rhythms, animated, climactic.
Que lindos olhos	Lyric, chordal, tune in inner voice, atmospheric pedal point, soft drum effects, calm ending, religioso.
Có có có	Animated, brilliant, rapidly alternating hands, some running left-hand figuration. (Sampaio Arraujo and Co.)
Cirandinhas	Collection of nine easy pieces on popular children's themes.

Prole do Bébé (Series I—The Baby's Dolls)

Branquinha (The Porcelain Doll)	Bell-like sonorities, problems in pedaling and balance.
Moreninha (The Paper Doll)	Brilliant, spirited, fast moving sixteenth-note tremolos, cross-rhythms.
Caboclinha (The Clay Doll)	Insistent samba rhythm, steady sixteenths, suave moderato, chordal textures.
Mulatinha (The Rubber Doll)	Free scherzo, improvisatory, changing textures and tempi from poco animato to prestissimo.
Negrinha (The Wooden Doll)	Lively, alternating hands in sixteenths throughout.
A Pobresinha (The Rag Doll)	Short melancholy lament, chordal, ostinato harmonies.
O Polichinello (Punch)	Breathless presto, alternating hands in rapid sixteenths, right hand on white keys, left hand on black.
Bruxa (The Witch Doll)	Extended piece, big scope, changing textures, climactic. (E. B. Marks, complete in one volume.)

Prole do Bébé (Series II—The Little Animals)

More difficult and extended than Series I.

A Baratinha de Papel (The Little Paper Bug)	Quizzical study in cross accents.
O Gatinho de Papelão (The Little Cardboard Cat)	Vague, wandering, atmospheric, ostinato figures.

O Camundongo de Massa (The Little Toy Mouse)	An extended piece, brilliant, difficult. Requires strong equipment, bravura.
O Cachorrinho de Borracha (The Little Rubber Dog)	Slow, vague opening mounting to huge, sonorous climax. Some rough barking at the end. Short.
O Cavalinho de Pau (The Little Wooden Horse)	Staccato double notes, animated, cross-rhythms, pesante climax ffff, quiet ending.
O Boisinho de Chumbo (The Little Tin Ox)	A big canvas. Lumbering rhythms, great sonorous scope, double notes, octaves, widespread chords. Difficult.
O Passarinho de Panno (The Little Cloth Bird)	Very difficult. Trills in both hands, cross-rhythms, powerful climax, catch ending.
O Ursozinho de Algodão (The Little Cotton Bear)	Animated. Double notes, alternating hands, dynamic rhythms, strong close. Requires power.
O Lobosinho de Vidro (The Little Glass Wolf)	A wild toccata. Fast repeated notes, octaves, fast parallel chords in fourths, sweeps up the keyboard. Requires virtuosity and power. (Eschig, through Associated Music)

Ciclo Brasileiro (1936-1937)

Plantio do Caboclo (Native Planting Song)	Warm, quiet. Widespread, broken-chord figuration in right hand, melody in tenor.
Impressões Seresteiras (Minstrel Impressions)	Extended, improvisatory, free pianistic treatment of sentimental waltz. Lush.
Festa no Sertao (Jungle Festival)	Brilliant, festive. Alternating hands, octaves, rapid right-hand figuration, cross-rhythms, climactic effects.
Dansa do Indio Branco (Dance of the White Indian)	Vigorous, uninhibited bravura treatment of simple tune. Alternating chords and octaves throughout. (Villa-Lobos Music Corp.)

Suite Floral (1916-1917)

Idilio na Rêde (Summer Idyll)	Lyric. Broken-chord figuration split between the hands.

Uma Camponeza
  Cantadeira (A Singing
  Country Girl)
	Melody over vague figuration, irregular groups, climactic point, quiet close.

Allegria na Horta (Joy in the Garden)	Best of the set. Animated, colorful dance. Wide variety of textures and figurations. Brilliant, difficult. (Villa-Lobos Music Corp.)

Saudades das Selvas
  Brasileiras (Brazilian
  Forest Memories)
	Two pieces. No. 1—animated fragmentary melodies over ostinato bass figures. Exotic. No. 2—Crisp chordal treatment of simple melody, four against three, "très rhythmé toujours."

Dansa (Miudinho, from Bachianas Brasileiras No. 4)	Animated. Broken-chord, prelude-like figures accompanying a Brazilian tune. Dissonant ostinato bass figures in middle section driving to a return. In <u>Latin American Art Music for the Piano</u>, Schirmer.
Alma Brasileira—Choros No. 5	Lament over a murmuring chord and broken-chord accompaniment. Brazilian syncopations, rubato. Not easy. (E. B. Marks)
Carnaval das Criancas Brasileiras (Brazilian Children's Carnival)	Eight pieces.
2—O Chicote do Diabinho (The Devil's Whip)	Molto allegro, trills, repeated chords, passage playing. Light, brilliant, short.
3—A Manha da Pierette (Pierette's Hands)	Playful, not difficult. (E. B. Marks)
Rudepoema	Large-scale virtuoso work. Literally a "rough poem." Villa Lobos's most extended piece for piano solo. (Eschig, through Associated Music)

HECTOR IGLESIAS VILLOUD (1913-   ) Argentina

Villoud draws his inspiration from indigenous popular and creole song. He is an authority on Indian music of Bolivia, Peru, Chile, Uruguay and Brazil. The many important posts he has held include his activity as Secretary of the Association of Argentine Composers and Professor of Advanced Harmony and Musical Culture in the Conservatorio Fracassi.

Provincianas	Series of pieces featuring dances of various provinces.
Catamarqueña	Energetic, rhythmic, rapid. Forceful syncopations. Catchy quality. Not difficult. ECIC, through Southern Music Publishing Co.
	The same series also includes: <u>Jujena</u>, <u>Santiaguena</u>, <u>Mendocina</u>, <u>Correntina</u>, <u>Saltena</u>, <u>Cordobesa</u>, <u>Pampeana</u>.
Brujo Ayrnara	From the series <u>Amerindia</u>. Furious <u>Allegro barbaro</u>. Strident, marcato dance. Percussive, short, not difficult. (Ricordi Americana)
Tres Piezas	
La chola apasionada	Predominantly animated dance, colorful, changing textures, irregular meters. Brilliant ending.
Camino de Tilcara Danza de los "Laikas"	Energetic, vivacious, pentatonic. Short, explosive phrases. (Ricordi Americana)

Part IV
Original Works for Four Hands

Music for One Piano—
Four Hands

The experience of playing four hands at one piano is, for the pianist, the most direct road to the more complex forms of ensemble playing. It plays a welcome role in the development of musicianly attitudes since good four-hand playing demands not only the basic give and take required of all good chamber music performances but, in addition, it calls for the development of a sympathetic pianism in achieving a well-integrated balance of sound between "primo" and "secundo" parts.

The literature of arrangements is not only large, it is incredible. Everything from the St. Matthew Passion of Bach to the Feu d'artifice of Stravinsky exists in a four-hand version. There is no better way for the pianist to become familiar with the great repertoire of symphonic and chamber music than to grapple with these scores in well-contrived adaptations for four hands.

However, in addition to arrangements, the repertoire boasts a number of original works by master composers some of which may be reckoned among the treasures of the pianist's repertoire. By and large our piano students are not sufficiently acquainted with these works in which the composer has accepted the medium seriously and produced bona fide pieces for concert performance.

The infinite mass of pedagogic material for young students is very sparsely represented in the following list. A number of composers have experimented with one easy part against a rather difficult one designed to sustain the interest of the student. A few of these are noted below.

The serious repertoire is larger than is commonly supposed and includes some noteworthy contributions by contemporary composers. The following list includes all the standard works and many additional pieces that may prove stimulating and fruitful.

Collections:

Tunes for Four Hands (L. J. Beer, ed.), 2 Vols. Universal; Associated Music. Original compositions from Mozart to Reger.

Classical Duets (Willy Rehberg, ed.), Schott; Associated Music. Original easy piano duets.

Vermischte Handstücke (Alfred Kreutz, ed.), Schott (through Associated Music). Little four-hand pieces from the eighteenth century by Beck, Geyer, Gläzer, Neefe, Saupe, Schneidler, Schuster.

Duet Album (Leopold Mannes, ed.), Mercury Music. Original compositions by Mozart, Schumann, Brahms, Dvorak (Legends, Op. 59), MacDowell (Poems, Op. 20), J. Strauss (Leaflet Waltzes). An excellent collection!

Classical Album, G. Schirmer. Twelve original pieces by Haydn, Mozart, Clementi, Kuhlau, Beethoven, Weber.

Festival Series of Piano Duets, J. Curwen and Sons. Original works of moderate length and difficulty by contemporary British composers.

JOHANN ANTON ANDRÉ (1775-1842)

Conversations Musicales   Moderately paced Marche with light contra-
                                                puntal elaboration, light Walse on two short

motives with coda. Not difficult. A library
item, should be reprinted.
(André)

ANTON ARENSKY (1861-1906)

Six Pièces Enfantines,
Op. 34

Pieces of moderate length and difficulty.
Neatly written, light and transparent in texture: Conte, Le Coucou, Les Larmes, Valse,
Berceuse and a Fugue sur un Thème Russe
done with a light, jovial touch.
Augener, Broude Bros. Reprinted by Leeds
as Six Recital Pieces.

Twelve Pieces, Op. 66

Medium length and difficulty. In four books;
1—Prelude, Gavotte, Ballade, 2—Menuetto,
Elégie, Consolation, 3—Valse, Marche, Romance,
4—Scherzo, Berceuse, Polka.
(P. Jurgenson)

RICHARD ARNELL (1917-   )

Sonatina, Op. 61

Vigorous, assertive work, crisp and strongly
marked. Fairly difficult, modern in idiom but
tonal. Introductory Andante e maestoso leading to linear Allegro in three and four voices;
short Andante and a vigorous, crisp, rhythmic
Poco Presto to close.
(Schott)

JOHANN CHRISTIAN BACH (1735-1782)

Three Sonatas
In C Major, Op. 15, No. 6
In A Major, Op. 18, No. 5
In F Major, Op. 18, No. 6

Light-textured, polished, suave, flowing
pieces in the "galant" style. Ingratiating
qualities. See especially the one in A; gently
singing Allegretto and a dignified Tempo di
Menuetto. Each sonata is in two movements.
(Peters)

WILHELM FRIEDRICH ERNST BACH (1759-1845)

The last male descendant in the Bach line.

Andante in A Minor

Wistful, melancholy, with some dramatic
moments. Not difficult. Touching qualities.
(Schott)

LUDWIG VAN BEETHOVEN (1770-1827)

Although the four-hand music of Beethoven must rank among his minor
efforts, the pieces are all diverting and, in several instances, reveal a
most delightful side of Beethoven's temperament. They are in no instance
of more than moderate difficulty and have been republished by International
Music Co.

Sonata in D Major, Op. 6	In two movements: <u>Allegro molto</u> and <u>Rondo-moderato</u>.
Three Marches, Op. 45	In C, E-flat and D major. The first and third are unusual and are decidedly worth playing.
Variations on an Air of Count Waldstein	Eight variations and coda. Somewhat over-long.
Six Variations on the song "Ich denke dein"	Light, sensitive, interesting, ingenious set, on a song to a Goethe text.

LORD GERALD TYRWHITT BERNERS (1883-   )

Valses bourgeoises	Three rather lengthy, sparkling pieces full of a wry wit: vigorous, swinging <u>Valse brillante</u>; scherzando <u>Valse Caprice</u> with sudden changes of character and a finale entitled <u>Strauss, Strauss et Strauss</u>—self-explanatory. Not easy. Require brilliance, neatness of touch and flexibility of rhythm. (J. & W. Chester)

GEORGES BIZET (1838-1875)

Jeux d'Enfants, Op. 22	Twelve descriptive pieces built around children's games: <u>Swinging</u> (Rêverie), <u>The Top</u> (Impromptu), <u>The Doll</u> (Berceuse), <u>Hobby Horses</u> (Scherzo), <u>Flying</u> (Fantaisie), <u>Trumpet and Drum</u> (March), <u>Soap Bubbles</u> (Rondino), <u>Four Corners</u> (Sketch), <u>Blind-Man's Buff</u> (Nocturne), <u>Leap-Frog</u> (Caprice), <u>Little Husband, Little Wife</u> (Duo), <u>The Ball</u> (Galop). Clever characterizations demanding lightness and humor. Not too easy. The Peters edition (Hug) omits Nos. 1, 5, 7, 8 and 10 of the original. Complete reprint by International Music Co.

ALEXANDER BORODIN (1833-1887)

Polka in D Major	Short, capricious salon piece, not difficult. (State Music Publishers, U.S.S.R.; Leeds Music)
Tarentelle in D Major (1862)	Lengthy, brilliant, bravura concert piece allegro molto vivo. Excellent closing piece to a group or program. Requires agility. (State Music Publishers, U.S.S.R.; Leeds Music)

JOHANNES BRAHMS (1833-1897)

Ten Variations on a Theme by Schumann, Op. 23 in E-flat Major	A personal tribute to Schumann (who imagined the theme to have been communicated to him by Schubert and Mendelssohn). Requires a discerning musicianship. (Augener, through Broude Bros.)

ixteen Waltzes, Op. 39	Predominantly Viennese with a tinge of Magyar flavor. Various reprints.
Eighteen Liebeslieder Waltzes, Op. 52a	After the Liebeslieder, Op. 52 ("For piano-forte duet and vocal parts ad libitum").
Fifteen New Liebeslieder Waltzes, Op. 65a	After the Neues Liebeslieder, Op. 65 ("For four voices and piano duet"). "Two books of innocent little waltzes in Schubertian form." (Associated Music)
Twenty-one Hungarian Dances	In four books. Original melodies from gipsy orchestras "arranged" by Brahms. Many reprints.

MAX BRUCH (1838-1920)

Swedish Dances, Op. 63	In two books, fifteen pieces in all, each book to be performed as a unit. Short, contrasting dances in a broad pianistic style requiring moderate facility, rhythmic impetus and a certain flair. No. 15 is No. 1 da capo serving to round out the cycle. There is also a version for violin and piano. (Simrock)

ANTON BRUCKNER (1824-1896)

Quadrille (1854)	In three parts, each with a middle section, then da capo: flowing Andante con moto with short, lively Allegretto; flowing Amabile with short Patetico; jumping Grazioso with flowing Poco animato. (Heinrichshofen)

There are also three very short, easy pieces by Bruckner for four hands published by Schott (through Associated Music).

ALFREDO CASELLA (1883-1947)

Pagine di Guerra (1915)	Four musical "films," descriptive pieces on war scenes: In Belgium (artillery attack), In France (atmospheric evocation of the Cathedral at Rheims), In Russia (cavalry charge), In Alsace (cradle song with siciliano rhythms). (Ricordi)
Pupazzetti (1916)	Five pieces for marionettes: vivacious, lively Marcietta; Berceuse; gently moving Serenata; atmospheric Nocturne and a grotesque Polka (allegro molto vivace). (J. & W. Chester)
Fox-Trot (1920)	Fairly long piece built on stylized dance music of the 1920's. (Universal Edition)

MUZIO CLEMENTI (1752-1832)

Seven Sonatas

In C, F, E-flat, G and C (all major). Some of these sonatas demand virtuosity in traditional piano techniques. They are in two and three movements. See especially No. 7 in C (a brilliant work with a short <u>Larghetto</u> slow movement.
(Breitkopf and Härtel)

CESAR CUI (1835-1918)

Ten Pieces for Five Keys, Op. 74

In two books. Short, easy, melodic, very moderate difficulty.
(Leeds Music)

CARL CZERNY (1791-1857)

It is worth mentioning, if only as a curiosity, the fact that Czerny's works for four hands are legion. They include thirty to forty sets of variations, twenty to thirty rondos, fifteen to twenty fantasies, nocturnes, marches, dances, études, etc. They are all out of print (perhaps justly so). They fall into the same class as the equally numerous works of Kalkbrenner, Field, Steibelt and other epigoni of the period.

CLAUDE DEBUSSY (1862-1918)

Six Épigraphes Antiques (1914)

Atmospheric, exotic, modal. <u>Pour invoquer Pan</u> (pastorale), <u>pour un tombeau sans nom</u> (slow, sombre), <u>pour que la nuit soit propice</u> (slow, expressive), <u>pour la danseuse aux crotales</u> (supple, flexible), <u>pour l'Egyptienne</u> (with gentle flow), <u>pour remercier la pluie au matin</u> (animated).
(Durand)

Marche Ecossaise (sur un thème populaire) (1891)

Written to order for a Scottish general on a traditional Scotch tune. Brilliant. Originally published by Fromont (Jobert) in 1903.

Petite Suite (1889)

Four pieces of moderate length and difficulty written in Debussy's early style. Melodic, graceful, not impressionistic. Flowing <u>En Bateau</u>, animated <u>Cortège</u>, gentle <u>Menuet</u>, vigorous <u>Ballet</u> with <u>Tempo di Valse</u> as middle and closing sections.
(Durand)

ANTON DIABELLI (1781-1858)

Melodious Pieces, Op. 149

Twenty-eight short studies within the compass of five notes. Easy to medium difficulty.
(Carl Fischer)

Pleasures of Youth, Op. 163

Six sonatinas on five notes, three movements in each.
(Schirmer)

Five Sonatinas, Op. 24,
54, 58, 60
Three Sonatas, Op. 32,
33, 37

Both sets published by Schirmer.

ERNST VON DOHNANYI (1877-   )

Walzer, Op. 3

A chain of waltzes with a recurring Tempo I,
<u>Allegro risoluto</u>. Not difficult.
(L. Doblinger)

LOUIS DUREY (1888-   )

Deux Pièces, Op. 7
(1916, 1918)

Two atmospheric pieces, lengthy and serious:
<u>Carillons</u>, proceeding from a hazy beginning
to a heavy, strident climax involving difficulties for both players; <u>Neiges</u>, quiet, crystal-
line textures, not as difficult as the above.
(Editions de la Sirène; Salabert)

JOHANN LADISLAUS DUSSEK (1760-1812)

Sonata in C Major,
Op. 43

Fluent, bright work in classic vein requiring
precise techniques in traditional pianistic
figures: lengthy <u>Allegro</u>; short, expressive,
singing <u>Larghetto</u>; tiny transitional <u>Intermezzo</u>
leading to a bright <u>Rondo</u>—<u>Allegro moderato</u>
requiring agility and lightness.
(Heugel, through Mercury Music)

There are also four other sonatas, three <u>Easy Sonatas</u>, three <u>Fugues</u>
<u>à la Camera</u> and an <u>Easy Sonata</u> op. posth. all for four hands by the same
composer.

ANTONIN DVORAK (1841-1904)

Slavic Dances, Op. 46

Two books, eight dances.

Slavic Dances, Op. 72

Two books, sequel to the above.
Many reprints.

Polonaise in E-flat
Major

Brilliant, vigorous, quite long, not easy.
(Edition Musicus)

Legends, Op. 59

In two books. A fine contribution to the four-
hand repertoire. Sensitive, skillfully written,
moderately long, poetic pieces in romantic
vein. See especially No. 6 (agitated, melancholy, brooding <u>Allegro con moto</u>) and No. 10
(gentle, lyric <u>Andante</u>). Nos. 6 to 10 are in
the duet album published by Mercury Music
(Leopold Mannes, ed.)

From the Bohemian
Forests, Op. 68

Six pieces, difficult.
(Simrock)

ELIZABETHAN KEYBOARD DUETS (Frank Dawes, ed.)

Nicholas Carlton (17th
century) A Verse
Thomas Tomkins (1573-
1656) A Fancy

Two of the earliest keyboard duets extant.
Both pieces are <u>Fancies</u>, works in fugal texture in the style of the English Virginalists.
<u>A Verse</u> is written in florid four part counter-
point with an <u>In Nomine</u> plain chant inserted
in the alto. <u>A Fancy</u> is shorter and features
antiphonal counterpoint and much imitative
writing.
(Schott)

PIERRE OCTAVE FERROUD (1900-1936)

Sérénade (1927)

Suite of three pieces; lengthy contrapuntal
<u>Berceuse</u>; short, expressive <u>Pavane</u>; lively,
rhythmic <u>Spiritual</u> with syncopated rhythms
and a quiet, surprise ending.
(Durand)

NIELS W. GADE (1817-1890)

Nordiske Tonebilleder,
Op. 4 (Norwegian Tone
Pictures)

Three fantasies of moderate length and difficulty: <u>Allegro risoluto</u> in strong dotted
rhythms; melancholy, flowing <u>Allegretto quasi
Andantino</u>; concluding <u>Allegro comodo</u>.
(Augener)

HENRY F. GILBERT (1868-1928)

Three American Dances

"N. B. These Ragtime Dances should be
played with nonchalant grace and in moderate
time" (Gilbert). <u>Uncle Remus</u> (<u>quasi nobil-
mente,</u> vigorous, brilliant climax), <u>Delphine</u>
(light, scherzando) and <u>Br'er Rabbit</u> (longest
of the set, varying moods).
(Boston Music Co.)

MICHEL GLINKA (1804-1857)

Capriccio sur des
Thêmes Russes (1834)

Opus posthumous published in 1904. Lengthy
piece built around three Russian folk tunes.
Varied textures including a fugato. Requires
some dexterity, but not really difficult.
(P. Jurgenson)

LEOPOLD GODOWSKY (1870-1938)

Miniatures

<u>Three Suites</u> (twelve pieces), <u>Seven Ancient
Dances</u>, <u>Seven Modern Dances</u>, and <u>Twenty
Miscellaneous Pieces</u>. One part is difficult,
often requiring virtuosity, the other part is
easy, written within the compass of five
notes. Godowsky lavished much care on these
pieces and considered them useful and important contributions to the four-hand repertoire.
(Carl Fischer)

EDVARD GRIEG (1843-1907)

Symphonic Pieces, Op. 14
Lengthy <u>Adagio cantabile</u> and <u>Allegro energico</u>. Requires some maturity and a moderately advanced pianism.
(Schirmer)

Waltz-Caprices, Op. 37
Two moderately difficult waltzes, the second requiring some agility in the "primo" part.
(Peters)

Norwegian Dances, Op. 35   (Peters)

MICHAEL GNESSIN (1883-   )

Variations on an "Orah," Op. 35
Seven short, characteristic variations and finale on a workingmen's dance in Galilee. Not difficult. Modal.
(Jibne Edition, Jerusalem)

Aux Enfants, Op. 27
Suite of pieces. Too difficult for children to play. Rhythmic problems. <u>Spring Song</u>, two contrasting <u>Oriental Dances</u>, energetic <u>Song of a Noble of the Middle Ages</u>, <u>Berceuse</u> and a waltz like <u>Air de Ballet</u>. Moderately difficult.
(State Edition, U. S. S.R.)

JOHANN WILHELM HÄSSLER (1747-1822)

Two Sonatas for Three and Four Hands (1786-1787)
In C: For three hands. In one movement, a classic <u>Allegro</u>. The third hand plays the uppermost voice. In C: Solemn introduction in pathetic genre, <u>Adagio mesto e sostenuto</u>; short, lively <u>Allegro di molto.</u>
Nagel's Musik-Archiv (possibly through Associated Music)

KURT HESSENBERG (1908-   )

Sonata in C Minor, Op. 34, No. 1
Three-movement work in quasi-Hindemithian vein. Conventional sonata structure. Light texture, linear throughout. Short <u>Adagio</u> intervenes between a <u>Moderato</u> opening movement and a closing <u>Vivace.</u>
(Schott, through Associated Music)

FERDINAND HILLER (1811-1885)

Operette ohne Text, Op. 106
An amusing lengthy and sometimes touching period piece retaining all the set numbers of the nineteenth-century operetta, complete without text: lengthy, brilliant, theatrical <u>Ouverture</u>; expressive, romantic <u>Maiden's Romanza</u>; vigorous, lusty, dancelike <u>Polterarie</u> (?); <u>Hunter's Chorus and Ensemble</u>; quiet <u>Romanza of the Youth</u>; agitated <u>Duettino</u>;

Drinking Song with Chorus (in 2/8 ‼); brisk,
lengthy March; gentle Terzett; graceful
Women's Chorus; fast lengthy Dance (waltz);
Closing Song as finale.
(Augener)

PAUL HINDEMITH (1895-   )

Sonata (1938)

Serious work in three movements on a fairly
large scale: Mässig bewegt, Lebhaft (tricky
syncopated rhythms), Ruhig bewegt (lyric
counterpoint) - sehr lebhaft (rapid interlude) -
im früheren Zeitmass (return to lyric section).
Difficult. Requires facility, musicianship,
strong rhythm, careful balance.
(Associated Music)

JOHANN NEPOMUK HUMMEL (1778-1837)

Sonata or Divertissement
in E-flat Major, Op. 51

Introductory Marcia and a light Andante
leading to a lengthy Rondo (con brio).
(Peters)

Grande Sonata in A-flat
Major, Op. 92

Solemn Grave introduction leading to a long
Allegro comodo requiring brilliant passage
work and sensitive phrasing. Dancelike Andantino sostenuto with vigorous middle section
and concluding Rondo; graceful, lengthy,
flowing and, at times, brilliant.
(Peters)

Nocturne in F Major,
Op. 99 (with two horns
ad lib.)

Declamatory Adagio; theme, four variations
and coda (Tempo di Valse) with brilliant
ending.
(Peters)

D. E. INGELBRECHT (1880-   )

La Nursery

Six collections of settings of French nursery
songs, each containing six pieces of moderate
length and difficulty. Tastefully and effectively written. An outstanding series for students
of very moderate advancement.
(Salabert)

ADOLPH JENSEN (1837-1879)

Jensen is a first-rate salon composer. His four-hand pieces evoke the
Schumann tradition from which he developed. They are unpretentious
well-contrived genre pieces of moderate difficulty within a traditional
nineteenth-century romantic pianistic idiom.

Wedding Music

Festive procession, bridal song and a nocturne.
(Schirmer)

Abendmusik, Op. 59

Six pieces: lyric, agitated, piquant, gentle,
expressive and brilliant. Require facility and
lightness.
(J. Hainauer)

See also Three Pieces, Op. 18, Idylls, Op. 43, and the Silhouettes, Op. 61.

PAUL JUON (1872-1940)

Tanzrytmen

Seven books of pieces, Op. 14 (2), Op. 24 (3), Op. 41 (2) containing seventeen pieces built on dance rhythms. Fairly long, not easy. See especially Op. 24, No. 1 (a piece in variable meters on the arithmetical series 123454321 repeated throughout). Compare with some of the more recent experiments of Boris Blacher's solo works. Also Op. 41, No. 2 - a rapid, engaging Waltz Vivace molto, clear and brilliant in texture. (Schlesinger)

JOHANNES A. JUST (c.1750-after 1785)

Two Little Sonatas

In C; Allegro assai, Theme and Three Variations.
In E-flat; Allegro maestoso, Minuetto (with trio in minor).
Short, graceful, unpretentious, not difficult. (Schott, through Associated Music)

Six Divertimentos for Two Performers

In two collections. No. 1 in D, A and F; No. 2 in B-flat, C and E-flat (all in the major key). Two- and three-movement works in classic vein, light texture, moderate difficulty. The two sonatas above are the fifth and sixth pieces in this group. A library item. (J. Bland)

CHARLES KOECHLIN (1867-1950)

Quatres Sonatines Françaises

Three to five movements in length. Completely linear in concept, sometimes approaching a rather intricate polyphony. See especially No. 4—(Romance, Autre Romance and a lengthy fugal Final). (Oxford University Press)

CONSTANT LAMBERT (1905-1951)

Trois Pieces Nègres (1949) (pour les touches blanches)

Pieces in Latin-American Negro idioms all on the white keys: lively, nervous, strongly marked Aubade with quiet ending; atmospheric Siesta with free melodic phrases and pastoral qualities; nonchalant, languorous Nocturne at times gay and robust, ending quietly. (Oxford University Press)

EDWARD MACDOWELL (1861-1908)

Three Poems, Op. 20 | Night by the Sea (atmospheric, calm), A Tale from Knightly Times (vigorous, heroic), Ballade (short allegretto placido with climactic points). Moderately difficult. (Schirmer) Nos. 1 and 3 are in the duet album published by Mercury Music (Leopold Mannes, ed.).

Lunar Pictures, Op. 21 | Cycle of five moderately long pieces of moderate difficulty. After H. C. Andersen's "Picture Book without Pictures." Lyric Hindumädchen, playful Storchgeschichte, In Tyrol (bell sonorities), Der Schwan (quiet, calm), Bärenbesuch (simple allegretto with climax alla marcia). (J. Hainauer)

FELIX MENDELSSOHN-BARTHOLDY (1809-1847)

Andante and Variations, Op. 83a | Originally for solo piano (Op. 83). Lengthy, not easy. Eight variations and coda. (International Music Co.)

Allegro Brillante, Op. 92 | A vivacious work requiring virtuosity, lightness, speed and a good staccato. Brilliant coda and ending. (International Music Co.)

IGNACE MOSCHELES (1794-1870)

The four-hand works of Moscheles are out of print and are available only in libraries.

La belle union, Op. 76 | Brilliant Rondo preceded by a slow introduction. (Societé pour la publication de musique classique et moderne)

Grand Duo, Op. 102 | On motives from Euryanthe and Oberon. (Kistner)

Sonate Symphonique, Op. 112 | Large-scale work; Andante patetico leading to an Allegro agitato; florid Andante espressivo; Scherzoso alla tedesca antica and a finale Allegro con brio preceded by the introductory Andante patetico. (Stern and Co.)

See also Les Contrastes, Op. 115.

MORITZ MOSZKOWSKI (1854-1925)

From Foreign Lands | Six pieces; Russian, German, Spanish, Polish, Italian, Hungarian. (Schirmer)

Spanish Dances, Op. 12
New Spanish Dances,
Op. 65

Both sets are published by G. Schirmer and
are too wellknown to require comment.

WOLFGANG AMADEUS MOZART (1756-1791)

The practice of playing four hands at one piano was a natural outgrowth
of Mozart's musical relationship with his sister. Various occasions
during his lifetime made it necessary for him to develop a small repertoire of four-hand music which resulted in a legacy of several sonatas, two
fantasies (originally for mechanical organ), a set of variations and a
fugue. At least one of these (Sonata in F) is a masterpiece. The remaining works are standard items in the four-hand repertoire. They are all
easily obtainable in various editions.

Sonata in D Major, K.381
Sonata in B-flat Major,
K.358

Bright, vivacious works in three movements.
Moderate difficulty.

Sonata in F Major, K.497

Large-scale work, weighty, mature, complex.
Difficult ensemble problems. Middle move-
ment (Andante) is a variant of the Horn
Concerto, K. 495.

Sonata in C Major, K.521

Solid, three-movement work of moderate
difficulty.

Fantasy in F Minor,
K. 594

Sombre introductory Adagio, brilliant
Allegro, Adagio da capo. Difficult, weighty,
serious.

Fantasy in F Minor,
K. 608

Complex Allegro, Andante, Allegro. Unusual
modulations, difficult.

Tema con Variazioni,
K. 501

Four variations, charming, dainty.

Fugue in G Minor, K. 401

Four voices, sustained, not difficult.

VINCENT PERSICHETTI (1915-)

Concerto for Piano,
Four Hands, Op. 56

Large-scale work in one movement built on a
single musical idea. Requires virtuosity in
both parts. Available at the Carnegie Institute Library, Pittsburgh.

IGNACE PLEYEL (1757-1830)

Three Original Duetts
(sic) for Two Performers

Two- and three-movement sonatas (C major,
G minor, A major) in classic vein employing
traditional techniques. See especially No. 2:
Allegro, Largo espressivo, Menuetto. A
library item.

There are numerous four-hand sonatas by Pleyel.

FRANCIS POULENC (1899-   )

Sonate (1918)

Gay, humorous work in three movements: Prelude, Rustique, Finale. Not long, not difficult.
(J. & W. Chester)

SERGE RACHMANINOFF (1873-1943)

Six Pieces, Op. 11

Barcarolle
Scherzo
Thème russe
Valse
Romance
Slava

Moderately long pieces of moderate difficulty. Occasionally require facility (Barcarolle, Slava). Often effective, brilliant and climactic. (Gutheil) The Thème Russe has been republished by International Music Co.

MAURICE RAVEL (1875-1937)

Ma Mère l'Oye

Mother Goose suite: short Pavane de la Belle au bois dormant (cool, clear, quiet counterpoint), Petit Poucet (wandering figures, descriptive bird calls), Laideronette, Impératrice des Pagodes (pentatonic, gamelan imitations, exotic bell-like sonorities), Les Entretiens de la Belle et de la Bête (moderate waltz characterizing the conversation between Beauty and the Beast), La Jardin Féerique (slow sarabande with pealing bells as conclusion. One of the gems of the repertoire.
(Durand, through Elkan-Vogel)

ALAN RAWSTHORNE (1905-   )

The Creel

Short suite after Izaak Walton: The Mighty Pike is the Tyrant of the Fresh Water (majestic, dissonant), The Sprat; A Fish that is ever in Motion (two-voice canon at the double octave, scherzando), The Carp is the Queen of the Rivers (stately, lyric Andante con moto), The Leap or Summersault of the Salmon (short caprice with a catch ending). Modern in spirit, witty, moderately difficult.
(Oxford University Press)

MAX REGER (1873-1916)

Waltz Caprices, Op. 9

A dozen pieces of moderate length. Quite difficult. The entire set inclines toward a thick texture and encompasses a variety of technical demands on the part of both players. See especially No. III (short, wistful Andante con passione, No. VII (short, lyric Moderato) and No. VIII (delicate caprice Allegro non tanto). (Schott, through Associated Music)

Six Waltzes, Op. 22	Much less complicated than the above. Considerably lighter in texture, in Brahmsian vein. See especially No. IV (wistful Moderato). (Universal Edition)
Cinq Pièces Pittoresques, Op. 34	Characteristic pieces in sharply delineated moods. Moderately long, not easy. Tendency toward the playful and grotesque. In two books. (Universal Edition)
Introduction and Passacaglia	Originally for organ, but set by the composer for four hands. Short, weighty, majestic introduction; eight-bar passacaglia theme and variations leading to a heavy climactic ending. Not long, relatively easy Reger, thoroughly baroque in concept. (Breitkopf and Härtel)

There are also some Deutsche Tänze, Op. 10, and Six Burlesques, Op. 58.

CARL REINECKE (1824-1910)

Reinecke has written several four-hand works in the Schumann tradition; genre pieces in descriptive vein, always pianistically apt, generally light in emotional content but worth exploring for the moderately advanced student as diversion from more serious and important music.

Nussknacker und Mause-König, Op. 46 (Nutcracker and the Mouse King)	After the fairy tale of E.T.A. Hoffmann. A program suite of considerable length and moderate difficulty. Music for the theatre with appropriate quotations from Hoffmann inserted in the score. (Schirmer)
From the Cradle to the Grave, Op. 202	A cycle of sixteen fantasy pieces with programmatic titles (Childhood Dreams, Play and Dance, Vigorous Work, etc.). Long, not difficult. (Edward Schuberth & Co.)
Improvisations on a Gavotte by Gluck, Op. 125	Also arranged for two pianos by the composer himself. (Peters)

VLADIMIR REBIKOV (1866-1920)

Petite Suite	Rather lengthy pieces of moderate difficulty; smoothly flowing Valse; short Danse des Myosotis; rather lengthy, rapid, clear, crisp Tarantelle; exotic Danse orientale; vigorous concluding Mazurka. A library item. (P. Jurgenson)

ANTON RUBINSTEIN (1820-1894)

Six Characteristic Pieces, Op. 50	Quiet <u>Nocturne</u>, vivacious <u>Scherzo</u>, short <u>Barcarolle</u>, <u>Capriccio</u> in waltz time, lengthy <u>Berceuse</u> with animated middle section, long <u>March</u> as finale. (Schirmer)
Bal Costumé, Op. 103	Suite of characteristic pieces in two volumes. A lengthy, difficult collection in free pianistic treatment set off by an introduction and a finale. Each piece takes its point of departure from a dancing couple at a costume ball representing a different national group in a different historical period, e.g. <u>Astrologue et Bohèmienne</u> (fifteenth century), <u>Chevalier et Châtelaine</u> (twelfth century), <u>Toréador et Andalouse</u> (eighteenth century), <u>Polonais et Polonaise</u> (seventeenth century), <u>Sauvage et Indienne,</u> etc. Twenty pieces in all. Both parts demand a developed pianism. (P. Jurgenson)

ERIK SATIE (1866-1925)

Trois Morceaux en forme de Poire (1903)	"Avec une manière de Commencement, une prolongation du même, un En Plus suivi d'une Redite." Actually seven pieces in all. Written as a rejoinder to Debussy's comment that his pieces had no form. Not difficult. Fresh, humorous, tongue-in-cheek. Clear textures. (Salabert)
Apercus Désagréables (1908-1912)	Three easy pieces on the serious, somber side: rather slow, short <u>Pastorale</u>; short, broad <u>Choral</u>; fairly long chromatic <u>Fugue</u> in four voices, <u>non vite</u>. (E. Demets)
En Habit de Cheval (1911)	Originally conceived for full orchestra but never realized in that medium. Short <u>Choral</u>. Slow, modal, sombre <u>Fugue Litanique</u> in free number of voices. Tiny, quiet <u>Autre Choral</u>. Bouncing <u>Fugue de Papier</u> in moderate tempo, free style, quiet ending. (Salabert)

FLORENT SCHMITT (1870-   )

Musiques Foraines, Op. 22 (1901)	Lengthy suite of six pieces on circus themes: animated <u>Parade</u>, vigorous, rhythmic fanfares; <u>Boniment de Clowns</u> in moderate waltz time, short; <u>La Belle Fathma</u>, short, slow, melodic; <u>Les Eléphants Savants</u>, pompous, solemn, vigorous, lengthy; <u>La Pythonisse</u>, short, melodic, rubato; lengthy, animated <u>Chevaux</u>

de Bois as finale, in fast waltz time. Not
easy.
(J. Hamelle)

Huit Courtes Pièces,
Op. 41

Eight not-so-short pieces preparatory to contemporary music, the pupil's part on the first
five notes of the scale: vigorous opening
Overture in march time; Menuet with strongly
contrasting phrases; quiet, legato Chanson;
rather long animated Sérénade; very brisk,
short Virelai; vigorous, lengthy, rhythmic
Bolero; quiet Complainte in irregular meters;
solemn, concluding Cortège. The entire set
implies a certain development above elementary levels on the part of the student.
(Heugel, through Mercury Music)

FRANZ SCHUBERT (1797-1828)

Schubert wrote more four-hand music than any other great composer.
Included in the list are not only compositions of charm, engaging delicacy
and grace but also several works that may be classed among this composer's
most important contributions to the piano repertoire. The Fantasy in F
Minor, Divertissement à l'Hongroise, and the Grand Duo in C Major are
pieces of great emotional range, intensity and lyric beauty. Less well
known, more intimate but nonetheless worthy of performance are the
Sonata in B-flat Major, Andantino Varié in B Minor and the Variations in
A-flat Major.

Such a treasure should be the companion of every student and devotee
of piano music. The works may be grouped into: 1) Overtures, 2) Dances,
3) Marches, 4) Variations, 5) Fantasies, 6) Rondos, 7) Sonatas, 8) Miscellaneous pieces. Separate pieces have been reprinted by International Music,
but a complete reprint is available in the Peters edition.

Sonata in B-flat Major,
Op. 30 (1818)

Predominantly a flowing lyricism. Allegro
moderato, Andante con moto leading into a
final Allegretto. Moderate difficulty.

Sonata in C Major, Op.140
(Grand Duo) (1824)

Major work on a large scale, symphonic in
style, orchestral throughout. Allegro moderato,
Andante, Scherzo, Allegro vivace. Requires
technical and musical maturity.

Divertissement à l'Hon-
groise (1824 ?)

Strongly Hungarian in its florid melodies,
characteristic rhythms, cembalom-like
cadenzas. Lengthy. Andante, Marcia,
Allegretto (long rondo). Requires flair and
rhythmic verve.
(International Music)

Lebensstürme (1828)

Lengthy allegro in A minor, spirited, impassioned.

Fantasy in F Minor,
Op. 103 (1828)

Major work on a large scale in several connected movements: Allegro molto moderato,
Largo, Allegro vivace, Tempo I (including a

fugue). Great variety of emotional content. Requires maturity. (International Music Co.)

Variations in A-flat Major, Op. 35 (1824)	Eight variations. Lengthy, subtle, not easy.
Andantino varié in B Minor, Op. 84 (c.1825)	On a French motive. Short, moderately difficult. Four variations. (International Music Co.)
Trois Marches militaires, Op. 51 (before 1824)	No. 1 is the famous March in D.
Deux Marches caractèr-istiques, Op. 121 (before 1826)	Impulsive, vivacious pieces in 6/8.
Rondeau in A Major, Op. 107 (1828)	Lengthy allegretto quasi andantino. Suave, lyric period piece demanding grace and finish.
Polonaises, Op. 61 and Op. 75 (c.1825)	Ten short pieces of moderate difficulty and great rhythmic charm.
Dances for Piano Duet	"Deutsche Tänze und Ländler." Easy. (Heritage Music Publications).

CYRIL SCOTT (1879-)

Three Dances	Short, not difficult: slow waltz, flowing waltz, rapid scherzando waltz. (Theodore Presser)

ROBERT SCHUMANN (1810-1856)

The four-hand music of Schumann abounds in the same warmth that characterizes his music at large. These are mostly genre pieces of middle difficulty for the home and studio, preeminently melodic in content with much emphasis on dance styles. They have been republished in numerous editions. In addition to the following list, the Universal catalogue lists Eight Polonaises (posthumous).

Bilder aus Osten, Op. 66 (Pictures from the East)	Six impromptus inspired by the Arabian tales of Rückert about Abu Seid (Arabian counterpart of Tyl Eulenspiegel). Require sensitivity. See especially No. 4 (Nicht schnell). (Mercury Music)
Twelve Piano Pieces, Op. 85	"Für kleine und grosse Kinder." Series of genre pieces of moderate difficulty. See especially No. 1 (a simple, straightforward birthday march), No. 2 (lumbering bear dance over drone basses), No. 9 (Am Springbrunnen, "as fast as possible") and No. 12 (the famous Abendlied). (Schirmer)
Scenes from the Ball, Op. 109	Nine pieces. See especially the Walzer.

Children's Ball, Op. 130   Polonaise (majestic, deliberate), Waltz (light, gay), Minuet (on the solemn side), Ecossaise (running, animated), Française (flowing), Round Dance (lively, full of vitality). (Edition Musicus)

CHRISTIAN SINDING (1856-1918)

Suite, Op. 35   Lengthy Tempo di Marcia, vigorous and bril- liant. Andante funèbre with heavy climax. An Allegretto somewhat like a short set of varia- tions. Vigorous, bravura Finale requiring energy and sharp rhythms. (Peters)

There is also a set of Norwegian Dances and Melodies, Op. 98.

IGOR STRAVINSKY (1882-   )

The four-hand music of Stravinsky is strictly tongue-in-cheek. One part is ridiculously easy; the other part usually plays a lampooning role often involving rhythmic difficulties. The resulting ensemble makes for a divert- ing, wry musical satire.

Five Easy Pieces   Andante, Espanola, Balalaika, Napolitana, (Easy Primo)   Galop. (Omega Music Edition).

Three Easy Pieces   March, Valse, Polka. (Easy Secondo)   (Omega Music Edition)

DONALD FRANCIS TOVEY (1875-1940)

Balliol Dances   Four-hand waltzes on the model of the Brahms waltzes—equally accomplished technically but rather more ponderous. Well worth performing. (Schott)

PETER ILICH TSCHAIKOWSKY (1840-1893)

Russian Folk Songs   Fifty tunes set by the composer. Each one is very short and not difficult. Excellent for browsing and sight reading. (Leeds Music). Peters publishes a selection of thirty-six from the above.

DANIEL GOTTLOB TÜRK (1750-1813)

Tonstücke für vier Hände   Short pieces of medium difficulty by a fine (Pieces for Four Hands)   pedagogue of the eighteenth century. (Schott, through Associated Music)

RICHARD WAGNER (1813-1883)

Polonaise in D Major   Vigorous piece with strong dotted rhythms and traditional diatonic harmony. (Breitkopf and Härtel)

PETER WARLOCK (Philip Heseltine) (1894-1930)

Capriol — Suite based on dances from Arbeau's Orchéso-graphie (1588): Basse-Danse, Pavane, Tordion, Bransles, Pieds-en-l'air, Mattachins. (J. Curwen and Sons). Also exists in a version for string orchestra.

CARL MARIA VON WEBER (1786-1826)

Six Pieces, Op. 3 — Short, not difficult: flowing Sonatina in one movement (moderato e con amore); florid melodic Romanze; vigorous Menuetto; quiet Andante with three variations; Marcia with trio; joyous Rondo (allegramente). (Peters)

Six Pieces, Op. 10 — Same genre as Opus 3. See especially No. 2 (melancholy Andante con moto) and No. 4 (vigorous Mazurka). (Peters)

Eight Pieces, Op. 60 — More difficult than either Opus 3 or 10. See especially No. 2 (vigorous Allegro), No. 4 (lusty dance in minor Allegro tutto ben marcato with trio in major), No. 6 (Tema Variata on the song "Ich hab' mir Eins erwahlet," requiring agility) and No. 8 (a scurrying, lively Rondo, vivacious and joking). (Peters)

ERNST WILHELM WOLF (1735-1792)

Sonata in C Major — Elegant, graceful work in three movements: Allegro, Andante and Allegro. Not difficult. A neat and tidy sonata. (Schott, through Associated Music)

GEORG FRIEDRICH WOLF (late eighteenth century?)

Sonata in F Major — "Composed for Amateurs," in four movements: lively Allegro; Larghetto e lagrimoso in minor; short, lusty Minuetto with lyric trio; short, lively Finale. Not difficult. Should be reprinted. A library item. (Breitkopf and Härtel)

Music for Two Pianos— Four Hands

The following list of original compositions for two pianos, four hands is by no means exhaustive or complete. It is confined to the standard works in the repertoire and some contemporary additions that are useful contributions to this branch of the literature. Supplementary material covering many minor composers may be found in Hans Moldenhauer's Duo-Pianism, Chicago Musical College Press, 1950.

ANTON ARENSKY (1861-1906)

Five Suites

Op. 15	Music of easy effectiveness and charm. Contains the popular Waltz.
Op. 23	Five program pieces called Silhouettes. (P. Jurgenson)
Op. 33	In the form of variations. See especially the Minuet and the brilliant Scherzo which requires a delicate and rapid staccato chord technique. (P. Jurgenson)
Op. 62	Four pieces. (Schirmer)
Op. 65	Children's suite consisting of eight canons. (Schirmer)

VICTOR BABIN (1908-)

Six Études	Concert studies of which number four is based on the "Flight of the Bumble Bee." (Universal Music Co.).
Three Fantasies on Old Themes	Hebrew Slumber Song, The Piper of Polmood, Russian Village. (Augener)

JOHANN CHRISTIAN BACH (1735-1782)

Sonata in G Major, Op. 15, No. 6	Light-textured, flowing music. Not difficult. (Schott)

JOHANN SEBASTIAN BACH (1685-1750)

Two Fugues from The Art of the Fugue	Versions for two claviers of the "mirror" fugues in Contrapunctus XIII of the Art of the Fugue. Bach adds free counterpoint to the original version to give both hands of each player enough to do. Tovey cautions that the dotted rhythms of the original should be supplied consistently in the two-clavier version. (Peters)

WILHELM FRIEDEMANN BACH (1710-1784)

Sonata in F Major	Three-movement work with much canonic and imitative writing, the last section especially lively and imaginative. (International Music Co.)

ERNST BACON (1898-   )

Kankakee River Burr Frolic	(Wesley Webster, California). (Associated Music)
Coal Scuttle Blues	Written with Otto Luening (Associated Music). Pieces of moderate length and difficulty exploiting various facets of American folklore.

BÉLA BARTÓK (1881-1945)

Sonata for Two Pianos and Percussion	Virtuoso work in three movements with involved contrapuntal and rhythmic problems. Requires strength, vitality, fluent chord techniques, mature musicianship. Also exists in version for two pianos and orchestra. (Boosey & Hawkes)
Seven Pieces from the Mikrokosmos	Short pieces of moderate difficulty, including Hungarian dances and two chromatic inventions. (Boosey & Hawkes)

STANLEY BATE (1912-   )

Three Pieces	Conceived as a suite; crisp, bright, lengthy Prelude; Pastoral on siciliano rhythms; driving Presto as finale. Each piece fairly long, moderately difficult. (Associated Music)

ARNOLD BAX (1883-   )

Moy Mell	One movement, romantic in character, moderately difficult. Requires careful tonal balance. (J. & W. Chester)
The Poisoned Fountain	Short, atmospheric program piece requiring color and flexibility. (Murdoch, Murdoch and Co.)
Hardanger	Short, vivacious, dancelike piece "with acknowledgments to Grieg." (Murdoch, Murdoch and Co.)
The Devil that Tempted St. Anthony	Atmospheric Lento languido with contrasting strident Allegro. Shrill, powerful ending. (Murdoch, Murdoch and Co.)

Sonata

Rhapsodic opening two movements with vigorous, energetic finale <u>Vivace e feroce</u>.
(Murdoch, Murdoch and Co.).

MRS. H. H. A. BEACH (1867-1944)

Suite

(John Church).

Variations on Balkan
  Themes, Op. 60

(Arthur P. Schmidt)

ARTHUR BENJAMIN (1893-)

Jamaican Rumba
From San Domingo

Light dance pieces.
(Boosey & Hawkes)

NICOLAI BEREZOWSKY (1900-1953)

Fantasy, Op. 9

Large-scale work in one movement exploring
many varied textures and ideas. Difficult.
Also exists in a version for two pianos and
orchestra.
(Associated Music)

LENNOX BERKELEY (1903-)

Capriccio, Nocturne and
  Polka

(J. & W. Chester)

ÉMILE BLANCHET (1877-)

Ballade Op. 57

(Eschig)

CHARLES BORDES (1863-1909)

Rapsodie Basque

(Salabert)

PAUL BOWLES (1911-)

Sonata

(Schirmer).

GEORGE BOYLE (1886-1948)

Danse Nègre

(Elkan-Vogel)

Minuet Antique

(Elkan-Vogel)

JOHANNES BRAHMS (1833-1897)

Sonata, Op. 34 bis

Another version of the work familiarly known
as the <u>Piano Quintet</u>. Requires mature pianism
and musicianship. Demanding in every respect.
(International Music Co.)

Variations on a Theme
  by Haydn, Op. 56b

One of the peaks of the two-piano repertoire.
Requires mature pianism and musicianship.
Should be studied in conjunction with the ver-
sion for orchestra.
(Schirmer)

HENRY BRANT (1913-   )

Sonata
Four Chorale Preludes
Two Jazz Toccatas on
    Themes of Haydn and
    Bach

All available at the American Music Center.

BENJAMIN BRITTEN (1913-   )

Introduction and Rondo
    alla Burlesca

Weighty, serious <u>Grave</u> leading to a spirited
<u>Allegro moderato</u>, neatly accented. Brilliant
ending.
(Boosey & Hawkes)

Mazurka Elegiaca

In memoriam I. J. Paderewski.
(Boosey & Hawkes).

ALAN D. BUSH (1900-   )

Three Pieces

(Murdoch, Murdoch and Co.)

FERRUCCIO BUSONI (1866-1924)

Duettino Concertante

"After Mozart." Requires facility.
(Breitkopf and Härtel)

ROBERT CASADESUS (1899-   )

Dances Mediterranéennes

Vigorous <u>Sardana</u>; quiet, expressive <u>Sarabande</u>
working to a heavy climax; brilliant, lively
concluding <u>Tarentelle</u>.
(Carl Fischer)

EMMANUEL CHABRIER (1841-1894)

Trois Valses Romantiques

Elegant, salon style requiring polish and grace.
(Enoch).

THEODORE CHANLER (1902-   )

The Second Joyful Mystery

One-movement fugal work after a quotation
from Dante's "Purgatory."
(Associated Music)

ABRAM CHASINS (1903-   )

Carmen Fantasy
Fledermaus Fantasy

(J. Fischer)
(Oliver Ditson)

Two brilliant concert paraphrases on themes
from the operas.

Period Suite

(Chappell).

FRÉDÉRIC CHOPIN (1810-1849)

Rondeau in C Major,
    Op. 73

Light, brilliant salon style requiring sensitive
rubato and facile finger technique.
(Schirmer)

MUZIO CLEMENTI (1746?-1832)

Two Sonatas in B-flat Major, Op. 12 and Op. 46 — Simple, graceful pieces about the difficulty of the average Mozart sonata. (Schirmer)

ULRIC COLE (1905-)

Divertimento — (J. Fischer).

AARON COPLAND (1900-)

Danzon Cubano — A driving piece stressing percussive sonorities and irregular, abrupt phrases. (Boosey & Hawkes).

Billy the Kid — A suite derived from the well-known ballet. Requires sensitivity and, at the climactic points, drive and power. (Boosey & Hawkes)

FRANÇOIS COUPERIN (1668-1733)

Allemande in A Major from the ninth "Ordre" — Complex texture, problems in ornamentation. (Oxford University Press).

The following pieces from the Pièces de Clavecin can be adapted for two keyboard instruments. Couperin's footnote to La Julliet is as follows: "This piece can be played on different instruments. But better yet on two Harpsichords or Spinets, i.e., the main voice ('sujet') with the bass on one instrument and the same bass with the countermelody ('contre-partie') on the other. The same goes for all the other pieces in three parts."

La Julliet — From the fourteenth Ordre. (Oxford University Press)

Musette de Choisi
Musette de Taverni — From the fifteenth Ordre. (Oxford University Press).

La Létiville — From the sixteenth Ordre. (Oxford University Press)

HENRY COWELL (1897-)

Celtic Set — (Schirmer)

CÉSAR CUI (1835-1918)

Trois Morceaux Op. 69 — (P. Jurgenson)

CLAUDE DEBUSSY (1862-1918)

Lindaraja — An early work, atmospheric, dancelike, based on habanera rhythms. (Jobert)

En Blanc et Noir — Three pieces of substantial length and emotional content: Avec emportement, in waltz rhythm with some cross-accentuation; Lent,

Sombre, an elegy on a friend killed in World
War I, with a tumultuous middle section;
Scherzando finale (to Stravinsky), rather
sardonically humorous.
(International Music Co.)

NORMAN DEMUTH (1898-   )

Rhapsody   All published by Oxford University Press.
Bolero
Habanera

CELIUS DOUGHERTY (1902-   )

Music from Seas and Ships (Schirmer)

JOHANN LADISLAUS DUSSEK (1760-1812)

Sonata in E-flat Major,   (Haslinger)
  Op. 38

There are also duos for two pianos Opus 11 and Opus 36, the latter with
horn ad libitum.

GEORGES ENESCO (1881-   )

Variations, Op. 5   (Enoch)

GILES FARNABY (c.1560-c.1600)

For Two Virginals   One of the earliest known pieces for two keyboard instruments. Very short, two phrases,
each varied once.
(Oxford University Press)

LUKAS FOSS (1922-   )

Set of Three Pieces   Spirited, contrapuntal March; lengthy Andante;
elaborate concluding Concertino.
(Schirmer)

MIRIAM GIDEON (1906-   )

Hommage à ma Jeunesse   Light, graceful, diatonic Sonatina in three
movements: Allegretto, Pastoral, Allegro.
Transparent, unencumbered writing. Not
difficult.
(Mercury Music)

ALEXANDER GLAZOUNOFF (1865-1936)

Fantasie, Op. 104   Lengthy three-movement work requiring complete pianistic equipment.
(M. P. Belaieff).

REINHOLD GLIÈRE (1875-1926)

Six Pieces, Op. 41   (Leeds Music)

LEOPOLD GODOWSKY (1870-1938)

Contrapuntal Paraphrases on Weber's "Invitation to the Dance" — With optional part for third piano. (Carl Fischer)

RICHARD FRANKO GOLDMAN (1910-)

Le Bobino — An evocation of the French music hall of that name. Burlesque in three scenes: lively Allegro, short Entr'Âcte and Le Jazz Cold recalling jazz style of the 1920's. Not difficult. (Southern Music Publishing Co.)

EDVARD GRIEG (1843-1907)

Variations on an Old Norwegian Romance, Op. 51 — (Peters)

RUDOLPH GRUEN (1900-)

Humoresque and Scherzo — (Associated Music)

TIBOR HARSANYI (1898-)

Pièce — Brilliant piece alternating a Tempo di Valse with a Fox-trot. Requires energetic bravura.

CHARLES HAUBIEL (1894-)

Suite Passacaille — (Composer's Press)

EVERETT HELM (1913-)

Eight Minutes for Two Pianos — (American Music Center)

EDWARD BURLINGAME HILL (1872-)

Four Jazz Studies — (Schirmer)

PAUL HINDEMITH (1895-)

Sonata (1942) — Long, elaborately-developed work: majestic opening in free vein entitled Chimes; incisive Allegro requiring clarity and rhythmic bite; slow movement in Canon; free recitative on a literary quotation from c. 1300 - "This World's Joy" leading into final powerful Fugue. Requires mature musicianship and an advanced pianism. (Associated Music)

ALAN HOVHANESS (1911-)

Mihr — "Imitating an Orchestra of Kanoons." In New Music, April, 1946.

JOHANN NEPOMUK HUMMEL (1778-1837)

Introduction and Rondo,   (Breitkopf and Härtel)
Op. Posth., No. 5

MANUEL INFANTE (1883-)

Trois Danses Anda-   Contains the well-known Ritmo.
louses   (Salabert).

Musiques d'Espagne   Suite on Spanish themes.
(Salabert)

ULYSSES KAY (1917-)

Baile   Spanish Dance.
(American Composer's Alliance Library)

WENDELL KEENEY (1903-)

Spanish Capriccio   (J. Fischer)

ARAM KHATCHATURIAN (1903-)

Suite   Ostinato, lyric Romance and a brilliant,
sweeping Fantastic Waltz as conclusion. Not
easy.
(Leeds Music)

JOHN KLEIN (1915-)

Three Dances   (Associated Music).

CHARLES KOECHLIN (1867-1950)

Suite, Op. 6   (Alphonse Leduc)

FRANZ LISZT (1811-1886)

Concerto Pathétique   Virtuoso work in one movement exploiting a
wide variety of pianistic problems.
(Schirmer)

NIKOLAI LOPATNIKOFF (1903-)

Arabesque   (Associated Music)

JEAN-LOUIS MARTINET (1912-)

Prélude et Fugue   Melodic Prelude; lengthy, sonorous Fugue
with brilliant pianistic figuration, quiet ending.
Not easy.
(Heugel)

GIUSEPPE MARTUCCI (1856-1909)

Variations in E-flat   Both published by Ricordi.
Major
Fantasy in D Minor,
Op. 32

DANIEL GREGORY MASON (1873-   )

Divertimento Op. 26a	March and Fugue after an unpublished wind quintet. (Carl Fischer)
Scherzo, Op. 22b	(Carl Fischer)
Prelude and Fugue, Op. 20	(J. Fischer)

OLIVIER MESSIAEN (1908-   )

Sept Visions de l'Amen	Lengthy, difficult, mystical work requiring strength and the most varied sonorities. "I have allotted to the first piano the rhythmic difficulties, chord clusters and all problems in velocity, charm and quality of sound: to the second piano I have allotted the principal melody, thematic elements and everything that demands emotion and power." (Durand).

COLIN McPHEE (1901-   )

Balinese Ceremonial Music	(Schirmer)

JACQUES DE MENASCE (1905-   )

Divertissement sur une Chanson d'Enfants	(Carl Fischer)

DARIUS MILHAUD (1892-   )

Le Bal Martiniquais	Short, chordal Chanson Créole in moderate tempo followed by brilliant, rhythmic Biguine.
Scaramouche Suite	A "clownish" set of three movements: humorous Vif; melancholy Modéré and concluding Brazileira in the style of a samba. (Elkan-Vogel)
Carnaval à la Nouvelle Orleans	(Leeds Music)
Kentuckiana	Piece built on twenty Kentucky mountain tunes. (Elkan-Vogel)
Les Songes	Suite in three movements: facile, clear opening Très vif; short Valse in moderate tempo; brilliant, animated Polka. (Elkan-Vogel)

IGNAZ MOSCHELES (1794-1870)

Hommage à Handel, Op. 92 (Augener)

MORITZ MOSZKOWSKI (1854-1925)

Caprice   All published by Ries and Erler, Berlin.
Mazurka
Deux Morceaux

WOLFGANG AMADEUS MOZART (1756-1791)

Fugue in C Minor,   Animated, contrapuntal tour de force. Com-
K. 426   plex counterpoint. Technically and rhythmic-
          ally difficult.
          (Schirmer)

Sonata in D Major,   In three movements: facile, flowing Allegro
K. 448   con spirito; rather lengthy Andante; brisk,
          concluding rondo, Allegro molto. Requires
          the utmost neatness, elegance and sensitivity.
          (Schirmer)

CHARLES HUBERT PARRY (1848-1918)

Grand Characteristic   (Breitkopf and Härtel)
Duo in E Minor

BERNARDO PASQUINI (1637-1710)

Sonatas in G Minor and (Durand)
F Major
Sonata in D Minor   Originally improvised by two players from
          figured bass parts.
          (Bärenreiter)

VINCENT PERSICHETTI (1915-)

Sonata   Broad, lengthy declamatory Lento rising to
          great climax with fugato interspersed; waltz-
          like Allegretto; short, sombre Largo; propul-
          sive, energetic Vivace as conclusion. Not
          easy.
          (Leeds Music)

FELIX PETYREK (1892-1919)

Six Concert Etudes   Short studies in velocity, double notes, ar-
          peggios, interlocking chords. Not easy.
          (Universal).

Toccata and Fugue in Broad, expansive Toccata on a chorale theme
Mixolydian Mode   later used in Fugue I; short, chordal Arioso
          concluding with a jovial Fugue II (mirror-
          fugue).
          (Universal Edition)

PAUL A. PISK (1893-)

My Pretty Little Pink Piece built on a Southern folk tune.
          (Leeds Music)

JOHN POWELL (1882-   )

Natchez-on-the-Hill	Both published by G. Schirmer.
Three Virginian Country Dances	

HENRI RABAUD (1873-   )

Divertissement sur des Chansons Russes	(Enoch)

SERGEI RACHMANINOFF (1873-1943)

Suite, Op. 5	Fantaisie consisting of <u>Barcarolle</u>, "Oh night, Oh love," <u>Tears</u>, <u>Easter</u>. (International Music Co.)
Suite, Op. 17	In four movements: <u>Introduction</u> with grandiose chords; <u>Waltz</u> requiring neat, precise ensemble; melodic <u>Romance</u>; brilliant <u>Tarentelle</u> as conclusion. (International Music Co.)

MAURICE RAVEL (1875-1937)

Les Sites Auriculaires	An early work (1895-1896) containing the <u>Habanera</u> and the <u>Entre Cloches</u>. (Unpublished)

MAX REGER (1873-1916)

Variations and Fugue on a Theme by Beethoven, Op. 86	Involved, massive work on a theme from the <u>Bagatelles</u>, Op. 119. (Bote & Bock)
Introduction, Passacaglia and Fugue, Op. 96	Thick, complicated style, much harmonic and contrapuntal interest. (Bote & Bock)

CARL REINECKE (1824-1910)

Andante and Variations, Op. 6	(Hofmeister)
Impromptu on a Motif from Schumann's "Manfred," Op. 66	(Associated Music)
Variations on a Sarabande by Bach, Op. 24b	(Edward Schuberth)
Improvisations on a French Folk Song, Op. 94	(Breitkopf and Härtel)
Improvisations on a Gavotte by Gluck, Op. 125	(Peters)

Variations on "A Mighty Fortress is our God," Op. 191	(Forberg)
Four Pieces, Op. 241	(Peters)
Three Sonatas Op. 240 in F Major Op. 275 in G Major Op. 275 in C Major	(Peters; Hofmeister)

WALLINGFORD RIEGGER (1885-   )

Dance Suite	Three pieces originally written for the modern dance: Evocation—for Martha Graham (Southern Music Publishing Co.); The Cry— for Hanya Holm (Southern Music Publishing Co.); New Dance—for Doris Humphrey (Arrow Music Press)

GUY ROPARTZ (1864-   )

Pièce in B Minor	An extended piece on a large scale. Florid pianistic writing in Franckian vein. (Durand)

BERYL RUBINSTEIN (1898-1952)

Suite	Light Prelude, lyric Canzonetta, an Irish Jig and Masks, a concluding piece featuring irregular meters. (Schirmer)

CAMILLE SAINT-SAËNS (1835-1921)

Caprice Héroique, Op. 16	
Variations on a Theme by Beethoven, Op. 35	An effective and glittering work on the Trio of the Minuet to the Sonata in E-flat, Op. 31, No. 3. Lively and telling fugue as conclusion. Moderate difficulty. Requires precision in rapidly alternating chords between the two instruments. (Schirmer).
Polonaise, Op. 77	(Durand)
Scherzo, Op. 87	Light, brilliant work requiring elegance and facility. (Durand)
Caprice Arabe, Op. 96	(Durand)
Fantasy and Fugue, Chorale, Scherzo and Finale	(Fromont)

FLORENT SCHMITT (1870-   )

Three Rhapsodies, Op. 53
Rather lengthy pieces in waltz-time: Française, Polonaise, Viennoise. The first and third are brilliant, the second more lyric in quality. (Durand)

ROBERT SCHUMANN (1810-1856)

Andante and Variations, Op. 46
Graceful, warmly emotional work with much back-and-forth dialogue between the instruments. Only one variation is really difficult. (Schirmer)

CYRIL SCOTT (1879-   )

Theme and Variations
An extended work featuring harmonies in fourths. Ten variations culminating in a climactic Quasi Fuga. Difficult. (Elkin and Co.)

CHRISTIAN SINDING (1856-   )

Variations, Op. 2
Virtuoso treatment of sombre theme. Requires facility in Lisztian techniques. (Wilhelm Hansen)

BEDRICH SMETANA (1824-1884)

Sonata in E Minor
For eight hands! (Peters)

CHARLES VILLIERS STANFORD (1852-1924)

Serenade, Op. 17
(Boosey & Hawkes)

IGOR STRAVINSKY (1882-   )

Concerto per Due Pianoforti Soli
Large-scale work in four movements: lengthy opening Con moto; atmospheric Notturno; Quattro variazioni leading to choral-like Preludio and a vigorous concluding Fuga. Requires high degree of virtuosity and musicianship. (Schott)

Sonata
Graceful chamber work: suave, flowing Moderato; broad, diatonic theme with four short variations; flowing Allegretto as conclusion. Moderately difficult. (Associated Music).

GERMAINE TAILLEFERRE (1892-   )

Jeux de Plein Air
(Durand)

LOUISE TALMA (1906-   )

Four-handed Fun

An <u>Allegro</u> movement; witty, light, primarily rhythmic in interest.
(Carl Fischer)

VIRGIL THOMSON (1896-   )

Synthetic Waltzes

A chain of easy waltzes, completely diatonic in style.
(Elkan-Vogel)

MICHAEL TIPPETT (1905-   )

Fantasia on a Theme of Handel

(Associated Music)

ERNEST WALKER (1870-   )

West Africa Fantasy, Op. 53
Waltz Suite, Op. 60

Both published by Oxford University Press.

HUGO WEISGALL (1912-   )

Fugue and Romance

(Mercury Music)

RALPH VAUGHAN WILLIAMS (1872-   )

Introduction and Fugue

An elaborate work; short, sonorous, chordal <u>Prelude</u> leading to a lengthy, complex <u>Fugue</u> with complicated pianistic textures. Requires good command of the piano in both parts.
(Oxford University Press)

ESTHER WILLIAMSON (1915-   )

Sonata

In three movements; moderato opening; short singing <u>Andante</u> leading to vigorous <u>Allegro vivace</u>. Moderately difficult.
(Mercury Music)

Part V
Music for Piano and Orchestra

Music for Solo Piano and Orchestra

EUGEN D'ALBERT (1864-1932)

Concerto No. 2, in E
Major, Op. 12

An expertly contrived work, in four linked
movements: An opening <u>Moderato</u>, starting
with an orchestral fanfare, which alternates
with passages for piano of a more lyrical
character, leading to a second theme in a
suave cantabile; an <u>Adagio</u>, quietly expressive,
with a more passionate central theme; a lively
<u>Scherzo</u>, which gives effective contrast; and a
final section, which develops some of the preceding material and ends with a grandiose
climax. The influence of Liszt is evident.
(Bote & Bock)

ANTON ARENSKY (1861-1906)

Concerto in F Minor,
Op. 2

This has a showy piano part. The material is
sometimes rather commonplace; and there is
a good deal of repetition with little real
development. The concerto is, however,
superficially effective.
(Rahter)

CARL PHILIPP EMANUEL BACH (1714-1788)

It is to be hoped that contemporary publishers will print reliable editions
of at least a representative selection of the concertos of C. P. E. Bach.
The remarkable collection of full scores in the Library of Congress provides ample material.

Concerto in D Minor

This concerto, at present not easily available,
is a work of importance both intrinsically and
historically, bridging as it does the gap between the clavier concerto of Johann Sebastian
Bach and the established classical form of
Mozart. It has a dignified first movement
with a short opening tutti, the latter part of
which is used to conclude the movement. The
rhythmical motives of the first subject appear
in the orchestra in combination with effective
keyboard passages, the soloist also having a
small amount of lyrical contrasting material.
An extended <u>Andante</u> consists of an expressive
dialogue between clavier and strings; the
lively finale has the same general structure
as the first movement, with an arresting subject whose rhythm dominates throughout.
(Steingräber)

JOHANN CHRISTIAN BACH (1735-1782)

Concerto in D Major,
Op. 13, No. 2
Concerto in B-flat Major,
Op. 13, No. 4

These are fair examples of the compositions of "the English Bach" for cembalo (or piano) and orchestra. It is easy to see their influence on the earliest work of Mozart; they are very naive and, to our ears, somewhat unenterprising in their conventional runs and arpeggio formulas. The concerto in B-flat has for a finale a set of variations on a Scottish folk tune; and the entire concerto was transcribed for pianoforte solo by Haydn.
(Peters)

JOHANN SEBASTIAN BACH (1685-1750)

The clavier concertos of J. S. Bach are in a category of their own, with the solo instrument not so much a "star" performer as part of the entire contrapuntal texture. There is still some controversy concerning the best way to treat the clavier part. Some players feel themselves at liberty to fill out the harmonies liberally - Busoni's edition is an example of this procedure - in accordance with the practice of the continuo player of Bach's day. On the other hand, the clavier part as printed gives us a text that is quite practicable as it stands, even with occasional omissions — e.g., of the first six bars of the clavier part in the D-minor concerto. The various editions stand between the two extremes of the Bach Society's and Busoni's text.

Concerto in D Minor

This is evidently a transcription of a violin concerto (as most of the clavier concertos appear to be); a restoration of the original has been made and has become familiar. The material of the first and second movements was also used by Bach in the Cantata Wir müssen durch viel Trübsal, the slow movement there actually having a chorus superimposed. The work is on a grand scale; the problems for a player on the modern pianoforte are in the first and last movements primarily problems of balance. The noble slow movement, with its expressive florid melody held together by a persistent bass figure, is of the same type as the central movements of the Italian Concerto for clavier alone and the E-major violin concerto.
Published by Peters; Schirmer; Breitkopf and Härtel (Busoni edition)

Concerto in F Minor

This charming work is on a comparatively small scale. The first movement at the start recalls the C-minor concerto for two claviers, in the echo effect at the end of the phrases; a smooth legato delivery of the rolling triplets that characterize this section

of the concerto seems essential. The very short <u>Largo</u>, with continuous pizzicato accompaniment, is an expressively ornamental version of a melody that has become familiar in its simpler form. A lively <u>Presto</u> completes the scheme.
(Peters; International Music Co.)

Concerto in A Major

Has a solid first movement with the musical interest alternating between strings and clavier; a flowing <u>Larghetto</u> with an almost uninterrupted solo for the clavier; and a third movement less brilliant than usual, owing to a good deal of florid passage work that enforces a moderate tempo.
(Peters)

Concerto in D Major for clavier, flute and violin

This, the fifth Brandenburg concerto, must be mentioned for the outstanding inspiration of its musical material, and the special prominence of the clavier in a long cadenza in the first movement - the remarkable climactic effect of this is most compelling. The second movement is an unaccompanied trio for the three solo instruments, and the last is a gigue-like movement with an irresistible rhythmic swing.
(Breitkopf and Härtel; Kalmus)

WILHELM FRIEDEMANN BACH (1710-1784)

Concerto in C Minor

The eldest son of John Sebastian Bach had probably a more original native talent than any of his brothers, though he had faults of character that prevented his making the most of his gifts. He makes use of the general structural principles of his father, with a texture that resembles more that of Carl Philipp Emanuel. His material has individuality, and there is a great deal of brilliant passage work for the solo instrument.
(Schott)

BÉLA BARTÓK (1881-1945)

Concerto No. 1 (1926)

In extreme dissonant idiom with, at times, constant changes of bar length and generally enterprising rhythmical treatment of material that is not always melodically striking. Various percussion instruments have a prominent part, as may be noted from the direction: "Percussion instruments, including timpani, are to be placed, if possible, directly behind the piano." The piano writing, it can be said, is itself largely percussive.
(Boosey & Hawkes)

Concerto No. 2 (1932)	This has many of the characteristics of the first concerto—extreme dissonance, emphasis of rhythmic interest with a certain barbaric quality in the persistent figures, and interesting orchestral color. The piano part is most taxing, with exacting chord and double-note passages. The uninterrupted rhythmic excitement of the first and last movements is contrasted with the chantlike opening and close of the middle movement, where two melodic lines, in the upper and lower registers of the orchestra, are each harmonized in unvarying major ninths, with a central fifth making a three-note chord. (Boosey & Hawkes)
Concerto No. 3 (1945)	Much more transparent and easily comprehended than the two earlier piano concertos. The thematic material has more direct melodic appeal, and the piano part is much less physically exacting. It should be noted that the final directions for performance were not all completed at the time of the composer's death. As a whole, the concerto shows a mitigation of the extreme harshness of some of Bartók's earlier work. The second movement - <u>Adagio religioso</u> - begins, like that of the second concerto, with a chant; now, however, having a contrapuntal character that suggests sixteenth-century influence. The middle section of the same movement, with its striking little wisps of sound against the tremolo of the orchestra, depends largely on effects of instrumental color. (Boosey & Hawkes)

LUDWIG VAN BEETHOVEN (1770-1827)

<u>Editions</u>

Each of Beethoven's five is in its way an outstanding landmark in the literature of the piano concerto. The Schirmer reprint of Kullak's edition is reliable, although here and there Beethoven's meager dynamic indications have to be supplemented. Max Pauer has more recently prepared for Peters an edition "based on the Beethoven manuscripts." Kalmus also prints the first, second, third and fourth concertos.

Concerto in C Major, Op. 15	Actually the second concerto in order of composition, and more weighty than the one in B-flat. The broken-chord and passage work in the first and last movements, while not excessively difficult, requires a good technique; the slow movement tests the player's cantabile. Beethoven's third cadenza, an extended and masterly "extemporization," should be noted.

Concerto in B-flat Major, Op. 19	This charming early work has a first movement with only one really taxing passage, with sixteenth-note runs alternately for right and left hand, near the end of the exposition and recapitulation. The slow movement is characteristically expressive, with an imaginative dialogue between piano and orchestra at the end. The humor of the finale, less boisterous than that of the C major, is equally pointed. Beethoven's cadenza is not specially interesting.
Concerto in C Minor, Op. 37	In this the style of Beethoven's middle period begins to emerge. The technical demands are on the whole greater than in Opus 15 and Opus 19, both in the first and last movements. The slow movement, opening with the piano alone and introducing a striking modulation in the course of the first theme, is one of Beethoven's finest. The composer's cadenza has been left in a rather sketchy condition, and does not defy competition.
Concerto in G Major, Op. 58	One of the great masterpieces in this form, perfect in its design, and most poetic in its content. It is a searching test of the artist's interpretative gifts, and on the technical side it has its pitfalls, in difficulties which do not always lie on the surface. Beethoven's cadenzas (particularly the second of the two he wrote for the first movement) are to be recommended.
Concerto in E-flat Major, Op. 73	The grandeur of this work has even given it the nickname "Emperor" in English-speaking countries. It calls for great breadth of style, a highly developed technique, and similar musical insight to that demanded by Opus 58. In striving for a correct balance of tone, the pianist has to bear in mind in certain passages the difference between the sonority of Beethoven's piano and that of a modern concert grand. Some fortes have to be modified accordingly.
Choral Fantasia, Op. 80	For piano, chorus and orchestra. This is interesting because of its latter part, which anticipates some of the material of the finale of the Ninth Symphony.
Triple Concerto, Op. 56	For piano, violin and violoncello. A somewhat austere work, which treats its special problem in a masterly manner; it is to be wished that it could be heard more often.

ARTHUR BENJAMIN (1893-   )

Concerto quasi una Fanta-
sia

An elaborate work employing a large orchestra
and extra percussion. In one continuous movement, its main sections are: A rhapsodical
opening, with frequently changing tempi, working up to a grandiose climax; a fanciful scherzo;
and a passacaglia with nine variations (the
ninth being a cadenza for the piano), leading
to a final version of the climax of the first
section. Some recapitulation of the material
of the opening of the whole work brings a brilliant conclusion. The piece has a unifying
thread in a figure of five notes, which introduces at the outset a furious descending string
passage and appears in various guises, ulti-
mately in a curious angular version, producing
the passacaglia theme. The piano writing has
a wide range and requires both power and delicacy. The final climax asks the soloist to
contend against the strings and full brass.
(Boosey & Hawkes)

LENNOX BERKELEY (1903-   )

Concerto in B-flat Major
(1952)

A piece of contemporary flavor, with a good
deal of effective writing for the soloist; it is
not unduly weighty, but requires expert pianism. The main theme of the final movement
has an engaging rhythmic character.
(J. & W. Chester)

ARTHUR BLISS (1891-   )

Concerto in B-flat Major

A lengthy and imposing work, idiomatically
written for the piano with resourceful treatment of the orchestra. It is harmonically
modern without abandoning tonality, and it is
extremely taxing for the soloist.
(Novello)

ERNEST BLOCH (1880-   )

Scherzo fantasque

This piece makes use of a number of very
short, sharply differentiated motives in a manner that recalls Debussy's Fêtes. The piano
is treated effectively, without excessive difficulty, in passages of wide technical variety;
the orchestration is colorful and brilliant,
with much astringent dissonance. The material
is mainly rhythmic in character; some contrast
comes in a short central section in slower tempo
where ideas presented previously in a driving
allegro appear in more meditative guise. When

the first tempo is resumed it leads to a coda where at last a sense of definite tonality is achieved in a striking peroration in A minor. (Schirmer)

Concerto symphonique

An important and highly organized work in three movements. At the outset fourteen bars for the piano alone present a pregnant motive, characterized by four ascending scale steps, which reappear throughout the concerto. Further introductory material, orchestra and piano taking part, leads to the statement of a main subject, in steady marching rhythm, by orchestra and piano alternately. This, too, is referred to in the later movements. After an extended cadenza for the piano, some condensed recapitulation and a quiet coda bring the movement to an end. In the second movement a whispering pizzicato bass introduces a strongly rhythmical subject for the piano, later taken up by the orchestra, which dominates, until an episode with a persistent bass recalling the opening of the whole work leads to a calm lyrical andante, in which the piano is joined in a succession of themes by a number of solo instruments. The movement closes calmly on a dissonance. The third movement, like the first, has a lengthy introduction, foreshadowing in fragmentary form material that afterward acquires more continuity—a subject of decided character, marked by a repeated-note figure, becomes prominent in the whole movement. There is some brief lyrical relief, a return to the rhythmical opening subject, and a close which harks back in the full orchestra to motives heard at the start of the concerto. In general, the scoring is heavy; and the piano has often to contend with a rather thick orchestral texture, rarely being heard in isolation. The composition, however, repays study and is stamped with the composer's individuality. (Boosey & Hawkes)

Concerto grosso, for piano and strings

One of Bloch's most immediately appealing works. In its four movements - Prelude, Dirge, Pastorale and Rustic Dances, and Fugue - the piano, however, has no real solo function and is employed almost entirely to double other instruments. (Birchard)

GEORGE BOYLE (1886-1948)

Concerto in D Minor, for piano and orchestra

An effective work, written in a vein of nineteenth century romanticism, but with a

definite creative impulse. It had in its day a
striking success, owing to its genuine emotional quality and technical expertness, and it
might well be revived.
(Schirmer)

JOHANES BRAHMS (1833-1897)

The concertos of Brahms reveal him as the outstanding inheritor of the
classical tradition of Mozart and Beethoven.

Concerto in D Minor,   A powerful and mature work, with a large
Op. 15   first movement of great tragic force, a serene
and profound adagio, and a vigorous and bril-
liant finale. In the first movement the chains
of trills, with octave stretch for right-hand
thumb and fourth finger, are only effective for
a large hand; for others it is expedient to re-
arrange them by some device of alternating
hands. The rondo follows in some of its main
features the shape of Beethoven's concerto
in C minor.

Concerto in B-flat Major,   A great work in the classical tradition (com-
Op. 83   pare the passage leading to the return of the
principal subject in the first movement with
the similar one in Beethoven's concerto in
E-flat). Great power and sweep are essential
for its full effect. The technical difficulties
are great, and are only slightly lessened by occasional redistribution of some passages.
A novelty is the addition, to the usual classical scheme, of a fourth movement (a scherzo)
between the opening movement and the Andante.

FRANK BRIDGE (1879-1941)

Phantasm, for piano and   An imaginative work, with expert idiomatic
orchestra   treatment of solo instrument and orchestra.
In Bridge's latest, atonal style.
(Augener)

BENJAMIN BRITTEN (1913-   )

Concerto in D Major,   A characteristically uninhibited example of
Op. 13   this composer's assured and striking talent.
The scheme is unconventional, with four move-
ments entitled: Toccata, Waltz, Impromptu,
March. The Toccata employs much energetic
percussive technique and a great deal of brilliant passage work; there is a showy cadenza;
there are interesting devices of augmentation
and diminution. The Waltz is graceful, with a
comparatively simple piano part. The Impromptu is actually an imaginative passacaglia, the

theme being given out by the piano and after-
wards left to the orchestra, with contrapuntal
elaboration by the soloist. It leads directly
to the final March, which has a main theme of
(possibly intentional) unabashed blatancy, a
"cadenza in tempo" embodying an exciting
crescendo in the march rhythm, and a glittering coda that ends the concerto with much solo
and orchestral brilliance. The idiom throughout is freely dissonant without any feeling of
atonality.
(Boosey & Hawkes)

Diversions on a theme, for left hand and orchestra, Op. 21	An ingenious set of variations exploiting vari- ous kinds of left-hand technique; the "theme" is hardly more than three notes, rising by perfect fifths. The eleven variations, the com- poser announces, do not attempt to imitate a two-handed technique; but they do traverse the possibilities of the single hand, giving it an elaborate work-out. (Boosey & Hawkes)

FERRUCIO BUSONI (1866-1924)

Indian Fantasy, Op. 44	An elaborate work with an extremely brilliant piano part and pleasing melodic material. It deserves more frequent performance. (Breitkopf & Härtel)

JOHN ALDEN CARPENTER (1876-1951)

Concertino for piano and orchestra	One continuous movement with varying tempi. It relies mainly on persistent rhythms for its interest, and is reminiscent of the methods of Albeniz in his Iberia. There is much piquant orchestration, and the piano part is not diffi- cult. (Schirmer)

ALFREDO CASELLA (1883-1947)

Partita for piano and orchestra	The orchestra consists of strings, oboe, three clarinets, three trumpets and timpani; and this distribution is cleverly handled, full ad- vantage being taken of the possibility of treat- ing the instruments in separate groups. The piano is given some grateful solo work, though it is more often absorbed in the or- chestral texture. The three movements are: A lively Sinfonia with busy counterpoint, of eighteenth-century type in spite of its disso- nances, having an almost incessant eighth- note pulse—a Passacaglia with twelve varia- tions and coda, the piano making its appearance

first in the fifth and sixth variations where it
has an elaborate solo part—and a <u>Burlesca</u>, in
which the trumpets open with a tune of almost
Sullivanesque character and the movement
pursues a high-spirited course, with the piano
mainly in the role of accompanist, though it
emerges at times to provide a link between
phrases, a glockenspiel-like effect in the upper
octaves, or some glittering climactic passages
with alternating hands.
(Universal Edition)

CÉCILE CHAMINADE (1857-1944)

Concertstück for piano
and orchestra, Op. 40

A short piece, not very significant, but
pleasant and effectively written; fairly easy.

FRÉDÉRIC CHOPIN (1810-1849)

Concerto in E Minor,
    Op. 11
Concerto in F Minor,
    Op. 21

The two concertos of Chopin make unique interpretative demands; they abound in extended
stretches of passage work, admirably adapted
to the instrument, which alternate between a
glittering brilliance and a peculiar expressiveness that is hardly approached in any other
works for piano and orchestra. These qualities are specially evident in the first movement
of the Concerto in F minor; in its second movement, together with the characteristic Chopin-
esque cantabile and graceful ornamentation,
there is a notable feature in a dramatic central
recitative, the hands playing an octave apart
over tremolo strings, which provides a most
effective contrast; the graceful main subject
of the finale has as a foil much brilliant finger
technique and a coda, the full effect of which
is hard to achieve unless the pianist has a
good-sized hand. The concerto in E minor has
less grace and subtlety than its companion,
with some compensation in the rhythmic vitality of the finale's principal theme. The coda
of the first movement has at its start a long
passage that taxes the outer fingers of the
right hand, with less than Chopin's usual
grateful quality; the second movement, entitled
<u>Romance</u>, recalls some of the nocturnes in its
emotional and decorative phrases and its
poetical close. In both concertos the orchestra,
except in the tuttis, gives only the barest support to the cominating piano part; the scoring
lacks effectiveness on the whole, and attempts
by Klindworth and others toward its improve-
ment have not appreciably bettered the situation.
(Schirmer; Augener; Breitkopf & Härtel;
Ricordi, etc.)

Variations on Mozart's "La ci darem," Op. 2	These effective variations, with their introductory <u>Largo</u>, make exacting technical demands of a varied character; the influence of Hummel is apparent.
Grand Fantasia on Polish Airs, Op. 13	This piece has qualities of elaborate technical display like those of the variations, Op. 2; musically, it is rather superficial.
Krakowiak, Op. 14	A short introduction leads to a lengthy and brilliant allegro with much taxing passage work. The main subjects are harmonically somewhat poverty-stricken; however, the solution of the interesting technical problems is worth while.
	The Schirmer edition of the above three pieces, and of the <u>Andante spianato</u> and <u>Polonaise</u>, Op. 22, has second piano parts printed separately.

AARON COPLAND (1900-   )

Concerto in one movement	This is characterized by persistent syncopated rhythms of a barbaric nature, and extreme dissonance. There is a strong suggestion of jazz influence. (Cos Cob Press)

FREDERICK DELIUS (1863-1934)

Concerto in C Minor	An early work of the composer, but later recast. It has much elaborate writing for the soloist, requiring a good double-note technique and powerful octaves and chords. The material is mainly of a cantabile character, with a final grandiose climax. There is an opening <u>Moderato</u>, a slower middle section, and a return to the material of the beginning—the whole being played without a break. (Universal Edition)

ERNST VON DOHNANYI (1877-   )

Variations on a Nursery Song, Op. 25	This delightful piece has a brilliant and grateful piano part, which presents the little theme ("Ah, vous dirai-je, maman"), after a mock-serious introduction for the orchestra, with comic simplicity but with the interpolation of two ridiculous gambolings that presage later humorous events. There are eleven variations, the tenth being a clever and serious passacaglia; a "fugato" finale follows, with a reference in a short coda to the original simple tune. (Associated Music)

ANTONIN DVORAK (1841-1904)

Concerto in G Minor, Op. 33

A work which has been rather underestimated, by reason, no doubt, of its lack of virtuoso display; the pianoforte writing has in general a character similar to that of Dvorak's chamber music for piano and strings. While not, perhaps, one of his greatest compositions, this concerto is decidedly worthy of revival for its melodic and rhythmic interest and its constant vitality. (J. Hainauer)

MANUEL DE FALLA (1876-1946)

Nights in the Gardens of Spain

Subtitled: "Symphonic Impressions for piano and orchestra," this is a colorful work with strong national flavor. Its three movements— the first, a tranquil atmospheric piece, and the others, dance movements of gradually mounting excitement—employ the piano partly as an orchestral instrument, doubling other strands of the texture, and also in solo passages of more independent character. A type of technique which divides the figuration conveniently between alternating hands, and simple passages in single notes for hands playing an octave apart, account for much of the material, which nevertheless calls for considerable brilliance. (Eschig)

Concerto in D Major for harpsichord or piano (With flute, oboe, clarinet, violin and violoncello)

Actually a piece of chamber music (the composer emphasizes that the string players are "soloists" and that their number is not to be increased). A very individual work. It has enterprising treatment of the combination, with polytonal contrasts, at times, between the different instrumental colors. It is rhythmically vital, and the composer's imagination has, it is easy to feel, been stimulated by the harpsichord's quality of tone, which (he suggests in a note) should be kept in mind when the piano is substituted. (Eschig)

GABRIEL FAURÉ (1845-1924)

Ballade for piano and orchestra, Op. 19, in F-sharp Major

This short work has all Fauré's usual finish of workmanship. Starting with a quiet cantabile for piano alone, it develops to a strong central climax, then recedes to a poetic close. It might be effectively placed in a program with some contrasting work of similar length. (J. Hamelle, through International Music Co.)

Fantaisie for piano and orchestra, Op. 111, in G Major

Opens vigorously and rhythmically, with the piano in dialogue with the clarinet; later, the violins in octaves have a cantilena which is taken up by the piano, followed by some development leading to a contrasting central section. The opening is recapitulated and the final climax is brilliant. It is not a piece that makes an easy appeal, in spite of its elaborate and skillful writing.
(Durand)

HOWARD FERGUSON (1908-   )

Concerto in D Major for piano and strings

A musicianly work, with individual touches though the idiom is mainly conservative. The first movement has a classical design, preserving even the opening orchestral tutti; the second is a set of variations that are, with one exception, plaintively expressive; and there is a lively finale. The pianoforte writing is expert and of not more than average difficulty.
(Boosey & Hawkes)

JEAN FRANÇAIX (1912-   )

Concertino for piano and orchestra

A short and slight work in four movements (<u>Prelude</u>, <u>Lento</u>, <u>Menuet</u> and <u>Rondo</u>). The first and last consist almost entirely of persistent, lively sixteenth-note passages, with moderately dissonant harmonies which give an attractive flavor. There is a continuous two-bar rhythm which would become tiresome in a longer work. The second and third movements are quite short and unambitious. The piece is entertaining, and not difficult for anyone with a good finger staccato.

CESAR FRANCK (1822-1890)

Variations Symphoniques

This short work is one of the most successful, structurally, that Franck has given us. It is founded on two distinct themes - one in 4/4 time which appears first in fragmentary and improvisatory phrases and is then stated complete by the soloist, and a second in 3/4 time which is treated in a continuous central series of variations in moderate and slow tempi. Finally, the first theme forms the main subject of a brilliant finale, with episodic reference to a version of the second theme, appearing as bass to a subordinate subject. A free rotational technique is needful throughout.

Some editions contain editorial treatment of the solo part in the final section, adding a question-

able semi-cantabile effect in the main theme
(given in the original in plain eighth-notes),
and also some doubtful phrasing in the piano
solo in E-flat.
(Litolff; Schirmer; Peters; Kalmus)

Les Djinns

This beautiful and little-known composition is
a musical illustration of a poem by Victor
Hugo, describing the emotions of a man pur-
sued by sinister spirits, which approach through
the air and gradually increase his terror; he
has recourse to prayer; the spirits recede and
he is left in silence. The crescendo- and-
diminuendo structure of the poem is followed
faithfully by Franck with striking musical
effect; the "prayer"—an expressive cantilena—
is notably moving. There is no element of
superficial virtuosity, which may account for
the fact that this sensitive and poetical work
has not received the attention it deserves.
(Litolff; Schirmer)

GEORGE GERSHWIN (1898-1937)

Rhapsody in Blue
Concerto in F Major

These two pieces employ a jazz idiom with a
striking effect that is aided by the composer's
real melodic gift. The Rhapsody is the more
successful of the two, the concerto showing to
a greater degree the lack of the technical
equipment that Gershwin, in his short life,
strove for but never quite achieved. Both
compositions call for an assured command of
the keyboard and great rhythmic verve.
(Harms)

C. ARMSTRONG GIBBS (1889-   )

Concertino for piano and
    string orchestra,
    Op. 103

This has no complexities in its three short
movements. The folk-song-like theme of the
second and the dance rhythm of the third have
particular charm, and a pianist of moderate
technical powers will find the work has unpretentious but rewarding qualities.
(Boosey & Hawkes)

ALEXANDER GLAZOUNOFF (1865-1936)

Concerto in F Minor,
    Op. 92

An impressive work, displaying much contrapuntal skill and ingenuity of development,
the material is graceful and pleasing without
striking individuality. The idiom is conservative, and some devices (e.g., the use of sequences and diminution) are a little overworked.
The concerto is in two sections - a movement
in free sonata form, and a set of variations,

worked out with great skill and much elaborate piano writing, which leads to a finale where various elements of the first movement are cleverly dovetailed with the theme of the variations.
(Belaieff)

EUGENE GOOSSENS (1893-)

Phantasy Concerto,
Op. 60

A very clever piece in four sections, played without break. The idiom is persistently dissonant, and the development relies largely on ingenious rhythmical transformations of a short four-note motive announced at the outset by the trumpet.
(J. & W. Chester)

EDVARD GRIEG (1848-1907)

Concerto in A Minor,
Op. 16

A romantic work with an obvious indebtedness, at the beginning, to Schumann's concerto in the same key, but thereafter following a structural plan that is even simpler than Schumann's. It is, however, suited to Grieg's individual personality, and it is carried out quite successfully and effectively, so that the concerto—Grieg's most important work in a large form—retains its popular appeal. A good deal of power is required; otherwise there are no excessive technical demands. It is one of the easiest works in the repertoire for the conductor.
Published by Peters, Schirmer, Ditson, Kalmus.
The Schirmer edition, by Percy Grainger, prints many alternatives in the piano part, as having been sanctioned by the composer.

ALEXEI HAIEFF (1914-)

Concerto for piano and
orchestra (1950)

Three descending-scale notes, the first harmonized with a sharp dissonance, set the stage for this three-movement concerto, which handles a contemporary idiom with considerable imagination. The tendency to insist on barbaric repetitions of abrupt rhythms suggests the influence of Stravinsky. The first movement contains much staccato octave and chord writing for the piano; the second opens with a few bars in slow tempo which present a dissonant arpeggio, providing the main material for a following scherzando section with some effective passage work for the soloist. The third movement (Andante, leading to a short concluding

<u>Allegro</u>), after a grave orchestral introduction, continues with piano passages which rely largely either on octave or on alternating-hand technique. There is much effective brilliance and a final insistence on the dissonant descending-scale figure with which the concerto starts. (Boosey & Hawkes)

HOWARD HANSON (1896-   )

Concerto in G Major, Op. 36

The four movements of this work contain material that alternates between the romantic and poetic feeling of the opening <u>Lento</u> and the rhythmic character of figures that build up climaxes through repetition and through increases of dynamic power. A certain improvisatory quality in the more reflective portions is characteristic. A somewhat restricted pianoforte technique is employed, with few difficulties; for much of the time the two hands double each other in octaves. (Carl Fischer)

JOSEF HAYDN (1732-1809)

Concerto in D Major

In this (so far, the most easily accessible of Haydn's keyboard concertos) the first movement consists mainly of a single theme and its development. There follows a <u>Larghetto</u> with a rather elaborately ornamented solo part. The finale is an engaging <u>Rondo all' Ongharese,</u> with a humorous echo effect in its main theme. The technical requirements are moderate. (Peters; Schirmer; International Music Co.) The Peters edition prints cadenzas by Haydn.

ADOLF HENSELT (1814-1889)

Concerto in F Minor, Op. 16

An imposing work, making severe technical demands, featuring the wide extensions in which this composer specialized; the material has less distinction than its treatment. (Breitkopf and Härtel)

FERDINAND HILLER (1811-1885)

Concerto in F-sharp Minor, Op. 69

The only work of its composer that has survived. It contains some effective piano writing and is not without character. (Schirmer—edited by Joseffy)

PAUL HINDEMITH (1895-   )

Concerto for piano obligato and 12 solo

This deserves mention for the abounding vitality of its four movements—the first built on a

instruments, Op. 36,
No. 1 (Chamber
Music No. 2)

single vigorous motive, the development of
which in a genially dissonant texture gives the
piano a prominent solo part—the second an
Adagio with much interest in the florid writing
for piano and the instrumental combinations—
the third a grotesquely humorous piece of
buffoonery entitled Little Potpourri—and the
last having a leading subject of decided rhythm
that dominates a characteristically dissonant
contrapuntal structure. The demands are on
the pianist's musicianship rather than on his
technique.
(Schott)

Concerto in A Minor, for
piano and orchestra
(1945)

This has a first movement in Hindemith's
more "difficult" manner—the main subject has
a melodic line featuring two successive descending perfect fourths, which dominate much
of the development. Rhythmic variation of
that subject is resorted to, a final phase coming in a quiet coda with a beautifully transparent texture. The slow middle movement,
with two themes that are subjected to complicated contrapuntal treatment, has beauties
that do not lie on the surface; its genuine expressiveness is felt only on close acquaintance.
The last movement, entitled a Medley, has a
chain of sections: Canzona, March, Valse lente,
Caprice, Medieval Dance. They present rhythmic transformations of the same theme, and
the final dance has a straightforward simplicity
that is surprising after the sophistication of so
much that has preceded it.
(Schott)

ARTHUR HONEGGER (1892-   )

Concertino for piano and
orchestra

In three sections which follow one another
without a break. 1. An Allegro, beginning with
a dialogue between dissonant syncopated chords
in the orchestra and simple answering phrases
in the piano; the piano passages become more
continuous, with a polytonal character, accompanying persistent rhythms in the orchestra;
the original dialogue is resumed, leading to
2. a short Larghetto, an expressive cantabile
for the piano with dissonant counterpoint in the
orchestra. To this succeeds 3. an Allegro
with a continuous march rhythm in the orchestra, again with a dissonant contrapuntal texture;
the piano contributing almost without cessation.
The movement dies down in a gradual diminuendo, cut short by a single final fortissimo

discord. The work has rhythmic vitality, and no real difficulties for the pianist. (Senart)

JOHANN NEPOMUK HUMMEL (1778-1837)

Concerto in A Minor, Op. 85

The concertos of Hummel, once so highly esteemed (by Chopin, among others), are now almost forgotten. This one is a good example of his special style, profusely ornamental in its details, and naive and formal in its essential structure. The technical passages have still some pedagogical use - they provide a drill like that of much of the material in Czerny's School of the Virtuoso. And anyone who has learned to execute the decorations of the slow movement both gracefully and rhythmically has an accomplishment, the value of which is not confined to the music of the early nineteenth century. (Breitkopf and Härtel)

VINCENT d'INDY (1851-1931)

Symphony on a French Mountain Song

The piano in this important work is used largely in accompanying figures, or in combination (frequently with the harp). But it has also vital solo functions—e.g., in the opening of the second of the three movements. The brilliant piano-and-harp passages that introduce the third movement have an arresting effect, and in general the orchestration is ingenious and effective. (Hamelle)

JOHN IRELAND (1879-   )

Concerto in E-flat Major

This employs a full orchestra reinforced by five percussion instruments in addition to timpani, and much of the concerto's effect is due to its instrumental color. The first of the two movements avoids any conventional concerto form; both of its main themes are referred to in the second part of the work, which consists of an expressive Lento (in irregular rhythm) leading to a rhythmical final section with a principal motive of a lively "cat-catching-its-own-tail" type, persistently doubling on itself. The Lento recurs momentarily and leads to a glittering martellato finish for the pianist. A mature technique is essential. (J. & W. Chester)

GORDON JACOB (1895-   )

Concerto for piano and orchestra	A quite short three-movement work. The material in itself does not make a strong impression, but in its treatment there is some brilliant pianoforte writing. (Oxford University Press)

FREDERICK JACOBI (1891-1952)

Concertino in C Major	This work has grateful pianoforte writing of not more than moderate difficulty. It is musically direct, with a strong feeling for tonality combined with modulatory freedom. The three short movements are: An opening <u>Allegro</u>, mainly of rhythmical character; a meditative <u>Andante</u>; and a lighthearted <u>Tarantella</u> with an engagingly humorous finish. (Elkan-Vogel)

DIMITRI KABALEVSKY (1904-   )

Concerto in A Minor, Op. 9	A concerto of some importance, with interesting material and much effective piano writing— the harmonic technique is somewhat conservative, but has an original flavor. The variations of the middle movement are founded on a theme of folk-song character and are interestingly elaborated. The finale is brilliant and has a resounding climax founded on a secondary theme of the first movement. (Universal Edition)
Concerto in G Minor, Op. 23	This fulfills the promise of the early Opus 9, with fine workmanship, and material that has character and individuality. The demands on the pianist's technical resources are taxing. Some of the devices recall those of the earlier concerto by Kabalevsky—e.g., the recurrence in the finale of material stated first in the opening movement. The concerto may be regarded as one of the outstanding productions of the contemporary Russian school. (Leeds Music)

ARAM KHATCHATURIAN (1903-   )

Concerto in D-flat Major	A concerto which combines a liberal use of dissonance with a strong feeling for tonality. Musically, it has not much depth, but it has a decided effectiveness and, especially in the slow movement, melodic charm. A powerful tone and rhythmic drive are required for its many martellato chord passages; and a brilliant finger technique is needed in the finale. (Leeds Music)

ERNST KRENEK (1900-   )

Concerto in F-sharp
Major, Op. 18

In one continuous movement, with varying tempi. There is a complicated contrapuntal texture, and the thematic material is generally a little elusive, with one of two exceptions in passages of startling naiveté. There is comparatively little "pianoforte writing" in the usual sense.
(Universal Edition)

CONSTANT LAMBERT (1905-1952)

Concerto for solo piano
and nine players

In three movements - Overture, Intermède and Finale. The Overture relies almost entirely on the exploiting of persistent syncopated rhythms—with such irregularities as 7/4, 11/8, 13/8, etc.—and includes a lengthy cadenza of the same character for the soloist. The Intermède has a similar rhythmic undercurrent, with expressive flute, trumpet and trombone solos. The Finale has for its only tempo indication the word "lugubre" and maintains its elegiac quality throughout, coming to a close with a pianissimo dissonance. There are no timpani in the score, but a single percussion player is called on to deal with a variety of exotic instruments, which contribute to the work's interesting and original atmosphere.
(Oxford University Press)

SERGEI LIAPOUNOFF (1859-1924)

Concerto in E-flat Minor,
Op. 4

A short work in one continuous movement with varying tempi. At the outset two contrasting ideas, one rhythmic and the other lyrical, are presented in the orchestra, and these serve as the main material throughout, with a third motive in slow tempo occupying two short sections. The pianoforte writing is brilliant, with imposing octave passages at the final climax.
(Bote & Bock)

FRANZ LISZT (1811-1886)

Concerto No. 1, in E-flat
Major
Concerto No. 2, in
A Major

Both of the piano concertos of Liszt exhibit a wide technical variety, with a maximum of brilliant effect which is often out of proportion to the actual difficulty. They make an obvious appeal to the pianist of virtuoso and dramatic temperament. Each consists of a number of sections, in varying tempi, which are played without break. They also have in common the device (which also characterizes Liszt's sonata in B minor) of rhythmical transformation of a few main themes.

The better known of the two works is that in E-flat; it presents in concentrated form the elements of a four-movement structure. Notable features are the piano's striking anti-phonal octaves in reply to the orchestra's opening theme, an expressive cantabile for the piano alone, a graceful scherzando section with piquant scoring, and a final summing-up with an exciting accelerando.

The second concerto is somewhat more diffuse; its piano technique has features similar to those of the concerto in E-flat—elaborate passage work, octave brilliance and expressive cantabile. The final climax, with a slight lapse of taste in a "marziale" transformation of the opening romantic theme in slow tempo, has an immense glitter.

In both works the total effect is much enhanced by the masterly orchestration. (Schirmer; Schott; Augener, etc.).

Hungarian Fantasia	This has the popular appeal of Liszt's Hungarian Rhapsodies for piano solo, and the same technical and temperamental requirements. The material is the same as that of the fourteenth Rhapsody for piano alone. (Schirmer; Durand; Augener, etc.)
Totentanz	A set of variations on Dies Irae. It produces a powerful effect when given a performance that does justice to its prevailingly grotesque and savage character, and to the virtuosity of the piano part—there is only occasional relief—e.g., in the legato episode in canon. At the same time there is no excessive technical difficulty, and such things as the startling glissandos for both hands require only a certain knack. (Breitkopf and Härtel)
Busoni's arrangement of	
Spanish Rhapsody	Busoni's arrangement for piano and orchestra of Liszt's original pianoforte solo decidedly enhances its effectiveness. After a short cadenza for the soloist there follows a series of variations on the Folies d'Espagne theme, building to a climax and subsiding into the lively Jota aragonese. This has its brilliancies cleverly distributed between piano and orchestra; a cadenza for piano anticipates a quieter

second theme, in this section, which has a brief development before the return of the first "Jota" tempo. These two themes are worked up with increasing excitement and lead to a grandiose statement, in the major, of <u>Folies d'Espagne</u>. A shower of Lisztian octaves is a feature of the close. It need not be said that the piece calls for the wide exploitation of a virtuoso technique. (Schirmer)

NIKOLAI LOPATNIKOFF (1903-   )

Concerto No. 2, in F Minor, Op. 15

A work characterized by an extreme, and almost constant, dissonant idiom, together with a firm grasp of formal organization. There is a vein of sardonic humor, especially in the finale; and an expressive quality emerges in the central <u>Andantino</u> against the background of dissonance. There is little technical difficulty for the soloist. (Schott)

EDWARD MacDOWELL (1861-1908)

Concerto No. 2 in D Minor, Op. 23

This has the distinction of being the only major piano concerto by an American that has so far established itself in the general concert repertoire. Its three movements—a prevailingly lyrical and romantic first movement, a most effective <u>Presto giocoso</u> embodying rapid passage work that demands a highly developed finger technique, and a rhythmically vital finale—while harmonically conservative, have genuine originality. It is perhaps MacDowell's strongest work; on the technical side it has a wide range, with Lisztian tendencies. (Breitkopf and Härtel; Schirmer)

Concerto in A Minor, Op. 15

MacDowell's earlier concerto suffers from repetitious treatment of rather undistinguished material. The last movement is influenced by the finale of the Grieg concerto - it has some effective passage work for the soloist; but this work has been overshadowed by the <u>Concerto in D minor</u>. (Breitkopf and Härtel)

G. FRANCESCO MALIPIERO (1882-   )

Concerto No. 1 for piano and orchestra

A short work in three movements in dissonant idiom. It has a good deal of rhythmic vitality and comparatively little technical difficulty. The structure is simple, but the texture is complicated. (Ricordi)

Concerto No. 2 for piano and orchestra

Another short three-movement work, characterized by persistent repetitious rhythms of somewhat barbaric flavor. Again there is not much technical difficulty. (Suvini-Zerboni)

BOHUSLAV MARTINU (1890-   )

Concerto No. 2 (1934)
Concerto No. 3 (1948)

These two concertos, written fourteen years apart, have yet similar characteristics, as is to be expected from a composer of marked individuality, with his own established technical procedures. In both works the traditional processes of thematic statement and development are often abandoned or obscured; a salient feature is a tendency toward the presentation of patterns, in extended stretches of quasi-sequential figuration, which hardly make themselves felt as definite themes. Any recapitulation is likely to be brief, and generally serves to lead to a short coda. An exception to this is to be noted in the finales of both concertos; there the aforementioned "pattern" becomes a theme which recurs in rondo-like fashion with a prevailing rhythm—alternating eighth and two-sixteenth notes—often used by Martinu. In each concerto, again, the piano has one or more cadenzas, constructed from non-thematic figuration, with an effect of toccata-like improvisation. The pianoforte writing is idiomatic, without breaking fresh ground apart from frequent harmonic sophistication; nor does it require exceptional virtuosity. (Boosey & Hawkes)

Sinfonietta giocosa, for piano and small orchestra (1940)

Written between the dates of the two works above-mentioned, this has a somewhat different character. Its four movements, with the exception of a short Andante introducing the final Allegro, are uniformly animated in mood. The first—Poco Allegro—has obvious "concerto grosso" influence, with a busy contrapuntal texture, developing a well-marked opening theme. The second movement is a cheerful Allegretto, with a theme in staccato chords and irregular rhythm given out by the orchestra and continued in delicate chromatic passages for the piano. A Scherzo, having as a main subject the alternation of only two chords in an engaging rhythm, and a placid trio constitute the third movement. In the finale a prefatory Andante for the orchestra, with constantly shifting bar lengths, leads to an Allegro with some of the rhythmic charac-

ter of the second movement. The work as a whole is an effective vehicle for a pianist with a well-rounded technique, and its demands are not unduly taxing.
(Boosey & Hawkes)

NICHOLAS MEDTNER (1879-1951)

Concerto in C Minor, Op. 33

A lengthy composition in one continuous structure, with varying tempi. There is much elaborate development, employing rhythmical transformation and contrapuntal treatment of a comparatively small number of themes, and displaying the composer's invariable technical mastery. The piece as a whole is a little austere, but the pianoforte writing is effective.
(State Music Publishers, U.S.S.R.)

FELIX MENDELSSOHN-BARTHOLDY (1809-1847)

Concerto in G Minor, Op. 25

This very effective work has all of Mendelssohn's virtues—idiomatic piano writing with a great deal of technical variety, mastery of design, and expert scoring for the combination of solo instrument and orchestra. The three movements are played without a break. The first departs considerably from the classical concerto form; brilliant rotation and finger technique predominates in the solo part. The slow movement has a main theme, in Mendelssohn's typical vein of romantic sentiment, which is later stated by the orchestra with feathery arpeggio piano accompaniment. In the finale the Mendelssohnian rotation passages alternate with staccato chords and octaves, all very gratefully written.
(Schirmer; Peters; Augener)

Concerto in D Minor, Op. 40

In this Mendelssohn's mannerisms are more obtrusive than in the earlier concerto, and the material is less inspired, rarely rising above the commonplace, and giving an impression of labor and repetitiousness.
(Schirmer; Augener)

Capriccio Brillante, Op. 22

An introduction with material like that of the introduction to the Rondo Capriccioso, Op. 16, leads to an Allegro recalling in its technical character the first movement of the G minor concerto. The second subject is a slightly comic march, which plays in combination with the principal theme a big part in the subsequent development.
(Schirmer; Augener)

Rondo Brillant, Op. 29,
in E-flat Major

A brilliant show piece; there is a large piano part with dazzling finger technique, staccato octaves and chords, broken chords, etc., in Mendelssohn's best vein. The scoring, it goes without saying, is unfailingly effective, with many individual captivating touches.
(Schirmer; Augener)

Serenade and Allegro
giocoso, Op. 43

A skillfully written short work. The introductory Serenade opens with an effective dialogue between piano and orchestra, continuing with some brilliant arpeggio passages for the solo instrument. Both in that and in the lively Allegro which follows the material is hardly worthy of the treatment accorded to it.
(Augener)

GIAN CARLO MENOTTI (1911-   )

Concerto in F Major

A lengthy and somewhat diffuse work in three movements. It displays extraordinary technical facility and a wealth of invention, with ideas of great variety and varying quality. In places a highly developed virtuoso technique is called for. (Some passages in the arrangement of the orchestral accompaniment are, as they stand, impracticable).
(Ricordi)

FRANCISCO MIGNONE (1897-   )

Fantasia Brasiliera

A piece that exploits primitive rhythms with orchestral and pianistic brilliance. Harmonically it is rather elementary. A lengthy cadenza leading to the final section gives opportunity to a pianist with temperament and wide tonal range; both power and delicacy are needed.
(Ricordi)

DARIUS MILHAUD (1892-   )

Le Carnaval d'Aix
(Fantaisie pour piano et
orchestre)

A suite of twelve short pieces, including some tone portraits, most of them humorous in intention and effect. They are frequently sharply dissonant, and they contain some entertaining march and dance rhythms.
(Heugel)

Ballade for piano and
orchestra

A short piece of polytonal character relying largely on syncopated and dance rhythms - not very difficult, but necessitating the span of a ninth.
(Universal Edition)

Five Etudes for piano and orchestra	These are experiments in extreme dissonance, the limit being reached perhaps in No. 3, entitled <u>Fugues</u>, in which four separate and conflicting fugues are played by woodwind, brass, strings and piano. (Universal Edition)
Concerto No. 1	A lively work in three movements, with frequent characteristic combinations of different tonalities. There is little actual development, but much rhythmic vitality in the first and last movements. The middle movement has a persistent barcarolle rhythm. The pianoforte writing lies well for the hand as a rule, but some passages in the last movement are a little awkward. (R. Deiss)
Concerto No. 2	In this the composer develops further, in the first and third movements, the carefree spirit that made itself felt in his first concerto. There is the same reliance upon a polytonal technique, and constant "busyness." The workmanship tends to become rather easygoing, especially in its treatment of basses. A facile pianism is needed. (Heugel, through Mercury Music)

WOLFGANG AMADEUS MOZART (1756-1791)

It is in the pianoforte concertos, much more than in the solo sonatas, that Mozart's genius is most fully displayed. The series of twenty-three contains many mature masterpieces, rivaling the greatest of the symphonies, and some of them are only now receiving the attention they deserve. On the technical side they do not at this day seem at first sight formidable, but there are treacherous passages in almost all, and occasional difficulties that tax the mental control, if not the physical power, of any pianist.

Orchestral scores

At present the complete full scores (published by Breitkopf and Härtel) are difficult of access except in libraries. But the orchestral scores of the following have been reprinted by Broude: K.V. 271, 413, 414, 415, 450, 453, 459, 466, 467, 482, 491, 503, 537 and 595.

Editions

The following editions of various concertos, with arrangement of the accompaniment for second piano, are available:

Schirmer: K.V. 271, 453, 459, 466, 467, 482, 488, 491, 537, 595.
International Music Company: K.V. 271, 382, 414, 449, 450, 453, 466, 488, 503, 595 (mostly unedited)
Peters: K.V. 271, 450, 466, 467, 482, 488, 491, 537.

Cadenzas

Thirty-six original cadenzas by Mozart are published by Broude.

The Piano Concertos

K. 37, 39, 40, 41	These four concertos, printed in the complete edition of Breitkopf and Härtel, were referred to by Mozart himself as "pasticci," and contain material from second-rate composers of the day, which either the boy Mozart or his father put together for use on their tours. They cannot be regarded very seriously.
K. 175, in D Major	This already employs one of Mozart's fullest orchestras, with oboes, horns, trumpets and timpani added to the strings. He displays, at the age of seventeen, immense assurance in the treatment of the form, with plenty of technical display for the soloist. At the outset the prevalence of three-bar rhythm is notable. This freedom of rhythmic structure continues in the Andante un poco Adagio. The finale, in sonata form, opens with a confident tutti— oboes and violins stating the theme·in canon with the brass and basses; a continuation in "fifth-species" counterpoint turns out to be the regular second subject. At the entry of the piano it, too, delivers in canon a brilliant variant of the first subject, left hand answering right, and the whole movement displays constant liveliness, with rapid broken chords and broken octaves much in evidence. Mozart has supplied cadenzas for the first and second movements that are quite sufficient.
K. 238, in B-flat Major	The first of three concertos for small orchestra, in two of which Mozart seems to be preparing for the astonishing flowering of his genius in the third. We have here an opening allegro which is technically expert without offering any outstanding feature, apart from the rhythmic interest of the syncopation in the latter part of the second subject. A slow movement, marked, like that of K. 175, Andante un poco Adagio, derives (also like that predecessor) a good deal of its attractiveness from the variety of its bar groupings. The Rondo is lively, with considerable technical brilliance.
K. 246, in C Major	A concerto on a small scale. It is less exacting technically than K. 238; the first movement's material is not specially striking, though attractive features such as the unexpected three measures for the soloist, just before the cadenza, are not lacking. There is a charming Andante, and, for a finale, a rondo in minuet tempo which, with all its simplicity, has an occasional touch of humor like the amusing fanfare for oboes and horns which corroborates a similar passage in the piano.

K. 271, in E-flat Major

One of the most startlingly original of all the Mozart concertos. The first movement begins unconventionally with a six-bar dialogue between orchestra and piano. The part for the solo instrument is brilliant, with striking features such as the entry with a trill, in the midst of the first orchestral tutti, introducing the first main section for the piano. The Andantino is in sonata form minus the development, with, after the cadenza, an imaginative little coda with a moving dialogue between orchestra and soloist, cut short by the two forte chords of the final cadence. The rondo finale is a bustling Presto, opening with no less than thirty-four measures for piano alone, and continuing with an extraordinary flow of high spirits until it is pulled up by a Menuetto, with phrases presented alternately by the piano alone and by piano accompanied by the orchestra. An elaborate short cadenza leads to the return of the Presto.

K. 413, in F Major

The first of three concertos written in close succession; this is the smallest in scale, and the scoring adds to the strings only oboes and horns. The first movement contains some passages—almost the only ones of any brilliance—with crossed hands as a feature. The central Larghetto, in prevailing 4/4 time, acquires an interesting rhythmical freedom in its main subject from the fact that its first three measures are actually the equivalent of two in 3/2 time. The finale, Tempo di Menuetto, is, like the rest of the concerto, of not more than moderate difficulty, with a few broken-third formulas providing contrast to its generally gentle character.

K. 414, in A Major

Written for the same small orchestra as its immediate predecessor, this concerto contains particularly characteristic material, and is said to have been a favorite of Mozart's which he was fond of teaching to his pupils. One or two of its passages require careful fingering, but there are no special technical hazards, and it forms an excellent introduction, for a musical student, to the concerto style. The full chords of the piano's opening solo in the Andante are somewhat exceptional; there should be noted also a second theme which clearly recalls the start of the whole work. The finale is even less given to display than that of K. 413, but it has a specially whimsical character that is most appealing.

Mozart's cadenzas—two complete sets—again indicate his affection for this work.

K. 415, in C Major

This delightful concerto has, rather unusually, most of its brilliance confined to the opening movement. The orchestra is larger, by the addition of bassoons, trumpets and timpani, than that of K. 413 and K. 414, and the extra brass and percussion make a striking contribution, together with pianoforte passages that show the soloist to advantage. The central _Andante_ is in the simplest song form, with some graceful ornamentation in the piano part. The final rondo has special originality, with a stroke of genius in the interruption (twice) of the main allegro by a mournful adagio of fifteen measures in C minor, given to the piano. The use of soft horns and trumpets is particularly charming, and the concluding fade-out—the full orchestra, pianissimo, accompanying the chords of the piano—is unforgettable. Mozart has provided excellent cadenzas.

K. 449, in E-flat Major

This was described by Mozart as "a concerto of quite another kind" (compared with the three following it), intended for a small orchestra. It makes use of no more instruments than K. 413 and K. 414. The opening movement is not very exacting, apart from the persistent trills (derived from the third bar of the concerto) in the development. Mozart's cadenza, using a motive at the start which does not appear elsewhere except in the orchestra, has points of interest that give it preference. The _Andantino's_ most notable structural feature is the transposition of a large portion of the material, in the middle of the movement, from B-flat to the unusual key (in relation to the main tonic) of A-flat. The frequency, in the ornamentation, of the turn may also be observed. The finale's lighthearted staccato theme is immediately captivating, and its varied statements in the piano add to the witty effect. The movement is full of a lively brilliance, with more technical difficulty than the rest of the concerto, and the final rhythmical transformation of the two main themes is most exhilarating.

K. 450, in B-flat Major

Mozart himself, and later commentators, have remarked on the difficulty of this concerto, and it is true that the first and last movements (especially the latter) have passages of exceptional trickiness. There is much interesting structural detail, with important new material introduced by the piano in the opening movement. The slow movement consists of a theme, two variations and coda. Both theme and variations have a double statement of each half, the melodic interest alternating in piano and orchestra, with much subtle expressiveness in the ornamentation. The finale is full of lighthearted humor and technical brilliance, with an entertaining fanfare, developed from a subordinate subject, for a coda. Cadenzas by Mozart are available, the two for the finale being specially substantial.

K. 451, in D Major

Here we have an example of Mozart's dexterity in producing an impressive composition with material that seems to fall short of his usual inventive power. The opening <u>Allegro</u> relies largely on themes of a marchlike character, and the frequent alternations of tonic and dominant harmony begin to sound somewhat perfunctory. Two chord progressions in the piano part are written in such a way as to invite further elaboration. The <u>Andante</u> is a simple rondo, charmingly orchestrated. The finale has more taxing technical material than the rest of the concerto, and an interesting feature is a coda which presents transformations, in 3/8 instead of 2/4 time, of the two main subjects. Mozart's cadenza for the first movement is rather slight; the one for the finale is more satisfying.

K. 453, in G Major

One of the most individual of the piano concertos, which might receive much more frequent performance. The orchestra is small, and the technical difficulties for the soloist are not excessive. Starting with a familiar rhythm, employed by Mozart for an opening over and over again (see K. 451, 456, 459, etc.), the first movement soon exhibits special beauties of its own. The slow movement is one of Mozart's most deeply felt and moving utterances, with beautiful use of the woodwind and some startling harmonic features. The set of variations that constitutes the finale is again one of Mozart's outstanding achievements in this form; the theme is notably witty, both in character and in orchestration - see the comical dotting of the i's at the cadences by oboes and bassoons. The whole is rounded off by what sounds like a parody of an operatic finale. The cadenzas of Mozart to the first and second movements are particularly satisfactory.

K. 456, in B-flat Major

A comparatively unfamiliar concerto, in spite of extremely interesting material and a very grateful piano part. In the first movement the almost exact recapitulation, in the latter part, of the piano's original exposition is unusual. The slow movement is a fine set of variations on a theme of attractively free rhythmic structure. The principal subject of the finale has something of the spirit of the last movement of K. 450, and a further reminder in a secondary transitional theme. A daring modulation to the remote key of B minor introduces a rare combination of 2/4 time in the orchestra with 6/8 in the piano, that relationship being later reversed. For this concerto, too, Mozart's cadenzas are to be recommended.

K. 459, in F Major

This delightful work has almost none of the customary opportunities for individual display that are expected from a solo concerto. Particularly in the first and second movements the piano makes one of a chamber music partnership, and much depends upon the quality of the wind-instrument players. The first movement has not a single really brilliant passage for the piano. In place of the usual slow movement there is a charming _Allegretto_, with a captivating five-measure phrase; throughout this, the dovetailing of the piano and orchestra is carried out in a manner to stimulate the soloist's musicianship indeed, but not to allow him more than an equal share in the artistic result. Only in the finale do the pianist's rushing scales give him at times a special prominence. The cadenzas of Mozart are short and quite adequate.

K. 466, in D Minor

The most familiar of Mozart's concertos, and one of the only two in the minor mode. The striking opening, with the throbbing syncopations over a dominating figure in the bass, has an almost tragic character. On the technical side the first movement asks for good broken octaves and broken chords. An occasional detail of the delightfully simple main subject of the central _Romanza_ may be discreetly varied, by a soloist properly conversant with Mozart's style, at its later repetitions; but actually the almost violent interruption by the brilliant episode in G minor gives sufficient contrast. The exciting finale has some of Mozart's most enchanting themes; its passage work makes insistent demands on finger and brain. In the coda, horn and trumpet introduce a touch of actual comedy. Note should be taken of the cadenzas (for the first and last movements) composed by Beethoven.

K. 467, in C Major

A very elaborate piano part is a leading feature. Mozart gives to the player some quite taxing passages of technical display, notably in the sections leading, at the end of the exposition and before the cadenza, to the two main cadences of the first movement, where he seems to delight in his digital dexterity and to leave the field to the orchestra with regret! The dominating part played by the detached eighth notes of the opening figure should be noted, their influence persisting in the slow movement's pizzicato basses. This Andante is one of Mozart's most placid movements; variety is secured through avoidance of "squareness" in the phrases, and a striking modulation, before the end, to A-flat, rather than through any change in the texture. In the spirited finale one should note the reference, at the start of the piano's second solo, to a subject which had stood in complete isolation and apparent irrelevance in the first movement—another instance of this concerto's high degree of organization.

K. 482, in E-flat Major

The first movement of this favorite concerto is remarkable, even for Mozart, for the number of new themes presented by the piano in its opening statements. These are mostly ignored in the recapitulation, which concerns itself more with restatement of material given by the orchestra at the beginning. Much of the development may be regarded as derived from the start of a theme stated in the exposition by the piano in B-flat minor, though the impression is rather of episodic material; and a completely new subject is thrown in for good measure. The slow movement also has an interesting structure, being a set of three variations on a theme given to the orchestra, which provides interludes of new material between the first and second variation (both, solos for the piano) and between the second and third. The third variation is a dialogue between piano and orchestra and is followed by an extended coda. The finale is of the same lighthearted type as that of K. 450, with a new feature—an expressive Andantino after the second appearance of the main rondo theme. A few measures of the piano part are written by Mozart in his familiar shorthand, and require filling in by the soloist.

K. 488, in A Major	One of Mozart's most appealing compositions. The first movement presents little technical difficulty, and the main subjects are most ingratiating. The cadenza by Mozart is more than usually slight and sketchy, and it is hard to believe that it gives anything but a hint of his wishes. The slow movement, in the unique key, for Mozart, of F-sharp minor, is touchingly pathetic; some passages are presented in skeleton and invite elaboration. The finale is exhilarating and brilliantly effective, with a large number of individual themes, and much passage work that tests the reliability of the pianist's fingers.
K. 491, in C Minor	This great concerto, like some other masterpieces of Mozart, was written very rapidly. Some passages in the piano part of the first movement are merely indicated by a single note to a measure, the actual figures in sixteenths having to be filled in by the soloist. Again, when the principal theme of the slow movement recurs after the first episode, the harmonization of the piano part is inconsistent with that of the orchestra and should be corrected accordingly. Mozart employs his largest orchestra, with both oboes and clarinets. The first movement has great structural interest through varied treatment of the opening tutti, the subsequent restatement by piano and orchestra, and the recapitulation; each of these has a different selection and arrangement of the thematic material. The slow movement is a rondo with, in contrast to the elaborate first movement, extremely simple rhythmic structure in its three childlike themes. The finale is a noble set of variations, with relief from the persistence of the key of C minor through the insertion, first, of a variation in A-flat major, and later, of one in C major. The pianoforte writing is extremely brilliant and more than usually exacting technically.
K. 503, in C Major	One of Mozart's most impressive works, which has not often found, in public performance, its proper appreciation. The opening allegro vies in grandeur with the great C-minor concerto, and has an equally complicated and highly organized structure, with immense contrapuntal mastery, especially in the development section. Instead of the simple rondo form of the Larghetto of K. 491 we have here a modification of the classical concerto's

first-movement form; there is an opening
ritornello for the orchestra, a restatement
for the piano with a swing to the dominant,
no development section, and a recapitulation
which redistributes ingeniously the preceding
material. The finale is an elaborate rondo
with a great variety of material and exceptional freedom in the rhythmic structure—note
the delightfully humorous expansion, before
the reappearance in the tonic of the first episode, of the passage on the dominant which
introduces it.

K. 537, in D Major
("Coronation" concerto)

The piano part of this well-known work was
not completely written out by Mozart though,
as printed, it represents him adequately. As
a whole it has been somewhat overestimated
in comparison with the greater but less familiar concertos on either side of it; the attached title may be partly a reason. The exposition of the first movement is on a large
scale, with the material of the opening tutti
developed and expanded by the piano; the central working-out is rather slight, however.
The principal theme of the Larghetto, relying
entirely on tonic and dominant harmony, has
a naive charm which is maintained in the
opening subject of the finale. It should be
noted that the Mozart cadenza printed in the
Schirmer edition belongs, not to this concerto,
but to the earlier one—K. 451.

K. 595, in B-flat Major

The whole concerto is of finest quality, opening with a movement exhibiting rhythmic and
harmonic subtleties that recall K. 503. Much
of its humor is derived from a little five-note
figure with which the wind instruments inter-
rupt the first violins at the fifth measure.
Later, in the development, this recurs with
daring modulations. The Larghetto is reminiscent, in the character of the main theme,
of the Larghetto of the C-minor concerto; and
in its structure, of the central movement of
the D major, K. 537. The finale, with its
prevailing dancing rhythm, has a playfulness
that is quite irresistible; it gives the soloist
a great opportunity for a display of both vitality and delicacy. Mozart uses with consum-
mate skill a small orchestra, without clari-
nets, trumpets or drums. His cadenzas—one
for the first movement and two for the finale—
should be used.

Rondos

Rondo, K. 382, in D Major	Originally intended as the finale of K. 451, this is actually a set of simple variations on a childlike tonic-and-dominant theme. One in the minor is, as usual, more interesting than the others. Seven variations lead to a transition with a cadenza, followed by a short coda.
Rondo, K. 386, in A Major (U.E.)	This piece, reconstructed by Alfred Einstein from fragmentary materials, probably represents the original finale of K. 414. It is slighter than the present one.

IGNACE JAN PADEREWSKI (1860-1941)

Concerto in A Minor, Op. 17 Polish Fantasy, Op. 19	Of these two pieces for piano and orchestra by Paderewski, the Polish Fantasia has the more interesting material, with some attractive tunes. Both works are somewhat diffuse, but the pianoforte writing is effective. (Bote & Bock)

RICCARDO PICK-MANGIAGALLI (1882-   )

Sortilegi	A symphonic poem illustrating, in imaginative fashion, an Oriental tale. It employs a large orchestra; the brilliant piano part is sometimes reminiscent, in its technical features, of the same composer's Danse d'Olaf. (Ricordi)

WILLEM PIJPER (1894-1947)

Concerto for piano and orchestra (1927)	A rather cryptic work, in one continuous movement and varying tempi. It suggests various influences - e.g., Debussy and Stravinsky, and it adds to dissonant harmony an extreme rhythmic sophistication, that interposes difficulties at a first hearing. The technical requirements of the piano part are not more than moderate. One obstacle to frequent performance is the orchestration, which includes a clarinet and saxophone in E-flat and several unusual percussion instruments. (Oxford University Press)

WALTER PISTON (1894-   )

Concertino for piano and chamber orchestra	A short work in contemporary dissonant idiom, consisting of a main section with two contrasted subjects, a scherzo-like central passage, recapitulation of the opening section, and a coda embodying new material and brilliant passage work for the pianist. For anyone with good fingers it presents no great difficulty. (Arrow Press)

FRANCIS POULENC (1899-   )

Concert Champêtre, for harpsichord or piano

In three movements. The first, after a brief introduction (adagio), presents in a brisk Allegro a variety of themes, starting with a tuneful one which suggests the title of the concerto; there is a lively and brilliant amount of orchestral color and liberal use of dissonance. The second movement (Andante) is a siciliano of ingratiating character and swinging rhythm. The finale, starting with a theme of dancelike nature for the soloist, proceeds in the boisterous spirit of the first movement with much dialogue between orchestra and solo, and a great deal of humorous contrast between successive phrases. There is little technical difficulty.
(Rouart, Lerolle and Co.)

JOHN POWELL (1882-   )

Rhapsodie nègre

Musicianly treatment of Negro rhythms and melodic material. The piano part is effective and brilliant, requiring a well-rounded technique.
(Schirmer)

SERGE PROKOFIEFF (1891-1953)

Concerto No. 1, in D-flat Major, Op. 10

A youthful work, with an opening section consisting of a series of themes, largely in four-bar rhythm, which are presented with a good deal of repetition but little development. The piano writing is percussive and brilliant. A central Andante provides contrasting cantabile with busy figuration in the pianoforte part, and the work ends with recapitulation in varied form of the earlier material, the first theme being presented triumphantly in the orchestra with accompanying counterpoint in octaves in the piano.
(Leeds Music)

Concerto No. 2, in G Minor, Op. 16

This opens with a declamatory Andante, the piano giving out the theme in octaves, with support of thick harmonies in the orchestra. To that succeeds a scherzo-like Allegretto with a theme of characteristically sardonic flavor. The first theme returns with complicated piano writing leading to a cadenza for pianoforte alone. A brilliant Scherzo follows, the piano playing rapid finger passages, right and left hand an octave apart, against some striking orchestration. A somewhat grotesque Intermezzo, of a marchlike character, is

again enhanced by ingenious orchestration.
The Finale opens with a brilliant staccato passage distributed equally to the orchestra and
the piano's glittering octaves; subsequently,
the piano takes charge with passages in alternating-hand technique over the whole keyboard.
A quiet theme in slower tempo gives contrast;
there is a piano cadenza, some further recapitulation and development, a biting bitonal
passage and a boisterous finish.
(Edition Gutheil; Breitkopf and Härtel)

Concerto No. 3, in C
Major, Op. 26

Perhaps the most important concerto for piano
by a contemporary composer. Its three movements display a wide imaginative range, original melodic invention, ingenious orchestration and expert treatment of the pianoforte.
The frequent use of a dissonant idiom is always logical and convincing. There is great
emotional variety - suave cantabile, brilliant
passage work and a grotesque, sardonic humor.
The texture is often complicated, and the pianist is called upon for a mental grasp that goes
beyond the demands of ordinary virtuosity.
(Leeds Music)

SERGEI RACHMANINOFF (1873-1943)

Concerto No. 1, in
F-sharp Minor, Op. 1

This early work was revised drastically by
the composer. It has long lyric lines and
brilliant and exacting pianoforte writing. Its
less direct melodic appeal and the rhythmic
complexity of certain parts of the finale make
it less immediately attractive than the popular
work in C minor; but it is well worth playing.
(Schirmer)

Concerto No. 2, in
C Minor, Op. 18

The popularity of this concerto is undoubtedly
due to its frank lyrical and romantic character;
its main themes, with the exception of the
first in the finale, are all of the sort that has
made the opening of Tschaikowsky's B-flat
minor concerto so instantly appealing. Structurally, Rachmaninoff's is the stronger of the
two. It offers few interpretative problems;
anyone with sufficient technical power and
emotional warmth can give a satisfying performance, and its climaxes are of an obvious
and straightforward kind that can be relied on
to win an average audience. It may be observed that the extremely simple rhythmic
structure of most of the work - repeated
groupings in four measures - helps the quick
grasp of its content.
(Schirmer; International Music Co.)

**Concerto No. 3, in
D Minor, Op. 30**

Rachmaninoff's third concerto has technical features of interest that place it in some respects above its more popular predecessor. It has more rhythmic variety and flexibility, as may be seen from the phrase-structure of the main theme of the first movement. Its treatment of the form is also more enterprising; here again the first movement may be adduced in evidence, with its departures from stereotyped procedure in the development, cadenza and recapitulation. The central movement, entitled Intermezzo, has an extended improvisation on a theme given out at first quietly by the orchestra and later developed in grandiose style by the piano; there follows a scherzo-like section in which the first movement's main theme is presented in a hardly recognizable rhythmic transformation—and a recurrence of the opening material of the movement leads, through a violent outburst of the piano, without break to the finale. This relies more on its rhythmic and dynamic interest than on melodic charm; there is again a great deal of interesting workmanship, including development and rhythmic variation of material from the first movement. The piano writing is, in the whole concerto, much more elaborate and complicated than in the Cminor concerto, and presents a formidable task to the soloist.
(Schirmer; International Music Co.)

**Concerto No. 4, in
G Minor, Op. 40**

The three movements have the same technical and harmonic mastery as his other concertos; there is only lacking Rachmaninoff's former melodic invention. The pianoforte writing is idiomatic and brilliant, with many effective features.

**Rhapsody on a theme by
Paganini, Op. 43**

An extended set of variations on the theme previously used by Liszt and Brahms. Technically grateful, they show much harmonic ingenuity, and dazzling effectiveness. A piece for a virtuoso pianist.

MAURICE RAVEL (1875-1937)

Concerto in G Major

A three-movement work, the first and last containing much brilliant writing for the piano, employing largely an alternating-hand technique of a familiar type. In the first movement there is a second-subject section with contrasting legato themes placed effectively in the centre of the keyboard; the finale is almost continuously a "moto perpetuo," requiring in addition to the alternating-hand mechanism of the first movement a glittering finger technique. The actual musical substance of these two movements resembles some of the lighter products of Ravel's younger compatriots. The middle movement is, on the other hand, an adagio of romantic character, with an extended cantilena for the piano, which is later repeated by the orchestra with accompanying figuration for the soloist. (Durand)

Concerto for the left hand

A short and powerful composition, in three main sections, played without a break - an opening Lento, a central Allegro, and a return to the first tempo. The resources of the single hand are taxed to the utmost; great physical power and technical dexterity are called for, the whole keyboard being covered. Naturally there is need for expert balancing of tone, when one hand has at times to supply both melody and accompaniment; this is specially the case in the very difficult cadenza just before the end. The middle part has a staccato theme, in a lively rhythm, that is reminiscent of one in the finale of the G major concerto mentioned above. (Durand)

ALAN RAWSTHORNE (1905-   )

Concerto No. 1

A three-movement work—Capriccio, Chaconne, Tarantella. Except for the short middle section, where the soloist finally caps a crescendo of the orchestra, developing contrapuntally a marchlike theme, the Capriccio consists almost entirely of rapid passage work for the piano, scampering over the whole keyboard. The idiom makes frequent use of astringent dissonance and the piano writing is effective. The Chaconne consists of variations on an eight-bar formula, starting with a series in which each successive statement is a half-tone above its predecessor. The working out of this is interesting. The Tarantella has the same restless activity as the Capriccio, with constantly shifting key centers; it ends with a surprising humorous touch when, after an extended passage for orchestra alone, the piano enters with half a dozen pianissimo chords and dies away with a whimsical reference to the opening of the movement. (Oxford University Press)

Concerto No. 2

The first of this concerto's four movements—
Allegro piacevole—opens with an extended
cantabile for the orchestra accompanied by the
piano; starting with F-sharp as a key center;
the tonality in general, however, is vague.
After a continuation by the piano, the latter
contributes some vigorous development in
diminution. In the middle of the movement a
marchlike subject (as in the first Rawsthorne
concerto) provides contrast; a very brief re-
capitulatory section ends the movement quietly. The second movement is a flying scherzo,
often piquantly dissonant, and rhythmically
easy to follow, as four-bar groupings prevail.
The piano writing is effective and brilliant.
The third movement, entitled Intermezzo,
consists of a meditative extended passage -
adagio - for the orchestra answered in florid
fashion by the piano and leading into a rapid
"sotto voce" section, including staccato
double-note passages for the soloist. These
are afterward taken up by the orchestra. Some
brief references to the adagio end in a striking
polytonal phrase - the piano first contradicting
and then agreeing with an orchestral chord of
B major. The finale has a main subject of
jocosely irregular rhythm given out softly by
the piano and continued, forte, by the orchestra.
A supplementary vigorous theme for the piano,
development of the first subject, and a forceful angular passage in the orchestra lead to
some recapitulation with new textural distribution and humorous dynamic contrasts. A coda,
beginning with a soft fugato derivative of the
main subject, ends in a martellato fortissimo.
(Oxford University Press)

MAX REGER (1873-1916)

Concerto in F Minor,
Op. 114

Contains a great deal of the thick, complicated
piano writing characteristic of this composer.
The harmonic progressions are rich and often
involved. Only a pianist of great intellectual
and physical power, and of compelling authority, can make this concerto effective.
(Eschig; Boston Music Co.; Schirmer)

NIKOLAI RIMSKY-KORSAKOFF (1844-1908)

Concerto in C-sharp
Minor, Op. 30

A single-movement work in various tempi,
strongly influenced by Liszt. An opening
phrase, delivered alternately in moderate and
slow tempo, (and its thematic transformations
through rhythmic variation account for much

of the material. A brilliant octave technique
is a main requirement for the soloist.
(Belaieff; International Music Co.)

EDMUND RUBBRA (1901-   )

Sinfonia Concertante, Op. 38

Fantasia	Two themes, one that rises in arpeggio and a second that moves up and down the scale, provide much of the material; they are insisted upon with striking effect, a short syncopated rhythm making a significant contribution. The piano has little independent solo function, being generally used in association and contention with a rather full orchestra.
Saltarella	This repeats, with cleverly varied scoring, a dance theme with some contrasting counterpoint to its triplet figures; there is little development apart from the appearance of the Saltarella theme in augmentation and a final 4/4 version in brilliant piano octaves.
Prelude and Fugue	The last movement's Prelude is founded on a solemn figure recalling one in the opening of the Fantasia; its elegiac character (it is subtitled - "In Memoriam Gustav Holst") is continued in a slow Fugue, at first developed in the orchestra alone, then with the assistance of a subsidiary theme, introduced by the piano, that has the last word in a fading pianissimo. (Universal Edition)

ANTON RUBINSTEIN (1830-1894)

Concerto No. 4, in D Minor, Op. 70	The most important product of Anton Rubinstein's too facile talent. The thematic material has more character and individuality than in his other pianoforte compositions, and in spite of the monotony of the phrase structure (the persistence of four-bar groups from beginning to end becomes undeniably tiresome) there is enough musical substance to hold the attention. The pianoforte writing is of course extremely grateful and effective, with a wide technical range. (Schirmer)

CAMILLE SAINT-SAËNS (1835-1921)

Concerto No. 2, in G Minor, Op. 22	Here are displayed all of Saint-Saens' qualities as a composer—skillful workmanship, clear texture, invariable effectiveness, with comparatively little emotional depth. The opening Andante sostenuto shows him in his most serious mood, with two gently expressive

themes and a powerful and brilliant climax for the solo instrument leading to the recapitulation of the first subject. The second movement is a delightful scherzo calling for light staccato chord playing of a Mendelssohnian type and brilliant finger technique. The finale, opening with a tarantella theme, is of similar light character; salient features are a central episode with trills for alternating hands and the interlocking passages of the dazzling coda. (Schirmer; Durand)

Concerto No. 4, in C Minor, Op. 44

This concerto has a more complicated and interesting structure than the G minor. There are two main divisions, each of which has again two subdivisions. At the start a simple theme, in broken rhythms alloted alternately to the orchestra and piano, is presented with two variations; a transitional passage (which later appears as a main theme in the opening of the second half of the work) leads to an Andante which, after a few introductory bars, states a chorale-like theme, pianissimo. This is developed with help from a subordinate subject in the piano, the latter bringing the movement to a quiet close. The aforementioned transitional passage from the first movement, now played in delicate octaves, opens the second; almost immediately a playful version of the first theme of the concerto enters, mainly in the orchestra with brilliant accompanying figures in the piano, and a crescendo leads to a new subject of an uninhibited rhythmic character. Some recapitulation leads to a close, pianissimo, on the dominant of C minor; a skillfully treated fugato for the orchestra, founded on material from the first movement, is continued by the piano, a crescendo leading finally into the last section. This is mainly concerned with a startlingly lively and forthright version in 3/4 time of what had been heard in the first movement as a grave chorale in 4/4. (Schirmer; Durand)

Concerto No. 5 in F Major, Op. 103

This makes a less immediate appeal than the two concertos above-mentioned, and its material is less striking. But it has similar qualities of neatness, finish and clarity; and in the central movement there are interesting effects of rhythm and instrumental color that give it individuality and atmosphere. The first movement, with its quiet opening in a broken rhythm that suggests the first theme of the C minor concerto, is pleasant without much distinction. The finale has a brilliant piano part that gives scope to the virtuoso; the material was also used by Saint-Saëns for the Toccata in his set of études, Op. 111. (Durand)

Rhapsodie d'Auvergne, Op. 73

A short and effective piece, musically quite simple. There are three main sections - an expressive Andante, an Allegretto of graceful rhythmic quality, and a brilliant Allegro which leads, with only a brief reference back to the Andante, to a lively climax. The thematic material is throughout of an attractively tuneful character. The difficulties are not excessive, but the rapid passage work of the third section requires good fingers. (Durand)

Fantasia - "Africa," Op. 89

This is an extremely clever piece with, in its short duration of only about ten minutes, much arresting thematic material of great variety and interest. The pianoforte writing is dazzlingly effective and requires good wrists — for the rapid staccato octaves and for the rapid repeated thirds in the final section. (Durand)

HENRI SAUGUET (1901-   )

Concerto in A Minor

A work which, like many of the contemporary French school, has vitality and liveliness without great depth of feeling; the texture is clear and comparatively thin. Fluent finger technique is a requisite, and a good finger and hand staccato for the finale. The short Lento has atmosphere, and needs delicate treatment of the pianoforte figuration in the latter part. (Eschig)

XAVER SCHARWENKA (1850-1924)

Concerto No. 1, in B-flat Minor, Op. 32

An extremely good work by a composer not of the front rank. It shows the solo instrument to advantage and contains some arresting thematic material, notably the opening subject, which recurs in the finale. A short slow section is incorporated in the development of the first movement, and there is no other slow movement, the second being an extensive scherzo. The finale, with less thematic distinction than the rest, is interesting from its gradual foreshadowing of the climax founded on the return of the material of the first movement. (Praeger & Meier; Schirmer)

ARNOLD SCHÖNBERG (1874-1951)

Concerto for piano and
orchestra

This has as its basis the composer's "twelve-tone" system; the logic of the concerto's development can be perceived by the average person visually, on the printed page, more easily than it can be aurally. The digital problems are simple, compared with the difficulty of obtaining a secure mental grasp of the work; it would be rash to pass a final judgment on its ultimate place.
(Universal Edition)

SCHUBERT-LISZT

Fantasia in C Major,
Op. 15

Liszt has made an able arrangement of Schubert's great Fantasia, though the principal argument in favor of the orchestral collaboration is the assistance the latter gives in concealing the weakness of the original finale.
(Schirmer)

WILLIAM SCHUMAN (1910-   )

Concerto for piano and
small orchestra

A vigorous piece in three movements, containing much dissonant harmonic and contrapuntal treatment of the material. The pianoforte technique is largely percussive, a notable exception is a smooth legato fugal passage for the soloist in the finale. This movement, starting with an ostinato bass and exhibiting a passacaglia-like character, subjects its opening six-note formula to a great deal of ingenious thematic transformation, which continues with increasingly brilliant piano writing up to an imposing close over an organ-point.
(Schirmer)

ROBERT SCHUMANN (1810-1856)

Concerto in A Minor,
Op. 54

This outstanding and romantically inspired work has a secure place in the repertory. Its technical difficulties are considerable without being extreme; they are presented in pianoforte writing that is always idiomatic and effective. The classical concerto form is not preserved in its strictness - there is no opening "tutti" - but the general outline of sonata form is maintained in the first and (more particularly) in the last movement. Schumann's fine cadenza in the first movement has a staccato chord passage that, together with the finale's non-legato brilliancies, offers the main technical hazards of the concerto.
(Peters; Kalmus; Augener)

Concertstück in G Major, Op. 92 (Introduction and Allegro appassionato)	This short composition is heard rather infrequently, but it is a characteristic and grateful piece, though it has less appeal for the virtuoso than the concerto in A minor. A brief adagio, with solo phrases for woodwind and horn, accompanied by arpeggios in the piano, leads to a vigorous allegro with much variety in its material—some of it already stated in the introduction. Apart from a double-note staccato passage requiring a good deal of power there are no serious technical problems. (Schirmer; Augener)
Concert-allegro in D Minor, Op. 134	A labored product of Schumann's declining powers, with little of his real quality. (Schirmer; Augener)

ALEXANDER SCRIABIN (1872-1915)

Concerto in F-sharp Minor. Op. 20	In Scriabin's early style. It makes considerable technical demands, with much elaborate figuration reminiscent of the concertos of Chopin. The three movements suffer somewhat from lack of contrast in the material. The central set of variations insists almost continuously, like so many Russian sets of variations, on the melodic outline of the theme. (Belaieff; Moscow State Music Ed.)

DIMITRI SHOSTAKOWITCH (1906-   )

Concerto in C Minor, Op. 35	Scored for an orchestra of strings and trumpet, this has three main movements, with a short interlude connecting the second and third. It is characterized by fluent invention and a tendency, instead of developing a theme, to supply fresh material of similar character. The trumpet has a prominent part both in the first and final sections; the latter is full of grotesque and uninhibited humor—sometimes deliberate vulgarity! As a whole, the work is not particularly difficult. (Leeds Music)

ARTHUR SOMERVELL (1863-1937)

Normandy: Symphonic Variations for piano and orchestra	Taking as its basis a French folk song, this work treats the variation form with great freedom and technical skill, and with a variety of tempo and emotional content that gives the whole an impact comparable to that of a complete symphony, ending in a passacaglia that culminates in a grandiose statement and

development of the folk-song theme. It is one
of its composer's most impressive achievements.
(Augener)

CHARLES VILLIERS STANFORD (1852-1924)

Concerto in C Minor,
Op. 126

A technically expert work which has a great
deal of melodic interest, especially in the
second and third movements. The pianoforte
writing is grateful, and while a mature pianism is required, there is no excessive
difficulty.
(Stainer & Bell)

SIGISMOND STOJOWSKI (1870-1946)

Prologue, Scherzo and
Variations

A musicianly work of romantic character, in
nineteenth-century idiom, with prominent use
of the device of rhythmic transformation of
its themes. The material of the Prologue is
developed in the finale of the variations. The
piano writing is skillful and grateful.
(Heugel, through Mercury Music)

RICHARD STRAUSS (1864-1951)

Burleske in D Minor for
piano and orchestra

A single-movement work, in sonata form,
which opens in a vigorous rhythmical fashion
that suggests the title, but also contains much
ingratiating lyrical material. It is Strauss's
most important piano composition, a comparatively early one, but showing expert technical mastery. The piano writing asks for a wide
tonal range, but it is grateful and not of excessive difficulty.
(E. B. Marks)

IGOR STRAVINSKY (1882-   )

Concerto (1924)

In three movements. The first opens with a
solemn march—largo—for the orchestra, the
piano breaking in with the principal subject of
the following allegro in decisive rhythmical
chords accompanied by the orchestra. The
movement continues with an almost uninterrupted flow of percussive chords and non-
legato finger passages, with immense rhythmic vitality and variety. A recapitulation of
the first part of the allegro leads to definite
assertion of the piano's predominance in a
lengthy solo with alternating-hand passages
and clashing chords, which finally reach a restatement by the orchestra of the opening slow
march, accompanied by the piano's arpeggios,

which ends the movement. The slow movement has expressive cantabile material for
both piano and orchestra, with dissonant har-
monization and two interruptions by cadenzas
for the soloist. In the finale the general character of the first movement is resumed, with
rhythmic interest prevailing, calling upon a
percussive non-legato and brilliant technique,
with a great deal of power; an alert rhythmic
sense for the frequent irregularities of pulse
is needed. A soft and brief reference to the
solemnity of the concerto's opening is followed by a violent martellato finish.
(Boosey & Hawkes)

Capriccio

A noteworthy feature of this brilliant work is
the welding together of the piano and orchestral parts, each being more continuously essential to the total effect than is usual, especially in the first and third movements. In
the central Andante rapsodico there is a more
independent role for the soloist. The technical difficulties are not excessive; clean
finger work is a main essential.
(Boosey & Hawkes)

KAROL SZYMANOWSKI (1883-1937)

**Symphonie Concertante,
Op. 60**

A complicated three-movement work. The
orchestra is a large one, with extra percussion instruments. The rhythmic element
predominates in the first and last movements,
with much of the piano's thematic material
assigned to the upper octaves; the soloist's
chord and double-note technique is taxed considerably. There is a poetic Andante with
solo passages for wind. A mature artistry
and musicianship are essential.
(Eschig)

GERMAINE TAILLEFERRE (1892-   )

Concerto in D Major

In three movements. The first has a continuous Bach-like contrapuntal texture and flow,
while employing a mildly dissonant idiom.
The short slow movement has an expressive
cantilena, the piano taking part in an ensemble
that includes solos for flute, oboe and trumpet.
The finale resumes the lighthearted mood of
the opening, with some engaging cross-rhythms.
An attractive, unpretentious and unexacting
piece.
(Heugel)

ALEXANDRE TANSMAN (1897-   )

Concerto No. 2, in
E Major

A lively work, in three movements—the first,
of decided rhythmical character, with some
difficult chord and double-note technique; the
second a brilliant moto perpetuo in its main
part, requiring dexterous finger work, with a
contrasting middle cantabile section; the
third consisting of an introductory lento,
developing a tune of folk-song type, leading
to a finale with jazz features. The musical
ideas are generally somewhat slight, but they
are presented with a good deal of sophistication, and with the use of familiar contemporary
devices like the simultaneous use in one chord
of triads whose roots are a diminished fifth
apart. Nevertheless there is no abandonment
of tonality.
(Eschig)

Concertino for piano and
orchestra

The opening Toccata has almost continuous
passages for piano, starting with a long unaccompanied solo, in chord and double-note
technique. There follows an Intermezzo
Chopiniano calling for much legato-chord
playing. A finale - Allegro risoluto - has
some of the rhythmic features of the Toccata,
and brilliant finger passages that make an
effective impression without any very significant thematic material.
(Eschig)

ERNST TOCH (1887-   )

Concerto for piano and
orchestra, Op. 38

The three movements of this work are written
in a dissonant contrapuntal style with a logic
that indicates an affinity with Hindemith. The
orchestral texture is often extremely complicated, and the solo part requires a facile
pianism. The third movement, curiously entitled Rondo disturbato, has a boisterous
humor.
(Schott)

DONALD FRANCIS TOVEY (1875-1940)

Concerto in A Major,
Op. 15

Like all the compositions of this amazing
musician, this employs a classical musical
vocabulary and technique. The concerto is a
work of great dignity, beauty and power with
a command of resource that actually chal-
lenges comparison with its great models. The
idiom, of course, belongs to a bygone day.
(Schott)

PETER ILICH TSCHAIKOWSKY (1840-1893)

Concerto in B-flat Minor, Op. 23	The piano part, as it stands, has been revised from the less practicable original - mainly by Edward Dannreuther. Its technical difficulties are considerable, and include virtuoso octaves of Lisztian type; there is no special idiomatic individuality. The concerto owes its popularity to the real originality and beauty of its thematic material, its warmth of feeling and its brilliant climactic effect. Great power, wide range of tone and rhythmic vitality are requisites; there is comparatively little demand for mere finger dexterity. (Schirmer)
Concerto in G Major, Op. 44	This work is hardly worthy of comparison with its famous predecessor, but it receives an occasional performance. The material and its development lack distinction, and the well-worn technical devices of the piano part become tiresome—even though their brilliance in the finale produces a superficial excitement. (Paragon Music)
Fantaisie de Concert in G Major, Op. 56	This is much more worthy of revival than the concerto in the same key. It is a short and attractive work with less pretentiousness than the second concerto. The two sections, entitled Quasi rondo and Contrastes, have much brilliant pianoforte writing, tuneful material and effective scoring. A mature technique and a great deal of power are needed. (P. Jurgenson)

A third concerto, Op. 75, in E-flat was finished by Taneieff; but it contains mechanical development of (mostly) poor material, and can be ignored.

WILLIAM WALTON (1902-   )

Sinfonia concertante, for orchestra with piano	The detailed title indicates the relative importance of orchestra and piano; the latter, from the opening bars where it supports with its chords a maestoso theme for the strings, is absorbed into the general texture of the work much more completely than in any composition that gives the soloist a star part. In the first movement an alternating Allegro spiritoso gives a few bars of effective octaves in the upper register to the piano, which for the most part engages in a dialogue with the orchestra. The placid central Andante has even less (about half a dozen bars) of piano solo. In the lively finale much of the piano's function is assigned to passage work in the

upper octaves, with the hands playing an octave apart; a short cadenza leads to a grandiose statement by full orchestra and piano of
the theme heard at the beginning of the work.
The pianist has to find, in the musical interest of the piece, compensation for its limited
technical range.

(Oxford University Press)

CARL MARIA VON WEBER (1786-1826)

Concertstück in
F Minor, Op. 79

It is hard to revive Weber's piano concertos,
but the Concertstück in F minor still shows a
healthy vitality, one not entirely confined to
the schoolroom. Its pedagogical usefulness is
of course undeniable. Its four sections—a romantic Larghetto, an agitated Allegro passio-
nato, a rhythmically stirring Tempo di Marcia
and the final brilliant Assai presto—exhibit
an astonishing technical range. Warm singing
tone, dazzling finger work, hand and rotation
technique, staccato chords and octaves are
all exercised without really excessive difficulty.

(Schirmer; Augener)

Music for Two or More Pianos and Orchestra

In recent years, after a long period during which little for the combination of two pianos and orchestra was produced, composers have begun again to turn their attention to a field distinguished by both Bach and Mozart. However, not all that is valuable has been made readily accessible at this time through publication. The most regrettable omission from the following list is the concerto, for two pianos, of Martinu—a work that has been widely and successfully performed, but which it has not been possible, so far, to obtain in print.

A large list of compositions, with and without publishers' names, is to be found in Hans Moldenhauer's Duo-pianism.

CARL PHILIPP EMANUEL BACH (1714-1788)

Concerto for two claviers and strings in E-flat Major

Concerto for two claviers and strings in F Major

These two works provide interesting anticipations of Mozart's treatment of this combination. The concerto in E-flat has a particularly delightful Haydnesque finale in humorous vein, while that in F is, in its first and second movements, the more enterprising in the combination of the two claviers. (Steingräber)

JOHANN SEBASTIAN BACH (1685-1750)

Concerto for two claviers and strings in C Major

Concerto for two claviers and strings in C Minor

Two concertos of uniformly fine quality. That in C major relegates the strings to a distinctly minor role; and though they enhance the general effect, mainly through occasional doubling of the claviers, the latter's sound and sense when played alone are not unsatisfactory. The placid middle movement has no string accompaniment. Perhaps the most notable feature is the final exhilarating fugue. In the concerto in C minor the strings have more importance both in the spirited first and last movements, where they make frequent independent contributions to the contrapuntal texture, and in the charmingly expressive slow movement where they accompany almost throughout with pizzicato chords. (Peters; International Music Co.; Breitkopf and Härtel)

Another concerto for two claviers and strings in C minor is a transcription of the well-known work in D minor for two violins.

Concerto for three claviers and strings in D Minor

Concerto for three claviers and strings in C Major

Of these two outstanding compositions, that in D minor has a special feature in the importance given to the first clavier, which has a part of more brilliance and prominence than the others. The slow movement is a

407

simple siciliano, first for all three claviers
in unison, then in a flowing variation for the
first clavier. The C-major concerto is a
more weighty work, with more elaborate
workmanship in the slow movement and an
imposing contrapuntal combination in the
main subject of the finale. Both concertos
demand painstaking rehearsal for the solution
of the frequent problems of ensemble balance.
(Breitkopf and Härtel)

Concerto for four claviers
and strings in A Minor

This is a transcription of Vivaldi's <u>Concerto
in B minor</u> for four violins. Bach has added
comparatively little, and has not altered the
essential fabric of the music.
(Breitkopf and Härtel)

ARTHUR BLISS (1891-   )

Concerto in D Minor for
two pianos and orchestra

In one movement, with varying tempi. Actually a short fantasia on a number of contrasting motives, using a large orchestra with two
timpani players and extra percussion. The
idiom is of a contemporary type, of freely
dissonant character; the writing for pianos
and orchestra is extremely brilliant and effective, with ingenious color combinations. The
total ensemble requires careful rehearsal and
two experienced pianists.
(Oxford University Press)

BENJAMIN BRITTEN (1913-   )

Scottish Ballad for two
pianos and orchestra,
Op. 26

At the outset the Scottish psalm tune "Dundee"
is quoted in heavy chords for both pianos, and
it reappears throughout the piece, even in
counterpoint against a lively "highland fling,"
which occupies the last section. Meanwhile
a solemn funeral march, with a contrasting
trio motive, has been developed at length,
rising to a fortissimo and subsiding into
some further "Dundee" references before
giving way to the concluding dance.
The piece can fairly be described as of the
"occasional" type; the resources of the two
keyboards are exploited effectively and gratefully and are enhanced by some brilliant
scoring.
(Boosey & Hawkes)

DARIUS MILHAUD (1892-   )

Concerto for two pianos
and orchestra (1950)

In the first movement (<u>Animé</u>)there is a continuous contrapuntal texture of concerto
grosso type, with the orchestra in attendance

except in a central cadenza for the two pianos.
The second (<u>Funèbre</u>) is introduced by the orchestra in a marchlike theme over an ostinato
bass; the rhythm of this continues through
most of the movement with complicated piano
writing. The third movement (<u>Vif et précis</u>)
has a general rhythmic flow like the first.
Throughout there is a free use of biting dissonance. Good chord, double-note and octave
technique is required.
(Elkan-Vogel)

WOLFGANG AMADEUS MOZART (1756-1791)

Concerto for two pianos
and orchestra (K.365)

A composition of a quality similar to that of
Mozart's sonata for two pianos in D, with the
same unfailing spontaneity and easy effectiveness. The regular design of the classical
concerto—opening orchestral tutti, fresh
thematic material introduced in the piano
part, etc.—is followed. There are: a dignified first movement, an expressively ornamental <u>Andante</u> and a lighthearted <u>Rondo</u>; the
technical demands are on a par with those of
the sonata for two pianos.
(Schirmer; International Music Co.)

Concerto for three pianos
and orchestra, K.242
(with an alternative ver-
sion by Mozart for two
pianos)

One of Mozart's lesser works. The piano
writing is easy for the individual instruments
and uncomplicated in ensemble. The thematic
material is pleasant without achieving any
great height of inspiration, and one feels that
it probably cost its composer very little effort. The final <u>Rondo</u> has less climax than
usual; it is in tranquil minuet rhythm.
(Breitkopf and Härtel)

FRANCIS POULENC (1899-   )

Concerto in D Minor for
two pianos and orchestra

In three movements—<u>Allegro ma non troppo</u>,
<u>Larghetto</u>, <u>Allegro molto</u>. A composition
that uses themes of a simple folk-song-like
character, harmonized in the first movement
in many cases with sharp dissonances; in the
second with ingratiating smoothness until the
final chord gives a slight shock. The <u>Finale</u>
is almost throughout in quick march rhythm.
A tendency to use two-bar phrases for much
of the material makes for easy comprehension, and the work has a popular flavor. The
piano writing lies for the most part easily
under the hand.

CAMILLE SAINT-SAËNS (1835-1921)

Carnaval des animaux
(Grande Fantaisie
zoölogique)

This most entertaining composition for two pianos and a small group of instruments imitates in a series of short pieces various animals of a zoo. Its performance imposes no special difficulties, and its humor makes its points with supreme effectiveness.

ALEXANDRE TANSMAN (1897-   )

Suite for two pianos and
orchestra

An elaborate work in four movements—Introduction and Allegro; Intermezzo; Perpetuum mobile; Variations, double fugue and finale. A strong finger and chord technique is needed for all but the simple little Intermezzo. An attractive and musicianly piece with clever dissonant technique that never loses contact with tonality.
(Eschig)

RALPH VAUGHAN WILLIAMS (1872-   )

Concerto for two pianos
and orchestra

In the three movements of this concerto— Toccata, Romanza, Fuga chromatica con Finale alla tedesca—we have a second version of a less effective earlier concerto for solo piano and orchestra. Even in this form the piano writing, though not technically exacting, is not always very resourceful; perhaps the movement in which the composer's musical personality appears most favorably is the Romanza, which has appealing lyrical quality. The Toccata has rhythmic vigor; the final fugue is somewhat severe.
(Oxford University Press)

Appendix

Anthologies of Early Keyboard Music

The most comprehensive anthology of keyboard music was compiled by Madame Louise Farrenc. It begins with the English Virginalists and early Italian masters of the sixteenth century and reaches as far forward as Chopin and Mendelssohn. It contains a mine of interesting material, some worthy of reprint. The second edition of Grove's Dictionary contained a listing of its contents, but since this is not readily available, the following tabulation may prove useful. It goes without saying that these volumes are library items and are not available on the commercial market.

Le Trésor des Pianistes (Louise Farrenc), in 23 volumes, 1861-1872, Leduc, Paris.

Vol. I
Preliminaries, History of the Piano, Treatise on Ornaments.
Vol. II
Parthenia (1611): 18 pieces by William Byrd (1542-1623), John Bull (1562-1628), Orlando Gibbons (1583-1625).
Various English composers.
Claudio Merulo (1533-1604): Toccatas.
Gerolamo Frescobaldi (1583-1643): Three Fugues (spurious), 6 Canzoni, various pieces.
Georg Muffat (1645-1704): 12 Toccatas.
Jacques Champion de Chambonnières (c.1602-1672): Pièces de Clavecin, 2 Bks.
Jean Henri d'Anglebert (1635-1691): Pièces de Clavecin.
Vol. III
Johann Kuhnau (1660-1722): 7 Sonatas, Neuer Clavier Übung, Toccatas.
Henry Purcell (1658-1695): Collection of pieces.
Johann Jakob Froberger (1616-1667): 5 Capricci, 6 Suites.
Louis Couperin (1626-1661).
Antoine Le Bègue (1630-1702).
Bernardo Pasquini (1637-1710)
Johann Kaspar Kerll (1627-1693)
Alessandro Scarlatti (1659-1725)
Vol. IV
François Couperin (1668-1733): Pièces de Clavecin, 3 Bks.
Vol. V
François Couperin: Pièces de Clavecin, Bk. 4.
George Frederick Handel (1685-1759): Suites, 3 Bks.; 6 Fugues.
Vol. VI
Domenico Scarlatti (1685-1757): 77 pieces.
Vol. VII
Domenico Scarlatti: 75 pieces.
Vol. VIII
J. S. Bach (1685-1750): 6 Partitas, 6 English Suites.
Jean Philippe Rameau (1683-1764): Pièces de Clavecin, 2 Bks.
Nicolo Porpora (1686-1766): 6 Fugues.
Vol. IX
Francesco Durante (1684-1755): 6 Sonatas.

413

François Dandrieu (1684-1740)
Benedetto Marcello (1686-1739)
Georg Telemann (1684-1740)
Giovanni Pescetti (c.1704-1766)
Claude Daquin (1694-1772): Pièces de Clavecin.
Padre Martini (1706-1784): 12 Sonatas.
Johann Ludwig Krebs (1713-1780): 3 Fugues.

Vol. X
Wilhelm Friedemann Bach (1710-1784): 12 Polonaises, Sonata, 8 Fugues, 1 Suite, 4 Fantasies.
Gottlieb Muffat (1690-1770): Collection of pieces.
Christoph Nichelmann (1717-1762): 11 Sonatas.

Vol. XI
Johann Gottlieb Goldberg (c.1720- ?): Prelude and Fugue.
Johann Ernst Eberlin (1702-1762): 6 Preludes and Fugues.
Johann Mattheson (1681-1764): Various pieces.
Domenico Zipoli (c.1675- ?): Pieces for Organ and Harpsichord.
John Christopher Smith (1712-1795): 9 Suites.
Chr. Schaffrath (18th cent.): 2 Sonatas.

Vol. XII
C.P.E. Bach (1714-1788): 30 Sonatas.

Vol. XIII
C.P.E. Bach: 35 Sonatas and 4 Rondos.

Vol. XIV
Domenico Paradies (1710-1792): 10 Sonatas.
Duphly (1716-1788): Pièces de Clavecin.
Johann Philipp Kirnberger (1721-1783): 6 Fugues, various pieces.
Johann Buttstedt (1666-1727): 2 Sonatas.
Georg Benda (1722-1795): 6 Sonatas.

Vol. XV
Christoph Friedrich Bach (1732-1795): Sonatas, various pieces.
Joseph Haydn (1732-1809): 16 Sonatas.
J. G. Albrechtsberger (1736-1809): 30 Fugues.
Karl Fasch (1736-1800): 2 Sonatas, 1 piece.

Vol. XVI
Muzio Clementi (1746-1832): 3 Sonatas, Op. 2; 2 Sonatas, Op. 7; 3 Sonatas, Op. 8; 4 Sonatas and a Toccata from Op. 9, 10, 14.
Johann Wilhelm Hässler (1747-1822): 2 Fantasies, 9 Sonatas, 4 Solos.
O. A. Lindemann (1769-1859): Various pieces.

Vol. XVII
W. A. Mozart (1756-1791): 16 Sonatas, Romance.

Vol. XVIII
Johann Christian Bach (1735-1782): 7 Sonatas.
Johann L. Dussek (1760-1812): 3 Grandes Sonates, Op. 35; Sonata, Op. 64.
J. G. Wernicke (?): 5 pieces.
Johann Schwanenberg (1740-1804): 2 Minuets.
Daniel Steibelt (1765-1823): Grande Sonate, Op. 64.
J. B. Cramer (1771-1858): 3 Sonatas.

Vol. XIX
L. van Beethoven (1770-1827): Sonatas (Op. 2 to Op. 27).

Vol. XX
Beethoven: Sonatas (Op. 28 to Op. 90).

Vol. XXI
Beethoven: Sonatas (Op. 101 to Op. 111): 6 Sets of Variations.

Vol. XXII
  Johann Nepomuk Hummel (1778-1837): 7 Sets of Variations; Intro. and
    Rondo, Op. 19; Rondo brillant, Op. 109; Sonatas, Op. 13, 20, 81; Adagio
    from Op. 38; Fantasie Op. 18.
Vol. XXIII
  Ferdinand Ries (1784-1838): L'Infortunée, Sonata, Op. 26.
  Carl Maria von Weber (1786-1826): 4 Sonatas.
  Felix Mendelssohn (1809-1847): Rondo capriccioso; 3 Fantasies or
    Caprices, Op. 16.
  Frédéric Chopin (1810-1849): 9 Nocturnes.

The second largest anthology of keyboard music was the work of Gino
Tagliapietra. It extends from the sixteenth century as far forward as
Busoni and Casella. At present writing it is available only in libraries but
it is to be hoped that a reprint by Ricordi will be forthcoming.

Antologia di musica antica e moderna per il pianoforte (TPA) (Gino
  Tagliapietra), 18 Vols., Ricordi.

Vol. I: 35 pieces
  Philippe Verdelot (before 1567).
  Adrián Willaert (c.1480-1562).
  Gerolamo Cavazzoni (c.1500- ?).
  Alonso de Mudarra (? -c.1570).
  Miguel de Fuenllana (16th cent.).
  Juan Bermudo (16th cent.).
  Cipriano de Rore (1516-1565).
  Andrea Gabrieli (c.1510-1586).
  Antonio de Cabezon (1510-1566).
  Annobale Padovano (1527-1575).
Vol. II: 31 pieces
  Claudio Merulo.
  Luzzasco Luzzaschi (? -1607).
  William Byrd.
  Thomas Morley (1557-1603).
  Ferdinando Richardson (c.1558-1618).
  Giovanni Gabrieli (1557-1612).
  Peter Philips (c.1550-1628).
  Giles Farnaby (c.1569- ?).
Vol. III: 38 pieces
  Jan Pieters Sweelinck (1562-1621).
  John Munday (c.1563- ?).
  John Bull.
  Jean Titelouze (1563-1633).
  Hans Leo Hassler (1564-1612).
  Andrea Banchieri (1565-1634).
  Christian Erbach (1570-1635).
  H. Praetorius (1560-1629) ?
  Orlando Gibbons.
Vol. IV: 24 pieces
  Frescobaldi.
Vol. V: 31 pieces
  Frescobaldi.
  Giovanni Maria Trabaci (early 17th cent.).

Giovanni Picchi (17th cent.).
Andrea Gabrieli.
Vol. VI: 30 pieces
  Samuel Scheidt (1587-1654).
  Hans Scheidemann.
  G. B. Fasolo.
  Michelangelo Rossi (17th cent.).
  Tarquinio Merula (17th cent.).
  Fabrizio Fontana.
  J. J. Froberger.
Vol. VII: 31 pieces
  Delphin Strungk (1601-1694).
  Wolfgang Ebner (c.1610-1665).
  Johann Elias Kindermann.
  François Roberday.
  Chambonnières.
  Henri Dumont.
  Johann Adam Reinken (1623-1722).
  Nicolas Gigault.
  J. K. Kerll.
  J. H. d'Anglebert.
  Jean Baptiste Lully (1633?-1687).
  J. Gaultier the elder.
Vol. VIII: 36 pieces
  Allessandro Poglietti (? -1683)
  Antoine Le Bègue.
  Louis Couperin.
  Georg Muffat.
  Dietrich Buxtehude (1637-1707).
  Bernardo Pasquini.
Vol. IX: 40 pieces
  Johann Christoph Bach (1642-1703).
  Johann Krieger (1651-1735).
  C. F. Pollaroli (1653-1722).
  Arcangelo Corelli (1653-1713).
  Johann Pachelbel (1653-1706).
  Henry Purcell (1658-1695).
  Alessandro Scarlatti (1659-60-1725).
Vol. X: 31 pieces
  Johann Kuhnau.
  F. X. Murschauser (1663-1738).
  J. K. F. Fischer (1650-1746).
  Jean Baptiste Loeillet (1680-1730).
  François Couperin.
  Louis Marchand (1669-1732).
  A. B. della Ciaja (1671-1755).
  Domenico Zipoli.
  George Telemann.
  Johann Mattheson.
Vol. XI: 18 pieces
  Rameau.
  Dandrieu.
  Durante.

Handel.
J. S. Bach.
D. Scarlatti.
Marcello.
Porpora.
Vol. XII: 21 pieces
Gottlieb Muffat.
Daquin.
Leonardo Leo (1694-1744).
Johann Adolph Hasse (1699-1783).
G. B. Sammartini (1701-1755).
G. A. Paganelli (1710-1765).
Giovanni Pescetti.
Padre Martini.
Baldassare Galuppi (1706-1784).
W. F. Bach.
Paradies.
Krebs.
Vol. XIII: 21 pieces
C.P.E. Bach.
F. W. Marpurg (1718-1795).
Kirnberger.
Georg Benda.
Johann Ernst Bach (c.1722-1777).
F. Bertoni (1725-1813).
Giovanni Rutini (c.1725-1797).
Joseph Haydn.
Antonio Sacchini (1730-1786)
Johann Christian Bach.
Johann Wilhelm Hässler.
F. Turini (1749-1812 ?).
G. B. Grazioli (c.1750-1820).
Muzio Clementi.
W. A. Mozart.
Vol. XIV: 28 pieces
Luigi Cherubini (1760-1842).
J. L. Dussek.
Francesco Pollini (1763-1846).
Daniel Steibelt.
Beethoven.
Cramer.
J. N. Hummel.
John Field (1782-1837).
F. Ries.
C. M. von Weber.
Vol. XV: 28 pieces
F. W. Kalkbrenner (1788-1849).
Carl Czerny (1791-1857).
Ignaz Moscheles (1794-1870).
Franz Schubert (1879-1828).
J. C. Kessler.
F. Mendelssohn.
Chopin.

Vol. XVI: 20 pieces
  Robert Schumann (1810-1856).
  Franz Liszt (1811-1886).
  Sigismund Thalberg (1812-1871).
  H. Kjerulf (1815-1868).
  S. Golinelli.
Vol. XVII: 20 pieces
  Joachim Raff (1822-1882).
  A. Fumagalli.
  Anton Rubinstein (1829-1894).
  Johannes Brahms (1833-1897).
  Giovanni Sgambati (1841-1914).
  M. Esposito (1855-1929).
  G. Martucci (1856-1909).
  C. Albanesi.
  N. v. Westerhout.
  Allessandro Longo (1864-   ).
  G. Orefice.
Vol. XVIII: 36 pieces
  Ferruccio Busoni (1866-1924).
  F. Cilea.
  A. Zanella (1873-   ).
  A. Savasta.
  D. Allaleona (1881-1928).
  R. Pick-Mangiagalli (1882-   ).
  L. Perrachio.
  Alfredo Casella (1883-1947).
  F. Santoliquido (1883-   ).
  A. Veretti.
  M. Castelnuovo-Tedesco (1895-   ).
  S. Musella (1896-   ).
  E. Masetti (1893-   ).
  M. Pilati (1903-   ).

The most easily accessible anthologies of early keyboard music are:

Early Keyboard Music (EKM), (Oesterle-Aldrich), 2 Vols., G. Schirmer.
  Vol. 1—Byrd, Bull, Gibbons, Frescobaldi, Froberger, Dumont, Chambon-
      nières, M.Rossi, Kerll, d'Anglebert, L. Couperin, Lully, Buxte-
      hude, B. Pasquini, John Blow, Pachelbel, Purcell, A. Scarlatti,
      Loeillet, Kuhnau.
  Vol. 2—F. Couperin, Murschhauser, Mattheson, Gottlieb Muffat, D. Scar-
      latti, Rameau.

Unfortunately these volumes are badly in need of re-editing. They may be
safely used in connection with more authoritative library editions. The
compositions are consistently overedited, misleading the student as to
style, tempo and phrasing. The fugue attributed to Frescobaldi is spurious, possibly by Poglietti. (Nevertheless it is a compelling work, chromatic and pathetic in style, certainly deserving of performance.) The Rossi
piece is also attributed to the wrong composer. As for the Couperin selections in Vol. II, a cursory glance at the fine Augener edition of the same
composer (ed. Brahms and Chrysander) will quickly indicate the cumber-
some editorial job that hampers the student.

The Art of the Suite: Eight suites of dances by masters of the 17th and 18th centuries, E. B. Marks.

An excellent collection of suites by Chambonnières, Froberger, Purcell, J. K. F. Fischer, F. Couperin, Dieupart, Daquin and Gottlieb Muffat, selected and edited by Yella Pessl. The edition is carefully done, authoritatively presented with biographical notes, a short essay on the suite in general, and a table of ornaments.

Old Masters of the Sixteenth, Seventeenth and Eighteenth Centuries (Walter Niemann), Kalmus.

A useful reprint of pieces by Böhm, J. K. F. Fischer, Froberger, C. H. Graun, Kerll, Kirnberger, Krieger, Kuhnau, Marpurg, Mattheson, Gottlieb Muffat, Murschhauser, Nichelmann, Pachelbel, Scheidt, Bull, Byrd, F. Couperin, Daquin, Durante, Frescobaldi, Galuppi, Marchand, Martini, Paradies, Poglietti, Rameau, D. Scarlatti, Zipoli.
Of especial interest are a brilliant Gigue in B-flat minor (Graun), using the wide skips and crossed-hands technique associated with the Italian masters; the Biblical Sonata of Kuhnau, The Battle between David and Goliath (an eighteenth-century example of program music), six short Fugues on the "Magnificat" by Pachelbel, and two interesting canzonas by Frescobaldi (all of which are excellent studies in polyphonic playing); The Bells of William Byrd (a sixteenth-century example of program music) and the two-movement Sonata in A of Paradies (sometimes Paradisi), the second movement of which is the famous Toccata, a short perpetual motion requiring clean finger work and lightness.
The Niemann volume is "arranged for the modern piano." This means that almost all indications of tempo, phrasing, accentuation, dynamics, pedaling, etc., have been added by the editor to suit his conception of how these compositions can best be transferred to the piano from the original harpsichord and clavichord for which they were written.

More authoritative, but extremely slight in content is a slim little volume edited and compiled by Curt Sachs, The Evolution of Piano Music, 1350-1700, E. B. Marks. A few interesting reproductions of paintings of the period and pertinent information on instruments and composers add to the charm of the collection. It contains at least one gem, the Toccata in D Minor by Froberger, a rich example of the baroque toccata, shorter than those of J. S. Bach, but with all the problems of free recitative, quiet polyphonic playing and vigorous concluding fugue to be met with in the toccatas of the Leipzig master.

Alte Hausmusik (1550-1780), (Willy Rehberg), 2 Vols., Schott (through Associated Music).

Short pieces by early German, English, French and Italian composers.

Sonatenbuch der Vorklassik für Klavier (Martin Frey), Schott (through Associated Music).

Fifteen sonatas and sonata movements by pre-classic composers: Kuhnau, Hasse, C. P. E. Bach, J. C. F. Bach, J. C. Bach, Paradies, Hässler, Türk, Méhul, Haydn. An interesting, carefully edited collection of only moderate difficulty.

The Sons of Bach (Willy Rehberg), Schott (through Associated Music).

Thirteen sonatas, pieces and single movements by W. F. Bach, C. P. E. Bach, J. C. F. Bach and J. C. Bach. The volume contains suggestions for practice.

Music of Early Times (1350-1650) (Willi Apel), 2 Vols., Schott Werkreihe (through Associated Music). Keyboard pieces from the Renaissance to early baroque.

Book I, Germany and Italy: (Paumann (1410-1475), Paumgartner (c. 1460), Kotter (1485-1541), Kleber (1490-1556), Neusiedler (1508-1563), Ammerbach (1530-1597), Normiger (c. 1548), Scheidt (1587-1654), Kindermann (1616-1655), Dalza (c.1508), Bossinensis (c. 1509), Cavazzoni (16th cent.), Bendusi (16th cent.), G. Gabrieli (1557-1612), Diruta (1560- ?), Trabaci (c. 1615), Banchieri (1565-1634), Frescobaldi.

Book II, England, Spain and France: Anon., Hughe Aston (? -1522), Bull, Byrd, Milan (c.1500-1560), Narvaez (1538), Valderravano (1547), Fuenllana (1554), Cabezon (1510-1566), Bešardus (1567- ?) Chambonnières, D. Gaultier (1600-1672), L. Couperin.

Alte Meister (E. Pauer), 6 Vols., Breitkopf and Härtel.

A famous anthology of early music (now out of print) compiled in the nineteenth century. The source for many subsequent reprints of works by eighteenth-century composers. Available only in libraries.

Thirteen Keyboard Sonatas of the 18th and 19th Centuries, edited with critical commentaries, by William S. Newman, The University of North Carolina Press.

A collection of unusual and out-of-the-way sonatas by Jean Barrière (flourished 1730-1750), Platti, Alberti, Georg Benda (1722-1795), J. J. Agrell (1701-1765), C. G. Neefe (1748-1798), Manuel Blasco de Nebra (c.1650-1784), Dittersdorf (1739-1799), Joseph Wölfl (1773-1812), E. T. A. Hoffmann (1776-1822), J. F. Reichardt, Loewe, Moscheles. A careful and scholarly edition.

A Program of Early American Piano Music (Collected, edited and arranged by John Tasker Howard), J. Fischer and Bro.

Pieces by Alexander Reinagle, James Bremner (? -1780), Raynor Taylor (late 18th cent.), John Palma (middle of the 18th cent.), Victor Pelissier (late 18th cent.), James Hewitt (1770-1827), Benjamin Carr (1769-1831), J. C. Moller (late 18th cent.). The Reinagle sonata here reprinted is shortened from the original version.

Some Further Reference Editions of Early Keyboard Music

The monumental series of publications by Breitkopf and Härtel known as the Denkmäler series includes many keyboard works by seventeenth- and eighteenth-century composers. They are Urtext editions, authoritative in every respect and are to be found in the larger libraries. The entire publication comprises the following three series:

Denkmäler der Tonkunst in Oesterreich (DTOe, 83 Vols. (1894-   ). (Monuments of Music in Austria).

Denkmaler der Tonkunst in Bayern (DTB, 36 Vols., 1900-1913). (Monuments of Music in Bavaria)

Denkmäler deutscher Tonkunst (DdT, 65 Vols., 1892-1931). (Monuments of German Music)

These were published in annual issues sometimes several volumes a year, thus the designation VI, 2 or III, 3.

The following keyboard composers are represented:

In DTOe
J. J. Froberger IV, 1; VI, 2; X, 2—Organ and Clavier Works.
Gottlieb Muffat III, 3—Componimenti Musicali.
            XXIX, 2—12 Toccatas and 72 Versetl.
J. Pachelbel VIII, 2—94 compositions mostly on the Magnificat.
A. Poglietti XIII, 2—Clavier and Organ Works.
G. Reutter XIII, 2—Clavier and Organ Works.
F. T. Richter XIII, 2—Clavier and Organ Works.
Viennese Clavier and Organ Works c.1650-1700, XIII, 2.

In DTB
Chr. Erbach IV, 2—Selected Works.
H. L. Hassler IV, 2—Works for Clavier and Organ.
J. K. Kerll II, 2—Selected Works.
J. and J. Ph. Krieger XVIII—Collected Works for Clavier and Organ.
F. X. Murschauser XVIII—Collected Works for Clavier and Organ.
J. and W. H. Pachelbel II, 1; IV, 1—Clavier and Organ Works.

In DdT
J. Kuhnau IV—Clavier Works.
S. Scheidt I—Tabulatura Nova.
J. G. Walther XXVI, XXVII—Collected Works for Organ.
F. W. Zachow XXI, XXII—Collected Works.

The keyboard works of Antonio de Cabezon, great Spanish composer of the sixteenth century (1510-1566) appear in volumes 3, 4, 7, 8 of Hispaniae Schola Music Sacra (ed. F. Pedrell, 1895-1898). A new Urtext reprint is available by Schott (through Associated Music).

Monumenta Musicae Belgicae (ed. J. Watelet, 1932-1938).
Vol. 1—J. B. Loeillet, Werken voor Clavecimbel.
Vol. 2—A. Kerckhoven, Werken voor Orgel.

Vol. 3—J. H. Fiocco, <u>Werken voor Clavecimbel</u>.
Vol. 4—Ch. Guillet, Giov. de Macque, C. Luython.

<u>Vereeinigung voor Noord Nederlands Muziekgeschiedenis</u>

Vol. 32—C. D. Hurlebusch, <u>Compositioni musicali per il Cembalo</u> (c.1750).
Vol. 19—A. van Noort, <u>Tabulatuur Boeck</u> (c.1659).
Vol. 37—<u>Oud-Nederlandsche Klaviermusiek</u> (music book of Anna Maria van Eijl, 1671).
Vol. XIV—A. Reinken, <u>Partite diverse</u>

List of Publishers

Publishing houses and other organizations which print or circulate compositions discussed in this book:

American Composers' Alliance (Library) - New York
American Music Center - New York
Am-Rus Edition (Leeds Music Corporation) - New York
Amphion - Paris
Arraujo and Co. - Rio de Janeiro
Arrow Music Press - New York
Associated Music Publishers - New York
Augener and Co. - London
Bärenreiter (Concordia Music Publishing House) - St. Louis
C. C. Birchard and Co. - Boston
Bomart Music Publications - Hillsdale, N. Y.
Boosey & Hawkes - London and New York
Boston Music Co. - Boston and New York
Bote & Bock - Berlin
Breitkopf and Härtel (Associated Music Publishers) - New York
Broude Bros.- New York
F. Bongiovanni - Bologna
A. Carisch and Co. - Milan
Chappell and Co. - London and New York
J. & W. Chester - London
John Church Co. - Cincinnati
Composers' Press - New York
Concordia Music Publishing Co. - St. Louis
Cos Cob Press (Arrow Music Press)
J. Curwen and Sons - London
De Santis - Rome
R. Deiss - Paris
E. Demets - Paris
Oliver Ditson (Musicians' Library) - (Theodore Presser) - Philadelphia
L. Doblinger - Vienna
A. Durand - Paris (Elkan-Vogel - Philadelphia)
Ediciones Musicales Poletonia - Buenos Aires
Edition Musicus - New York
Edition Mutuelle - Paris
J. W. Edwards - Ann Arbor, Michigan
Elkan-Vogel Co. - Philadelphia
Elkin and Co. - London
Enoch et Cie. - Paris
Max Eschig - Paris
Carl Fischer - New York
J. Fischer and Bro. - New York
D. A. Forlivesi - Florence
E. Fromont - Paris
Galaxy Music Corporation - New York
Grupo de Renovacion Musical - Buenos Aires and Havana
J. Hamelle - Paris

Hargail Music Press - New York
T. B. Harms - New York
William Hansen - Copenhagen
Heritage Music Publications - New York
H. Heugel - Paris
Hinrichsen (Peters) - New York
F. Hofmeister - Leipzig
International Music Company - New York
J. Jobert - Paris
P. Jurgenson - Leningrad
E. F. Kalmus - New York
A. Leduc - Paris
Leeds Music Corporation - New York
Alfred Lengnick - London
Lyrebird Press - Paris
E. B. Marks Music Corporation - New York
A. Z. Mathot - Paris
Mercury Music - New York
Merrymount Music Press (Mercury Music) - New York
Mills Music Co. - New York
Murdoch, Murdoch and Co. - London
New Music Press - New York
New World Music Corp. - New York
Novello and Co. - London
Omega Music Edition - New York
Oxford University Press - London and New York
Paragon Music Publishers - New York
C. F. Peters - New York
Theodore Presser Co., - Philadelphia
G. Ricordi and Co., Milan, London, Paris, New York
Riker, Brown and Wellington - Boston
Rouart, Lerolle et Cie - Paris
Rozsavolgyi & Co. - Budapest
Russian State Music Publications - Moscow
Salabert - Paris, Brussels, Rome, New York
Savini-Zerboni, Milan
E. C. Schirmer - Boston
G. Schirmer - New York
A. P. Schmidt - Boston
Schott & Co. - London, Brussels
Schroeder and Gunther - New York
Edward Schuberth & Co. - Leipzig, New York
Senart - Paris
Sirène Musicale - Paris
Simrock - Leipzig (Associated Music Publishers)
Société pour la publication de musique classique et moderne - Paris
Southern Music Publishing Co. - London, Mexico, New York
Albert Stahl - Berlin
Stainer & Bell, London (Galaxy Music Corp. - New York)
Clayton F. Summy, Chicago
Stern and Co. - Berlin
Universal Edition - London, Vienna
Universal Music Corporation - New York

Urbanek a Synove - Prague
Valley Music Press - Northampton, Mass.
Villa- Lobos Music Corp. - New York
Weintraub Music Co. - New York
Joseph Williams - London
Willis Music Co. - Cincinnati
M. Witmark & Sons - New York

New Biographical Appendix

Alphabetical list of composers in *Music for the Piano* who have died since its original publication, including a few whose death dates were omitted in the original text.

Allende, L. Humberto: 1885-1959
Babin, Victor: 1908-1972
Bate, Stanley: 1911-1959
Bauer, Marion: 1887-1955
Bax, Arnold: 1883-1953
Benjamin, Arthur: 1893-1960
Berners, Lord Gerald Tyrwhitt: 1883-1950
Blanchet, Emile: 1877-1943
Bloch, Ernest: 1880-1959
Bogdanov-Berezovsky, Valerian: 1903-1971
Boscovich, Alexander Uriah: 1907-1964
Casadesus, Robert: 1899-1972
Castelnuovo-Tedesco, Mario: 1895-1968
Castro, José Maria: 1892-1964
Castro, Juan José: 1895-1968
Chanler, Theodore: 1902-1961
Cowell, Henry: 1897-1965
Crawford, Ruth: 1901-1953
Demuth, Norman: 1898-1968
Dohnanyi, Ernst von: 1877-1960
Dvorsky, Michel: 1876-1957
Eisler, Hanns: 1898-1962
Eitler, Estaban: 1913-1960
Enesco, Georges: 1881-1955
Feinberg, Samuel: 1890-1962
Fine, Irving: 1914-1962
Freed, Isadore: 1900-1960
Fuleihan, Anis: 1900-1970
Giannini, Vittorio: 1903-1966
Gibbs, C. Armstrong: 1889-1960
Gnessin, Mikhail: 1883-1957
Goossens, Eugene: 1893-1962
Grainger, Percy: 1882-1961
Gretchaninoff, Alexander: 1864-1956
Grovlez, Gabriel: 1879-1944
Gruenberg, Louis: 1884-1964
Harsanyi, Tibor: 1898-1954
Hill, Edward Burlingame: 1872-1960

Hindemith, Paul: 1895-1963
Honegger, Arthur: 1892-1955
Ibert, Jacques: 1890-1962
Infante, Manuel: 1883-1958
Inghelbrecht, D. E.: 1880-1965
Ireland, John: 1879-1962
Ives, Charles: 1874-1954
Jelobinsky, Valery: 1912-1946
Kodály, Zoltán: 1882-1967
Koutzen, Boris: 1901-1966
Kurka, Robert: 1921-1957
Longo, Allessandro: 1864-1945
Martinu, Bohuslav: 1890-1959
Mason, Daniel Gregory: 1873-1953
McPhee, Colin: 1901-1964
Menasce, Jacques de: 1905-1960
Moore, Douglas: 1893-1969
Nin, Joaquin: 1879-1949
Palmgren, Selim: 1878-1951
Philipp, Isidor: 1863-1958
Pick-Mangiagalli, Ricardo: 1882-1949
Plaza, Juan Bautista: 1898-1964
Polovinkin, Leonid: 1894-1949
Ponce, Manuel: 1882-1948
Poulenc, Francis: 1899-1963
Powell, John: 1882-1963
Rabaud, Henri: 1873-1949
Rathaus, Karol: 1895-1954
Rawsthorne, Alan: 1905-1971
Riegger, Wallingford: 1885-1961
Roger-Ducasse, Jean Jules: 1873-1954
Ropartz, Guy: 1864-1955
Roussel, Albert: 1869-1937
Santoliquido, F.: 1883-1971
Sás, Andrés: 1900-1967
Schmitt, Florent: 1870-1958
Scott, Cyril: 1879-1971
Shebalin, Vissarion: 1902-1963
Shepherd, Arthur: 1880-1958
Sibelius, Jean: 1865-1957
Sowerby, Leo: 1895-1968
Stravinsky, Igor: 1882-1971

Toch, Ernst: 1887-1964
Turina, Joaquin: 1882-1949
Turner, Godfrey: 1913-1948
Valen, Fartein: 1887-1952
Villa-Lobos, Heitor: 1894-1959
Wagenaar, Bernard: 1894-1971

Walker, Ernest: 1870-1949
Whithorne, Emerson: 1884-1958
Williams, Ralph Vaughan:
  1872-1958
Wolpe, Stefan: 1902-1972

Index of Composers

A CATALOG OF SELECTED
DOVER BOOKS
IN ALL FIELDS OF INTEREST

A CATALOG OF SELECTED DOVER
BOOKS IN ALL FIELDS OF INTEREST

DRAWINGS OF REMBRANDT, edited by Seymour Slive. Updated Lippmann, Hofstede de Groot edition, with definitive scholarly apparatus. All portraits, biblical sketches, landscapes, nudes. Oriental figures, classical studies, together with selection of work by followers. 550 illustrations. Total of 630pp. 9⅛ × 12¼.
21485-0, 21486-9 Pa., Two-vol. set $25.00

GHOST AND HORROR STORIES OF AMBROSE BIERCE, Ambrose Bierce. 24 tales vividly imagined, strangely prophetic, and decades ahead of their time in technical skill: "The Damned Thing," "An Inhabitant of Carcosa," "The Eyes of the Panther," "Moxon's Master," and 20 more. 199pp. 5⅜ × 8½. 20767-6 Pa. $3.95

ETHICAL WRITINGS OF MAIMONIDES, Maimonides. Most significant ethical works of great medieval sage, newly translated for utmost precision, readability. Laws Concerning Character Traits, Eight Chapters, more. 192pp. 5⅜ × 8½.
24522-5 Pa. $4.50

THE EXPLORATION OF THE COLORADO RIVER AND ITS CANYONS, J. W. Powell. Full text of Powell's 1,000-mile expedition down the fabled Colorado in 1869. Superb account of terrain, geology, vegetation, Indians, famine, mutiny, treacherous rapids, mighty canyons, during exploration of last unknown part of continental U.S. 400pp. 5⅜ × 8½. 20094-9 Pa. $6.95

HISTORY OF PHILOSOPHY, Julián Marías. Clearest one-volume history on the market. Every major philosopher and dozens of others, to Existentialism and later. 505pp. 5⅜ × 8½. 21739-6 Pa. $8.50

ALL ABOUT LIGHTNING, Martin A. Uman. Highly readable non-technical survey of nature and causes of lightning, thunderstorms, ball lightning, St. Elmo's Fire, much more. Illustrated. 192pp. 5⅜ × 8½. 25237-X Pa. $5.95

SAILING ALONE AROUND THE WORLD, Captain Joshua Slocum. First man to sail around the world, alone, in small boat. One of great feats of seamanship told in delightful manner. 67 illustrations. 294pp. 5⅜ × 8½. 20326-3 Pa. $4.95

LETTERS AND NOTES ON THE MANNERS, CUSTOMS AND CONDITIONS OF THE NORTH AMERICAN INDIANS, George Catlin. Classic account of life among Plains Indians: ceremonies, hunt, warfare, etc. 312 plates. 572pp. of text. 6⅛ × 9¼. 22118-0, 22119-9 Pa. Two-vol. set $15.90

ALASKA: The Harriman Expedition, 1899, John Burroughs, John Muir, et al. Informative, engrossing accounts of two-month, 9,000-mile expedition. Native peoples, wildlife, forests, geography, salmon industry, glaciers, more. Profusely illustrated. 240 black-and-white line drawings. 124 black-and-white photographs. 3 maps. Index. 576pp. 5⅜ × 8½. 25109-8 Pa. $11.95

THE BOOK OF BEASTS: Being a Translation from a Latin Bestiary of the Twelfth Century, T. H. White. Wonderful catalog real and fanciful beasts: manticore, griffin, phoenix, amphivius, jaculus, many more. White's witty erudite commentary on scientific, historical aspects. Fascinating glimpse of medieval mind. Illustrated. 296pp. 5⅜ × 8¼. (Available in U.S. only) 24609-4 Pa. $5.95

FRANK LLOYD WRIGHT: ARCHITECTURE AND NATURE With 160 Illustrations, Donald Hoffmann. Profusely illustrated study of influence of nature—especially prairie—on Wright's designs for Fallingwater, Robie House, Guggenheim Museum, other masterpieces. 96pp. 9¼ × 10¾. 25098-9 Pa. $7.95

FRANK LLOYD WRIGHT'S FALLINGWATER, Donald Hoffmann. Wright's famous waterfall house: planning and construction of organic idea. History of site, owners, Wright's personal involvement. Photographs of various stages of building. Preface by Edgar Kaufmann, Jr. 100 illustrations. 112pp. 9¼ × 10. 23671-4 Pa. $7.95

YEARS WITH FRANK LLOYD WRIGHT: Apprentice to Genius, Edgar Tafel. Insightful memoir by a former apprentice presents a revealing portrait of Wright the man, the inspired teacher, the greatest American architect. 372 black-and-white illustrations. Preface. Index. vi + 228pp. 8¼ × 11. 24801-1 Pa. $9.95

THE STORY OF KING ARTHUR AND HIS KNIGHTS, Howard Pyle. Enchanting version of King Arthur fable has delighted generations with imaginative narratives of exciting adventures and unforgettable illustrations by the author. 41 illustrations. xviii + 313pp. 6⅛ × 9¼. 21445-1 Pa. $5.95

THE GODS OF THE EGYPTIANS, E. A. Wallis Budge. Thorough coverage of numerous gods of ancient Egypt by foremost Egyptologist. Information on evolution of cults, rites and gods; the cult of Osiris; the Book of the Dead and its rites; the sacred animals and birds; Heaven and Hell; and more. 956pp. 6⅛ × 9¼. 22055-9, 22056-7 Pa., Two-vol. set $21.90

A THEOLOGICO-POLITICAL TREATISE, Benedict Spinoza. Also contains unfinished *Political Treatise*. Great classic on religious liberty, theory of government on common consent. R. Elwes translation. Total of 421pp. 5⅜ × 8½. 20249-6 Pa. $6.95

INCIDENTS OF TRAVEL IN CENTRAL AMERICA, CHIAPAS, AND YUCATAN, John L. Stephens. Almost single-handed discovery of Maya culture; exploration of ruined cities, monuments, temples; customs of Indians. 115 drawings. 892pp. 5⅜ × 8½. 22404-X, 22405-8 Pa., Two-vol. set $15.90

LOS CAPRICHOS, Francisco Goya. 80 plates of wild, grotesque monsters and caricatures. Prado manuscript included. 183pp. 6⅝ × 9⅝. 22384-1 Pa. $4.95

AUTOBIOGRAPHY: The Story of My Experiments with Truth, Mohandas K. Gandhi. Not hagiography, but Gandhi in his own words. Boyhood, legal studies, purification, the growth of the Satyagraha (nonviolent protest) movement. Critical, inspiring work of the man who freed India. 480pp. 5⅜ × 8½. (Available in U.S. only) 24593-4 Pa. $6.95

ILLUSTRATED DICTIONARY OF HISTORIC ARCHITECTURE, edited by Cyril M. Harris. Extraordinary compendium of clear, concise definitions for over 5,000 important architectural terms complemented by over 2,000 line drawings. Covers full spectrum of architecture from ancient ruins to 20th-century Modernism. Preface. 592pp. 7½ × 9⅜. 24444-X Pa. $14.95

THE NIGHT BEFORE CHRISTMAS, Clement Moore. Full text, and woodcuts from original 1848 book. Also critical, historical material. 19 illustrations. 40pp. 4⅝ × 6. 22797-9 Pa. $2.50

THE LESSON OF JAPANESE ARCHITECTURE: 165 Photographs, Jiro Harada. Memorable gallery of 165 photographs taken in the 1930's of exquisite Japanese homes of the well-to-do and historic buildings. 13 line diagrams. 192pp. 8⅜ × 11¼. 24778-3 Pa. $8.95

THE AUTOBIOGRAPHY OF CHARLES DARWIN AND SELECTED LETTERS, edited by Francis Darwin. The fascinating life of eccentric genius composed of an intimate memoir by Darwin (intended for his children); commentary by his son, Francis; hundreds of fragments from notebooks, journals, papers; and letters to and from Lyell, Hooker, Huxley, Wallace and Henslow. xi + 365pp. 5⅜ × 8. 20479-0 Pa. $5.95

WONDERS OF THE SKY: Observing Rainbows, Comets, Eclipses, the Stars and Other Phenomena, Fred Schaaf. Charming, easy-to-read poetic guide to all manner of celestial events visible to the naked eye. Mock suns, glories, Belt of Venus, more. Illustrated. 299pp. 5¼ × 8¼. 24402-4 Pa. $7.95

BURNHAM'S CELESTIAL HANDBOOK, Robert Burnham, Jr. Thorough guide to the stars beyond our solar system. Exhaustive treatment. Alphabetical by constellation: Andromeda to Cetus in Vol. 1; Chamaeleon to Orion in Vol. 2; and Pavo to Vulpecula in Vol. 3. Hundreds of illustrations. Index in Vol. 3. 2,000pp. 6⅛ × 9¼. 23567-X, 23568-8, 23673-0 Pa., Three-vol. set $37.85

STAR NAMES: Their Lore and Meaning, Richard Hinckley Allen. Fascinating history of names various cultures have given to constellations and literary and folkloristic uses that have been made of stars. Indexes to subjects. Arabic and Greek names. Biblical references. Bibliography. 563pp. 5⅜ × 8½. 21079-0 Pa. $7.95

THIRTY YEARS THAT SHOOK PHYSICS: The Story of Quantum Theory, George Gamow. Lucid, accessible introduction to influential theory of energy and matter. Careful explanations of Dirac's anti-particles, Bohr's model of the atom, much more. 12 plates. Numerous drawings. 240pp. 5⅜ × 8½. 24895-X Pa. $4.95

CHINESE DOMESTIC FURNITURE IN PHOTOGRAPHS AND MEASURED DRAWINGS, Gustav Ecke. A rare volume, now affordably priced for antique collectors, furniture buffs and art historians. Detailed review of styles ranging from early Shang to late Ming. Unabridged republication. 161 black-and-white drawings, photos. Total of 224pp. 8⅜ × 11¼. (Available in U.S. only) 25171-3 Pa. $12.95

VINCENT VAN GOGH: A Biography, Julius Meier-Graefe. Dynamic, penetrating study of artist's life, relationship with brother, Theo, painting techniques, travels, more. Readable, engrossing. 160pp. 5⅜ × 8½. (Available in U.S. only) 25253-1 Pa. $3.95

HOW TO WRITE, Gertrude Stein. Gertrude Stein claimed anyone could understand her unconventional writing—here are clues to help. Fascinating improvisations, language experiments, explanations illuminate Stein's craft and the art of writing. Total of 414pp. 4⅝ × 6⅜. 23144-5 Pa. $5.95

ADVENTURES AT SEA IN THE GREAT AGE OF SAIL: Five Firsthand Narratives, edited by Elliot Snow. Rare true accounts of exploration, whaling, shipwreck, fierce natives, trade, shipboard life, more. 33 illustrations. Introduction. 353pp. 5⅜ × 8½. 25177-2 Pa. $7.95

THE HERBAL OR GENERAL HISTORY OF PLANTS, John Gerard. Classic descriptions of about 2,850 plants—with over 2,700 illustrations—includes Latin and English names, physical descriptions, varieties, time and place of growth, more. 2,706 illustrations. xlv + 1,678pp. 8½ × 12¼. 23147-X Cloth. $75.00

DOROTHY AND THE WIZARD IN OZ, L. Frank Baum. Dorothy and the Wizard visit the center of the Earth, where people are vegetables, glass houses grow and Oz characters reappear. Classic sequel to Wizard of Oz. 256pp. 5⅜ × 8. 24714-7 Pa. $4.95

SONGS OF EXPERIENCE: Facsimile Reproduction with 26 Plates in Full Color, William Blake. This facsimile of Blake's original "Illuminated Book" reproduces 26 full-color plates from a rare 1826 edition. Includes "The Tyger," "London," "Holy Thursday," and other immortal poems. 26 color plates. Printed text of poems. 48pp. 5¼ × 7. 24636-1 Pa. $3.50

SONGS OF INNOCENCE, William Blake. The first and most popular of Blake's famous "Illuminated Books," in a facsimile edition reproducing all 31 brightly colored plates. Additional printed text of each poem. 64pp. 5¼ × 7. 22764-2 Pa. $3.50

PRECIOUS STONES, Max Bauer. Classic, thorough study of diamonds, rubies, emeralds, garnets, etc.: physical character, occurrence, properties, use, similar topics. 20 plates, 8 in color. 94 figures. 659pp. 6⅛ × 9¼. 21910-0, 21911-9 Pa., Two-vol. set $15.90

ENCYCLOPEDIA OF VICTORIAN NEEDLEWORK, S. F. A. Caulfeild and Blanche Saward. Full, precise descriptions of stitches, techniques for dozens of needlecrafts—most exhaustive reference of its kind. Over 800 figures. Total of 679pp. 8⅜ × 11. Two volumes. Vol. 1 22800-2 Pa. $11.95 Vol. 2 22801-0 Pa. $11.95

THE MARVELOUS LAND OF OZ, L. Frank Baum. Second Oz book, the Scarecrow and Tin Woodman are back with hero named Tip, Oz magic. 136 illustrations. 287pp. 5⅜ × 8½. 20692-0 Pa. $5.95

WILD FOWL DECOYS, Joel Barber. Basic book on the subject, by foremost authority and collector. Reveals history of decoy making and rigging, place in American culture, different kinds of decoys, how to make them, and how to use them. 140 plates. 156pp. 7⅞ × 10¾. 20011-6 Pa. $8.95

HISTORY OF LACE, Mrs. Bury Palliser. Definitive, profusely illustrated chronicle of lace from earliest times to late 19th century. Laces of Italy, Greece, England, France, Belgium, etc. Landmark of needlework scholarship. 266 illustrations. 672pp. 6⅛ × 9¼. 24742-2 Pa. $14.95

ILLUSTRATED GUIDE TO SHAKER FURNITURE, Robert Meader. All furniture and appurtenances, with much on unknown local styles. 235 photos. 146pp. 9 × 12. 22819-3 Pa. $7.95

WHALE SHIPS AND WHALING: A Pictorial Survey, George Francis Dow. Over 200 vintage engravings, drawings, photographs of barks, brigs, cutters, other vessels. Also harpoons, lances, whaling guns, many other artifacts. Comprehensive text by foremost authority. 207 black-and-white illustrations. 288pp. 6 × 9. 24808-9 Pa. $8.95

THE BERTRAMS, Anthony Trollope. Powerful portrayal of blind self-will and thwarted ambition includes one of Trollope's most heartrending love stories. 497pp. 5⅜ × 8½. 25119-5 Pa. $8.95

ADVENTURES WITH A HAND LENS, Richard Headstrom. Clearly written guide to observing and studying flowers and grasses, fish scales, moth and insect wings, egg cases, buds, feathers, seeds, leaf scars, moss, molds, ferns, common crystals, etc.—all with an ordinary, inexpensive magnifying glass. 209 exact line drawings aid in your discoveries. 220pp. 5⅜ × 8½. 23330-8 Pa. $4.50

RODIN ON ART AND ARTISTS, Auguste Rodin. Great sculptor's candid, wide-ranging comments on meaning of art; great artists; relation of sculpture to poetry, painting, music; philosophy of life, more. 76 superb black-and-white illustrations of Rodin's sculpture, drawings and prints. 119pp. 8⅜ × 11¼. 24487-3 Pa. $6.95

FIFTY CLASSIC FRENCH FILMS, 1912–1982: A Pictorial Record, Anthony Slide. Memorable stills from Grand Illusion, Beauty and the Beast, Hiroshima, Mon Amour, many more. Credits, plot synopses, reviews, etc. 160pp. 8¼ × 11. 25256-6 Pa. $11.95

THE PRINCIPLES OF PSYCHOLOGY, William James. Famous long course complete, unabridged. Stream of thought, time perception, memory, experimental methods; great work decades ahead of its time. 94 figures. 1,391pp. 5⅜ × 8½. 20381-6, 20382-4 Pa., Two-vol. set $19.90

BODIES IN A BOOKSHOP, R. T. Campbell. Challenging mystery of blackmail and murder with ingenious plot and superbly drawn characters. In the best tradition of British suspense fiction. 192pp. 5⅜ × 8½. 24720-1 Pa. $3.95

CALLAS: PORTRAIT OF A PRIMA DONNA, George Jellinek. Renowned commentator on the musical scene chronicles incredible career and life of the most controversial, fascinating, influential operatic personality of our time. 64 black-and-white photographs. 416pp. 5⅜ × 8¼. 25047-4 Pa. $7.95

GEOMETRY, RELATIVITY AND THE FOURTH DIMENSION, Rudolph Rucker. Exposition of fourth dimension, concepts of relativity as Flatland characters continue adventures. Popular, easily followed yet accurate, profound. 141 illustrations. 133pp. 5⅜ × 8½. 23400-2 Pa. $3.50

HOUSEHOLD STORIES BY THE BROTHERS GRIMM, with pictures by Walter Crane. 53 classic stories—Rumpelstiltskin, Rapunzel, Hansel and Gretel, the Fisherman and his Wife, Snow White, Tom Thumb, Sleeping Beauty, Cinderella, and so much more—lavishly illustrated with original 19th century drawings. 114 illustrations. x + 269pp. 5⅜ × 8½. 21080-4 Pa. $4.50

SUNDIALS, Albert Waugh. Far and away the best, most thorough coverage of ideas, mathematics concerned, types, construction, adjusting anywhere. Over 100 illustrations. 230pp. 5⅜ × 8½. 22947-5 Pa. $4.50

PICTURE HISTORY OF THE NORMANDIE: With 190 Illustrations, Frank O. Braynard. Full story of legendary French ocean liner: Art Deco interiors, design innovations, furnishings, celebrities, maiden voyage, tragic fire, much more. Extensive text. 144pp. 8⅞ × 11¾. 25257-4 Pa. $9.95

THE FIRST AMERICAN COOKBOOK: A Facsimile of "American Cookery," 1796, Amelia Simmons. Facsimile of the first American-written cookbook published in the United States contains authentic recipes for colonial favorites—pumpkin pudding, winter squash pudding, spruce beer, Indian slapjacks, and more. Introductory Essay and Glossary of colonial cooking terms. 80pp. 5⅜ × 8½. 24710-4 Pa. $3.50

101 PUZZLES IN THOUGHT AND LOGIC, C. R. Wylie, Jr. Solve murders and robberies, find out which fishermen are liars, how a blind man could possibly identify a color—purely by your own reasoning! 107pp. 5⅜ × 8½. 20367-0 Pa. $2.50

THE BOOK OF WORLD-FAMOUS MUSIC—CLASSICAL, POPULAR AND FOLK, James J. Fuld. Revised and enlarged republication of landmark work in musico-bibliography. Full information about nearly 1,000 songs and compositions including first lines of music and lyrics. New supplement. Index. 800pp. 5⅜ × 8¼. 24857-7 Pa. $14.95

ANTHROPOLOGY AND MODERN LIFE, Franz Boas. Great anthropologist's classic treatise on race and culture. Introduction by Ruth Bunzel. Only inexpensive paperback edition. 255pp. 5⅜ × 8½. 25245-0 Pa. $5.95

THE TALE OF PETER RABBIT, Beatrix Potter. The inimitable Peter's terrifying adventure in Mr. McGregor's garden, with all 27 wonderful, full-color Potter illustrations. 55pp. 4¼ × 5½. (Available in U.S. only) 22827-4 Pa. $1.75

THREE PROPHETIC SCIENCE FICTION NOVELS, H. G. Wells. *When the Sleeper Wakes, A Story of the Days to Come* and *The Time Machine* (full version). 335pp. 5⅜ × 8½. (Available in U.S. only) 20605-X Pa. $5.95

APICIUS COOKERY AND DINING IN IMPERIAL ROME, edited and translated by Joseph Dommers Vehling. Oldest known cookbook in existence offers readers a clear picture of what foods Romans ate, how they prepared them, etc. 49 illustrations. 301pp. 6⅛ × 9¼. 23563-7 Pa. $6.50

SHAKESPEARE LEXICON AND QUOTATION DICTIONARY, Alexander Schmidt. Full definitions, locations, shades of meaning of every word in plays and poems. More than 50,000 exact quotations. 1,485pp. 6½ × 9¼. 22726-X, 22727-8 Pa., Two-vol. set $27.90

THE WORLD'S GREAT SPEECHES, edited by Lewis Copeland and Lawrence W. Lamm. Vast collection of 278 speeches from Greeks to 1970. Powerful and effective models; unique look at history. 842pp. 5⅜ × 8½. 20468-5 Pa. $11.95

THE BLUE FAIRY BOOK, Andrew Lang. The first, most famous collection, with many familiar tales: Little Red Riding Hood, Aladdin and the Wonderful Lamp, Puss in Boots, Sleeping Beauty, Hansel and Gretel, Rumpelstiltskin; 37 in all. 138 illustrations. 390pp. 5⅜ × 8½.   21437-0 Pa. $5.95

THE STORY OF THE CHAMPIONS OF THE ROUND TABLE, Howard Pyle. Sir Launcelot, Sir Tristram and Sir Percival in spirited adventures of love and triumph retold in Pyle's inimitable style. 50 drawings, 31 full-page. xviii + 329pp. 6½ × 9¼.   21883-X Pa. $6.95

AUDUBON AND HIS JOURNALS, Maria Audubon. Unmatched two-volume portrait of the great artist, naturalist and author contains his journals, an excellent biography by his granddaughter, expert annotations by the noted ornithologist, Dr. Elliott Coues, and 37 superb illustrations. Total of 1,200pp. 5⅜ × 8.
                                                              Vol. I 25143-8 Pa. $8.95
                                                              Vol. II 25144-6 Pa. $8.95

GREAT DINOSAUR HUNTERS AND THEIR DISCOVERIES, Edwin H. Colbert. Fascinating, lavishly illustrated chronicle of dinosaur research, 1820's to 1960. Achievements of Cope, Marsh, Brown, Buckland, Mantell, Huxley, many others. 384pp. 5¼ × 8¼.   24701-5 Pa. $6.95

THE TASTEMAKERS, Russell Lynes. Informal, illustrated social history of American taste 1850's–1950's. First popularized categories Highbrow, Lowbrow, Middlebrow. 129 illustrations. New (1979) afterword. 384pp. 6 × 9.
                                                                    23993-4 Pa. $6.95

DOUBLE CROSS PURPOSES, Ronald A. Knox. A treasure hunt in the Scottish Highlands, an old map, unidentified corpse, surprise discoveries keep reader guessing in this cleverly intricate tale of financial skullduggery. 2 black-and-white maps. 320pp. 5⅜ × 8½. (Available in U.S. only)   25032-6 Pa. $5.95

AUTHENTIC VICTORIAN DECORATION AND ORNAMENTATION IN FULL COLOR: 46 Plates from "Studies in Design," Christopher Dresser. Superb full-color lithographs reproduced from rare original portfolio of a major Victorian designer. 48pp. 9¼ × 12¼.   25083-0 Pa. $7.95

PRIMITIVE ART, Franz Boas. Remains the best text ever prepared on subject, thoroughly discussing Indian, African, Asian, Australian, and, especially, Northern American primitive art. Over 950 illustrations show ceramics, masks, totem poles, weapons, textiles, paintings, much more. 376pp. 5⅜ × 8.   20025-6 Pa. $6.95

SIDELIGHTS ON RELATIVITY, Albert Einstein. Unabridged republication of two lectures delivered by the great physicist in 1920–21. *Ether and Relativity* and *Geometry and Experience*. Elegant ideas in non-mathematical form, accessible to intelligent layman. vi + 56pp. 5⅜ × 8½.   24511-X Pa. $2.95

THE WIT AND HUMOR OF OSCAR WILDE, edited by Alvin Redman. More than 1,000 ripostes, paradoxes, wisecracks: Work is the curse of the drinking classes, I can resist everything except temptation, etc. 258pp. 5⅜ × 8½.   20602-5 Pa. $4.50

ADVENTURES WITH A MICROSCOPE, Richard Headstrom. 59 adventures with clothing fibers, protozoa, ferns and lichens, roots and leaves, much more. 142 illustrations. 232pp. 5⅜ × 8½.   23471-1 Pa. $3.95

PLANTS OF THE BIBLE, Harold N. Moldenke and Alma L. Moldenke. Standard reference to all 230 plants mentioned in Scriptures. Latin name, biblical reference, uses, modern identity, much more. Unsurpassed encyclopedic resource for scholars, botanists, nature lovers, students of Bible. Bibliography. Indexes. 123 black-and-white illustrations. 384pp. 6 × 9. 25069-5 Pa. $8.95

FAMOUS AMERICAN WOMEN: A Biographical Dictionary from Colonial Times to the Present, Robert McHenry, ed. From Pocahontas to Rosa Parks, 1,035 distinguished American women documented in separate biographical entries. Accurate, up-to-date data, numerous categories, spans 400 years. Indices. 493pp. 6½ × 9¼. 24523-3 Pa. $9.95

THE FABULOUS INTERIORS OF THE GREAT OCEAN LINERS IN HISTORIC PHOTOGRAPHS, William H. Miller, Jr. Some 200 superb photographs capture exquisite interiors of world's great "floating palaces"—1890's to 1980's: *Titanic, Ile de France, Queen Elizabeth, United States, Europa,* more. Approx. 200 black-and-white photographs. Captions. Text. Introduction. 160pp. 8⅞ × 11¾. 24756-2 Pa. $9.95

THE GREAT LUXURY LINERS, 1927–1954: A Photographic Record, William H. Miller, Jr. Nostalgic tribute to heyday of ocean liners. 186 photos of Ile de France, Normandie, Leviathan, Queen Elizabeth, United States, many others. Interior and exterior views. Introduction. Captions. 160pp. 9 × 12. 24056-8 Pa. $9.95

A NATURAL HISTORY OF THE DUCKS, John Charles Phillips. Great landmark of ornithology offers complete detailed coverage of nearly 200 species and subspecies of ducks: gadwall, sheldrake, merganser, pintail, many more. 74 full-color plates, 102 black-and-white. Bibliography. Total of 1,920pp. 8⅝ × 11¼. 25141-1, 25142-X Cloth. Two-vol. set $100.00

THE SEAWEED HANDBOOK: An Illustrated Guide to Seaweeds from North Carolina to Canada, Thomas F. Lee. Concise reference covers 78 species. Scientific and common names, habitat, distribution, more. Finding keys for easy identification. 224pp. 5⅝ × 8½. 25215-9 Pa. $5.95

THE TEN BOOKS OF ARCHITECTURE: The 1755 Leoni Edition, Leon Battista Alberti. Rare classic helped introduce the glories of ancient architecture to the Renaissance. 68 black-and-white plates. 336pp. 8⅝ × 11¼. 25239-6 Pa. $14.95

MISS MACKENZIE, Anthony Trollope. Minor masterpieces by Victorian master unmasks many truths about life in 19th-century England. First inexpensive edition in years. 392pp. 5⅜ × 8½. 25201-9 Pa. $7.95

THE RIME OF THE ANCIENT MARINER, Gustave Doré, Samuel Taylor Coleridge. Dramatic engravings considered by many to be his greatest work. The terrifying space of the open sea, the storms and whirlpools of an unknown ocean, the ice of Antarctica, more—all rendered in a powerful, chilling manner. Full text. 38 plates. 77pp. 9¼ × 12. 22305-1 Pa. $4.95

THE EXPEDITIONS OF ZEBULON MONTGOMERY PIKE, Zebulon Montgomery Pike. Fascinating first-hand accounts (1805–6) of exploration of Mississippi River, Indian wars, capture by Spanish dragoons, much more. 1,088pp. 5⅜ × 8½. 25254-X, 25255-8 Pa. Two-vol. set $23.90

A CONCISE HISTORY OF PHOTOGRAPHY: Third Revised Edition, Helmut Gernsheim. Best one-volume history—camera obscura, photochemistry, daguerreotypes, evolution of cameras, film, more. Also artistic aspects—landscape, portraits, fine art, etc. 281 black-and-white photographs. 26 in color. 176pp. 8⅜ × 11¼. 25128-4 Pa. $12.95

THE DORÉ BIBLE ILLUSTRATIONS, Gustave Doré. 241 detailed plates from the Bible: the Creation scenes, Adam and Eve, Flood, Babylon, battle sequences, life of Jesus, etc. Each plate is accompanied by the verses from the King James version of the Bible. 241pp. 9 × 12. 23004-X Pa. $8.95

HUGGER-MUGGER IN THE LOUVRE, Elliot Paul. Second Homer Evans mystery-comedy. Theft at the Louvre involves sleuth in hilarious, madcap caper. "A knockout."—Books. 336pp. 5⅜ × 8½. 25185-3 Pa. $5.95

FLATLAND, E. A. Abbott. Intriguing and enormously popular science-fiction classic explores the complexities of trying to survive as a two-dimensional being in a three-dimensional world. Amusingly illustrated by the author. 16 illustrations. 103pp. 5⅜ × 8½. 20001-9 Pa. $2.25

THE HISTORY OF THE LEWIS AND CLARK EXPEDITION, Meriwether Lewis and William Clark, edited by Elliott Coues. Classic edition of Lewis and Clark's day-by-day journals that later became the basis for U.S. claims to Oregon and the West. Accurate and invaluable geographical, botanical, biological, meteorological and anthropological material. Total of 1,508pp. 5⅜ × 8½. 21268-8, 21269-6, 21270-X Pa. Three-vol. set $25.50

LANGUAGE, TRUTH AND LOGIC, Alfred J. Ayer. Famous, clear introduction to Vienna, Cambridge schools of Logical Positivism. Role of philosophy, elimination of metaphysics, nature of analysis, etc. 160pp. 5⅜ × 8½. (Available in U.S. and Canada only) 20010-8 Pa. $2.95

MATHEMATICS FOR THE NONMATHEMATICIAN, Morris Kline. Detailed, college-level treatment of mathematics in cultural and historical context, with numerous exercises. For liberal arts students. Preface. Recommended Reading Lists. Tables. Index. Numerous black-and-white figures. xvi + 641pp. 5⅜ × 8½. 24823-2 Pa. $11.95

28 SCIENCE FICTION STORIES, H. G. Wells. Novels, *Star Begotten* and *Men Like Gods,* plus 26 short stories: "Empire of the Ants," "A Story of the Stone Age," "The Stolen Bacillus," "In the Abyss," etc. 915pp. 5⅜ × 8½. (Available in U.S. only) 20265-8 Cloth. $10.95

HANDBOOK OF PICTORIAL SYMBOLS, Rudolph Modley. 3,250 signs and symbols, many systems in full; official or heavy commercial use. Arranged by subject. Most in Pictorial Archive series. 143pp. 8⅛ × 11. 23357-X Pa. $5.95

INCIDENTS OF TRAVEL IN YUCATAN, John L. Stephens. Classic (1843) exploration of jungles of Yucatan, looking for evidences of Maya civilization. Travel adventures, Mexican and Indian culture, etc. Total of 669pp. 5⅜ × 8½. 20926-1, 20927-X Pa., Two-vol. set $9.90

DEGAS: An Intimate Portrait, Ambroise Vollard. Charming, anecdotal memoir by famous art dealer of one of the greatest 19th-century French painters. 14 black-and-white illustrations. Introduction by Harold L. Van Doren. 96pp. 5⅜ × 8½.
25131-4 Pa. $3.95

PERSONAL NARRATIVE OF A PILGRIMAGE TO ALMANDINAH AND MECCAH, Richard Burton. Great travel classic by remarkably colorful personality. Burton, disguised as a Moroccan, visited sacred shrines of Islam, narrowly escaping death. 47 illustrations. 959pp. 5⅜ × 8½.   21217-3, 21218-1 Pa., Two-vol. set $17.90

PHRASE AND WORD ORIGINS, A. H. Holt. Entertaining, reliable, modern study of more than 1,200 colorful words, phrases, origins and histories. Much unexpected information. 254pp. 5⅜ × 8½.   20758-7 Pa. $5.95

THE RED THUMB MARK, R. Austin Freeman. In this first Dr. Thorndyke case, the great scientific detective draws fascinating conclusions from the nature of a single fingerprint. Exciting story, authentic science. 320pp. 5⅜ × 8½. (Available in U.S. only)   25210-8 Pa. $5.95

AN EGYPTIAN HIEROGLYPHIC DICTIONARY, E. A. Wallis Budge. Monumental work containing about 25,000 words or terms that occur in texts ranging from 3000 B.C. to 600 A.D. Each entry consists of a transliteration of the word, the word in hieroglyphs, and the meaning in English. 1,314pp. 6⅜ × 10.
23615-3, 23616-1 Pa., Two-vol. set $27.90

THE COMPLEAT STRATEGYST: Being a Primer on the Theory of Games of Strategy, J. D. Williams. Highly entertaining classic describes, with many illustrated examples, how to select best strategies in conflict situations. Prefaces. Appendices. xvi + 268pp. 5⅜ × 8½.   25101-2 Pa. $5.95

THE ROAD TO OZ, L. Frank Baum. Dorothy meets the Shaggy Man, little Button-Bright and the Rainbow's beautiful daughter in this delightful trip to the magical Land of Oz. 272pp. 5⅜ × 8.   25208-6 Pa. $4.95

POINT AND LINE TO PLANE, Wassily Kandinsky. Seminal exposition of role of point, line, other elements in non-objective painting. Essential to understanding 20th-century art. 127 illustrations. 192pp. 6½ × 9¼.   23808-3 Pa. $4.50

LADY ANNA, Anthony Trollope. Moving chronicle of Countess Lovel's bitter struggle to win for herself and daughter Anna their rightful rank and fortune—perhaps at cost of sanity itself. 384pp. 5⅜ × 8½.   24669-8 Pa. $6.95

EGYPTIAN MAGIC, E. A. Wallis Budge. Sums up all that is known about magic in Ancient Egypt: the role of magic in controlling the gods, powerful amulets that warded off evil spirits, scarabs of immortality, use of wax images, formulas and spells, the secret name, much more. 253pp. 5⅜ × 8½.   22681-6 Pa. $4.50

THE DANCE OF SIVA, Ananda Coomaraswamy. Preeminent authority unfolds the vast metaphysic of India: the revelation of her art, conception of the universe, social organization, etc. 27 reproductions of art masterpieces. 192pp. 5⅜ × 8½.
24817-8 Pa. $5.95

CHRISTMAS CUSTOMS AND TRADITIONS, Clement A. Miles. Origin, evolution, significance of religious, secular practices. Caroling, gifts, yule logs, much more. Full, scholarly yet fascinating; non-sectarian. 400pp. 5⅜ × 8½.
23354-5 Pa. $6.50

THE HUMAN FIGURE IN MOTION, Eadweard Muybridge. More than 4,500 stopped-action photos, in action series, showing undraped men, women, children jumping, lying down, throwing, sitting, wrestling, carrying, etc. 390pp. 7⅞ × 10⅝.
20204-6 Cloth. $19.95

THE MAN WHO WAS THURSDAY, Gilbert Keith Chesterton. Witty, fast-paced novel about a club of anarchists in turn-of-the-century London. Brilliant social, religious, philosophical speculations. 128pp. 5⅜ × 8½.
25121-7 Pa. $3.95

A CEZANNE SKETCHBOOK: Figures, Portraits, Landscapes and Still Lifes, Paul Cezanne. Great artist experiments with tonal effects, light, mass, other qualities in over 100 drawings. A revealing view of developing master painter, precursor of Cubism. 102 black-and-white illustrations. 144pp. 8¾ × 6⅜.
24790-2 Pa. $5.95

AN ENCYCLOPEDIA OF BATTLES: Accounts of Over 1,560 Battles from 1479 B.C. to the Present, David Eggenberger. Presents essential details of every major battle in recorded history, from the first battle of Megiddo in 1479 B.C. to Grenada in 1984. List of Battle Maps. New Appendix covering the years 1967–1984. Index. 99 illustrations. 544pp. 6½ × 9¼.
24913-1 Pa. $14.95

AN ETYMOLOGICAL DICTIONARY OF MODERN ENGLISH, Ernest Weekley. Richest, fullest work, by foremost British lexicographer. Detailed word histories. Inexhaustible. Total of 856pp. 6½ × 9¼.
21873-2, 21874-0 Pa., Two-vol. set $17.00

WEBSTER'S AMERICAN MILITARY BIOGRAPHIES, edited by Robert McHenry. Over 1,000 figures who shaped 3 centuries of American military history. Detailed biographies of Nathan Hale, Douglas MacArthur, Mary Hallaren, others. Chronologies of engagements, more. Introduction. Addenda. 1,033 entries in alphabetical order. xi + 548pp. 6½ × 9¼. (Available in U.S. only)
24758-9 Pa. $11.95

LIFE IN ANCIENT EGYPT, Adolf Erman. Detailed older account, with much not in more recent books: domestic life, religion, magic, medicine, commerce, and whatever else needed for complete picture. Many illustrations. 597pp. 5⅜ × 8½.
22632-8 Pa. $8.95

HISTORIC COSTUME IN PICTURES, Braun & Schneider. Over 1,450 costumed figures shown, covering a wide variety of peoples: kings, emperors, nobles, priests, servants, soldiers, scholars, townsfolk, peasants, merchants, courtiers, cavaliers, and more. 256pp. 8⅜ × 11¼.
23150-X Pa. $7.95

THE NOTEBOOKS OF LEONARDO DA VINCI, edited by J. P. Richter. Extracts from manuscripts reveal great genius; on painting, sculpture, anatomy, sciences, geography, etc. Both Italian and English. 186 ms. pages reproduced, plus 500 additional drawings, including studies for *Last Supper, Sforza* monument, etc. 860pp. 7⅞ × 10¾. (Available in U.S. only) 22572-0, 22573-9 Pa., Two-vol. set $25.90

THE ART NOUVEAU STYLE BOOK OF ALPHONSE MUCHA: All 72 Plates from "Documents Decoratifs" in Original Color, Alphonse Mucha. Rare copyright-free design portfolio by high priest of Art Nouveau. Jewelry, wallpaper, stained glass, furniture, figure studies, plant and animal motifs, etc. Only complete one-volume edition. 80pp. 9⅜ × 12¼. 24044-4 Pa. $8.95

ANIMALS: 1,419 COPYRIGHT-FREE ILLUSTRATIONS OF MAMMALS, BIRDS, FISH, INSECTS, ETC., edited by Jim Harter. Clear wood engravings present, in extremely lifelike poses, over 1,000 species of animals. One of the most extensive pictorial sourcebooks of its kind. Captions. Index. 284pp. 9 × 12.
23766-4 Pa. $9.95

OBELISTS FLY HIGH, C. Daly King. Masterpiece of American detective fiction, long out of print, involves murder on a 1935 transcontinental flight—"a very thrilling story"—NY Times. Unabridged and unaltered republication of the edition published by William Collins Sons & Co. Ltd., London, 1935. 288pp. 5⅜ × 8½. (Available in U.S. only) 25036-9 Pa. $4.95

VICTORIAN AND EDWARDIAN FASHION: A Photographic Survey, Alison Gernsheim. First fashion history completely illustrated by contemporary photographs. Full text plus 235 photos, 1840–1914, in which many celebrities appear. 240pp. 6½ × 9¼. 24205-6 Pa. $6.00

THE ART OF THE FRENCH ILLUSTRATED BOOK, 1700–1914, Gordon N. Ray. Over 630 superb book illustrations by Fragonard, Delacroix, Daumier, Doré, Grandville, Manet, Mucha, Steinlen, Toulouse-Lautrec and many others. Preface. Introduction. 633 halftones. Indices of artists, authors & titles, binders and provenances. Appendices. Bibliography. 608pp. 8⅜ × 11¼. 25086-5 Pa. $24.95

THE WONDERFUL WIZARD OF OZ, L. Frank Baum. Facsimile in full color of America's finest children's classic. 143 illustrations by W. W. Denslow. 267pp. 5⅜ × 8½. 20691-2 Pa. $5.95

FRONTIERS OF MODERN PHYSICS: New Perspectives on Cosmology, Relativity, Black Holes and Extraterrestrial Intelligence, Tony Rothman, et al. For the intelligent layman. Subjects include: cosmological models of the universe; black holes; the neutrino; the search for extraterrestrial intelligence. Introduction. 46 black-and-white illustrations. 192pp. 5⅜ × 8½. 24587-X Pa. $6.95

THE FRIENDLY STARS, Martha Evans Martin & Donald Howard Menzel. Classic text marshalls the stars together in an engaging, non-technical survey, presenting them as sources of beauty in night sky. 23 illustrations. Foreword. 2 star charts. Index. 147pp. 5⅜ × 8½. 21099-5 Pa. $3.50

FADS AND FALLACIES IN THE NAME OF SCIENCE, Martin Gardner. Fair, witty appraisal of cranks, quacks, and quackeries of science and pseudoscience: hollow earth, Velikovsky, orgone energy, Dianetics, flying saucers, Bridey Murphy, food and medical fads, etc. Revised, expanded In the Name of Science. "A very able and even-tempered presentation."—The New Yorker. 363pp. 5⅜ × 8.
20394-8 Pa. $6.50

ANCIENT EGYPT: ITS CULTURE AND HISTORY, J. E Manchip White. From pre-dynastics through Ptolemies: society, history, political structure, religion, daily life, literature, cultural heritage. 48 plates. 217pp. 5⅜ × 8½. 22548-8 Pa. $4.95

SIR HARRY HOTSPUR OF HUMBLETHWAITE, Anthony Trollope. Incisive, unconventional psychological study of a conflict between a wealthy baronet, his idealistic daughter, and their scapegrace cousin. The 1870 novel in its first inexpensive edition in years. 250pp. 5⅜ × 8½. 24953-0 Pa. $5.95

LASERS AND HOLOGRAPHY, Winston E. Kock. Sound introduction to burgeoning field, expanded (1981) for second edition. Wave patterns, coherence, lasers, diffraction, zone plates, properties of holograms, recent advances. 84 illustrations. 160pp. 5⅜ × 8¼. (Except in United Kingdom) 24041-X Pa. $3.50

INTRODUCTION TO ARTIFICIAL INTELLIGENCE: SECOND, EN-LARGED EDITION, Philip C. Jackson, Jr. Comprehensive survey of artificial intelligence—the study of how machines (computers) can be made to act intelligently. Includes introductory and advanced material. Extensive notes updating the main text. 132 black-and-white illustrations. 512pp. 5⅜ × 8½. 24864-X Pa. $8.95

HISTORY OF INDIAN AND INDONESIAN ART, Ananda K. Coomaraswamy. Over 400 illustrations illuminate classic study of Indian art from earliest Harappa finds to early 20th century. Provides philosophical, religious and social insights. 304pp. 6⅜ × 9⅜. 25005-9 Pa. $8.95

THE GOLEM, Gustav Meyrink. Most famous supernatural novel in modern European literature, set in Ghetto of Old Prague around 1890. Compelling story of mystical experiences, strange transformations, profound terror. 13 black-and-white illustrations. 224pp. 5⅜ × 8½. (Available in U.S. only) 25025-3 Pa. $5.95

ARMADALE, Wilkie Collins. Third great mystery novel by the author of *The Woman in White* and *The Moonstone*. Original magazine version with 40 illustrations. 597pp. 5⅜ × 8½. 23429-0 Pa. $9.95

PICTORIAL ENCYCLOPEDIA OF HISTORIC ARCHITECTURAL PLANS, DETAILS AND ELEMENTS: With 1,880 Line Drawings of Arches, Domes, Doorways, Facades, Gables, Windows, etc., John Theodore Haneman. Sourcebook of inspiration for architects, designers, others. Bibliography. Captions. 141pp. 9 × 12. 24605-1 Pa. $6.95

BENCHLEY LOST AND FOUND, Robert Benchley. Finest humor from early 30's, about pet peeves, child psychologists, post office and others. Mostly unavailable elsewhere. 73 illustrations by Peter Arno and others. 183pp. 5⅜ × 8½. 22410-4 Pa. $3.95

ERTÉ GRAPHICS, Erté. Collection of striking color graphics: *Seasons, Alphabet, Numerals, Aces* and *Precious Stones*. 50 plates, including 4 on covers. 48pp. 9⅜ × 12¼. 23580-7 Pa. $6.95

THE JOURNAL OF HENRY D. THOREAU, edited by Bradford Torrey, F. H. Allen. Complete reprinting of 14 volumes, 1837-61, over two million words; the sourcebooks for *Walden*, etc. Definitive. All original sketches, plus 75 photographs. 1,804pp. 8½ × 12¼. 20312-3, 20313-1 Cloth., Two-vol. set $80.00

CASTLES: THEIR CONSTRUCTION AND HISTORY, Sidney Toy. Traces castle development from ancient roots. Nearly 200 photographs and drawings illustrate moats, keeps, baileys, many other features. Caernarvon, Dover Castles, Hadrian's Wall, Tower of London, dozens more. 256pp. 5⅜ × 8¼. 24898-4 Pa. $5.95

AMERICAN CLIPPER SHIPS: 1833–1858, Octavius T. Howe & Frederick C. Matthews. Fully-illustrated, encyclopedic review of 352 clipper ships from the period of America's greatest maritime supremacy. Introduction. 109 halftones. 5 black-and-white line illustrations. Index. Total of 928pp. 5⅜ × 8½.
25115-2, 25116-0 Pa., Two-vol. set $17.90

TOWARDS A NEW ARCHITECTURE, Le Corbusier. Pioneering manifesto by great architect, near legendary founder of "International School." Technical and aesthetic theories, views on industry, economics, relation of form to function, "mass-production spirit," much more. Profusely illustrated. Unabridged translation of 13th French edition. Introduction by Frederick Etchells. 320pp. 6⅛ × 9¼. (Available in U.S. only)
25023-7 Pa. $8.95

THE BOOK OF KELLS, edited by Blanche Cirker. Inexpensive collection of 32 full-color, full-page plates from the greatest illuminated manuscript of the Middle Ages, painstakingly reproduced from rare facsimile edition. Publisher's Note. Captions. 32pp. 9⅜ × 12¼.
24345-1 Pa. $4.95

BEST SCIENCE FICTION STORIES OF H. G. WELLS, H. G. Wells. Full novel *The Invisible Man*, plus 17 short stories: "The Crystal Egg," "Aepyornis Island," "The Strange Orchid," etc. 303pp. 5⅜ × 8½. (Available in U.S. only)
21531-8 Pa. $4.95

AMERICAN SAILING SHIPS: Their Plans and History, Charles G. Davis. Photos, construction details of schooners, frigates, clippers, other sailcraft of 18th to early 20th centuries—plus entertaining discourse on design, rigging, nautical lore, much more. 137 black-and-white illustrations. 240pp. 6⅛ × 9¼.
24658-2 Pa. $5.95

ENTERTAINING MATHEMATICAL PUZZLES, Martin Gardner. Selection of author's favorite conundrums involving arithmetic, money, speed, etc., with lively commentary. Complete solutions. 112pp. 5⅜ × 8½.
25211-6 Pa. $2.95

THE WILL TO BELIEVE, HUMAN IMMORTALITY, William James. Two books bound together. Effect of irrational on logical, and arguments for human immortality. 402pp. 5⅜ × 8½.
20291-7 Pa. $7.50

THE HAUNTED MONASTERY and THE CHINESE MAZE MURDERS, Robert Van Gulik. 2 full novels by Van Gulik continue adventures of Judge Dee and his companions. An evil Taoist monastery, seemingly supernatural events; overgrown topiary maze that hides strange crimes. Set in 7th-century China. 27 illustrations. 328pp. 5⅜ × 8½.
23502-5 Pa. $5.95

CELEBRATED CASES OF JUDGE DEE (DEE GOONG AN), translated by Robert Van Gulik. Authentic 18th-century Chinese detective novel; Dee and associates solve three interlocked cases. Led to Van Gulik's own stories with same characters. Extensive introduction. 9 illustrations. 237pp. 5⅜ × 8½.
23337-5 Pa. $4.95

Prices subject to change without notice.

Available at your book dealer or write for free catalog to Dept. GI, Dover Publications, Inc., 31 East 2nd St., Mineola, N.Y. 11501. Dover publishes more than 175 books each year on science, elementary and advanced mathematics, biology, music, art, literary history, social sciences and other areas.